A Gift For:

from:

HOPE
for Each Day

MORNING & EVENING DEVOTIONS

BILLY GRAHAM

A Division of Thomas Nelson Publishers

THOMAS NELSON
Since 1798

NASHVILLE   DALLAS   MEXICO CITY   RIO DE JANEIRO

Published by in Nashville, Tennessee, by Thomas Nelson. Thomas Nelson is a registered trademark of Thomas Nelson, Inc.

Thomas Nelson, Inc., titles may be purchased in bulk for educational, business, fund-raising, or sales promotional use. For information, please e-mail SpecialMarkets@ThomasNelson.com.

These meditations include edited excerpts from *Unto the Hills: A Daily Devotional* by Billy Graham and edited sermons from Billy Graham that were previously published in *Decision* magazine. These are used with the author's permission. Other meditations from the author have been prepared specifically for this volume.

ISBN-13: 978-1-4041-8970-6

12 13 14 15 TIMS 9 8 7

www.thomasnelson.com

Therefore I live for today—
Certain of finding at sunrise
Guidance and strength for the way.
Power for each moment of weakness,
Hope for each moment of pain,
Comfort for every sorrow,
Sunshine and joy after rain!

—Anonymous

Preface

For many years I have sought to walk with God every day. What a joy it is to wake up in the morning and know He is with me, no matter what the day has in store. What a joy it is to look back in the evening and be able to thank Him for His faithfulness and to experience His peace. What a joy it is to know that someday soon the burdens of this life will be over and I will awaken in His presence!

When I think about God's love, I tend to dwell upon all the good things He has done for me. But then I must stop and realize that even when circumstances have been hard or the way unclear, God has still surrounded me with His love. God's love is just as real and just as powerful in the darkness as it is in the light. And that is why we can have hope!

Every day I turn to the Bible to give me strength and wisdom for the day and hope for the future. Its words have seen me through good times and bad—through times of happiness and grief, health and sickness, victory and disappointment. God's Word can do the same for you.

May God use these daily selections to encourage you and give you hope. May they also challenge you both to live more fully for Christ each day and to trust His great love—no matter what comes your way.

—BILLY GRAHAM

JANUARY

New Year, New Ways

"Consider your ways."
HAGGAI 1:5

Making New Year's resolutions and not keeping them is a universal experience. We may be sincere when we make them, but then we find them too hard to keep, or perhaps we forget all about them.

Let me give you two reasons why it can be good to make resolutions at the beginning of a new year. First, it forces us to look at ourselves—to be honest about our failures and our need to change. Many New Year's resolutions are unrealistic or only wishful thinking, but the exercise of examining ourselves—with God's help—and seeing where we fall short is important.

Second, making a list of resolutions can turn us to God. If we are honest, we know we fall far short of being what we ought to be—and because of that, we need God's forgiveness. We'll also realize that we can't live the way we should in our own strength. We need God's help.

Begin this year by making resolutions—especially the resolution to open your heart and life to Jesus Christ more than you ever have before.

In Tune with the Master

You shall surround me with songs of deliverance.

PSALM 32:7

Out West an old sheepherder had a violin, but it was out of tune. He had no way of tuning it, so in desperation he wrote to one of the radio stations and asked them at a certain hour on a certain day to strike the tone A. The officials of the station decided they would accommodate the old fellow, and on that particular day the true tone of A was broadcast. His fiddle was thus tuned, and once more his cabin echoed with joyful music.

When we live apart from God, our lives get out of tune—out of harmony with others and with God. But if we live in tune with the Master, we, too, will find ourselves surrounded by His beautiful music.

As this new year begins, ask God to help you tune your life every day to His Word, so you can bring harmony and joy to those around you.

Hope for the Future

If anyone is in Christ, he is a new creation; old things have passed away; behold, all things have become new.
2 CORINTHIANS 5:17

As we start a new year, the Bible tells us there can be hope for the future.

First, there is hope of a changed person. No matter how hard we try, we are incapable of ridding ourselves of the selfishness and greed that cause conflict and strife and war. Our only hope is a changed heart—and Jesus is in the business of changing hearts.

Second, there is hope of a changed world. When we know Christ, He gives us by His Spirit a new love and concern for others. We can no longer be indifferent to their sufferings, and we'll want to do something about them. Changed by Christ, we can begin to change our world.

Third, there is hope of an unchanging eternity in Heaven. This world is not all there is. Someday all its pain and heartache will come to an end for those who know Christ (Revelation 21:4). Evil and death will be abolished, and we will be safely in God's presence forever.

As you read the headlines or look at your own life, you may be wondering if there is any hope. The answer from the Bible is a resounding yes.

The Sun Still Shining

They looked . . . and behold, the glory of the
LORD appeared in the cloud.

EXODUS 16:10

Without the clouds we would not be shielded from the burning sun. Without the clouds there would be no lavish sunsets, no beneficial rain, no beautiful landscapes.

The same is true with life's clouds. When hard times come, we easily get discouraged. But behind the clouds God is still present, and can even use them to water our souls with unexpected blessings. Longfellow once wrote: "Be still, sad heart, and cease repining; behind the clouds is the sun still shining." As God's people wandered in the wilderness, He declared, "Behold, I come to you in the thick cloud" (Exodus 19:9).

Each of us experiences clouds in life—sometimes slight, but sometimes dark and frightening. Whatever clouds you face today, ask Jesus, the Light of the World, to help you look behind the cloud to see His glory and His plans for you.

Your Purpose in Life

Teach me Your way, O LORD,
And lead me in a smooth path.
PSALM 27:11

God has a plan or purpose for every person, although many people go through life without ever thinking about it. But their lack of awareness doesn't change the fact that God put each of us here for a purpose.

We aren't here by accident. We are here because God put us here. And He put us here for a reason: so we could come to know Him in a personal way and then live in a way that brings glory to His name.

This is the greatest discovery you will ever make: you were created to know God and to be His friend forever. When I was young, my mother taught me from our church's catechism that "the chief end [or purpose] of man is to glorify God and enjoy Him forever."

But God not only has a general purpose for each of us; He also has a specific plan for each of our lives. Don't wander through life without any purpose or direction, but pray and seek God's will, and learn to follow Him.

A Spring for the Soul

For with You is the fountain of life;
In Your light we see light.

PSALM 36:9

Sadly, many people get their happiness only from outward circumstances. As long as their lives are untroubled, they feel happy. But when illness strikes, a relationship breaks down, or any other unexpected troubles engulfs them, then happiness flees.

Near my home is a spring that never varies its flow. Floods may rage, but its output doesn't increase. A long summer's drought may come, but it won't decrease. Its flow is steady, reliable, and unending.

Such is the peace we all yearn for—and such is the peace Jesus promises to all who trust in Him: "The water that I shall give him will become in him a fountain of water springing up into everlasting life. . . . My peace I give to you" (John 4:14; 14:27).

Have you come to that unending spring—which is Christ? Are you coming to Him each day?

Revival Begins with You

"Repent, for the kingdom of heaven is at hand."
MATTHEW 4:17

If Christianity is important at all, then it is all-important. If it is anything at all, then it is everything. It is either the most vital thing in your life, or it isn't worth bothering with.

So don't give the lie to the Christian faith by professing Christ without possessing Him. Don't lock the church door with the key of inconsistency and keep the lost from coming to Christ. Don't hinder revival by your unbelief and prayerlessness. Don't cheat yourself out of spiritual victory by allowing sin to imprison you. Seek God's face and turn from your wicked ways. Then you will hear from Heaven and true revival will begin—starting with you.

The Church holds the key to revival. It is within our grasp. Will we rise to the challenge? Will we dare pay the price? The supply of Heaven is adequate for the demands of our spiritually starved world. Will we offer that supply to the hungry masses?

May the revival that the world needs begin in you—starting today.

The Promise Is Ours

"I am with you always, even to the end of the age."

MATTHEW 28:20

When David Livingstone returned to his native Scotland after sixteen difficult years as a missionary and explorer in Africa, his body was emaciated by the ravages of some twenty-seven fevers that had coursed through his veins during the years of his service. His left arm hung useless at his side, the result of his being mangled by a lion.

Speaking to the students at Glasgow University, he said, "Shall I tell you what sustained me during the hardship and loneliness of my exile? It was Christ's promise, 'Lo, I am with you always, even to the end of the age.'"

That promise is ours as well. No matter what trials we face, Christ never leaves us. He is with us every step of the way! Keep that promise before you today—and always.

He Is Here to Help

Who shall separate us from the love of Christ?
ROMANS 8:35

After His resurrection Jesus came to His disciples, meeting them between the garden with its empty tomb and the city with its mob still passionate with hate. He said to them, "Do not be afraid. Go and tell My brethren" (Matthew 28:10).

In the midst of a world filled with danger, hatred, and war, the words of our Lord Jesus Christ are just as relevant as when He spoke them. He still says to all who love Him, "Do not be afraid."

He comes to you in the hospital room or in the midst of a family tragedy. He comes to you in the midst of an unexpected business reversal or health crisis. And He says, "Don't be afraid. I'm alive, and I'm here to help you. The cross shows the depth of My love, and the resurrection shows the extent of My power. Nothing can ever separate you from Me!"

Tending to Our Earthly Tent

We know that if our earthly house, this tent, is destroyed, we have a building from God, a house not made with hands, eternal in the heavens.

2 CORINTHIANS 5:1

Her uncle had some very bad health habits that would kill him if he didn't stop them. But when she shared her concern, he laughed and said he'd rather enjoy his life, even if it shortened his days. Why, she asked me, would anyone act like this?

I was first struck by his self-centeredness. Deliberately doing something that will cut short his life revealed that he was thinking only about himself, and ignoring all the hurt and sorrow his premature death would bring to his family. Perhaps, I suggested, she could remind him of this—as well as urge him to give his life to Christ.

But his situation got me to thinking: In what ways might we be like him? What health rules are we violating? In what ways are we not taking care of the body God has given us?

Someday each one of us who follows Jesus as our Savior and Lord will leave behind our Earthly tent—our flesh-and-bone body—and join Him in Heaven for eternity. But until that day—as the Bible says—"Glorify God in your body" (1 Corinthians 6:20).

Vision, Integrity, Presence

Do not be conformed to this world, but be transformed by the renewing of your mind.

ROMANS 12:2

In many contexts, *VIP* means "Very Important Person." But the acronym also offers us a character test.

The *V* stands for VISION, for "where there is no vision, the people perish" (Proverbs 29:18 KJV). Having a vision means seeing what can be done, what ought to be done, and how to get it done. The highest vision we can have is to glorify God by discovering God's will for our lives—and then doing it.

The letter *I* stands for INTEGRITY, meaning that a person is the same on the inside as he or she appears on the outside. There must be no discrepancy between what we say and what we do, between our walk and our talk.

The *P* stands for PRESENCE—God's presence in our lives. Without God's help we are doomed. Only in Christ do we find out who we are, why we are here, and where we are going—and only in Him do we find the power to fulfill our God-given vision.

So be steadfast in your commitment to Christ, and be a real VIP—a person with vision, integrity, and God's presence.

The Glory of God

*"In My Father's house are many mansions. . . .
I go to prepare a place for you."*

JOHN 14:2

There was once a little boy who was riding alone on a train, and the scenery was not too interesting. A woman sitting beside him asked, "Are you tired of the long ride?"

The boy smiled and said, "I'm a little tired, but I don't mind it much. You see, my father is going to meet me when I get there."

Sometimes we get tired of the burdens of life, but we know that Jesus Christ will meet us at the end of our life's journey—and that makes all the difference. Paul wrote, "Therefore we do not lose heart. . . . For the things which are seen are temporary, but the things which are not seen are eternal" (2 Corinthians 4:16, 18). Knowing we will be with Christ forever far outweighs our burdens today! Keep your eyes on eternity!

How Will We Learn?

The unfolding of your words gives light;
it gives understanding to the simple.
PSALM 119:130 NIV

We know we ought to know more about the Bible—but perhaps you're like many Christians: it's so overwhelming you've never really gotten into it.

The first step is to realize what it is: God's love letter to you.

From one end to the other, it tells of God's love for us—a love so great that He sent His Son into the world to redeem us. You wouldn't ignore a letter from someone who loved you; don't ignore God's love letter either.

Then think of ways you can learn about the Bible from others—gifted teachers on the radio, your pastor's sermons, group Bible studies, even books like this. Some people have a special God-given gift for teaching His Word, and they can help you learn more about it.

Finally, get acquainted with the Bible on your own. Set aside a few quiet minutes and begin reading through one of the gospels (such as John)—perhaps only a paragraph or two at first. Ask God to help you understand it and apply it to your life every day.

A Spirit of Thankfulness

*I have learned the secret of being content in
any and every situation.*

Philippians 4:12 niv

Some years ago I visited a man who was wealthy and successful, the envy of all his friends and business associates. But as we talked, he broke down in tears, confessing that he was miserable inside. Wealth had not been able to fill the empty place in his heart.

A few hours later I visited another man who lived only a few miles away. His cottage was humble, and he had almost nothing in the way of this world's possessions. Yet his face was radiant as he told me about the work he was doing for Christ and how Christ had filled his life with meaning and purpose.

I went away convinced that the second man was really the richer man. Although he had very little, he had learned to be thankful for everything God had given him. A spirit of thankfulness makes all the difference.

Eyes That Refuse to See

"They have eyes to see but do not see and ears to hear but do not hear, for they are a rebellious people."
EZEKIEL 12:2 NIV

The Bible tells us that we have two sets of eyes. We have physical eyes—but we also have spiritual eyes. With one set we see the physical world around us, while with the other we discern the spiritual truths God has set forth for us in His Word. Tragically, some who are able to see physically do not see spiritually—and spiritual blindness keeps us from knowing God.

Sometimes physical blindness can be prevented or cured. Spiritual blindness, however, is caused by sin—and only the Lord Jesus Christ can cure spiritual blindness because only He can take away our sin.

When we come to Christ, He comes to live within us by His Holy Spirit—and He then opens our spiritual eyes to God's truth. This is one reason why the Bible is important, because God uses it to help us discern His truth.

May you turn to God and receive from Him the cure for your spiritual blindness. May He open your eyes to His love, so you learn to trust Him no matter what troubles you. And may He guide you as He opens your eyes to His will every day.

The Triumphs of Grace

"I, even I, am He who blots out your transgressions."

ISAIAH 43:25

When Charles Wesley experienced the joy of divine forgiveness, he told a Moravian friend of his new sense of pardon, adding, "I suppose I had better keep silent about it."

"Oh, no, my brother," came the reply. "If you had a thousand tongues, you should go and use them all for Jesus."

Charles Wesley went home and wrote the great hymn: "O for a thousand tongues to sing / My great Redeemer's praise, / The glories of my God and King, / The triumphs of His grace!"

To a burdened, benighted world, crushed under the weight of its own wickedness, God says, "I, even I, am He who blots out your transgressions." This is glorious news, and it applies to all people everywhere—including you. Have you received God's gift of forgiveness? If you have, thank Him for it—and if not, by faith invite Christ into your life today.

God's Desire for You

*We . . . are being transformed into [Christ's]
likeness with ever-increasing glory.*
2 Corinthians 3:18 niv

God can seem near to us when we walk in the woods or are surrounded by the grandeur of a starry night, and that is a wonderful experience. But it shouldn't become a substitute for going to church.

Never forget: God doesn't want us to just feel His presence. He wants to change our lives. He wants to take away our self-centeredness and make us more like Christ. He also wants to teach us His truth and prepare us to become His servants.

How does this happen? How does God change us into the people He wants us to be? Not just by a walk in the woods, as pleasant as that may be. No, God mainly changes us by His Word, the Bible, as we listen to its truth and allow it to shape our lives. That is one reason I urge you to become active in a church where God's Word is taught and lived. You will become more like Christ as you hear and obey His Word.

Love Pays the Price

In Him we have redemption through His blood.

Ephesians 1:7

A loving mother who saved her little girl from a burning house suffered severe burns on her hands and arms. When the girl grew older, not knowing how her mother's arms had become so seared, the girl was ashamed of those scarred, gnarled hands and always insisted that her mother wear long gloves to cover up the ugliness.

But one day the daughter asked her mother how her hands had become so scarred. The mother, for the first time, told her the story of how she had saved the daughter's life with those hands. The daughter wept tears of gratitude and said, "Oh, Mother, those are beautiful hands, the most beautiful in the world. Don't ever hide them again!"

Just so, the blood of Christ may seem to be a grim, repulsive subject to those who do not realize its true significance; but to those who have been rescued from sin's chains, Christ's nail-pierced hands are beautiful beyond measure, for they tell us of His love and His willingness to save us regardless of the cost.

New Hearts, New World

"I will give you a new heart and put a new spirit within you; I will take the heart of stone out of your flesh and give you a heart of flesh."

EZEKIEL 36:26

Today we have more knowledge than at any other time in history. In seconds our laptops or smartphones can call up information about a topic that would have taken years to collect formerly. Young people graduate from high schools, colleges, and universities with more knowledge than ever before—but they are not always acquiring the wisdom to use it. In spite of their knowledge, they are confused, bewildered, frustrated, and without moral moorings.

Why is there so little peace in a world of unprecedented knowledge and unlimited potential? The problem, Jesus said, is the human heart: "out of the heart proceed evil thoughts, murders, adulteries" (Matthew 15:19). The new world will come about only when Jesus Christ, the King of kings and the Lord of lords, reigns supreme in people's hearts. At the end of the present age, God will act, and Scripture promises that He will act dramatically and decisively. But before that time comes, God wants to rule in our hearts.

Is He ruling in yours?

Think Eternity

"Seek first the kingdom of God."

MATTHEW 6:33

King George V wrote on the flyleaf of the Bible of a friend: "The secret of happiness is not to do what you like to do, but to learn to like what you have to do."

Too many people think happiness is an elusive, will-o'-the-wisp thing to be found only by constant pursuit and relentless searching. But happiness is not an end in itself; it is the byproduct of something far greater. Jesus told His disciples: "Seek first the kingdom of God and His righteousness, and all these things shall be added to you" (Matthew 6:33). The "things" He spoke of were the basic needs of life: food, drink, clothes, shelter. He told us not to make these things the chief goal of our lives, but to "seek . . . the kingdom."

There, if we will take it, is the secret of happiness: "Seek first the kingdom of God." How do we do this? By submitting ourselves without reserve to Jesus Christ as King of our lives every day. This is the path of true happiness.

What Are You Pursuing?

I denied myself nothing. . . .
Yet when I surveyed all that my hands had done
and what I had toiled to achieve,
everything was meaningless.

ECCLESIASTES 2:10–11 NIV

King Solomon was convinced he knew how to find happiness—and with his vast resources, he was able to pursue it. Wealth, fame, pleasure, power, lavish houses, a reputation for wisdom—you name it, King Solomon had it. Yet after gaining everything he had ever wanted, he reluctantly concluded that his life was still empty and without meaning. His search for lasting happiness had failed; his soul was empty.

Are you like King Solomon—convinced that the things of this world will bring you happiness and peace, and pursuing them with all your might? Don't be deceived; they never will. And the reason is because you were made to know God.

Later, King Solomon realized this. He should have known it sooner; after all, his father, David, was a man after God's own heart, and Solomon himself had vowed to live according to God's wisdom. Don't be misled (as he was). Make Christ the center and foundation of your life—beginning today.

Faith Grows by Expression

"You are the light of the world."

MATTHEW 5:14

Tom Allan, Scotland's famous preacher, was brought to Christ while a soldier was singing, "Were you there when they crucified my Lord?" He said it was neither the song nor the voice, but the spirit in which that soldier sang—something about his manner, something about his sincerity of expression—that convicted Allan of his wicked life and turned him to the Savior.

Jesus said, "You are the light of the world. . . . Let your light so shine before [others], that they may see your good works and glorify your Father in heaven" (Matthew 5:14, 16).

Our faith becomes stronger as we express it; a growing faith is a sharing faith. Pray now for those you know who need Christ, and ask God to help you be a witness to them—by the life you live and the words you speak.

All for Jesus

We are in Him who is true, in His Son Jesus Christ.
1 JOHN 5:20

In His Steps, by Charles M. Sheldon, tells of a pastor who challenged his congregation to pledge for one year not to do anything without first asking the question, "What would Jesus do?"

This challenge was kindled when a shabby man, mourning his wife who had died in poverty, stumbled into a wealthy church and addressed the congregation. He said, "I heard some people singing at a church prayer meeting the other night: 'All for Jesus! All for Jesus! / All my being's ransomed powers; / All my thoughts and words and doings, / All my days and all my hours.' I kept wondering as I sat on the steps outside just what they meant by it. It seems to me there's an awful lot of trouble in the world that somehow wouldn't exist if all the people who sing such songs went and lived them out."

If someone posed the same question to us, what would be our response? Do we live our lives with the thought, *What would Jesus do?* Do we put it into practice every day?

True Worship

Come, let us bow down in worship,
let us kneel before the Lord our Maker;
for he is our God
and we are the people of his pasture,
the flock under his care.

PSALM 95:6–7 NIV

When was the last time you truly worshipped God? What is worship, anyway?

Worship in the truest sense takes place only when our full attention is on God—on His glory, His power, His majesty, His love, His compassion. And if we're honest, this doesn't happen very often, because even in church or in our times of quiet devotion, we get distracted.

Notice in these verses what prompted the psalmist's worship. First, he recognized that God is the Lord—the sovereign, all-powerful God of the universe. He recognized, too, that God had made him; he wasn't here by accident, but by God's perfect plan. Finally, he worshipped God because God had made him part of His flock, constantly watching over him and providing for his every need.

Learn to shut out the distractions that keep you from truly worshipping God. Then turn your mind and heart to Him every day, praising Him for who He is and thanking Him for His love for you in Christ.

God's Blessings

Every good gift and every perfect gift is from above.
JAMES 1:17

In the midst of the Lord's Prayer are these familiar words: "Give us this day our daily bread" (Matthew 6:11). They remind us that we are dependent on God for everything, and He is the giver of every blessing. "Every good gift and every perfect gift is from above, and comes down from the Father of lights" (James 1:17).

Some people say, "Why should I pray for my daily bread? I can take care of my own needs!" But listen: if it weren't for God's love and grace, you wouldn't have anything. We need to pray this prayer every day, because we need to be reminded to trust God in everything.

This prayer reminds us also of Jesus' words: "I am the bread of life. He who comes to Me shall never hunger" (John 6:35). Thank God for all His gifts—especially Christ, the greatest gift of all.

God's Life-Changing Word

They asked each other, "Were not our hearts burning within us while he talked with us on the road and opened the Scriptures to us?"

LUKE 24:32 NIV

Can an ancient book that was written by many people over the course of many centuries have anything to say to us today? Is the Bible's message honestly relevant?

Yes, it is—as millions of believers around the world would attest. If anything, in fact, it's more relevant today than ever before, as we see the storm clouds gathering and events taking place that herald the second coming of Jesus Christ. As the Bible says, "Our salvation is nearer than when we first believed" (Romans 13:11).

But the Bible is as up-to-date as tomorrow for another reason: it alone answers the deepest questions of the human heart—questions that have not changed over the centuries: *Who am I? Why am I here? Where did I come from? Where am I going when I die? How should I live?* Only the Bible gives us firm answers to these questions—and the reason is because it is God's Word, given by Him to guide us and point us to Christ. Is the Bible the foundation of your life?

Love in Action

Since God so loved us, we also ought to love one another. No one has ever seen God; but if we love one another, God lives in us and his love is made complete in us.

1 JOHN 4:11–12 NIV

Jesus said, "All men will know that you are my disciples, if you love one another" (John 13:35 NIV). But how do we put that love into action?

Serve one another. The Lord modeled this when He washed His disciples' feet. Be patient with one another. This is possible because of the Spirit's presence in us. Be courteous to one another. Even if someone is difficult or disagreeable, treat them with gentleness and love. Set an example for one another "in speech, in life, in love, in faith and in purity" (1 Timothy 4:12 NIV). Forgive one another because God forgave you. If you do not extend forgiveness, God "will not forgive your sins" (Matthew 6:15 NIV).

We are not to judge one another. That is the Lord's job. We may be called to rebuke or reprove in love, but we are not to judge. Be subject one to another. That will mean not always having things our way. Edify one another. We are to encourage and build up our brothers and sisters in Christ. Pray for one another. What a privilege to come before the Lord on another's behalf.

Christ Provides the Cure

If anyone is in Christ, he is a new creation.

2 CORINTHIANS 5:17

Wouldn't it be wonderful if we could find a medicine that would absolutely cure human nature's weaknesses and failures? Conflict, discontent, and unhappiness plague people everywhere. But suppose a cure could be found for humanity's ills. It would cause a worldwide stampede!

The most thrilling news in the world is that there is a cure! God has provided the medicine—and that "medicine" is Christ. Through Him our sins can be forgiven, and by His Holy Spirit within us, our lives can be changed and renewed.

Sin, confusion, and disillusionment can be replaced by righteousness, joy, and hope. Our souls can know peace, a peace that is not dependent on outward circumstances. This cure was provided two thousand years ago by Jesus Christ's death and resurrection for us. Is He working daily in your life, changing you and making you more like Him?

Looking for Lasting Joy

May the God of hope fill you with all joy.
ROMANS 15:13

How often have you found what you were looking for in life, only to realize it didn't bring you the satisfaction you thought it would?

It is life's ultimate frustration—thinking we will find fulfillment in the things of this world. But they can never bring lasting happiness. As one bumper sticker I saw expressed it, "All I want is a little more than I have now."

We look for love, security, and happiness through our jobs, our possessions, our relationships—but if they really brought lasting joy, wouldn't we have testimonies to that effect from millions of people all over the world? Instead, we find emptiness, discontent, and hopelessness.

Try putting Christ first and watch how your life is turned around. You will discover that He alone is the source of the love, peace, and joy you have been searching for.

Seeking the Truth

While Paul was . . . in Athens . . . he reasoned in the synagogue with the Jews and the God-fearing Greeks, as well as in the marketplace day by day with those who happened to be there.

ACTS 17:16–17 NIV

When the apostle Paul came to Athens, Greece, he saw people who were like many in our world today: they were trying to put together the puzzle of life.

The average Athenian of that day was a religious person. In fact, the people in Athens had numerous gods, and their city was sprinkled with numerous idols and temples. They also followed numerous philosophies in their search for truth.

The philosophers of Athens argued with Paul—but some who heard him were serious searchers after truth. The religions and philosophies of the day had left them empty, and they wanted to know the truth. And they heard it as they listened to Paul tell them about Jesus, and the hope we can have because of Him.

Are you searching for the truth? Don't let anything—or anyone—keep you from Jesus, who alone is "the way and the truth and the life" (John 14:6 NIV).

Enjoying God's Presence

In Your presence is fullness of joy.
PSALM 16:11

Have you ever watched a young couple communicate their love for each other without even saying a word? Maybe you have experienced it yourself. Every glance, every touch, every smile conveys love. People deeply in love find absolute bliss simply being in each other's presence.

In the same way, simply being in the presence of God brings us great joy. It happens as we listen to Him speak in His Word; it happens as we pray. But it also happens as we simply enjoy His presence—meditating on His goodness, delighting in the beauty of His creation, rejoicing in the life of a new baby or the surprise of an unexpected blessing. The Bible says, "Be still, and know that I am God" (Psalm 46:10).

Someday we will be in His presence forever; the Bible says, "God Himself will be with them" (Revelation 21:3). What joy that will be! But in the meantime, delight in His presence right now, for He is with you every hour of the day.

Ask . . . and Receive

"Ask and it will be given to you; seek and you will find; knock and the door will be opened to you."

LUKE 11:9 NIV

How can you know that you will go to Heaven when you die?

Suppose a friend comes by your house and offers you a gift. What would you do? Would you refuse to take it until you had paid him for it? Would you decline it because you felt you weren't worthy of it? No, of course not. Your friend wants you to have it and has already paid for it; all you must do is accept it.

In a far greater way, this is what Jesus Christ did for you. By His death on the cross, He paid the price for your salvation—completely and fully. Now He offers it to you as a free gift—and all you have to do is receive it. The Bible says, "For the wages of sin is death, but the gift of God is eternal life in Christ Jesus our Lord" (Romans 6:23 NIV).

Have you received this gift? If not, you can, by confessing to God your sins and your need of Christ, and then asking Him to come into your life. Salvation is God's free gift; why not receive it today?

Problems—and Peace

Present your requests to God. And the peace of God,
which transcends all understanding, will guard your
hearts and your minds in Christ Jesus.

PHILIPPIANS 4:6–7 NIV

God doesn't necessarily remove all our problems when we become followers of Christ. But He has promised to be with us and help us and encourage us in the midst of those problems. Jesus' promise to His disciples is still true: "Peace I leave with you; my peace I give you. . . . Do not let your hearts be troubled and do not be afraid" (John 14:27 NIV).

How is it possible to experience this kind of peace? It's possible first of all because we are never alone if we know Christ. He loves us and is with us, and nothing we will ever face takes Him by surprise. This peace is also possible because the Holy Spirit gives us patience and joy even in the midst of life's difficulties. And peace is possible because we know our problems are only temporary; someday they will all come to an end.

Which is better: facing life's problems and hurts without God—or facing them with Him? Which are you choosing today?

Serving Eternally

*You have a better and an enduring
possession for yourselves in heaven.*

HEBREWS 10:34

Some people think Heaven will be dull and boring, but nothing could be further from the truth. The Father's house will be a happy home because there will be work to do there. John wrote in Revelation 22:3, "His servants shall serve Him." Each one will be given exactly the task that suits his powers, his tastes, and his abilities.

And the Father's house will be a happy home because friends will be there. Have you ever been to a strange place and had the joy of seeing a familiar face? Not one of us who enters the Father's house will feel lonely or strange, for we who have put our trust in Christ are part of His family, sharing Heaven's joys forever with all our brothers and sisters in Christ.

Alexander MacLaren described Heaven this way: "The joys of heaven are not the joys of passive contemplation, of dreamy remembrance . . . but they are described thus, 'They rest not night or day,' and 'His servants serve Him and see His face.'" In the midst of Earth's turmoil, keep your eyes on Heaven!

God's Presence

"I am with you always, to the very end of the age."
MATTHEW 28:20 NIV

These words are Christ's promise to all His disciples, and it is a promise that is marvelously inclusive. No situation is excluded; no challenge is omitted.

Dr. Handley Moule, the noted Greek scholar and Anglican Bishop of Durham (England) in another generation, maintained that the word always could be paraphrased, "I am with you all the days, all day long." That means we can count on Christ's presence not only every day, but every moment of every day.

Of the fact of His presence there can be no doubt, for His Word cannot fail. What we need is to cultivate the sense of His presence, every day, every hour, every moment. This happens as we speak to Him in worship and prayer, and listen to Him speak to us through His Word, the Bible.

Putting the Pieces Back Together

Though I walk in the midst of trouble,
You will recieve me.

PSALM 138:7

D o you feel as if you've let God down? Let me reassure you that He loves you no matter what you've done. The last thing God wants you to do is to spend your life filled with guilt and shame and remorse.

May that truth give you hope, because it means that God wants to help you. He wants to put back together the pieces of your life and make you whole.

Think about the apostle Peter. After Jesus' arrest, Peter denied three times that he was a follower of Jesus and that he even knew Him (Matthew 26:69–75). But God forgave Peter, and he went on to help build the early Church. He's still ministering to believers today through his New Testament letters.

So if you feel as if you've failed God, ask for His forgiveness—and ask Him also to help you forgive yourself for what you have done. Then commit your future to Him. God will be with you, and you can trust Him to help you.

Words for the Crossroads

*I will instruct you and teach you in the way you
should go;
I will counsel you and watch over you.*

PSALM 32:8 NIV

Sometimes we face a major crossroad in life, and when we do, we find ourselves wondering what God's will is for the decision we must make. Maybe that's where you are right now.

The most important advice for life's crossroads is this: "Seek God's will." He knows what's best for you, and He doesn't want you to wander aimlessly through life.

Never forget: God made you, and He knows all about you—including the gifts and abilities He gave you. More than that, He loves you and wants what is best for you. Maybe you've been living for yourself and for the moment rather than for Him and for things eternal. But don't stay on that path; you will only end up at a blank wall if you ignore God's plan for your life.

Ask God to guide you as you make decisions about your future. He may not show you everything at once, but with Christ in your heart, you can face the future with confidence, knowing He will lead you in His perfect way.

The Tug of God's Love

The Spirit Himself bears witness with our
spirit that we are children of God.

ROMANS 8:16

Whenever anyone asks me how I can be so certain about who and what God really is, I am
reminded of the story of the little boy who was out flying a kite. It was a fine day for kite flying. The wind was
brisk, and large billowy clouds were blowing across the
sky. The kite went up and up until it was entirely hidden
by the clouds.

"What are you doing?" a man asked the little boy.

"I'm flying a kite," he replied.

"Flying a kite?" the man said. "How can you be
sure? You can't see the kite."

"No," said the boy, "I can't see it, but every little
while I feel a tug, so I know for sure that it's there!"

Don't take anyone else's word for God. Find Him for
yourself by inviting Jesus Christ to come into your life.
Then you, too, will know by the wonderful, warm tug
on your heartstrings that He is there for sure.

Rest for the Weary

"Come to Me, all you who labor and are heavy laden, and I will give you rest."

MATTHEW 11:28

Few people know how to rest these days. Even on vacation, many people rush to cram in as much as they can before returning to their jobs, where they spend twice as much energy catching up on the work and mail that piled up in their absence. Many of us need vacations just to rest from our vacations! Perhaps we have been looking for rest in the wrong places.

Jesus said, "Come to Me . . . and I will give you rest." Like peace, rest and contentment can be found only in one place, from one source, and that is the Lord Jesus Christ.

Jesus gives us the ultimate rest, the confidence we need, to escape the frustration and chaos of the world around us. Rest in Him and don't worry about what lies ahead. Jesus Christ has already taken care of tomorrow.

Good Reason

He had no beauty or majesty to attract us to him,
nothing in his appearance that we should desire him.

ISAIAH 53:2 NIV

It has always been interesting to me that—outside of the hints given in Isaiah 53—the Bible does not tell us what Jesus looked like, nor were paintings or drawings made of Him during His lifetime. Artists throughout the centuries have tried to imagine what He must have looked like, but the truth is, we don't know.

And I believe there is a very good reason for this: God knew that if we had an accurate portrait of Jesus, we would be tempted to worship it instead of worshipping Jesus Himself. We could even lapse into a type of idolatry, and that would be wrong.

But someday we will know what the risen Christ looks like, for someday we will enter into His presence forever. And when we do, the Bible says, "we shall be like Him, for we shall see Him as He is" (1 John 3:2). Then we will share in His resurrection glory, and we will share in His sinless perfection.

Are you ready for that glorious day? You can be, by committing yourself to Christ and opening your heart and life to Him.

Keep on Being Filled

Be filled with the Spirit.

EPHESIANS 5:18

The command to "be filled with the Spirit" actually has the idea of continuously being filled in the original Greek language. We are not filled once for all, like a bucket. Instead, we are to be filled constantly. This verse might be translated, "Be filled and keep on being filled."

Dr. Merrill C. Tenney has compared this to the situation of an old-time farmhouse kitchen. In one corner was a sink; above it was a pipe through which came a continuous stream of water from the spring outside. The water, by running constantly, kept the sink brimful of good water.

In the same way, we are not to let ourselves be filled and then emptied of the Spirit—like a leaky bucket—only to be refilled later on, again and again. Rather, the Holy Spirit should flow within us constantly—and He will as we yield ourselves to Christ's presence and power every day.

Choosing the Minority

*"If the world hates you, keep in mind
that it hated me first."*

JOHN 15:18 NIV

People often have one of three reactions to the message of the gospel.

First, some people will deny the gospel is true. They laugh and scoff and say, "This talk about sin and resurrection is foolish and ridiculous." Pride may prompt this scorn. Others fear what people would think, so they don't give credence to God's truth. Other fears also can keep us from committing our lives to Christ and following Him closely.

Second, some people delay: "I'll think about it and maybe make a commitment to follow Jesus some other time." But it's dangerous to delay making a decision. You may never hear the gospel again, or you may not see another tomorrow.

Third, some people will make a decision for Christ even though they know that being a believer may place them in a minority. It's tough to be a Christian in our world. We need to be willing to take on Jesus' unpopularity and the scorn that is often heaped on Him.

What is your response to Jesus? Denial . . . delay . . . or decision?

Physical and Spiritual Health

*For physical training is of some value, but godliness
has value for all things, holding promise for both the
present life and the life to come.*

1 TIMOTHY 4:8 NIV

Eating right, exercising regularly, and sleeping adequately—these are some of the components of a
physically healthy life. And God wants us to take care
of the body He has given us. The Bible says, "Your body
is a temple of the Holy Spirit. . . . Therefore honor God
with your body" (1 Corinthians 6:19–20 NIV).

But we can give too much attention to our bodies
and almost worship them by giving them the amount
of attention that only God deserves. We can focus on
our physical health so much that we ignore the health
of our soul.

Has this happened to you? Only you can answer
that question, and I hope you will face it honestly. Only
God should have first place in your life, for only He is
worthy of your worship.

Someday your life will be over, no matter how much
attention you give to your health. Will you look back with
regret, because you nourished your body but starved
your soul?

Children of Light

You, brethren, are not in darkness. . . .
You are all sons of light.
1 THESSALONIANS 5:4–5

T he born-again Christian sees life not as a blurred, confused, meaningless mass, but as something planned and purposeful. His eyes have been opened to spiritual truth.

In Christ's first sermon at Nazareth, He said that one of the reasons He had come to Earth was to preach "recovery of sight to the blind" (Luke 4:18). By nature we are all spiritually blind because of sin. But the Spirit of God helps us see our sin and our helplessness and shows us God's redeeming grace in Christ. The Spirit reveals the truth of Jesus' declaration: "I am the light of the world. He who follows Me shall not walk in darkness, but have the light of life" (John 8:12).

In the Bible we are called "children of light and children of the day" (1 Thessalonians 5:5 NRSV), because it pleased God to share His mysteries and secrets with us. We are no longer in the dark—we know where we came from, we know why we are here, and we know where we are going. In the midst of a world living in spiritual darkness, walk as a child of the light!

Hope for the Hopeless

As a father has compassion on his children,
*so the L*ORD *has compassion on those who fear him;*
for he knows how we are formed.

PSALM 103:13–14 NIV

Discouragement, hopelessness, despair—so many situations in this fallen world can make us feel this way. Problems and struggles can wear us down physically, emotionally, and mentally—and can even erode our faith.

But God, our loving Heavenly Father, understands our feelings at times like these, and He wants to help us. After all, His Son, Jesus Christ, went through the same experiences we do—although without sinning (Hebrews 4:15). We are never alone when we know Christ, and we can trust Him to lead us out of our dilemma.

Life sometimes takes us through hard places. But even in the midst of them, God is with us, and nothing can happen to us that is beyond His ability to help.

The Bible says we can "rejoice in our sufferings, because we know that suffering produces perseverance; perseverance, character; and character, hope" (Romans 5:3–4 NIV). Being joyful may seem hard to you right now, but put your hope in Christ, and thank Him that He will never abandon you.

Life After Death

For to me, to live is Christ, and to die is gain.

PHILIPPIANS 1:21

I have asked a number of scientists questions concerning life after death, and most of them say, "We just do not know." Science deals in formulas and test tubes. But there is a spiritual world science knows nothing about.

Because many do not believe in life after death, we find writings filled with tragedy and pessimism. The writings of William Faulkner, James Joyce, and many others are filled with pessimism, darkness, and tragedy. Sadly, the same was often true of their lives.

How different from Jesus Christ who said, "I am the resurrection and the life. He who believes in Me, though he may die, he shall live. And whoever lives and believes in Me shall never die" (John 11:25–26). Our hope of immortality is based on Christ alone—not on our desires, longings, arguments, or instincts of immortality. And because we know Christ is alive, we have hope—hope for the present and hope for life beyond the grave.

Only . . .

"We have no more than five loaves and two fish."

LUKE 9:13

"We have only . . ." Little did the disciples know what Jesus would do with only five loaves and two fish. The Bible tells us that everyone in the crowd ate—and there were twelve basketfuls of leftovers. And the men alone numbered five thousand.

Perhaps when you give to your church or some other ministry, your thinking is like that of the disciples: "I can only give . . ." But let me challenge you to do just that! Give what you can give—and give in faith.

After all, Jesus only had a few loaves of bread and a couple of fish, but in His hands God multiplied it, and it became a huge feast for the crowd. In the same way God is able to take even a very small amount of money and use it to accomplish His purposes—if we dedicate it to Him.

Jesus gave everything for your salvation, even His life. Have you given everything back to Him in return—including your finances? Make it your goal to serve Christ in every way you can, including with your money.

Because of Prayer

The effective, fervent prayer of a
righteous man avails much.

JAMES 5:16

John Knox prayed, and God's responses to his prayers caused Queen Mary to say that she feared the prayers of John Knox more than she feared all the armies of Scotland. John Wesley prayed, and revival came to England, sparing that nation the horrors of the French Revolution. Jonathan Edwards prayed, and revival spread throughout the American colonies.

History has been changed time after time because of prayer. I tell you, history could be changed again if people went to their knees in believing prayer. Even when times are bleak and the world scorns God, He still works through the prayers of His people. Pray today for revival in your nation, and around the world.

Suffering and Success

Whenever you face trials of any kind,
consider it nothing but joy.

JAMES 1:2 NRSV

Before the power of the atom was discovered, science had to devise a way to smash the atom. The secret of the atom's immeasurable and limitless power was in its being crushed.

Some of the most godly people I've ever known were men and women who were called upon to endure great suffering. They could have grown bitter and resentful . . . yet, because they knew Christ and walked in the joy of His presence every day, God blessed them and turned them into people who reflected Christ.

Dr. Edward Judson, at the dedication of a church in New York City, said, "Suffering and success go together. If you are succeeding without suffering, it is because others before you have suffered; if you are suffering without succeeding, it is that others after you may succeed."

Admittedly it's hard to "count it all joy" (James 1:2) when suffering comes. But when it does, ask God to sanctify it and use it to make you steadfast in your faith.

Looking into the Mirror

*No one will be declared righteous in [God's]
sight by observing the law; rather, through the
law we become conscious of sin.*

ROMANS 3:20 NIV

Why did God give us the Ten Commandments when He knew we would break them?

He gave them in order to show us that we are sinful and weak, and that we need His mercy. When I look into the "mirror" of the Ten Commandments, I see that I am a sinner. Then I cry out, "God, be merciful to me!"

It is significant that after the giving of the commandments is the story of the building of the sacrificial altar. The Ten Commandments were given first, but the law and the altar go together. The law reveals that we are sinners and that we need forgiveness. But the law also reveals that the only path to forgiveness is through sacrifice. The law enables us to see ourselves as morally dirty and in need of cleansing. But it also points us to the place of cleansing: the cross of Christ.

God's law shows us what we really are: sinners who need God's grace and mercy. May the law continue to be the schoolmaster that leads us to Christ and His forgiveness.

Talking to God

*Oh that men would praise the LORD for his goodness,
and for his wonderful works to the children of men!*

PSALM 107:8 KJV

When you were very young and first started speaking, did you talk to your parents in long sentences and for great lengths of time? I doubt it. And yet they weren't disappointed in you; they were delighted by your first attempts to speak.

In the same way, when we truly understand that God is our loving Heavenly Father and we are His children, then we won't worry so much about disappointing Him by our prayers. Don't worry about your lack of eloquence; no matter how simple they are, God delights in our prayers when they truly express the feelings and desires of our heart.

If prayer feels uncomfortable to you, begin by thanking God for all He has done for you, and praising Him for His love and goodness. Then confess your sins and ask for His forgiveness. Finally, bring your concerns to Him. You may even find it helpful to keep a list of people for whom you are praying.

Remember: Jesus Christ opened Heaven's door for us by His death on the cross. When we know Him, we can be sure God hears our prayers.

When Christ Comes

Abide in Him, that when He appears, we may . . .
not be ashamed before Him at His coming.

1 JOHN 2:28

Almost two thousand years ago, Jesus Christ won the decisive battle against sin and Satan through His death and resurrection. Satan did his best to overthrow God's plans, but he could not win against God's overwhelming power.

Yet the war continues, for although Satan is a defeated foe, he is still alive and does everything he can to block God's work. But when Christ comes again, the war will be over. His victory over evil will be complete, and He will usher in an age in which sin and death will no longer rule, and cruelty and suffering will no longer exist.

For you who believe in Jesus Christ, the future is assured. Tomorrow belongs to you! You await the distant trumpet announcing the coming of Jesus Christ. In the meantime let nothing discourage you. Keep your eyes on Christ and live each day as if He were coming tomorrow. After all, He might!

Above the Din

Let this mind be in you which was also in Christ Jesus.
Philippians 2:5

We Christians are not to be conformed to this world in the way we think. The world by its advertisements, its conversation, and its philosophy is engaged in a gigantic brainwashing. Not always consciously but sometimes unconsciously, the Christian is beset by secular and worldly propaganda, calling us to live for ourselves and to put things and selfish pleasures ahead of God. The world's sewage system threatens to contaminate the stream of Christian thought.

However, above the din we can hear the voice of Scripture: "Do not be conformed to this world, but be transformed by the renewing of your mind, that you may prove what is that good and acceptable and perfect will of God" (Romans 12:2).

Time yourself the next time you read the Bible and pray. Compare it to the amount of time you spend watching television or surfing the Internet. Is God getting His share of your time and attention?

Is the world shaping your mind—or is Christ?

No Secrets from God

You alone know the hearts of all men.

1 KINGS 8:39 NIV

Do these words frighten you? They well might, because they remind us of a truth we often forget: God knows everything about us, even our deepest thoughts and motives. We can hide them from other people; we may even hide them from ourselves. But we can't hide them from God.

This shouldn't surprise us; after all, God knows everything. The Bible says, "Nothing in all creation is hidden from God's sight. Everything is uncovered and laid bare before the eyes of him to whom we must give account" (Hebrews 4:13 NIV). Think back over just the last twenty-four hours at all the thoughts you didn't want anyone else to know. But God knew them—every one of them.

But something should surprise us: in spite of all He knows about us, God still loves us. In fact, the verse above occurs in a prayer by King Solomon, thanking God for His love and forgiveness. Thank God for His grace and thank Him that, in spite of all He knows about us, in Christ "He has forgiven [us] all trespasses" (Colossians 2:13).

Letting Go of the Past

Get rid of all bitterness, rage and anger, brawling and slander, along with every form of malice.

EPHESIANS 4:31 NIV

Have you ever noticed that if you continue to hate someone, whatever that person did will continue to hurt you? Our anger and hatred just keep reopening the emotional wounds of the past.

This is one reason why we need to let go of the past and—with God's help—release our anger and hatred and replace them with His love. If we don't, our souls will be poisoned the rest of our life by bitterness and resentment, instead of reflecting the love and mercy of Christ. Remember Jesus' command: "Love your enemies and pray for those who persecute you" (Matthew 5:44 NIV).

Admittedly this isn't easy to do. That is why I urge you to turn to Christ and seek His forgiveness for all the ways you have hurt Him. When we realize how much we have hurt God, the hurts we have received from others will begin to fade.

Borrowed Troubles

*Let your requests be made known to God; and the
peace of God . . . will guard your hearts and minds.*

PHILIPPIANS 4:6-7

No troubles distress the mind and wear upon the
nerves like borrowed troubles. As someone has
written, "Worry is an old man with a bent head, carrying a load of feathers he thinks is lead."

Worry about what might happen makes even the
smallest trouble seem huge. Nervously anticipating
troubles that may never happen can crush our spirit.
Instead of "borrowing trouble" by constantly worrying about the future, listen instead to Jesus' promise:
"Peace I leave with you, My peace I give to you; not as
the world gives do I give to you. Let not your heart be
troubled, neither let it be afraid" (John 14:27).

Whatever is worrying you right now, give it to Jesus
and trust Him to take care of it. Let His peace replace
your worry.

Using Our Gifts

*We have different gifts. . . . If it is serving, let
him serve; if it is teaching, let him teach; if it is
encouraging, let him encourage . . . if it is showing
mercy, let him do it cheerfully.*

ROMANS 12:6–8 NIV

One of Satan's oldest tricks is to make us think we aren't worth anything and that God can't use us. But it simply isn't true. From one end to the other, the Bible tells us that God loves us. If He didn't, Christ would never have died for our sins. But He did—because God loves us. And God also wants to use us—He has equipped every one of us with the gifts we need to serve Him.

What spiritual gifts has God given you? They won't be the same as someone else's gifts—but they are the ones God knew you needed. Don't say your gifts are insignificant or don't matter; God didn't make a mistake when He gave them to you. You may have a special gift for welcoming visitors to your church, or helping the church's nursery, or praying for others, or running errands for sick people. It may be helping in a homeless shelter or packing boxes of clothing to ship overseas.

Ask God to show you your gifts—and then ask Him to help you use them for His glory.

Glorious Responsibilities

"If anyone serves Me, him My Father will honor."

JOHN 12:26

Young people seek adventure and excitement and, more important, something to believe in. Young people want a cause to give themselves to and a flag to follow. Without a purpose greater than themselves, many young people know they will end up with empty hearts and meaningless lives.

The only cause that is big enough to satisfy the yearning of our hearts—whatever our age—is the cause of Jesus Christ; and its flag is the blood-stained body that was lifted on the cross of Calvary for the redemption of the world.

This invitation to discipleship is the most thrilling cause we could ever imagine. Think of it: the God of the universe invites us to become His partners in reclaiming the world for Him! We can each have a part, using the unique gifts and opportunities God has given us.

Christ's call is for us to be His disciples every day. How are you responding to His call?

Living Stones

*You also, as living stones, are being built up a
spiritual house.*
1 PETER 2:5

I have a friend who lost his job, a fortune, his wife,
and his home. But he tenaciously held to his faith in
Christ—the only thing he had left. Like Job in the Old
Testament, he would not abandon God, no matter what
happened. And yet, like Job, he couldn't help but wonder why.

One day he stopped to watch some men doing stone-
work on a huge church. One of them was chiseling a
triangular piece of stone.

"What are you going to do with that?" asked my
friend.

The workman said, "See that little opening away up
there near the spire? Well, I'm shaping this down here
so it will fit in up there."

Tears filled my friend's eyes as he walked away, for
it seemed that God had spoken through the workman to
explain the ordeal through which he was passing: "I'm
shaping you down here so you'll fit in up there."

He Can Be Trusted

God is not a man, that he should lie,
nor a son of man, that he should change his mind.

NUMBERS 23:19 NIV

Can God's promises be trusted? Take, for example, His promise to be with us in every situation: "Never will I leave you; never will I forsake you" (Hebrews 13:5 NIV). Is it really true? When life turns against us and we can't see any way out of our problems, is He still with us—even if it looks as if He has abandoned us? Can His promises really be trusted?

Yes, we can trust His promises—because God does not lie, nor does He change His mind. What if He did? Then we wouldn't have any reason to depend on Him; His Word could not be trusted. But He doesn't lie, and He doesn't change His mind—because He is perfect and holy, and He loves us.

Perhaps this is a discouraging time for you. But God knows your problems, and He can be trusted to be with you. God hasn't promised that our way will always be smooth and free of problems, but He has promised to be with us—and that should give us great comfort.

Godly Thoughts

Be transformed by the renewing of your mind.
ROMANS 12:2

The Bible teaches that our minds are to be brought under the control of Christ. The reason? How we act will be determined by how we think. If God is to change our lives, He must first change our minds.

The human mind cannot exist as a vacuum. It will be filled either with good or with evil. It will be filled either with Christ or with carnality. What will make the difference? It depends on us, on what we allow to enter our minds.

Negatively, we must turn our minds away from evil. We must be careful what kind of television programs we see, what kind of books we read, what things occupy our thoughts.

But it isn't enough to put bad thoughts out of our minds. Positively, those bad thoughts must be replaced with good thoughts—thoughts that are shaped by God and His Word, by prayer and worship, by fellowship with other Christians.

Deliberately turn away from every evil thought today and ask God to fill your mind instead with Himself from this moment on.

The Trap of Laziness

*Be diligent in these matters; give yourself wholly to
them, so that everyone may see your progress.*

1 TIMOTHY 4:15 NIV

L et me suggest a little exercise, the results of which
may surprise you. Take a piece of paper and write
down all the things you do in an average twenty-four-hour
day—sleeping, eating, working, shopping, watching television, surfing the Internet, etc. Then put beside each item
how much time you spend on it during an average day.

Now look at your list. How much of your time is
used for things that really aren't important or may even
be morally or spiritually harmful? Take television or the
Internet, for example. We all need to relax, and I'm not
suggesting all entertainment is harmful or bad—not at
all. But how much of your spare time is simply wasted?

One last question: How much time did you give to
God? Remember: Satan doesn't need for us to fall into
gross sin in order to defeat us; a large dose of laziness
will do the trick just as well. Put Christ first in your life,
and then commit every hour of the day to Him.

FEBRUARY

A Glorious Opportunity

May the glory of the LORD endure forever;
May the LORD rejoice in His works.

PSALM 104:31

C. T. Studd, the famous Cambridge cricketer and missionary pioneer, wrote the following couplet while still a student at Cambridge:

Only one life, 'twill soon be past;
Only what's done for Christ will last.

Life is a glorious opportunity if it is used to condition us for eternity. If we fail in this, though we succeed in everything else, our life will have been a failure. There is no escape for the man who squanders his opportunity to prepare to meet God.

You will never live this day again; once it is gone, it is gone forever. How will you spend it—for yourself or for Christ? Remember: "Only what's done for Christ will last."

Right and Fair

Masters, give your bondservants what is just and fair, knowing that you also have a Master in heaven.

Colossians 4:1

Thankfully, slavery is a thing of the past for us—but the underlying principle the apostle Paul addresses above still stands: if we are employers or supervisors, we are to do "what is right and fair" to those who work under us. After all, he reminds us, we, too, have a Master, and someday we'll give an account of our lives to Him—including how we treated others.

Admittedly this isn't always easy to put into action. In some situations it's not always clear what is right and fair, and sometimes people react negatively even when we do treat them fairly. Human beings can be very difficult to deal with—as you've probably discovered! But the principle still holds, and we should seek God's wisdom to carry it out.

But this principle holds for all of us—for it is just another way of expressing Jesus' words to His disciples: "In everything, do to others what you would have them do to you" (Matthew 7:12 niv). Write this principle on your heart—and put it into action every day.

Always with Us

*No good thing will He withhold
from those who walk uprightly.*

PSALM 84:11

Many times, we make the mistake of thinking that Christ's help is needed only for sickrooms or in times of overwhelming sorrow and suffering. This is not true. Certainly, God is with us in times of distress, and that is a comforting truth. But listen: Jesus wants to be part of every experience and every moment of our lives.

He went to the wedding at Cana as well as to the home of Mary and Martha when Lazarus died. He wept with those who wept, and rejoiced with those who rejoiced. Someone has said, "There are just as many stars in the sky at noon as at midnight, although we cannot see them in the sun's glare."

I seriously doubt if we will ever understand our trials and adversities until we are safely in Heaven. Then when we look back, we are going to be absolutely amazed at how God took care of us and blessed us even in the storms of life. But God is with us in the good times also, and we should thank Him for them and commit them to Him just as surely as we do the hard times.

God's Love and Judgment

*The Lord is gracious and full of compassion,
slow to anger and great in mercy.*

Psalm 145:8

Imagine what the world would be like if God were only a God of love, who never judged evil or tried to stop it. Evil men could carry out their plans without fear. They would never have to worry that God would judge them or try to stop them.

Now imagine what the world would be like if God were only a God of judgment, who punished us every time we did wrong. If God were like that, none of us would ever have a chance, for we sin every day. Sometimes, however, God does correct and discipline us—not because He hates us, but because He loves us and wants us to turn from the destructive path we are on.

If you are a parent, you love your children, but at times, you need to discipline them for their good. In a far greater way, God loves us, so He also disciplines us when we need it for our good. The Bible says, "Do not . . . be discouraged when you are rebuked by Him; for whom the Lord loves He chastens" (Hebrews 12:5–6).

Who's to Blame?

"For God did not send His Son into the world to condemn the world, but that the world through Him might be saved."

JOHN 3:17

Why would a loving God send anyone to Hell? Let me answer that question with a question.

If someone deliberately commits a crime and is caught, who is to blame if that person is found guilty and sentenced to jail? Is the judge to blame—or is the criminal?

The lawbreaker is to blame for what has happened to him, not the judge. Yes, the judge sentenced him, but he alone broke the law, and he alone is to blame for the penalty he received. The judge was only following the law. The lawbreaker can't blame the judge; he can only blame himself.

Likewise, when we break God's law, we stand condemned, and we ourselves are to blame for what happens to us, not God. We can only blame ourselves for the consequences.

But we don't have to pay the penalty for our sins because Christ has already paid it for us. By His death on the cross, Jesus took the punishment you and I deserve. Jesus suffered judgment and Hell for us. Praise God, for His love!

Above the Clouds

Your faithfulness reaches to the clouds.

PSALM 36:5

My home is on a mountain nearly four thousand feet high. Many times we can see below us the clouds in the valley. Some mornings we wake up to find that we are in lovely sunshine, but the valley below is covered with clouds. At other times thunderstorms come up, and we can see the lightning flash and hear the thunder roar down below, while we are enjoying beautiful sunlight and clear skies above.

Many times I have sat on our rustic front porch and watched the clouds below. I have thought of the clouds of discouragement and suffering that temporarily veil the sunlight of God's love from us. Many people live with a cloud hanging over their lives.

The Bible has a great deal to say about clouds, for they sometimes symbolize the spiritual forces that obscure the face of God. But He has not abandoned us. He is still there, and in faith we know we can trust His promise: "I will never leave you nor forsake you" (Hebrews 13:5).

Love Demonstrated

He loved us and sent His Son to be the
propitiation for our sins.
1 JOHN 4:10

The word *love* is used to mean many different things. We say that we "love" the house that we have just bought or that we "love" a particular vacation spot or that we "love" a peanut butter and jelly sandwich. We also "love" a certain television program, and we "love" our husband or wife. Hopefully we don't love our spouse the same way we love a peanut butter and jelly sandwich!

The greatest love of all, however, is God's love for us—a love that showed itself in action. A friend once observed, "Love talked about is easily ignored, but love demonstrated is irresistible." The Bible says, "God demonstrates His own love toward us, in that while we were still sinners, Christ died for us" (Romans 5:8). Now that is real love! How will you respond to His love today?

God's Sovereign Power and Constant Presence

The LORD shall reign forever.

PSALM 146:10

If we looked only at the headlines every day, we would have good reason to be pessimistic about the future. But don't forget two important truths.

First, the future is in God's hands, and nothing takes Him by surprise. He is sovereign over the history of the world as well as our own personal histories, and behind the scenes He is at work to accomplish His purposes. Even when the future seems dark, we can turn to God—who "reigns forever"—and trust the future into His hands.

Second, never forget that even when the future is unclear, God is with those of us who are trusting Christ as our Savior and Lord, and He helps us. The apostle Paul faced great danger and uncertainty, but he could still say, "I can do all things through Christ who strengthens me" (Philippians 4:13). No matter what the future holds for you—no matter what today holds for you—you do not face it alone if you know Christ.

Longing for Perfection

*Now the Lord God had planted a garden in the east,
in Eden; and there he put the man he had formed.*

GENESIS 2:8 NIV

The garden of Eden is not just a symbol. It was a real place—just as real as Adam and Eve themselves. The garden's exact location is not known, although it was apparently somewhere in the Middle East.

The opening chapters of the Bible tell us that the garden of Eden was perfect—a place given by God to Adam and Eve so that their every need would be met. The reason the garden was perfect was because sin had not yet entered the world. But when Adam and Eve listened to Satan and turned against God—when Adam and Eve sinned—that perfect garden was no longer perfect. God banished them from the garden, and they would never return.

Since that time, the human race has been searching for the peace and perfection Eden once provided—but without success, because sin has ravaged our world and our hearts.

But that is not the end of the story. Christ came to conquer sin and death—and He has! In Him there is hope!

Longing for God

My heart and my flesh cry out for the living God.

PSALM 84:2

Have you ever been under water for a period of time that is longer than you had expected? You know, as the time ticks away, how desperate you become to reach the surface and breathe the air. The greater the time you are under water, the more you long for a breath of air until that desire overwhelms you, and you rush to get to the surface as rapidly as possible. You have no other thoughts but quenching your need for air.

That is what it means to long for God, to feel unfulfilled without Him. It means we know we desperately need Him, even more than we need air, and we yearn to be filled with His presence. "My heart and my flesh cry out for the living God."

God wants us to be satisfied with nothing less than Himself. And we are never more fulfilled than when we know Him. Ask God to give you a new hunger for Him, so you may become filled with "the fullness of Christ" (Ephesians 4:13).

Triumph and Glory

The day of the Lord so comes as a thief in the night.
1 Thessalonians 5:2

Christians have no cause to go around wringing their hands, wondering what they will do in the face of the present world situation. The Scripture says that in the midst of persecution, confusion, wars, and rumors of wars, we are to comfort one another with the knowledge that Jesus Christ is coming back in triumph, glory, and majesty.

Many times when I go to bed at night, I think that before I awaken, Christ may come. Sometimes when I get up and look at the dawn, I think that perhaps this is the day He will return.

But until that day, God is still working—and so should we. In a world filled with turmoil and hopelessness, we are to pray, and we are to do all we can to alleviate suffering and bring Christ's love to others. May Jesus' words become true in your life: "Let your light so shine before men, that they may see your good works and glorify your Father in heaven" (Matthew 5:16).

Meet Me in Heaven

At the name of Jesus every knee should bow,
in heaven and on earth and under the earth,
and every tongue confess that Jesus Christ is Lord,
to the glory of God the Father.

PHILIPPIANS 2:10–11 NIV

Once I read a biography of Queen Victoria, and I learned that she would sometimes go into the slums of London. One day, she went into a home to have tea with an older woman. When she rose to leave, the queen asked, "Is there anything I can do for you?"

The woman said, "Yes, Your Majesty. You can meet me in Heaven."

The queen turned to her and said softly, "Yes. I'll be there, but only because of the blood that was shed on the cross for you and for me."

Queen Victoria, in her day the most powerful woman in the world, had to depend on the blood of Christ for her salvation. And so do we. God provided the way of salvation: He accepted as a covering for your sin and mine Jesus' blood, shed on the cross for us. The war that exists between Holy God and us sinful human beings can be over! The peace treaty was signed more than two thousand years ago in the blood of His Son, Jesus Christ.

The Bread of Life

He who wins souls is wise.

PROVERBS 11:30

We have bread to give to a hungry world—the Bread of Life, Jesus Christ. People may be so busy feeding on other things that they ignore Him or refuse Him, but we must keep offering Christ to a spiritually dying world.

We have water to give to a thirsting world—the Living Water, Jesus Christ. People may seek to quench the thirst of their souls in a hundred other ways, but we must keep crying out, "Ho! Everyone who thirsts, come to the waters" (Isaiah 55:1). Sometimes they can't come, and we have to carry it to them.

We must persevere. We must never give up. Christ never gave up, but "became obedient to the point of death" (Philippians 2:8).

All around you are people who hunger and thirst for God, although they may not even realize it. Will you point them to Christ, who alone can satisfy their deepest longings?

The Deceiver at Work

*"Beware of false prophets, who come to you
in sheep's clothing, but inwardly they are
ravenous wolves."*

MATTHEW 7:15

Sometimes it is extremely difficult for us to recognize a false prophet—someone who claims to speak for God, but in reality does not.

The underlying principle of all of Satan's tactics is deception, and no Christian, however spiritual, is beyond the seductive assaults of this crafty and clever enemy. He began his work of deception in the garden of Eden, and it continues to this day. Satan does not build a church and call it the First Church of Satan—he is far too clever for that. Instead, he tries to infiltrate the theological seminary and the pulpit, invading the Church under the cover of an orthodox vocabulary—but emptying sacred terms of their true biblical meaning or denying their truth.

The sword of the Spirit—the Bible—is the weapon God has provided for us to use in this battle between truth and deception. Make it a priority to wield that sword skillfully. God's followers need to know the truth He sets forth in His Word so that we can confidently discern between His truth and Satan's lies.

The Storm Is Behind Us

You have cast all my sins behind Your back.
ISAIAH 38:17

We shall never understand the extent of God's love in Christ at the cross until we understand that we shall never have to stand before the judgment of God for our sins. All our sins—without exception—were placed on Christ, and He took the judgment we deserve. He accomplished the work of redemption.

Once, while crossing the North Atlantic in a ship, I looked out my porthole when I got up in the morning and saw one of the blackest clouds I had ever seen. I was certain that we were in for a terrible storm. I ordered my breakfast sent to my room and spoke to the steward about the storm. He said, "Oh, we've already come through that storm. It's behind us."

If we are believers in Jesus Christ, we have already come through the storm of judgment. It happened at the cross. Don't be bound by your guilt or your fears any longer, but realize that sin's penalty has already been paid by Christ—completely and fully.

Children of God

*Behold what manner of love the Father has
bestowed on us, that we should be called
children of God!*

1 JOHN 3:1

When we commit our lives to Jesus as our Savior and Lord, we become His sons and daughters. Because God is responsible for our welfare, we are told to cast all our cares and anxieties upon Him (1 Peter 5:7). Because we are depending on God, Jesus said, "Let not your heart be troubled" (John 14:1).

Children are not shy about asking for things. They would not be normal if they didn't boldly make their desires known. God is keenly aware that we are dependent on Him for life's necessities, so we can freely ask Him for those things. God loves us, He knows our needs, and He wants to grant them to us. The Bible says, "No good thing will He withhold from those who walk uprightly" (Psalm 84:11).

But as God's children we are not meant just to sit back and selfishly enjoy our privileges. Instead, God wants us to serve Him and to help others.

Are you trusting your Heavenly Father to provide for you? Are you boldly asking Him for what you need?

How's Your Heart?

"Man looks at the outward appearance,
but the LORD looks at the heart."
1 SAMUEL 16:7

Your heart beats about 100,000 strokes every twenty-four hours. It contracts about 4,000 times an hour. Our entire blood supply circulates through our hearts every four minutes. No wonder doctors urge us to take care of our hearts!

As amazing as it is, when Scripture talks about the heart, it's not talking about that life-sustaining muscle. It's talking about our entire inner being. The heart is the seat of our emotions, the seat of decisive action, and the seat of belief as well as doubt. The heart symbolizes the center of our moral, spiritual, and intellectual life. It is the seat of our conscience and life.

And God knows our heart well. The Almighty God searches our heart, weighs our heart by the teaching of Scripture, opens our heart to His truth, and gives us a new heart when we come to Christ—a heart of flesh sensitive to His presence, His leading, and His love. Don't ever hesitate to take to Him whatever is on your heart. He already knows it anyway, but He doesn't want you to bear its pain or celebrate its joy alone.

Power to Change the World

You are my hope, O Lord GOD;
You are my trust from my youth.

PSALM 71:5

We still wrestle with the same problems that preoccupied Plato and Aristotle centuries ago: Where did we come from? Why are we here? Where are we going? We search for answers, but the signs all seem to say "No exit."

But the cross boldly stands against the confusion of our world, a beacon of hope in the midst of darkness and doubt. On the cross, Christ not only bridged the gap between God and us, but there we find the answers to life's deepest questions. There we discover our true identity: forgiven sinners who now belong to God. There we discover our true destiny: a glorious eternity with God in Heaven. There we discover our true purpose: to love God and serve Him with all our might.

Never underestimate what Christ did for us through the cross. By His death our salvation was won, and by His death our lives—and our world—can be transformed. What difference does the cross make in your life?

Reprogramming Our Hearts

*"You are precious and honored in my sight,
and . . . I love you."*

ISAIAH 43:4 NIV

One thing a computer manufacturer does is program each machine. At the factory, a set of instructions is inserted into the computer's memory, and those instructions tell the computer what to do.

In a sense, you and I get programmed. When we are young, our minds are constantly being programmed by the experiences we have. Later on, those instructions that have been inserted into our brains will try to tell us what to do and think. This programming happens to all of us. But when the things that have been put into our memories are bad or untrue, we will have problems later in life.

In that case, we need to reprogram our mind and heart; we need to replace the bad things that have taken root there with good and true things. And that is where God can help. In His Word, He provides truths to replace the lies you've believed about yourself.

Open your heart to Christ and ask Him to help you see yourself the way He sees you—as His beloved child, "precious and honored in my sight."

The Master Key

*The LORD our God we will serve, and
His voice we will obey!*

JOSHUA 24:24

I knew a wealthy father who refused to get his son a bicycle because the boy's report card showed disgracefully low marks, the yard was not raked, and other assignments had not been carried out. I'm sure the father would not have been wise to lavish gifts upon such a disobedient and ungrateful son. He wasn't being cruel or stingy; he simply knew his son needed to learn responsibility.

God, too, wants us to learn responsibility. Yes, we are saved by His grace—but we are also called to be responsible disciples, learning to follow Christ by obeying God's will. The Bible warns, "If you do not obey the voice of the LORD, but rebel against the commandment of the LORD, then the hand of the LORD will be against you" (1 Samuel 12:15).

If you want God to hear your prayers, surrender your selfishness and stubbornness to Him, and then humbly seek His will. Obedience is the master key to effective prayer.

Not Sight, But Faith

*"The Son of Man will come in the glory of
His Father with His angels."*
MATTHEW 16:27

Today, Christ is hidden from our view (although
through the Holy Spirit He lives in our hearts).
Today is the day of faith; as Paul wrote, "We walk by
faith, not by sight" (2 Corinthians 5:7). Only in the
future will we "see Him as He is" (1 John 3:2).

Christ's first appearing was quiet, almost unnoticed—
a humble manger, simple shepherds, an insignificant
corner of the Roman Empire. His second appearing will
be glorious and universal. He will be accompanied by
His angels and will defeat every enemy until He sub-
dues the whole Earth.

How easily the events of the moment crowd out
the promise of eternity! The present seems so real; the
unseen future seems so illusory. But in reality the opposite is true. Don't let the present consume you. Instead,
"seek those things which are above, where Christ is"
(Colossians 3:1).

Ruling in Your Heart

"The kingdom of God is within you."

LUKE 17:21

Too many people think God is to be found by looking within their own minds and souls, and they often cite these words of Jesus in support of their claim.

Jesus, however, wasn't teaching that God is within us and that all we need to do is look inward to find God. Instead, Jesus was talking to people who believed that the Messiah would establish an Earthly, political kingdom—and Jesus said that wasn't His goal. "My kingdom is not of this world," Jesus told Pilate (John 18:36). His goal instead was to rule in the hearts of men and women.

And that is exactly what happens when we give our life to Christ. When we turn to Him in repentance and faith, He cleanses us of our sins, and He comes to live within us by His Holy Spirit. Once that happens, He begins to rule in our lives. In other words, He sets up His Kingdom—His rule—within us.

More and more each day, may your life clearly reflect the Christ's kingship over every area of your life!

The Power of Touch

*Filled with compassion, Jesus reached out his
hand and touched the man.*

MARK 1:41 NIV

As was the custom of the day, the man afflicted
with leprosy had called out "Unclean! Unclean!"
to warn people of his presence so they could avoid him.
Who knows how long it had been since he had experienced a human touch—a warm embrace, an encouraging
pat on the back, a friendly handshake? Had it been
months, or even years?

Jesus knew the man needed relief from this disease, but before Jesus dealt with his skin, He healed the
man's emotional pain. Jesus reached out and touched
him. Can you imagine how that leper felt when someone actually touched him? Then Jesus freed him from
his leprosy.

Jesus was teaching us by example that often the
best way to help the oppressed, the sick, and the poor is
to touch them with our compassion. Jesus had compassion on people; we should have compassion too.

Today, whom will you touch—literally as well as
figuratively—in the name of Christ?

We Wait on God

*But those who wait on the L*ORD
shall renew their strength;
they shall mount up with wings like eagles.

ISAIAH 40:31

Nowhere does the Bible teach that Christians are exempt from tribulation and natural disaster. We live in a world infected with the disease of sin, and we share in its misery and pain.

But the Bible does teach that we can face trials with a power others do not have—the power of God. As we trust Him, God helps us endure, and even discern His purposes in the midst of suffering. Christiana Tsai, the Christian daughter of a former governor in China, wrote, "Throughout my many years of illness, I have never dared to ask God why He allowed me to suffer so long. I only ask what He wants me to do."

The eagle has the unique ability to lock its joints and soar effortlessly on an updraft instead of flapping its wings. As we wait on God, He helps us use the winds of adversity to soar above our problems. As the Bible says, "Those who wait on the L ORD . . . shall mount up with wings like eagles."

A Joyful Life

Rejoice in the Lord always.

PHILIPPIANS 4:4

When our hearts are surrendered totally to the will of God, then we delight in seeing Him use us in any way He pleases. Our plans and desires begin to agree with His, and we accept His direction in our lives. Our sense of joy, satisfaction, and fulfillment in life increases, no matter what the circumstances, if we are in the center of God's will.

The Christian life is a joyful life. Christianity was never meant to be something to make people miserable. The ministry of Jesus Christ was one of joy. The Bible teaches that a life of inward peace and outward victory is a Christian's birthright.

"What a witness to the world Christians would be," wrote Amy Carmichael, "if only they were more evidently very happy people." Joy is one of the marks of a true believer. Will others see the joy of Christ in your life today?

Rebuilding Relationships

*Make every effort to live in peace with
all men and to be holy.*

HEBREWS 12:14 NIV

Is there a relationship you need to rebuild?

Too often people are filled with regret and guilt because they failed to reach out to someone with whom they were at odds—and then death intervenes and it's too late. Don't let this happen to you.

If a broken relationship comes to mind, know that the place to begin is within yourself. Are you convinced that rebuilding this relationship is something God wants you to do?

Then let the person know that you care and that you want your relationship to be different. Don't use words alone; back up your words with action. A small gift or an invitation to dinner can show that you mean what you say.

Most of all, seek God's forgiveness for anything you did to harm the relationship. Then trust Him to help you set aside the past. Don't argue about the past or who was at fault; that only reopens old wounds. Instead, focus on your hopes for the future. Change may take time, but with God's help it can happen.

Love One Another

Let no debt remain outstanding, except the continuing debt to love one another, for he who loves his fellowman has fulfilled the law.

ROMANS 13:8 NIV

Prejudice or hatred of any person because of his or her racial, ethnic, or religious background is wrong. God labels it sin.

After all, God created every one of us, and when we hate someone who is different from us, we are hating someone whom God has made and who is valuable in His sight. Every human being is created in God's image, and although sin has blurred that image in all of us, every single one of us still bears the mark of our Creator.

We also must never hate people who are different from us because Jesus Christ died for them. Jesus didn't die to save just one race or one group of people; Jesus died for all. The Bible says that "God so loved the world that he gave his one and only Son" (John 3:16 NIV). Heaven will include individuals "from every tribe and language and people and nation" (Revelation 5:9 NIV).

Ask God to free you from any prejudice that lurks in your heart. Ask Christ to fill you with His love. Prejudice flees when we see others through Jesus' eyes.

Christian Virtues at Home

"I am the vine, you are the branches. He who abides in Me, and I in him, bears much fruit."

JOHN 15:5

How we live at home is the acid test for any Christian man or woman. It is far easier to live an excellent life among our friends, when we are putting our best foot forward and are conscious of public opinion, than it is to live for Christ in our home.

Our own family circle sees us in our unguarded moments. They see us when exhaustion and stress fray our nerves. Our own family circle knows whether Christ lives in and through us.

If I am a genuine Christian, I will not give way at home to bad temper, impatience, faultfinding, sarcasm, unkindness, suspicion, selfishness, or laziness. Instead, each day my life will display the fruit of the Spirit, which is "love, joy, peace, patience, kindness, goodness, faithfulness, gentleness and self-control" (Galatians 5:22–23 NIV). How different would your home be if you consistently practiced these Christlike virtues?

Filled with the Spirit

They were all filled with the Holy Spirit.
ACTS 2:4

The early Christians had no buildings, no airplanes, no automobiles, no printing presses or televisions or radios. Yet they turned their world upside down for Christ. They started a spiritual revolution that shook the very foundations of the Roman Empire.

In the face of opposition and overwhelming odds, they stayed courageous, bold, dauntless, and full of faith. They lived their lives daily for Christ, no matter what others thought. They gladly suffered scorn, persecution, and even death for their faith in Christ.

What was their secret? The Bible gives us the key: "They were all filled with the Holy Spirit." The Holy Spirit changed their lives, and those they met couldn't help but be impressed by their love and the quality and purity of their lives. What keeps us from turning our world upside down for Christ?

With God's Help

Bear with each other and forgive whatever
grievances you may have against one another.
Forgive as the Lord forgave you.

COLOSSIANS 3:13 NIV

The command to forgive as we have been forgiven is difficult to obey, but we need to forgive people who have wronged us—even if we don't think they deserve it. If we don't, the poisons of anger and bitterness will eat away at our souls, but with God's help, we can deal with them in a way that honors Him.

First, if we were at fault in any way, we need to face it honestly and seek God's forgiveness. Then we need to ask the person to forgive us as well—even if they may refuse.

The next step is to ask God to help you forgive the one who hurt you. The only way to do this, I believe, is to realize how fully God has forgiven us in Christ. We don't deserve His forgiveness, yet we are "justified freely by His grace" (Romans 3:24). Open your heart to Christ, and then ask Him to replace your hurt and anger with His love—and He will.

Serving God Forever

Because of His great love . . . [He] made us alive together with Christ.

Ephesians 2:4–5

Your life may seem monotonous and filled with drudgery. Yet remember, if you are a Christian, you are not working for an hour or for a day but for eternity. When this body of corruption shall take on immortality, another part of our work will begin, for the Scripture teaches that God's servants shall serve Him forever. The difference is that in Heaven we will never grow bored or weary!

Some time ago a man said to me, "You might be mistaken, for no one has ever come back from the grave to tell us."

I replied, "Sir, that's exactly where you are wrong. Someone *has* returned—His name is Jesus Christ, our Lord."

That makes all the difference! Because Christ is alive, we have "an inheritance incorruptible and undefiled . . . reserved in heaven" (1 Peter 1:4). And this truth helps us persevere, even when life seems dull.

"I'm Sorry"

Be completely humble and gentle.
EPHESIANS 4:2 NIV

Apologizing doesn't come easily to most of us. The Bible, however, offers us instances of people who apologized when they acted wrongly, and we can learn from their example.

On one occasion, for instance, the apostle Paul was arrested and taken before an assembly of religious leaders. He spoke very bluntly to the high priest, not realizing who he was, and was rebuked for speaking disrespectfully to such an important official. Paul immediately apologized for his action, enabling him to continue with his defense.

Have you ever asked yourself why it's so hard to apologize? One reason is pride: we hate to admit we were wrong. But the Bible says that pride is sin: "I hate pride and arrogance" (Proverbs 8:13 NIV).

So if apologizing is difficult for you, ask God to help you overcome your pride—or whatever else is holding you back. Seek out one person you may have hurt and say very simply, "I'm sorry." Next time, apologizing will be even easier.

Power for Life

> *"The Spirit of truth . . . dwells with*
> *you and will be in you."*
> JOHN 14:17

Walter Knight tells the story about a little boy who had recently received Christ. "Daddy, how can I believe in the Holy Spirit when I have never seen Him?" asked Jim.

"I'll show you how," said his father, who was an electrician. The father took Jim to a power plant and showed him the generators. "This is where the power comes from to heat our stove and to give us light. We can't see the power, but it's in that machine and in the power lines," said the father.

"Now, son, let me ask you a question: Do you believe in electricity?" he asked.

"Yes, I believe in electricity," said Jim.

"Of course you do," said his father, "but you don't believe in it because you see it. You believe in it because you see what it can do. Likewise, you can believe in the Holy Spirit not because you see Him, but you see what He does in people's lives when they are surrendered to Christ and possess His power."

A Picture of Forgiveness

You have been set free from sin.

ROMANS 6:22 NIV

Imagine for a minute that you committed a crime, were arrested, and were sent to jail. The day has now come for you to appear in court.

As you stand before the judge, there is absolutely no doubt: you are guilty of the charges against you. According to the law, you must pay for this crime, and in this case the penalty is a year in jail. The judge issues his verdict and pronounces your sentence. At once the bailiff comes over to lead you away to prison.

But then something almost beyond belief happens. The judge steps down from the bench, stops the bailiff, and takes your place. He is innocent—but he goes to prison and pays the penalty for the crime you committed. You, on the other hand, are free!

This is a picture of what Jesus Christ did for you and me. We are guilty before God and deserve nothing less than death. But the Judge—Jesus Christ—took our place. By His death on the cross, He took the penalty we deserve, and we are free. Sin's penalty has been fully paid. Believe it!

God Takes the Burden

As a father pities his children,
*so the L*ORD *pities those who fear Him.*

PSALM 103:13

As God's children, we are His dependents. Dependent children spend little time worrying about meals, clothing, and shelter. They assume—and they have a right to—that their parents will provide everything they need.

Jesus said, "Do not worry, saying, 'What shall we eat?' or 'What shall we drink?' or 'What shall we wear?' . . . But seek first the kingdom of God . . . and all these things shall be added to you" (Matthew 6:31, 33).

Unfortunately, worry is an ingrained habit for most of us. But because we are God's children, He is responsible for our welfare. That is why you should be "casting all your care upon Him, for He cares for you" (1 Peter 5:7). In other words, let God do the worrying! He says, "I'll take the burden—don't give it a thought—leave it to Me."

Never forget: God is bigger than your problems. Whatever worries press upon you today, put them in God's hands—and leave them there.

Our Hardest Task

*"You have heard that it was said, 'Love your neighbor
and hate your enemy.' But I tell you: Love your enemies,
and pray for those who persecute you."*

MATTHEW 5:43–44 NIV

You've heard the expression "Forgive and forget"—but is it really possible? Perhaps someone once hurt you very deeply—and the emotional scars still ache. The last thing you think you could ever do is forgive and forget.

And yet Jesus goes even further: He not only tells us to forgive and forget, but to love the one who hurt us and pray for that person's welfare. We aren't to erase them from our memories; we are to keep them in our prayers!

Impossible? Yes—without God's help. What must we do? First, remember how generously Christ forgave you. You hurt God far more than anyone ever hurt you—and yet He willingly sent His Son to die in your place so you could be forgiven. Never forget how much it cost Christ to forgive you.

Second, begin seeing the other person through God's eyes. He loves them just as He loves you. Don't hold on to your hurts any longer, but turn them over to Christ and ask Him to help you forgive others—and then love them just as He does.

A Formula for Peace

Great peace have those who love Your law,
and nothing causes them to stumble.

PSALM 119:165

God has a plan for peace, and it is found in His Son, whom the Bible calls the "Prince of Peace" (Isaiah 9:6). But we have rejected God's plan. Wars still ravage our world—and our lives.

Why? Jesus said the problem is within us: "Out of the heart . . . proceed evil thoughts, adulteries, fornications, murders, thefts, covetousness, wickedness, deceit, lewdness, an evil eye, blasphemy, pride, foolishness" (Mark 7:21–22). What a list! Our real war is a rebellion against God—and it brings unending misery.

But God longs to see this rebellion cease. That is why Christ came. By His death He provided the way for us to be reconciled to God. And when we have peace with God, we have peace in our hearts—and peace with each other.

This happens as we repent and receive Christ. The war is over, for God extends a peace treaty to all who come to Christ.

We Need One Another

Woe to him who is alone when he falls, for he
has no one to help him up.

ECCLESIASTES 4:10

Have you ever met someone who was known as a rugged individualist? You probably have; you may even consider yourself to be one. And even if you aren't, you probably secretly admire them, with their drive, their independent attitude, and their lack of concern about what others think of them.

Anyone who has made a commitment to Jesus Christ is something of a rugged individualist. He or she isn't going to live the same way everyone else lives; a believer's goal now is to follow Christ. This may mean being scorned by family or friends, or taking a stand for what is right instead of what is popular.

But in other ways, a Christian must not be a rugged, independent individualist. Instead, when we come to Christ we become part of a family—the body of Christ, the Church. Instead of being concerned only about ourselves, we become concerned about others in the family of Christ and their needs. We become concerned, too, about those who do not yet know Christ. Is this concern becoming a reality in your life?

The Trap of Busyness

Then, because so many people were coming and going that they did not even have a chance to eat, [Jesus] said to [His disciples], "Come with me by yourselves to a quiet place and get some rest."

MARK 6:31 TNIV

Do you have days like this one in Jesus' ministry—days when you have so many demands on you that you don't see how you'll ever get everything done?

Why, in the midst of such a busy day, did Jesus insist His disciples leave the crowds to rest and be alone with Him? Because Jesus knew that the busier they were, the more they needed to rest and be alone with Him. If they didn't, eventually they would hurt both themselves and those they were seeking to help. The same is true of us.

God knows the demands and responsibilities you face—at home, on the job, even in your church. But God also knows you need His wisdom to keep those things in perspective, and you need His strength to get them done well. Begin each day with a brief prayer, committing the day to God and asking Him to guide you. Then set aside time—even just a few minutes at first—to be alone with God in His Word and in prayer. If Jesus found it important, shouldn't you?

A Warning Light

If your heart is wise,
My heart will rejoice.

PROVERBS 23:15

One of the ways God has revealed Himself to us is in the conscience. Conscience has been described as the light of the soul. Even when it is dulled or darkened by sin, it can still bear witness to the reality of good and evil, and to the holiness of God.

What causes this warning light to go on inside me when I do wrong? It is my conscience, given by God to steer me away from evil and toward good. Conscience can be our gentlest teacher and friend—and sometimes our worst enemy (or so we think) when we sin.

The Scripture says, "Man's conscience is the lamp of the eternal" (Proverbs 20:27 MOFFATT). In other words, conscience is God's lamp within the human breast. In his *Critique of Pure Reason*, Immanuel Kant said there were just two things that filled him with awe—the starry Heavens above and human conscience within.

Persistent sin can dull and even silence our conscience. On the other hand, persistent attention to God's Word will sharpen our conscience and make us more sensitive to moral and spiritual danger. Is this happening in your life?

Pray Anywhere, Anytime

Rejoice always, pray without ceasing.

1 THESSALONIANS 5:16–17

Prayer is an essential part of a healthy Christian life. Just as omitting an essential vitamin from our diet will make us physically weak, so a lack of prayer will make us spiritually anemic.

The Bible says, "Pray without ceasing." It isn't enough to get out of bed in the morning, quickly bow our head, and repeat a few sentences. Instead, we need to set aside specific times to be alone with God, speaking to Him in prayer and listening to Him speak through His Word. If you set aside special times for prayer, your unconscious mind will be saturated with prayer all day long.

For the overworked mother or other busy person, this may seem impossible (although even a few minutes alone with God can reap rich rewards). But even when we are busy, we can "pray without ceasing" in our hearts and minds. We can pray anywhere, anytime— and God will hear us. Today let prayer saturate your life "without ceasing."

Take Aim!

Set your minds on things above, not on earthly things.

COLOSSIANS 3:2 NIV

During the Second World War, the words of General Douglas MacArthur echoed in the hearts of the people of the Philippines while they were under enemy occupation. He promised, "I shall return"—and he kept that promise. Jesus Christ has also promised, "I shall return"—and He, too, will keep that promise.

A continual looking forward to the eternal world Jesus will usher in is not a form of escapism or wishful thinking. We Christians look forward with anticipation to Christ's return and spending eternity with Him.

The promise of that new world, however, does not mean that we are to leave the present world as it is. If you read history, you will find that the Christians who did the most for the present world were those who thought the most of the next. Only Christians who cease thinking of the next world become ineffective in this one.

"Aim at heaven," said C. S. Lewis, "and you will get earth thrown in. Aim at earth, and you will get neither." At what are you aiming?

Trust Crowds Out Worry

Commit your way to the LORD . . .
and He shall bring it to pass.

PSALM 37:5

You cannot stop a baby's cry by giving him a rattle when he is hungry. He will keep on crying until his hunger is satisfied by the food his little body demands. Neither can the soul of a mature person be satisfied apart from God. David described the hunger of every human being when he said, "As the deer pants for the water brooks, so pants my soul for You, O God" (Psalm 42:1).

Two conflicting forces cannot exist in one human heart. When doubt reigns, faith cannot abide. Where hatred rules, love is crowded out. Where selfishness rules, there love cannot dwell. When worry is present, trust cannot crowd its way in.

In the same way, God will not share His rightful place in our lives with anything or anyone less than Himself. Is anything crowding God out of your heart today? Don't give first place to anything less than Christ, but "commit your way to the LORD."

Life-Giving Faith

*But to all who did accept him and believe in him he
gave the right to become children of God.*

JOHN 1:12 NCV

The ugly larva in its cocoon spends sometimes many months in almost unnoticeable growth and change. But no matter how great that growth may be, there comes a moment when the little creature passes through a crisis and emerges a beautiful butterfly. The weeks of silent growth are important, but they cannot take the place of that event when the old and the ugly are left behind, and the new and the beautiful come into being.

Many Christians whose faith and lives testify that they have been converted to Christ do not know the exact day or hour that they left behind the old and the ugly and came to know Him. Whether or not they can remember the specific time, however, they can be sure there was a moment when they crossed over the line from death to life.

That moment comes when we put our faith in certain objective facts—in the work of Christ, His cross, His tomb, and His resurrection. Praise God for calling you to this life-giving faith!

Let It Shine!

The light of the righteous rejoices.
PROVERBS 13:9

We are holding a light. We are to let it shine! Though it may seem but a twinkling candle in a world of blackness, it is our business to let it shine. Light dispels darkness, and it attracts people in darkness to it.

We are blowing a trumpet. In the din and noise of battle the sound of our little trumpet may seem lost, but we must keep sounding the alarm to those who are in spiritual danger.

We are kindling a fire. In this cold world full of hatred and selfishness our little blaze may seem unavailing, but we must keep our fire burning.

A light, a trumpet, a fire ... they seem so little amidst the darkness and violence of the world. But "with God all things are possible" (Matthew 19:26), and He will bless our efforts to bring the good news of Jesus to a weary and strife-torn world.

Fully Trustworthy

Righteous are you, O LORD,
And your laws are right.
The statutes you have laid down are righteous;
they are fully trustworthy.

PSALM 119:137–138 NIV

It took sixteen hundred years to write. More than thirty authors acting as secretaries for God wrote its sixty-six books. Over those sixteen hundred years, these individual authors wrote the same message, and so unified is the message that the sixty-six books actually comprise one Book.

In the pages of the Bible, the sins of small and great are frankly addressed, the weaknesses of human nature are admitted, and life is presented as it actually is found. The message of the Bible is the story of God's redemption humanity through Jesus Christ.

And the truth in its pages is eminently practical. General Robert E. Lee observed, "The Bible is a book in comparison with which all others in my eyes are of minor importance, and which in all my complexities and distresses has never failed to give me light and strength."

Find in its pages the light and strength you need for each and every day of your life.

The Focal Point

"I am the Alpha and the Omega, the Beginning and the End, the First and the Last."

REVELATION 22:13

The central message of the Bible is Jesus Christ.

In Genesis, Jesus is the Seed of the Woman. In Exodus, He is the Passover Lamb. In Leviticus, He is the atoning Sacrifice. In Numbers, the Smitten Rock. In Deuteronomy, the Prophet. In Joshua, the Captain of the Lord's hosts. In Judges, the Deliverer. In Ruth, the Heavenly Kinsman. In the six books of Kings, the Promised King. In Nehemiah, the Restorer of the nation. In Esther, the Advocate. In Job, my Redeemer. In Psalms, my Strength. In Proverbs, my Pattern. In Ecclesiastes, my Goal. In the Song of Solomon, my Satisfier. In the prophets, the coming Prince of Peace. In the gospels, He is the Christ who came to seek and to save. In Acts, He is Christ risen. In the epistles, He is Christ exalted. In Revelation, He is Christ returning and reigning.

The message of the Bible is the story of salvation through Jesus—and the whole world needs to know this story. Whom will you tell today?

No Bargain, No Barter

"Come, buy . . .
without money and without price."

ISAIAH 55:1

God does not bargain with us, nor can we barter with Him. He holds our eternal salvation in His omnipotent hand, and He bids us take it as a free gift, "without money and without price."

Yet this is hard for us to accept. Surely something as precious as salvation must cost us greatly! Surely God must demand we work for it!

But that is wrong—and the reason is because the price has already been paid! Salvation is free—but it wasn't cheap. It cost the dear Son of God His very life.

Only cheap, tawdry things have a price tag on them. The best things in life are free—the air we breathe, the stars at night, the wonder of human love. But the greatest gift of all is our salvation, purchased for us by Jesus Christ. "Thanks be to God for His indescribable gift!" (2 Corinthians 9:15).

Now!

"As long as it is day, we must do the work of him who sent me. Night is coming, when no one can work."

John 9:4 niv

Dr. Samuel Johnson wore engraved on his watch the words "The night cometh," from John 9:4. Likewise, we Christians ought to carry written on our hearts the solemn truth of how short a time we have to witness for God. Whatever we are going to do for Christ we had better do now.

A dying Christian, who had been very reticent about sharing his testimony all his life, said to the man who sat beside him, "If I had the power, I'd shout, 'Glory to God.'" The companion answered, "It's a pity you didn't shout, 'Glory!' when you had the power."

We had better be sharing our testimony while we have the power. If we are ever to study the Scriptures, if we are ever to spend time in prayer, if we are ever to win souls for Christ, if we are ever to invest our finances for His Kingdom, it must be now.

You may not have tomorrow—but you do have today. What will you do for the Lord?

The Divine Flame

"You shall receive power when the Holy Spirit has come upon you; and you shall be witnesses to Me."

ACTS 1:8

Simon Peter was so spiritually weak before Pentecost that, in spite of his bragging to the contrary, he swore and denied Christ. He was cowed by the crowd, shamed by a little maid, and took his place with the enemies of Christ.

But see him after he was baptized with fire—the fire of the Holy Spirit! He stood boldly before the same rabble that had crucified Jesus, looked into their faces, and fearlessly proclaimed the good news of salvation (Acts 2:36). Peter, the weak, was transformed into Peter, the rock.

So it was with the early disciples. The Holy Spirit changed them from ordinary individuals into firebrands for God. Their faith and zeal started a conflagration that spread throughout the Roman Empire.

Their secret? Total submission to Jesus Christ and His will. What keeps you from being used of God to touch your world for Christ?

Standing Against Satan

Be self-controlled and alert. Your enemy the devil prowls around like a roaring lion looking for someone to devour. Resist him, standing firm in the faith.

1 PETER 5:8–9 NIV

No Christian is exempt from the attacks of Satan. Our adversary is personal, aggressive, intelligent, cunning, and destructive, and every day Satan must be resisted.

The earthly weapons we might try to use in spiritual warfare against the devil have no power against his cunning schemes and fierce attacks. Instead, the greatest hindrance to Satan's destructive efforts is our standing strong in the knowledge and fear of the Lord. The greatest roadblock to Satan's work is the Christian who, above all else, lives for God, walks with integrity, is filled with the Spirit, and obeys God's law.

Your greatest contribution to God's Kingdom work—and to defeating the Enemy's efforts against this Kingdom—is to keep up your daily devotions; live a clean, honest, humble, Spirit-filled life; trust God to guard and protect you morally, physically, and spiritually; and openly witness for Jesus Christ. Don't be a pawn of the devil, but a servant of Christ.

The Hand of God

No good thing will He withhold
from those who walk uprightly.

PSALM 84:11

In the midst of sorrow and trouble, this life has many blessings and enjoyments that have come from the hand of God.

Think of the blessings we so easily take for granted: life itself; preservation from danger; every bit of health we enjoy; every hour of liberty; the ability to see, to hear, to speak, to think, and to imagine—all this comes from the hand of God. Even our capacity to love is a gift from God. Most of all, God has given us the gift of Christ.

What should our response be? We can put it in one word: *gratitude*. But how do we show our gratitude? By giving back to God a part of what He has given us.

What have you done lately to show your gratitude to God for all that He has done—and is doing—for you?

Who Will Go?

How can they believe in the one of whom they have not heard? And how can they hear without someone preaching to them?

Romans 10:14 niv

The risen Christ commands His followers to "go into all the world and preach the gospel" (Mark 16:15).

God doesn't promise that obedience will be easy, or glamorous, or romantic. Oh, I know it's exciting to get on a plane and travel to another land. And perhaps while we're flying, God will fill us with His Spirit so that when we reach our destination, we will be prepared to serve Him. But if we are not winning people to Christ here, if we are not witnessing here, if we are not serving Christ here, God can't use us there. We must be faithful here first.

God is calling us to consider His call and wrestle in prayer over the mission He has for us in life. Will you go into the world for Him? There are a thousand things you can do with your life, a thousand ways you can spend it—but how many of them will enable you to have no regrets at the end? Obedience to Jesus is the only path of no regrets.

A Prepared Place

"In my Father's house are many mansions."

JOHN 14:2

As much as our homes mean to us, they are not permanent. Sometimes I look at my own adult children and can hardly believe they are all grown and on their own. The house that once rang with the laughter of children now seems empty.

Those disciples who for Christ's sake gave up houses and lands and loved ones knew little of home life or home joys. It was as if Jesus were saying to them, "We have no lasting home here on Earth, but My Father's house is a home where we will be together for all eternity."

The venerable Bishop Ryle is reputed to have said, "Heaven is a prepared place for a prepared people, and those who enter shall find that they are neither unknown nor unexpected."

Even life's happiest experiences last but a moment, yet Heaven's joy is eternal. Someday we will go to our eternal Home—and Christ will be there to welcome us!

The Fiery Furnace

"Be faithful, even to the point of death, and
I will give you the crown of life."
REVELATION 2:10 NIV

Shadrach, Meshach, and Abednego were Jewish captives in Babylon—and they refused to worship the golden image set up by King Nebuchadnezzar.

They could have bowed down and avoided trouble, but that would have compromised all that they believed.

They could have rationalized and said, "It is our duty to obey the king." But they had a higher law: God's law. They could have said, "It's just a matter of form. God knows that inwardly we are true to Him." Or they could have stayed indoors that day.

Instead, they risked the tyrant's rage and refused to bow before the idol. They proclaimed, "We take our stand for the living God, even if it means death." Then they were condemned and thrown into the fiery furnace, but God delivered them.

God is with His people in the fiery furnaces of life—our times of temptation, trouble, and trial. The Bible says that nothing—absolutely nothing—"shall be able to separate us from the love of God which is in Christ Jesus our Lord" (Romans 8:39).

A Passion to Please God

I have learned in whatever state I am, to be content.

PHILIPPIANS 4:11

Popularity and praise can be far more dangerous for the Christian than persecution. They can turn us away from God without our even being aware of it, making us like those in Jesus' day who "loved the praise of men more than the praise of God" (John 12:43).

Unfortunately, it is easy when all goes well to lose our perspective. Instead, we must learn like Paul to be content in whatever state we find ourselves. The important thing is to have one consuming passion: to please Christ. Then, whatever happens, we know He has permitted it to take place to teach us and to perfect us for His service. He will enrich our circumstances, be they pleasant or disagreeable, by His presence with us.

Ask God to keep you from worrying about what others think and to make you content with whatever He sends your way. All the tomorrows of our lives have to pass Him before they get to us!

MARCH

In the World, Not of the World

They are of the world. . . . We are of God.
1 JOHN 4:5–6

The Gulf Stream flows in the ocean, and yet it is not absorbed by it. It maintains its warm temperatures even in the icy waters of the North Atlantic.

Believers are in the world, yet we must not be absorbed by it. If Christians are to fulfill their purposes in the world, they must not be chilled by the indifferent, godless society in which they live. The Bible says, "Do not be conformed to this world" (Romans 12:2). It is true that Jesus dined with publicans and sinners, but He did not allow the social group to overwhelm Him and conform Him to its ways. Instead, He seized every opportunity to present spiritual truth and to lead a soul from death to life.

Our social contacts should not only be pleasant; they should be opportunities to share our faith with those who do not yet know Christ. As you have contact with others this day, will they sense the warmth of Christ's presence through you?

God's Perfection

As for God, his way is perfect;
the word of the LORD is flawless.

PSALM 18:30 NIV

H as it ever struck you how important it is that God is perfect? We know God is all-powerful, all-knowing, all-loving, and absolutely pure and holy and just. But He is also absolutely perfect.

What if He weren't perfect? What if He made mistakes . . . or failed to keep His promises . . . or did things only halfway . . . or occasionally told a lie . . . or slipped up and forgot to do what He said He would—all the things, in other words, that we often do (or fail to do)? If God were this way, why bother to trust Him? Why bother to worship Him?

But God isn't like this! God is perfect—absolutely, totally perfect in all He is and all He does. And because He is perfect, you can trust Him. You can trust His love, and you can trust His promises. You can trust Him to guide you, and you can trust Him to be with you even in life's darkest times. Most of all you can trust Him to save you through Christ—because His way of salvation is perfect.

Growing Stronger

Grow in the grace and knowledge of our Lord and Savior Jesus Christ.

2 PETER 3:18

So how do we grow spiritually? We grow through the study of God's Word. We will never grow in grace and in the knowledge of God until the Bible becomes part of our lives every day.

We grow through prayer. We should be in an attitude of prayer every minute of the day; we are to be praying constantly. In every choice we make, we should ask our Heavenly Father which way we should go and listen for Him to say, "This is the way, walk ye in it" (Isaiah 30:21 KJV).

We grow as well through our fellowship with other believers. Through worship, through hearing His Word preached and taught, through interaction with more mature believers—we need each other in order to grow.

Finally, we grow by witnessing. Just as exercise makes us physically stronger, exercising our faith by sharing it with others makes us spiritually stronger. Are you sharing the story of His love with others?

Make it your goal—beginning today—to grow closer to Christ.

People of Prayer

"Lord, teach us to pray."

LUKE 11:1

Thousands pray only in times of great stress, danger, or uncertainty. I have flown through bad storms and found myself surrounded by people praying for the first time in their lives. It is instinctive for us to pray in times of trouble. Only then do we realize our helplessness.

But, both by His teaching and His example, Christ instructed His followers to pray at all times. So fervent and so direct were Jesus' prayers that once, after He finished praying, His followers pleaded, "Lord, teach us to pray." They yearned to be in touch with God in the way they knew Christ to be.

Have you ever said, "Lord, teach me to pray"? Prayer shouldn't be casual or sporadic, dictated only by the needs of the moment. Prayer should be as much a part of our lives as breathing. Never has our world stood in greater need of people who will pray. Will you be one of them?

We Can Count on Him

Blessed is the man whose strength is in You.
PSALM 84:5

Someone has written a little verse that goes like this:

Said the robin to the sparrow,
I should really like to know,
Why these anxious human beings
Rush about and worry so.
Said the sparrow to the robin,
Friend, I think that it must be,
That they have no heavenly Father
Such as cares for you and me.

Jesus used the carefree attitude of the birds to underscore the fact that worrying is unnatural. "Look at the birds of the air, for they neither sow nor reap . . . yet your heavenly Father feeds them" (Matthew 6:26). If He cares for tiny birds and frail flowers, why can't we count on Him for every aspect of our lives? After all, He loves us so much that He sent His Son into the world to save us. We are that valuable to Him!

The Young Jesus

Jesus increased in wisdom and stature,
and in favor with God and men.

LUKE 2:52

The Bible doesn't tell us much about Jesus' child-hood, but the one incident it does record reveals that He was already aware of His unique status as God's Son, sent from Heaven to save us from our sins.

The incident occurred when Jesus was twelve. As was their custom every year, Mary and Joseph took Him on the long trip to Jerusalem for Passover, one of the most important Jewish feasts. Afterward, they became separated from Him, and when they finally found Him several days later, He was in the Temple listening to teachers of the Old Testament and asking them ques-tions. When Mary and Joseph rebuked Him, He replied, "Why were you searching for me? Didn't you know I had to be in my Father's house?" (Luke 2:49 NIV).

If Jesus found it important to be in God's House learning more about God's Word, shouldn't we as well? And shouldn't we ask God to help us instill the same priorities in our children?

Which Is Hardest?

As God's chosen people, holy and dearly loved, clothe yourselves with compassion, kindness, humility, gentleness and patience.

COLOSSIANS 3:12 NIV

With a twinkle in his eyes, my friend says that his favorite prayer is, "Lord, give me patience—and give it to me right now!" Patience, he admits, has been the hardest virtue for him to acquire.

Look at the five things Paul lists that should be part of our character as Christians: compassion, kindness, humility, gentleness, patience. Which is the hardest for you? Every one of them strikes a blow at our natural selfishness.

But for many of us, patience is the hardest. For one thing, our patience is probably tested every day—even every hour. But patience is also critical, for without it, the other four—compassion, kindness, humility, and gentleness—are impossible.

When impatience threatens to overwhelm you, ask God to take it away and replace it with His patience. Remember: His patience with you is beyond measure.

Life Plus Love

All the law is fulfilled in one word . . . "love your neighbor as yourself."

GALATIANS 5:14

Suppose I gave everything I had to charity. You probably would say I was a very good person, a fine Christian. But Paul said that unless I acted out of love, "I am nothing" (1 Corinthians 13:2). George Sweeting has said, "Life minus love equals nothing!"

Do you have this kind of love—a love that puts others ahead of yourself? Without Jesus Christ in your heart, without the Holy Spirit in your life, you can't produce this love. This is the kind of love Jesus had for us, when He willingly left the glory of Heaven and went to the cross for our salvation.

Only God can give us a selfless love for others, as the Holy Spirit changes us from within. This is one reason we must receive Christ, for apart from His Spirit we can never be freed from the chains of selfishness, jealousy, and indifference. Will others see Christ's love in your life today?

The Spirit of God

"I will pray the Father, and He will give you another Helper, that He may abide with you forever."
JOHN 14:16

During His lifetime on Earth, Christ's presence could be experienced by only a small group of people at any given time. Now Christ dwells through the Spirit in the hearts of all who have received Him as Savior and Lord. The apostle Paul wrote, "Do you not know . . . that the Spirit of God dwells in you?" (1 Corinthians 3:16).

The Holy Spirit is given to every believer—not for a limited time, but forever. If He left us for one moment, we would be in deep trouble. But He doesn't! He is there to give you both the gifts and the power to work for Christ. He is there to give you strength in the moment of temptation. He is there to produce the fruit of "love, joy, peace, longsuffering, kindness, goodness, faithfulness, gentleness, self-control" (Galatians 5:22–23).

You will never have more of the Holy Spirit than you do right now. But will He have more of you?

The Lamb's Book of Life

Only those who are written in the Lamb's Book of Life
[will enter the glory of Heaven].

REVELATION 21:27

You and I will never be good enough to get into Heaven on our own. The reason is because God is pure and holy, and even one sin—just one—would be enough to keep us out of Heaven. Any and every sin is an offense to God. He does not take our good deeds and bad deeds and weigh them against each other. Instead, the Bible says, "whoever keeps the whole law and yet stumbles at just one point is guilty of breaking all of it" (James 2:10 NIV).

That is why we need Christ, for He came into the world to take away our sins. We cannot remove our sins and guilt—but Christ can, because He was the sinless Son of God. When we come by faith to Him, all our sins are transferred to Him, and we are forgiven. Our names are written in God's Book of Life because of Christ.

We can't trust in our own goodness—but we can trust in Christ and in what He has done for us. Are you trusting Him alone for your salvation?

Glorious Giving

"Give, and it will be given to you."
Luke 6:38

"Give," Christ commanded. Yet it was more than a command. It was an invitation to glorious and abundant living. If we get our attitude toward money right, it will help straighten out almost every other area of our lives.

Have you ever realized just how cruel and deceptive a master money can be? Some people spend their entire lives slavishly serving it—often without even realizing it. No wonder Jesus warned, "You cannot serve both God and Money" (Matthew 6:24 NIV).

The chief motive of the selfish, unregenerate person is "get." The chief motive of the dedicated Christian should be "give." Jesus said, "Give, and it will be given to you." It's a promise, and we know Jesus never breaks His promises.

Getting . . . or giving? Which is true of you?

Sincere—or Genuine?

"Not everyone who says to Me, 'Lord, Lord,' shall enter the kingdom of heaven, but he who does the will of My Father in heaven."

MATTHEW 7:21

Did you know that the word *Christian* actually means "a partisan for Christ"? It means that you have chosen Christ and are following Him. Partisans are not neutral—they are committed.

Now I want to ask you: Are you a Christian? I mean a true Christian, a real Christian. Many people have a wrong idea of what a Christian is. They say, "A Christian is a person who prays" or "A Christian lives by the golden rule." But praying or living by the golden rule doesn't make someone a Christian. A person may be sincere, but that doesn't make him a Christian.

When I was a little boy, my mother was sincere when she gave me what she thought was cough syrup for my cold. Instead she gave me iodine. She quickly called the doctor, and he said, "Give him some cream." She almost filled me up with cream to neutralize the iodine. Sincerity doesn't necessarily accomplish what you want it to!

Are you a Christian? Have you confessed your sins and your need for forgiveness to Christ, and have you committed yourself to Him as your Lord and Savior?

A Solid Foundation

Thus says the Lord GOD: "Behold, I am against your magic charms by which you hunt souls there like birds."
Ezekiel 13:20

I t was a very difficult time to be a prophet of God. The Jewish nation was on the brink of an invasion that would soon destroy it and send most of its inhabitants into exile. And yet few wanted to hear what Ezekiel had to say, for his message warned of God's impending judgment.

Instead, they wanted to listen to prophets who spoke soothing words, telling them that Ezekiel was wrong and that soon the nation would experience peace. The people also flocked to magicians and astrologers and fortune-tellers who claimed to know the future and promised them better days. They, too, told people that Ezekiel's message was a lie.

Walk into any bookstore and you'll find hundreds of books telling you how to live. Turn on the television or radio, and many talk-show gurus promise better days. Some of their words may have value—but many are like the false prophets and charm merchants of Ezekiel's day. Don't be misled and don't be deceived! Instead, build your life on the truth God has given us in His Word.

Life in Christ Works

I know whom I have believed.

2 TIMOTHY 1:12

Does Christianity work? Does anything really happen when a person repents of sin and receives Christ by faith?

I can only tell you that it worked in my own life. I was reared during the Depression on a farm in North Carolina. My parents weren't able to give me the advantages most young people enjoy today. I grew up in a Christian home, but by the time I was fifteen, I was in full revolt against all religion—against God, the Bible, the Church.

But one night I committed my life to Jesus Christ, and He gave me a whole new direction. My grades picked up. My attitude toward others changed. I began to seek God's will instead of my own way. No, I didn't become perfect, but my life was changed.

I have been all over the world, and I have never met anyone who regretted giving his or her life to Christ. And neither will you.

Words That Help

Do not let any unwholesome talk come out of your mouths, but only what is helpful for building others up according to their needs.

EPHESIANS 4:29 NIV

We've all met people who seem to enjoy correcting others and telling them what is wrong with them. Sometimes it's done with an arrogant attitude—"I'm better than you, and I know what's wrong with you." Sometimes it's done with false humility: "I humbly hope I can help you become a better person."

If you're like most of us, however, you probably don't care much for people like this, and (rightly or wrongly) you probably don't listen to their advice. You sense that their real motive is pride, and their main goal is to impress you with how wise and perfect they are.

This is the opposite of what the Bible says here about the way we should speak to others. Instead of pride, our motive should be love. Instead of criticism, our goal should be to encourage and uplift. Instead of impressing others with ourselves, we want them to be impressed with Christ. Learn to avoid hurtful and useless words, and ask God to help you to encourage and help someone for Christ's sake today.

The Brightness of God's Love

*My flesh and my heart fail; but God is the strength
of my heart and my portion forever.*

PSALM 73:26

Trouble will not hurt us unless it does what many of us too often allow it to do—harden us, making us sour, bitter, and skeptical. But it need not be this way. Troubles we bear with trust in our Savior can bring us a fresh vision of God and a new outlook on life—an outlook of peace and hope.

If we make our troubles an opportunity to learn more of God's love and His power to aid and bless, then they will teach us to have a firmer confidence in His providence. As a result, the brightness of His love will fill our lives.

Learn to trust God with a childlike dependence on Him as your loving Heavenly Father, and no trouble can destroy you. In those darkest hours before the crucifixion, Jesus could still say, "I am not alone, because the Father is with Me" (John 16:32).

The same is true for you. Even in that last dark hour of death, when your flesh and your heart fail, you will be able to depend in peace upon Him who "is the strength of my heart and my portion forever."

Poor in Spirit, Part I

"Blessed are the poor in spirit."
MATTHEW 5:3

At first these words of Jesus sound like a contradiction. What did He mean by being "poor in spirit"—and how could it lead to blessing?

If we are to be poor in spirit, we must be aware of our spiritual poverty. (No one is more pathetic than the person who is in great need and is not aware of it!) Only God can satisfy our soul's emptiness—its deepest longings, desires, and appetites—but not everyone recognizes that truth and turns to Him.

The soul requires as much attention as the body. It demands fellowship and communion with God. It demands worship, quietness, and meditation. Unless the soul is fed and exercised daily, it becomes weak and shriveled.

Wise, then, is the person who openly confesses their lack of spiritual wealth and in humility cries out, "God, be merciful to me a sinner!" (Luke 18:13). In God's economy, spiritual emptiness comes before filling, and spiritual poverty before riches. Happiness, Jesus said, comes from admitting our spiritual poverty, and then asking Him to come into our lives. Have you done this?

Poor in Spirit, Part II

You are all children of God through faith in Christ Jesus.

GALATIANS 3:26 NLT

Being poor in spirit means being aware of our spiritual poverty. Being poor in spirit also means being conscious of our constant dependence on God.

Children depend on their parents for protection and care. Because of that relationship, children are not poor; but if it weren't for their relationship with their parents, they would be helpless and poor indeed.

Dependent children spend little time worrying about meals, clothing, and shelter. They assume—and they have a right to—that all will be provided by their parents.

When we come to Christ, we become children of God, and we can trust our Heavenly Father to provide for us. Jesus said, "What man is there among you who, if his son asks for bread, will give him a stone? . . . How much more will your Father who is in heaven give good things to those who ask Him!" (Matthew 7:9, 11).

We must admit we are poor before we can be made rich. We must admit we are destitute before we can become children of God through faith in Jesus Christ. C. H. Spurgeon said, "The first link between my soul and Christ is . . . not my riches but my need."

The Mind of Christ

Let this mind be in you which was also in Christ Jesus.
PHILIPPIANS 2:5

Jesus had the purest mind this world has ever seen. His convictions were so strong, so unswerving that He was not afraid to mingle with any group, secure in the knowledge that He would not be contaminated or swayed.

Fear—fear of rejection, fear our beliefs will be attacked, fear our faith might be shaken—makes us unwilling to give voice to our convictions or to listen to those of others. But if that is the case, perhaps we need to examine just how deep our convictions really are.

Jesus had no such fear, no need to fence Himself off from others for His own protection. He knew the difference between graciousness and compromise, and we would do well to follow His example.

Jesus alone is "the way, the truth, and the life" (John 14:6). Never lose your confidence in the truth of the gospel! And—like Jesus—may you always be "speaking the truth in love" (Ephesians 4:15).

A Mighty Fortress

He is my refuge and my fortress;
my God, in Him I will trust.

PSALM 91:2

A refuge is a place safely out of harm's way. A fortress is a fortified building that is virtually impenetrable by conventional means.

Martin Luther wrote a wonderful hymn that says, "A mighty fortress is our God, a bulwark never failing; Our helper He amidst the flood of mortal ills prevailing." What a statement about the magnificent power and protection of God!

Does God care for you and me? Can we turn to Him in trust and faith when troubles and temptations threaten to overwhelm us? Yes! A thousand times yes! What greater proof do we need than that He sent His Son, Jesus Christ, to die in our place?

Come Boldly

"Ask, and it will be given to you; seek, and you will find."
MATTHEW 7:7

Children are not bashful about asking for things. They would not be normal if they did not boldly make their needs known.

God has said to His children, "Let us . . . come boldly to the throne of grace, that we may obtain mercy and find grace to help in time of need" (Hebrews 4:16). God is keenly aware that we are dependent upon Him for life's necessities. It was for that reason that Jesus said, "Ask, and it will be given to you; seek, and you will find; knock, and it will be opened to you" (Matthew 7:7).

What is troubling you today? Is your heart burdened because of some problem that threatens to overcome you? Are you filled with anxiety and worry, wondering what will happen next? Listen: as a child of God through faith in Christ, you can turn these over to Christ, knowing that He loves you and is able to help you. Don't carry your burden any longer, but bring it "boldly to the throne of grace"—and leave it there.

Trusting His Word

All your words are true;
all your righteous laws are eternal.

PSALM 119:160 NIV

When you were young, your parents probably warned you not to believe everything you read. Their advice was sound: just because something is in print doesn't necessarily make it true. But why, then, should you believe the Bible? Why trust what it says?

One reason is that it tells about real people and real events. It doesn't consist of stories someone made up (unlike many other ancient books); the Bible's stories have the ring of truth about them, because they actually happened.

We can trust the Bible because it was written by people who actually witnessed what happened and wrote it down so future generations would have an accurate record of events. Peter, an eyewitness to Jesus' ministry, wrote, "We did not follow cunningly devised fables . . . but were eyewitnesses" (2 Peter 1:16).

Most of all, we can trust the Bible because it points us to the most important event in human history: the life, death, and resurrection of Jesus Christ. Through the written Word we discover the Living Word—Jesus Christ.

Healing or Harm?

Reckless words pierce like a sword,
but the tongue of the wise brings healing.

PROVERBS 12:18 NIV

How often have you had to apologize for something you said just because you didn't stop to think? You weren't trying to hurt someone; you didn't intend to be malicious; you may not even have been engaged in a serious conversation. But the reckless word slipped out—and once it was spoken, the damage was done. Jesus warned that people "will have to give account on the day of judgment for every careless word they have spoken" (Matthew 12:36 NIV). Those are sobering words.

But the answer to reckless words isn't to try to keep silent! Instead, the Bible says, we should seek to do good with our speech: "The tongue of the wise brings healing." Think back over the people who have encouraged or helped you over the years. Weren't they examples of this proverb?

Remember: Jesus Christ wants to be Ruler over every part of your life—including your tongue. Commit it to Him and ask Him for the wisdom to know when to speak and when to keep silent, and how to use your tongue to encourage and help others.

God's Kingdom, God's Way

Your throne, O God, is forever and ever.

PSALM 45:6

Many intellectuals are asking where history is going. Will society get better and better—or will we end up destroying ourselves?

Christ prayed, "Thy kingdom come, Thy will be done in earth, as it is in heaven" (Matthew 6:10 KJV). Someday that prayer—a prayer that you and I often pray—is going to be answered. The last chapter of history will not be written by any human leader, however good or bad. Only God will write it. And write it He will!

Someday, when the human race stands at the edge of the abyss of self-destruction, God will intervene. It may be tomorrow, it may be a thousand years from now. But the outcome is certain: the future belongs to the Kingdom of God.

Never forget: if you belong to the King, you are on the winning side!

Testifying to the Truth

*Always be ready to give a defense to everyone
who asks you a reason for the hope that is in you.*
1 PETER 3:15

One night, my wife and I were guests at a dinner with one of America's most brilliant scientists. He told us that he had been an agnostic, but through his study of science, he had come to believe that there must be a personal God. So he got a Bible and began to read it—and by reading the Bible, he came to know Jesus Christ as his personal Lord and Savior.

Another time, I received a letter from a man who was reared in a good family. He wrote, "I always thought I was a Christian. But my first weeks at the university showed me that my religion was more external than internal, and I set it aside. I was successful on my chosen path. Then I received a glimmer of revelation: if Jesus Christ is the Son of God, as He claims, I'm a fool not to follow Him."

What is your story? Be ready to share it when the Lord gives you the opportunity. God can use it to point others to Christ's transforming power.

From Dull to Dazzling

Stand fast in the Lord.

PHILIPPIANS 4:1

A bar of raw steel may be purchased for a few dollars. But when that bar of steel has been thrust into the fires and processed, when it has been tempered and forged and made into tiny watch springs for expensive watches, it is worth thousands of dollars. Fire and the skilled hands of master artisans made the difference, enhancing the value.

Just as the sun by its heat and light performs a thousand miracles a day in the plant kingdom, God, through the refining fire of His Spirit, performs a thousand miracles a day in the spiritual realm. His regenerating power can take the dull and ordinary things of our lives—even the burned-out ashes of our past—and forge them into something useful, even beautiful, for His purposes.

Head Back Home!

You may be sure that your sin will find you out.
NUMBERS 32:23 NIV

We don't need the Bible to tell us (as it does) that there can be pleasure in sin. We know this from our own experience. But the Bible also says that sin's pleasure is only for a season (Hebrews 11:25). Then it's over, leaving us bitter, and finally destroying us. A day of reckoning always comes. No one has ever committed a sin that he or she did not have to pay for.

In Luke 15 we read of a loving father and his son who learned this lesson the hard way. The boy had been reared in a wonderful home, with a father and mother who worshipped God. They loved their children and tried to raise them right. But this young man left home and wasted his inheritance on foolish and sinful living—and he paid the price. Eventually he found himself living in a pigpen and eating with the pigs. That is how low he sank . . . before he headed back home.

What sin do you need to leave behind? Repent and return to your Father today. He wants to welcome you home!

Rescuing Angels

The angel of the LORD encamps all around
those who fear Him,
and delivers them.

PSALM 34:7

During World War II, Captain Eddie Rickenbacker and his crew ran out of fuel and ditched their B-17 in the Pacific Ocean. For weeks nothing was heard of him, and across the country thousands of people prayed.

Then he returned and wrote about what had happened. "This part I would hesitate to tell," he wrote, "except that there were six witnesses who saw it with me. A gull came out of nowhere, and lighted on my head—I reached up my hand very gently—I killed him and then we divided him equally among us. We ate every bit, even the little bones. Nothing ever tasted so good." This gull saved them from starvation.

Years later, I asked him to tell me the story personally, because it was through this experience that he came to know Christ. He said, "I have no explanation except that God sent one of His angels to rescue us." We may never see them, but God still sends His angels to surround and protect His children—including you.

Standing Strong

*[Take up] the sword of the Spirit,
which is the word of God.*
EPHESIANS 6:17

Temptation is exactly the same for us as it was for Adam and Eve in the garden of Eden. And Satan also tempts us in the same way that he tempted Jesus—through "the lust of the flesh, and the lust of the eyes, and the pride of life" (1 John 2:16 KJV).

It is not a sin to be tempted, for everyone is tempted. The devil tempts, but he can tempt you only so far as God permits—and God always provides a way to escape (1 Corinthians 10:13). The sin is in yielding to temptation instead of seeking God's power to escape.

When you face temptation, follow Jesus' example. Satan will say, "For a moment's bowing of your head to me, the money, the fame, the business, the success, and the power will be yours." But do what Jesus did. Jesus didn't argue with Satan; Jesus didn't debate with him; Jesus didn't rationalize. Instead, He replied, "It is written . . ." Jesus responded to the Enemy's temptation with the simple but strong truth of God's Word, Scripture.

Do the same today—and always.

Joyous Optimism

My soul shall be joyful in the Lord.

PSALM 35:9

When Jesus Christ is the source of our joy, no words can describe it. It is a joy "inexpressible and glorious" (1 Peter 1:8 NIV). Christ is the answer to the sadness and discouragement, the discord and division in our world. He can take discouragement and despondence out of our lives and replace them with optimism and hope.

If our hearts have been attuned to God through an abiding faith in Christ, the result will be joyous optimism and good cheer. The reason? Because we know He loves us and that nothing "shall be able to separate us from the love of God which is in Christ Jesus our Lord" (Romans 8:39).

When our confidence is in Him, discouragement gets crowded out. May that be true in your life today!

By Birth, By Choice, By Practice

Who will rescue me from this body of death? Thanks be to God—through Jesus Christ our Lord!

ROMANS 7:24–25 NIV

As much as we hate to admit it, we are sinners by birth. The Bible is clear: "Surely I was sinful at birth, sinful from the time my mother conceived me" (Psalm 51:5 NIV).

We are also sinners by choice. There comes a time—actually it happens several times a day—when we deliberately choose to tell a lie, to steal, to covet, to gossip, to rage. Or we deliberately choose to not be kind, to not serve, or to not help. Sins of commission, sins of omission—we choose both.

We are also sinners by practice. The more we do it, the easier it is to practice lust, greed, hate, lying, stealing, pride, jealousy, anger, or whatever it may be. These things beset all of us. And the more we yield to the pressure, the more easily we will yield next time.

So we join with Paul: "What a wretched man I am! Who will rescue me?" And then with the apostle we thank God for sending His Son, our Savior and Deliverer!

Right on the Beam

*"Narrow is the gate and difficult is the
way which leads to life."*
MATTHEW 7:14

O nce when we were on a flight from Korea to Japan, we ran through a rough snowstorm. When we arrived over the airport in Tokyo, visibility was almost zero, so the pilot had to make an instrument landing. I sat up in the cockpit with him and watched him sweat it out as the watchful men in the airport tower guided him in.

I did not want these men to be broad-minded. I did not want them to say to the pilot, "Oh well, just land any way you want to. We don't think it'll matter what altitude you keep or how fast you land." I knew that our lives depended on their precise instructions.

Just so, when we come in for the landing in the great airport of Heaven, I don't want any broad-minded advice. I don't want anyone to tell me that it doesn't really matter what I believe as long as I'm sincere—for Jesus said otherwise. I want to come in on the beam, and even though I may be considered narrow-minded here, I want to be sure of a safe landing there. And I *am* sure, because Christ has gone before me and has provided the way.

Unload Your Distress

Casting all your care upon Him, for He cares for you.
1 PETER 5:7

I've been told that the French translation of the verse "Casting all your care upon Him" is "Unloading your distresses upon God."

Have you ever seen a dump truck get rid of its load? The driver simply pushes a button or pulls on a lever, and the heavy load is discharged at the prescribed spot. The truck would be of no use if it carried its burden forever.

We were never meant to be crushed under the weight of care. We can push the button of faith or pull the lever of trust, and our burden is discharged upon the shoulder of Him who said He would gladly bear it. Unload the anxieties of the present moment upon Him, for He cares for you. If He loved you enough to take away the burden of your sins, can't you trust Him to take away every lesser burden as well?

O Lord, Make Me Pure

If we confess our sins, He is faithful and just to forgive us our sins and to cleanse us from all unrighteousness.

1 JOHN 1:9

Saint Augustine was one of the greatest theologians who ever lived. But before he surrendered his heart and his life to Christ, he was a wicked young man, and his besetting sin was lust.

When he was first convicted of his sin, Augustine prayed, "O Lord, make me pure—but not yet." Only when he prayed, "Now, Lord, now. Do it now, Lord," was he forgiven and cleansed.

Augustine was converted to Christ, and God made him pure. When Augustine started following Jesus sixteen hundred years ago, he changed the direction of Christianity by calling on people to rediscover the Scriptures and focus on Christ.

What besetting sin do you struggle with? Sin is often, if not always, the perversion of something good. In the midst of all our sinning, though, God is willing to forgive us, change us, and give us a new power to overcome that sin.

Are you praying, "Make me pure—but not yet"? Maybe today is the day to say, "Do it now, Lord. Now."

Fear—and Fear Not!

*Now, O Israel, what does the LORD your God ask
of you but to fear the LORD your God, to walk in
all his ways, to love him?*

DEUTERONOMY 10:12 NIV

The Bible says, "Fear not, for I am with thee" (Genesis 26:24 KJV). But the Bible also says, "Fear the Lord." If God's Word says, "Fear not," and yet it also says, "Fear," which does it mean? The answer is: both.

Fear is a two-fold word. It refers to an emotion marked by dread and anxious concern. But it also means awe, and wonder, and profound reverence. This latter is the fear that inspires trust and confidence. The Bible calls us to have the latter kind of fear.

When we fear God, we don't cringe before Him like a prisoner robbed of freedom by a ruthless dictator. Our fear causes us to treat God with respect and trust. It is a reverence that comes from seeing the majesty and holiness and power of our loving Heavenly Father.

There is no shame in being afraid. We're all afraid from time to time. But there's an interesting paradox here, in that if we truly fear God with all our heart, then we have nothing to fear.

Material Gods

"What will it profit a man if he gains the whole world, and loses his own soul?"

MARK 8:36

The Bible does not condemn money or material possessions. Money and possessions can do great good when they are used wisely and kept in proper perspective. Some of the great people of the Bible were very rich. Abraham, Isaac, and Solomon were perhaps the richest men of their day.

God's quarrel is not with material goods but with material gods. Materialism has become the god of too many of us. Our material possessions are elevated to the central place in our lives, and we give them the attention only God deserves.

The Bible teaches that preoccupation with material possessions is a form of idolatry. And God hates idolatry. It poisons every other phase of our lives, including our family life.

The problem, the Bible says, is not with money itself, but with our love of money: "The love of money is a root of all kinds of evil" (1 Timothy 6:10). Don't let money, or anything else, take God's rightful place in your life.

Love by Your Actions

*"'Love the Lord your God with all your heart and with
all your soul and with all your strength and with all
your mind'; and, 'Love your neighbor as yourself.'"*
LUKE 10:27 NIV

Did you know that the religious leaders of Jesus'
day had more than six hundred man-made laws
they were required to obey? The people couldn't keep
all those laws; it was impossible. Yet the rulers believed
that those laws had to be obeyed in order to win God's
favor.

But Jesus summed up God's law with only two
commands: "Love the Lord your God" and "Love your
neighbor." And He used a special, all-encompassing
word for love, a word that includes everyone. We are to
love our neighbors, He said, even though they may have
a different color skin, ethnic background, or language;
even though they look different, walk differently, or act
differently. We are also to help our neighbors who are
poor. The gospel of Christ has no meaning unless it is
applied to those who are in need.

The Greek word for *love* that Jesus used implies
action. It is not a passive word; it is an action word. We
are to love by our actions. What will you do today to
show God's love by your actions?

Soaring in Victory

*"Unless one is born again, he cannot
see the kingdom of God."*

JOHN 3:3

In the third chapter of John, Jesus teaches that the new birth is something God does for us as we yield ourselves to Him and put our faith and trust in Christ. We do not have within ourselves the seed of the new life; this must come from God.

One day, an ugly caterpillar climbs into a tree and spins a silky robe about itself. It goes to sleep and, in a few weeks, emerges a beautiful butterfly.

So we—discouraged, unhappy, hounded by guilt, confused, depressed, vainly looking for an escape—can come by faith to Christ and emerge a new person. We can be born again! It sounds incredible, even impossible—and yet it is precisely what happens. We become members of God's family, looking forward to our eternal home in Heaven.

Do you feel you are in a cocoon? Turn to Christ and ask Him to give you your beautiful wings so that you might soar above your problems and be victorious over them.

Life with a Capital *L*

"The Son gives life to whom He will."
JOHN 5:21

The moment you come to Christ, the Spirit of God brings the life of God into you, and you begin to live. For the first time you begin to live with a capital *L*. There's a spring in your step, a joy in your soul, and a peace in your heart. Life has taken on a new outlook.

There's a whole new direction to your life, because now the Spirit of God has implanted within you the very life of God Himself, who is eternal. And that means you will live as long as God lives!

Too many Christians let themselves get bogged down by the cares and routines of daily living. Don't let that happen to you. Ask God to help you live each day with eternity in view.

Responding to God's Call

There are different kinds of gifts, but the same Spirit.
There are different kinds of service, but the same
Lord. There are different kinds of working, but the
same God works all of them in all men.

1 CORINTHIANS 12:4–6 NIV

I can remember when God first called me, calling me into His ministry. I thought of all the things I would have to give up or change. I wept, and I fought, and I battled. But ultimately I answered the Lord's call and began to serve Jesus Christ in a new way. I promised God then that I would never do anything as long as I lived except preach the gospel.

God's call on your life may not be as dramatic as mine was, and the ministry that results from your obedience may not be the same as mine. But none of that takes away from the significance of what you are doing with your life in the service of your King.

William Borden, heir to a large fortune and graduate of Yale, sacrificed everything to go to China as a missionary. He got as far as Egypt before he died of cerebral meningitis in Cairo. Later it was written of him that he had "no reserve, no retreat, no regrets." May you and I also live for Christ with no reserve, no retreat, and no regrets.

The Bottom Line

I resolved to know nothing while I was with you except Jesus Christ and him crucified.

1 CORINTHIANS 2:2 NIV

I remember preaching in Dallas, Texas, early in our ministry. It was 1953. Many thousands attended each night, but one evening only a few people responded to the appeal to receive Jesus Christ. Discouraged, I left the platform.

A German businessman was there, a devout man of God. He put his arm around me and said, "Billy, do you know what was wrong tonight? You didn't preach the cross." He was right.

The next night I preached on Christ and His sacrificial death for us, and a great host of people received Christ as Savior. When we preach Christ crucified and risen, that message has built-in spiritual power. The Holy Spirit takes the simple message of the cross, with its theme of redemptive love and grace, and infuses it with authority. This supernatural act of God's Spirit breaks down barriers in people's hearts.

So whether you're preaching with actions or words—in your home, neighborhood, or workplace—be sure that you're preaching the cross. The Spirit will be at work.

God's Great Heart

*"'Love the L*ORD* your God with all your heart' . . .*
and 'your neighbor as yourself.'"

LUKE 10:27

Divine love, like a reflected sunbeam, shines down before it radiates out. Unless our hearts are conditioned by the Holy Spirit to receive and reflect the warmth of God's compassion, we cannot love others as we ought.

Jesus wept tears of compassion at the graveside of a friend. He mourned over Jerusalem because its people had lost their sensitivity to God and His Word. His great heart was always sensitive to the needs of others. When challenged to state the most important commandment, He replied, "'You shall love the LORD your God with all your heart' . . . [and] 'your neighbor as yourself'" (Matthew 22:37, 39).

Jesus' love was more than human compassion, however; it was in the fullest sense divine love, for He was God in human flesh. This is the kind of love He calls us to have—and the kind He will give us as we seek it from Him.

Tears of Love

*Dear children, let us not love with words or
tongue but with actions and in truth.*

1 JOHN 3:18 NIV

One of our associate evangelists was preaching at a university. He yearned to win the students to Christ, but their reaction was hostile. One young woman was especially antagonistic. After the lecture she came to him and said, "I don't believe anything you said."

He replied, "I'm sorry that you don't agree, but do you mind if I pray for you?"

She answered, "Nobody has ever prayed for me before. I guess it won't do any harm."

He bowed his head and began to pray. She stood looking straight ahead. But suddenly she noticed that while he was praying, tears were coming down his cheeks. When he opened his eyes, she herself was in tears. She said, "No one in my entire life has ever shed a tear for me." They sat on a bench, and that woman accepted Christ as her Savior.

May the Lord use you today to help bring someone into His Kingdom by your love and your witness.

Earnest Prayer

*Continue earnestly in prayer, being vigilant
in it with thanksgiving.*

COLOSSIANS 4:2

We have learned to harness the power of the atom, but very few of us have learned how to fully develop the power of prayer. We have not yet learned that a man can be more powerful on his knees than behind the most powerful weapons ever developed.

We have not learned that a nation is more powerful when it unites in earnest prayer to God than when its resources are channeled into weapons. We have not discovered that the answer to our problems can come through contact with the living God.

Weapons by themselves will not keep us safe or solve the world's problems. Our basic problems are spiritual in nature, and only spiritual solutions will solve them. That is why prayer is so vital, for only God can change the human heart.

Who knows what might happen if millions of believers around the world availed themselves of the greatest privilege this side of Heaven—the privilege of intercessory prayer? Will you be one of them?

Read the Label

For the wages of sin is death, but the gift of God is eternal life in Christ Jesus our Lord.

Romans 6:23

After a minister had spoken strongly against sin one morning, one of the church members said, "We don't want you to talk so plainly about sin, because if our children hear you mention it, they will more easily become sinners. Call it a mistake, if you will, but do not speak so bluntly about sin."

The minister went to his medicine shelf and brought back a bottle of strychnine marked "Poison." He said, "I understand what you want me to do. You want me to change the label. Suppose I take this 'Poison' label off the bottle and put on a label like 'Peppermint Candy.' Can't you see the problem? The milder you make the label, the more dangerous the poison's presence."

It is high time we put a "Poison" label back on the poison of sin. We must not be afraid to be as plain as the Bible is about the tragic consequences of sin—or about the antidote for that poison: the blood of Christ.

Claim a Larger Blessing

Through God we will do valiantly.

Psalm 108:13

There are two ways of getting out of a trial. One is to simply try to get rid of the trial and be thankful when it is over. The other is to recognize the trial as a challenge from God to claim a larger blessing than we have ever had.

Sometimes God removes our trials, and it isn't necessarily wrong to ask Him to do that. But often the trials remain, and when they do, we should accept them and ask God to teach us from them.

As Peter Marshall once put it, "God will not permit any troubles to come upon us, unless He has a specific plan by which great blessing can come out of the difficulty."

During the suffering, the tests, and the trials of life, we can choose to draw near to God. A. B. Simpson once heard a man say something he never forgot: "When God tests you, it is a good time for you to test Him by putting His promises to the proof, and claiming from Him just as much as your trials have rendered necessary."

Cowardly or Courageous?

If God is for us, who can be against us?

ROMANS 8:31

The chairman of the history department of one of our great universities once stated his opinion to me: "We have become a nation of cowards." I challenged his statement, but he argued that many people have become reluctant to follow a course if it isn't popular. I had to admit he was right.

Even if, deep inside, we know a certain path to be right, we draw back because we are afraid of the consequences. If the odds are in our favor, we will take a stand; but if there is any risk involved in standing up for what we know to be right, we will play it safe.

How different from the early Christians! From one end of the Roman Empire to the other they boldly proclaimed the gospel in the face of hostility, persecution, scorn, and even death. The apostle Paul knew the key: "For God has not given us a spirit of fear, but of power and of love and of a sound mind" (2 Timothy 1:7).

You may never face the same dangers those early Christians did, but don't take the road of cowardice; don't give in to fear. Remember: "If God is for us, who can be against us?"

The Poison of Pride

"The LORD detests all the proud of heart.
Be sure of this: They will not go unpunished."

PROVERBS 16:5 NIV

The pride that God loathes is not a healthy self-respect or a legitimate sense of personal dignity. It is the haughty, undue self-esteem out of all proportion to our actual worth. It is the repugnant egotism that is repulsive to both man and God. It is that revolting conceit that swaggers before men and struts in the presence of the Almighty. And God hates it.

Pride may take various forms. Spiritual pride trusts in one's own virtue rather than in the grace of God. Intellectual pride gives its possessor self-confidence rather than God-confidence. Pride in material things enthrones self and displaces God; secondary things are exalted to the place of first importance. Social pride manifests itself in arrogance and status. All forms of pride emanate from the haughty human heart, and pride is the sin that God hates most.

What can you do about it? Confess your pride. Humble yourself in the sight of God. Look then at Christ, who "humbled himself and became obedient to death—even death on a cross!" (Philippians 2:8 NIV).

The Poison of Anger

A fool gives full vent to his anger.
Proverbs 29:11 niv

Anger is one sin that everyone is capable of committing. The tiny baby has a tantrum and spits up her dinner. The little boy has a tantrum and ruins the family gathering. The wife loses her temper and wounds her child's heart. The husband gets angry and terrifies his family. Homes can be destroyed by the swirling tornadoes of anger. Business relations can be shattered by fits of violent temper. Friendships can be broken by anger.

Anger causes murders, assaults, and conflicts. Anger brings out the animal nature of human beings. It hinders our Christian testimony and causes people to lose the joy of living. Too many of us excuse our anger by blaming our natural disposition, but anger is sin.

The first step in finding victory over anger is to want to get rid of it. Next comes confession. Then comes a yielding to God. His Spirit can tame your tongue and your passions when you surrender your heart to Jesus. He who calmed the turbulent Sea of Galilee can calm the tempestuous sea of your anger with His love.

The Poison of Envy

A heart at peace gives life to the body,
but envy rots the bones.

PROVERBS 14:30 NIV

In ancient Greece, the citizens of a certain city erected a statue of a celebrated champion in the public games. But his rival was so envious that he vowed to destroy that statue. Every night he went after dark and chiseled away at its base in an effort to undermine its foundation and make it fall. At last he succeeded. It did fall—but it fell on him. The jealous athlete died, a victim of his own envy.

Envy dethrones God. Envy destroys our spiritual health, and it takes the joy, happiness, and contentment out of living. Envy becomes a spiritual leprosy, isolating us from both God and other human beings. No wonder God ranks envy on the same level as sexual immorality, idolatry, witchcraft, and drunkenness (Galatians 5:19–21).

To get rid of this devastating poison, first recognize that you have it. Then confess your sin to God and renounce it. Finally, since envy cannot be overcome in your own strength, open your heart to the transforming power of Christ.

The Poison of Impurity

Among you there must not be even a hint of sexual immorality, or of any kind of impurity . . . because these are improper for God's holy people.

EPHESIANS 5:3 NIV

In God's eyes, impurity is one of the most revolting sins, because it twists and distorts one of God's most precious gifts: human love. Impurity drags this gift down to the level of the beast.

Yet impurity—surrounding us as it does in the form of filthy stories, suggestive remarks, open vulgarity; in magazines, on television, in the movies, through the Internet—has a better press agent than purity. Purity is considered smug, but impurity is considered smart—and the consequences of this vicious sin are played down. Satan fails to speak of the remorse, the futility, the loneliness, and the spiritual devastation that go hand in hand with immorality.

But Christ will cleanse you and give you victory over your sin. Jesus said to the immoral woman, "Go and sin no more" (John 8:11). He says that to you as well—and He never told anyone to do something without also offering the power to do it.

The Poison of Gluttony

Whether you eat or drink, or whatever you do,
do all to the glory of God.

1 CORINTHIANS 10:31

Before the fall of Rome, the Romans were known for gluttony, immorality, and drunkenness. They dug their grave with their teeth, killed themselves by illicit indulgence, and embalmed themselves with alcohol. It is said that, at their sumptuous banquets, men would rush to the windows, eject the contents of their stomachs, and then return to the table for further indulgence. No individual or nation given to drunkenness and gluttony can expect the blessing of God. Rome fell because she overstuffed her body and starved her soul.

Such gluttony is a perversion of a natural, God-given appetite. The gratification of our fleshly appetites is not to receive first importance in our lives. When we cater to the appetites of the flesh—when a normal hunger is extended into abnormality so that it harms the body, dulls the mind, and causes us to neglect the soul—we become guilty of the sin of gluttony.

When we acknowledge and confess our sin, Jesus will forgive the past and give us power of self-discipline, temperance, and restraint for the days ahead.

The Poison of Sloth

The sluggard's craving will be the death of him,
because his hands refuse to work.

PROVERBS 21:25 NIV

Webster's defines *sloth* as "a disinclination to action or labor; sluggishness, laziness, idleness." In theological contexts, *sloth* carries with it not only the idea of laziness in spiritual things, but also apathy and inactivity in the practice of our everyday lives.

The slothful person is like a piece of driftwood floating effortlessly and heedlessly downstream with the current. It takes no effort, no strength to be lost. A drifting boat always goes downstream, never up. Likewise, a drifting, slothful soul is inevitably moving toward an eternity of destruction.

The sin of doing nothing—the sin of omission—is just as dangerous as any sin of action—of commission. You don't have to do anything to be lost; just do nothing. Just be slothful about your soul. Tragically, thousands of us Christians are slothful when it comes to prayer, worship, reading the Bible, witnessing for Christ, helping neighbors in need, or giving to charity.

A stubborn, slothful spirit is a great hindrance to receiving Jesus' forgiveness and transforming power. Don't let it overcome you.

The Poison of Greed

From the least to the greatest,
all are greedy for gain.

JEREMIAH 6:13 NIV

A close relative of covetousness, greed is quite possibly the parent of more evil than any other sin. Greed cheats, robs, murders, and slanders in order to achieve its desires—and each of us is born with greed in our nature.

The Bible teaches that greed is idolatry, because it places things at the center of our lives instead of God. We in America, for instance, are so bent on making money that we do not have time for God and the spiritual disciplines. It is not a sin to be rich, but if our riches have choked out our spiritual life, then being rich has become sin—and we are poverty-stricken in God's sight. Furthermore, the love of money corrodes the human heart, spoiling our happiness and setting us in conflict with one another. The Bible says that "the love of money is a root of all kinds of evil" (1 Timothy 6:10).

As long as the prodigal son sang the song of "Give me," his lot was misery, want, loneliness, and famine. But when he changed his song to "Forgive me," he found himself in a state of fellowship, comfort, and plenty. What song are you singing?

The Spirit Within You

Do you not know that your body is the temple of the Holy Spirit who is in you, whom you have from God?

1 CORINTHIANS 6:19

If you have truly asked Christ to come into your life, you can be confident that the Holy Spirit resides in you—whether or not you feel His presence. The Bible says, "For you . . . received the Spirit of adoption" (Romans 8:15).

Even though the Spirit lives within us, however, we must yield our lives to Him every day because our old nature is still present. Furthermore, Satan will try to tempt us and convince us we must fight our spiritual battles alone. That's why every day we should pray something like this: "Lord, I know that on my own I can't live the way You want me to live—but with Your help I can. Please help me today to step aside and allow Your Holy Spirit to work in me and through me."

Yielding to God's Spirit doesn't mean all your problems will vanish; you and I are engaged in a spiritual battle that will last as long as we live. But we are not alone in that battle. God has provided His armor—including His Spirit—to help us (Ephesians 6:10–18).

Thank God that He lives within you by His Holy Spirit!

Forgiveness and Fellowship

*"I will forgive their iniquity, and their sin
I will remember no more."*

JEREMIAH 31:34

There is no possibility of true happiness until we have established friendship and fellowship with God. And there is no possibility of establishing this fellowship apart from the cross of His Son, Jesus Christ.

God says, "I will forgive you, but I will forgive only at the foot of the cross." He says, "I will fellowship with you, but I will fellowship with you only at the cross."

Why is this? Because only through Christ's death on the cross can we be forgiven and reconciled to God.

This is why we must come to the cross, repenting of our sins and trusting Christ alone to save us. Human pride gets in the way: we don't want to admit that we are sinners or that we are too weak to save ourselves. Only when we leave our pride at the cross can our hearts be open to God's redeeming grace.

When we come to Christ, God imparts His righteousness to us. It is as if an accounting entry had been made in the books of Heaven, declaring us righteous for Christ's sake. The Divine Bookkeeper cancels our debt!

Patience and Prayer

We . . . do not cease to pray for you.

COLOSSIANS 1:9

Some years ago, a woman wrote me that she had pleaded for ten years for the conversion of her husband, but that he was more hardened than ever. I advised her to continue to plead. Sometime later I heard from her again. She said her husband was gloriously and miraculously converted in the eleventh year of her prayer vigil. How thankful she was that she had kept on praying!

Scripture says, "Pray without ceasing" (1 Thessalonians 5:17). This should be the motto of every true follower of Jesus Christ. Never stop praying, no matter how dark and hopeless your case may seem. Your responsibility isn't to tell God when He must act or even how He must act. Your responsibility is simply to "pray without ceasing," trusting Him to act according to His perfect will.

God Cares for You

God is not the author of confusion but of peace.
1 CORINTHIANS 14:33

Who of us has not asked in times of affliction and difficulty, "Does God care for me?" The psalmist said, "Refuge failed me; no man cared for my soul" (142:4 KJV). Martha, overly concerned with her workaday duties, said to Jesus, "Lord, do You not care?" (Luke 10:40). How many faithful, loving mothers, overwhelmed by the burdens of motherhood, have cried anxiously, "Lord, do You not care?"

That question is forever answered in those reassuring words of Peter: "He cares for you" (1 Peter 5:7). This is the Word of God. Even if the world passes away, His Word will not change.

You can be confident God cares for you. If He didn't, would He have sent Christ into the world to die for you? Of course not! That is why you can always turn to Him for the strength and encouragement you need.

Yes, life can be overwhelming at times. But when it is, remember this: God knows what you are facing, and "He cares for you."

The Peace of God

Let the peace of God rule in your hearts.
COLOSSIANS 3:15

Science has confirmed what the Bible taught centuries ago: there is a close relationship between our minds and bodies. Proverbs puts it this way: "A cheerful heart is good medicine, but a crushed spirit dries up the bones" (17:22 NIV).

But there is also a close relationship between our mental and physical health and the health of our spiritual lives. Guilt, fear, jealousy, bitterness, futility, escapism—these and a host of other problems are spiritual ills brought about by the disease of sin. Like poison, they can sicken us in mind and body.

But when Christ comes into our lives, He removes our guilt and takes away our fears. He gives us love for others and a new purpose in life. His joy and peace neutralize sin's poison and promote emotional and physical health.

Does that mean our emotional and physical problems will vanish? Not necessarily. But like a spring of pure water, God's peace in our hearts brings cleansing and refreshment to our minds and bodies.

The Good Shepherd

"The good shepherd lays down his life for the sheep."

JOHN 10:11 NIV

One of the figures of speech Jesus applied to Himself was that of a shepherd. He said, "I am the good shepherd. The good shepherd lays down his life for the sheep. The hired hand is not the shepherd who owns the sheep. . . . I know my sheep and my sheep know me" (John 10:11–12, 14 NIV).

Note four things about Jesus, the Good Shepherd. He owns the sheep; they belong to Him. Next, He guards the sheep; He never abandons them when danger approaches. Also, He knows the sheep; He calls them by name and they follow Him. Finally, He lays down His life for the sheep; their salvation is His primary concern.

The Bible says, "We are His people and the sheep of His pasture" (Psalm 100:3). Because we belong to Christ, we can be secure and at rest.

We Can't Outgive God

The generous soul will be made rich.
PROVERBS 11:25

The Bible teaches that blessings follow those who give liberally. Proverbs 11:25 says, "The generous soul will be made rich, and he who waters will also be watered himself."

I've heard countless testimonies from men and women who were afraid to put to the test God's promise to bless those who are generous. They feared they would not have enough. Then, when at last they decided to tithe (to give a tenth of their income) in accordance with the Bible's standard, they began to prosper. They discovered what countless others have known across the ages: you can't outgive God.

What keeps you from being more generous in supporting God's work? Selfishness? Fear? Insecurity? Even a sinful habit you would rather support? Whatever the reason, repent of it and discover the blessedness of generosity. Remember: "God loves a cheerful giver" (2 Corinthians 9:7).

God's Only Son, Our Savior

*Praise be to God and Father of our Lord Jesus Christ,
who has blessed us in the heavenly realms with every
spiritual blessing in Christ.*

EPHESIANS 1:3 NIV

It has often been pointed out that Jesus lived in a small country and never went beyond its borders. He was so poor that He said He had nowhere to lay His head. His only pocketbook was the mouth of a fish. He rode on another man's beast. He cruised the lake in another man's boat. He was buried in another man's grave. And He had laid aside a royal robe for all this.

He never wrote a book. His recorded words would hardly make a pocket edition. Yet if all the words that have been written about Him were brought together, they would fill a thousand libraries.

He never founded a college to perpetuate His doctrines. Yet His teachings have endured for more than two thousand years.

He never carried a sword, He never organized an army, He never built a navy, and He never had an air force. Yet He founded an empire in which there are millions today who would die for Him.

His name is "Wonderful Counselor, Mighty God, Everlasting Father, Prince of Peace" (Isaiah 9:6). Praise His name!

APRIL

A Purpose and a Power

Go quickly and tell . . . that He is risen from the dead.
MATTHEW 28:7

When Samuel Morse, inventor of the telegraph, sent his first message, he telegraphed these words: "What hath God wrought!"

The greatest news ever sent tells of a far greater event God has wrought: Christ is risen. On that first resurrection day, the angel at the tomb delivered the most important message anyone can ever hear: "He is not here; for He is risen" (Matthew 28:6).

When Adam and Eve first sinned, God's warning became a reality: "You shall surely die" (Genesis 2:17). From that moment on, death reigned over the human race—and with it, fear, dread, and superstition.

But Christ's resurrection changed all that, bringing hope and salvation to all who put their trust in Him. Listen: Death is a defeated foe! Christ has won the victory. That is why Paul could say, "Thanks be to God, who gives us the victory through our Lord Jesus Christ" (1 Corinthians 15:57). Is your confidence in Jesus Christ, the risen Lord?

The Cross of Christ

*For the message of the cross is foolishness to
those who are perishing, but to us who are
being saved it is the power of God.*

1 Corinthians 1:18

Why is the cross an offense?

First, the cross is an offense because it condemns the world. It says, "You are sinners"—and we don't like someone pointing out our faults, failures, mistakes, and especially our sins.

The cross also offends and confuses an unbelieving world because blood was shed, and blood is repulsive. But by Christ's blood—by His death on the cross—we are released from the guilt of sin and accepted as righteous in God's sight (Colossians 1:20).

The cross is also an offense because it demands a disciplined life: following Jesus will mean denying self and bearing one's own cross.

In addition, the cross offends because it points to the end of the world as we know it, and that end will be marked by the return of Jesus Christ.

Finally, the cross of Christ is an offense because it claims to be the only way of salvation, the only way to God. Have you chosen to follow the way of the cross?

The Light of God's Love

O LORD my God, You are very great. . . .
You who laid the foundations of the earth.
PSALM 104:1, 5

God's love did not begin at Calvary. Before the morning stars sang together, before the world was baptized with the first light, before the first blades of tender grass peeped out, God was love.

Turn back to the unwritten pages of countless eons before God spoke this present Earth into existence, when the Earth was "without form and void" (Genesis 1:2) and the deep, silent darkness of space stood in stark contrast to the brilliance of God's glory and His cherubim and seraphim.

Even then, God was love. Before the worlds were created, He knew all about us and the need we would have someday for Christ to die for us. So in His love "he chose us in him before the creation of the world" (Ephesians 1:4 NIV).

God does not change—and neither does His love. He loved you before you were born . . . He loves you now . . . and He will love you forever. Will you love Him in return?

Glory in the Cross

*God forbid that I should glory, save in the
cross of our Lord Jesus Christ.*

GALATIANS 6:14 KJV

Why did the apostle Paul say that he gloried in the
cross of Christ above everything else?

Paul could have gloried in many things about himself. He could have gloried in his education: he was
one of the most brilliant men of his day. A Jew and a
Pharisee, Paul could have gloried in his religion. And he
could have gloried in his Roman citizenship.

Or Paul could have gloried in other aspects of Jesus'
life. He could have gloried in His birth: Jesus was virgin born. Or in the teachings of Jesus: no one had ever
taught like Jesus. Paul could have gloried in the resurrection of Jesus or in His future glory when He will
return as the victorious and conquering King.

But Paul gloried in the cross. Why? The cross shows
the seriousness of our sin—but it also shows us the
immeasurable love of God. Furthermore, the cross is
the only way of salvation. And the cross gives a new
purpose to life. Once you have been to the cross, you
will never be the same.

No wonder Paul—and you and I—can glory in the
cross.

The Future Life

As for man, his days are like grass;
As a flower of the field, so he flourishes.

PSALM 103:15

The Bible reminds us that our days are as grass. For a brief time we flourish, but soon we wither and die. Yet the minutes of our lives can be flecked with the gold of eternity. Instead of wasting our lives—as we so easily do—God exhorts us to redeem the time.

But we are also immortal. God made us different from the other creatures. He made us in His own image, a living soul. Don't let anyone tell you that we are simply a higher species of animal. If you believe that, you will begin to act like one. No! You are far greater.

One thousand years from this day, you will be more alive than you are at this moment. The Bible teaches that life does not end at the cemetery. There is a future life with God for those who put their trust in His Son, Jesus Christ. There is also a future Hell of separation from God for all who have refused, rejected, or neglected to receive His Son, Jesus Christ.

Make sure of your relationship to Christ, and then ask God to help you live each day for His glory.

Love and Justice Meet

*Then Jesus came with them to a place called Gethsemane
. . . and He began to be sorrowful and deeply distressed.*

MATTHEW 26:36–37

Gethsemane means "an oil press." When olives are harvested, they are squeezed under an enormous revolving stone that mashes the fruit to pulp and recovers the valuable oil.

In the Garden of Gethsemane, the wheel of humiliation and death would squeeze Jesus to the point of His greatest agony, so He pleaded with His Father for release—but only if it were the Almighty's will.

God did not grant release, for there was no other way for our just and loving God to deal with our sins. Sin must be punished. If God were simply to forgive our sins without judging them, then there would be no justice, no accountability for wrongdoing. God would not be truly holy and just.

But if God were simply to judge us for our sins as we deserve, there would be no hope of salvation for any of us. His love would have failed to provide what we need.

The cross was the only way to resolve the problem of sin. At the cross God's love and justice came together. Jesus took the punishment we deserved, and now we are clothed in His perfect righteousness.

Caving In to the Crowd

Then Pilate announced . . . "I find no basis for a charge against this man." . . . But with loud shouts they insistently demanded that he be crucified, and their shouts prevailed.

LUKE 23:4, 23 NIV

The name of Pontius Pilate will be forever linked to the death of Jesus Christ, for it was he, as Roman governor, who gave the final order condemning Jesus to death by crucifixion.

But the name of Pontius Pilate will also stand forever as a prime example of someone who knew what was right—but failed to do it. Repeatedly, he told the mob clamoring for Jesus' death that he found no basis for condemning Him—but in the end, he caved in to the pressures of the crowd and ordered His death. Publicly he washed his hands and told the crowd that they alone were responsible for Jesus' death (Matthew 27:24), but in reality Pilate's cowardice sent Jesus to the cross.

How often do you cave in to the pressures of the crowd, seeking the approval of others instead of the approval of God? We all like to be liked—but that can be a very dangerous thing. Make it your goal to live for Christ and be faithful to Him, regardless of what the crowd demands.

A Living Sacrifice

Present yourselves to God as being alive . . . and your members as instruments of righteousness to God.

ROMANS 6:13

The apostle Paul, who was a splendid example of a disciplined Christian, said, "I beseech you therefore, brethren, by the mercies of God, that ye present your bodies a living sacrifice, holy, acceptable unto God, which is your reasonable service" (Romans 12:1 KJV).

If we have given ourselves to Christ, then He has come to live within us, and our bodies are now the temples—the dwelling places—of the Holy Spirit. Now we must act worthy of Him who lives within us, disciplining both our bodies and minds so we do not bring dishonor to Him. We must pray as Jeremy Taylor once prayed, "Let my body be a servant of my spirit, and both body and spirit servants of Jesus."

Paul knew Christ had sacrificed His body for his salvation, and the only reasonable thing to do in response was to give his body as a living sacrifice to Christ.

Let me challenge you to commit your body and your mind to Christ, "which is your reasonable service."

The Living Christ

It is no longer I who live, but Christ lives in me.
GALATIANS 2:20

Jesus Christ was crucified between two thieves on a rugged cross on Calvary, just outside Jerusalem. Think of it: the very Son of God came down from Heaven and "humbled Himself and became obedient to the point of death, even the death of the cross" (Philippians 2:8).

Jesus gave His head to the crown of thorns for us. He gave His face to the human spittle for us. He gave His cheeks and His beard to be plucked out for us. He gave His back to the lash for us. He gave His side to the spear for us. He gave His hands and feet to the spikes for us. He gave His blood for us. Jesus Christ, dying in our place, taking our sins on that cross, is God's love in action.

But that's not the end of the story. He rose again, and He is the living Christ. If Christ is not alive, there is no hope for any of us. But He is alive! And because He is, "he is able to save completely those who come to God through him, because he always lives to intercede for them" (Hebrews 7:25 NIV). Hallelujah!

All for Love

He was pierced for our transgressions,
he was crushed for our iniquities;
the punishment that brought us peace was upon him,
and by his wounds we are healed.

ISAIAH 53:5 NIV

Flogged . . . Bits of glass and rocks shredded the flesh of His back . . . Crucified . . . Nailed to the rough wood of the cross and left hanging there to experience the excruciating pain of death by suffocation . . .

Why did Jesus willingly die such a violent death? The Bible says He went to the cross for one reason: to become the final and complete sacrifice for our sins. Each of us has sinned; each of us is guilty before God; each of us deserves to die. God is holy and just, and sin must be punished.

But Christ became our substitute; He died in our place. He was without sin, but all our sins were placed on Him, and He willingly took the punishment and death we deserve. The Bible says, "Christ died for sins once for all, the righteous for the unrighteous, to bring you to God" (1 Peter 3:18 NIV). Christ died for you!

Why did He do this? He did it because He loves you, and He wants you to spend eternity with Him in Heaven. Have you responded to His love?

"It Is Finished"

He was wounded for our transgressions.

ISAIAH 53:5

On a hill overlooking the harbor of Macao, Portuguese settlers built a massive cathedral. But over time it fell in ruins, except for one wall. On the top of that high, jutting wall, challenging the elements down through the years, was a huge bronze cross.

It is said that when Sir John Bowring saw it, he was moved to write these words: "In the cross of Christ I glory, / Tow'ring o'er the wrecks of time."

When Jesus lifted up His voice and cried, "It is finished," He did not mean His life was ebbing away or God's plan had been foiled. Though death was near, Jesus realized the last obstacle had been hurdled and the last enemy destroyed. He had successfully and triumphantly completed the task of redemption. With the words "It is finished," He announced that Heaven's door was open.

Kingdoms and empires come and go, but the cross and all it stands for will always remain, "tow'ring o'er the wrecks of time."

He Suffered for You

His visage was marred more than any man.

ISAIAH 52:14

When Jesus Christ was on the cross, His blood draining the life from His body, He knew what it was like to be alone and racked with pain. But Jesus' pain was far more than just physical pain, for He was suffering God's judgment on all the sins of the ages—the greatest darkness of the soul ever known. As the divine Son of God, He was perfect and without sin. But all our sins were placed on Him, and He took the judgment and Hell we alone deserve. He died in our place.

Why did Jesus suffer? For you. For me. That we might have eternal life and have His peace in the midst of life's storms. That we might know that He understands our pain and suffering and stands ready to help.

Why did Jesus suffer? Because God loves us. Because God loves you, Christ willingly went to the cross for you. There was no other way for sin's penalty to be paid, and for us to be redeemed. The cross is the measure of God's love.

How will you respond to His love, poured out on the cross for you?

The Key Moment in History

"I am the resurrection and the life. He who believes in me will live, even though he dies; and whoever lives and believes in me will never die."

JOHN 11:25–26 NIV

On that first Easter morning, something happened that had never happened before in the history of the human race—and would never happen again: someone came back from the dead, never to die again.

What difference does that event make? It makes all the difference in the world to us! For one thing, the resurrection proved beyond all doubt that Jesus was who He claimed to be: the Son of God sent from Heaven to save us from our sins. Because He rose from the dead, our salvation is secure.

But Jesus' resurrection also tells us that there is life beyond the grave. This world is not all there is; when we die, we continue to live—either in the place of utter darkness the Bible calls Hell or in the place of endless joy the Bible calls Heaven. And Jesus has opened the way to Heaven for us by His death and resurrection. Because Jesus rose from the dead, death has been defeated and Heaven awaits us. Hallelujah!

The Choice

Being in anguish, [Jesus] prayed more earnestly, and his sweat was like drops of blood falling to the ground.

LUKE 22:44 NIV

The Garden of Gethsemane is the place where Jesus was revealed to be truly human. There He faced the choice between obedience and disobedience. He was not a robot programmed to obey God automatically. He knows what it's like to be tempted. And, after three years of selfless giving and the stress of that final week, Jesus was never more vulnerable to temptation than at this moment in Gethsemane.

Some skeptics have said that Jesus' agony in Gethsemane was a sign of weakness. They point out that many martyrs have died without the intense emotional wrestling of Jesus. But it is one thing to die for a cause or for a country. It is quite another to die for an entire world—for all the accumulated sins of generations past and generations to come.

No one ever experienced greater spiritual suffering than Jesus. His death was a spiritual battle against the powers of darkness, and His resurrection meant the triumph of God over Satan. No mere man could defeat Satan. Only Jesus.

Let us give praise to the Man who was also God—Jesus Christ!

Christ Is Risen

He is not here, but is risen!
LUKE 24:6

Easter Sunday is the most triumphant and joyous day in the calendar of the Christian Church—and it should be!

For many people the resurrection of Jesus Christ is symbolized by new Easter clothes, the bright color of daffodils, and beautiful white Easter lilies. But most of all, the wonder of His resurrection is symbolized in the hope that beats in the hearts of believers everywhere as they sing triumphantly: "Christ the Lord is risen today."

It is the message "Jesus is alive!" that lifts Christianity out of the category of dead superstitions and archaic religions and makes it the abiding faith of millions. The angel's message is true: "He is not here, but is risen!" And now God's promise is for you: "If you confess with your mouth the Lord Jesus and believe in your heart that God has raised Him from the dead, you will be saved" (Romans 10:9).

The Message of Easter

He has risen! He is not here.

MARK 16:6 NIV

The message of Easter is the central focus of Christianity.

The apostle Paul said, "If Christ has not been raised, your faith is futile; you are still in your sins" (1 Corinthians 15:17 NIV). It is as simple as that. If Christ is still dead, then He cannot be our Savior, for He was not the Son of God, and He died like all men. More than that, Heaven's doors are still locked.

But if Christ is risen, as the Scriptures teach and as hundreds of witnesses testified (none of whom ever recanted that testimony despite threats and death for many of them), then we have the ultimate hope of humanity—eternal life with the God who made us and the certainty of life beyond the grave.

What does Easter mean to you? It should mean everything, because Christ has conquered death! And that makes all the difference—now and forever!

Risen and Returning

This same Jesus . . . will so come in like manner as you saw Him go.

ACTS 1:11

The resurrection of Jesus Christ is the key to God's plan for the future. Unless Christ was raised from the dead, there can be no future Kingdom and no returning King. Unless Christ was raised from the dead, sin and death still reign, and God's plan of redemption remains unfulfilled. But Christ has been raised!

As the disciples stood watching after Jesus ascended into the Heavens, the angels assured them that the risen Christ would someday be the returning Christ. "Men of Galilee, why do you stand gazing up into heaven? This same Jesus, who was taken up from you into heaven, will so come in like manner as you saw Him go into heaven" (Acts 1:11).

Just as surely as Christ rose from the dead, so He will return and take us to Himself. Every promise—without exception—will be fulfilled.

Jesus Is Alive!

[May you know] his incomparably great power for
us who believe. That power is like the working of
his mighty strength, which he exerted in Christ
when he raised him from the dead.

EPHESIANS 1:19–20 NIV

Did you know that the same power that raised Christ from the dead is available to you and me today? The moment we receive Jesus as Savior, the Holy Spirit comes into our hearts. He gives us supernatural power to overcome temptations, to smile through tears, to experience joy despite life's burdens and trials. The Holy Spirit will raise you out of your spiritual lifelessness and transform you.

In fact, imagine what a difference it would make if people understood that Christ is risen and the Holy Spirit has been given! What a transformation would take place in our families! What a reversal there would be in our culture's deteriorating morals! What a lessening of tensions we would see between individuals, groups, and even nations! And what new purpose and power we would experience if we caught the wonder of the biblical truth that Jesus is alive!

Believe and share the truth that can fuel this transformation: Jesus is alive!

The Victorious Chime

"I, even I, am the LORD,
and besides Me there is no savior."

ISAIAH 43:11

I t is said that during Napoleon's Austrian campaign, his army advanced to within six miles of the town of Feldkirch. It looked as though his men would take it without resistance. But as Napoleon's army advanced toward their objective in the night, the Christians of Feldkirch gathered in their little church to pray. It was Easter eve.

The next morning at sunrise, the bells of the village pealed out across the countryside. Napoleon's army, not realizing it was Easter Sunday, thought that in the night the Austrian army had moved into Feldkirch and the bells were ringing in jubilation. Napoleon ordered a retreat, and the battle at Feldkirch never took place. The Easter bells caused the enemy to flee, and peace reigned in the Austrian countryside.

As Easter is celebrated each year, churches and cathedrals around the world will ring their bells—not to sound Christ's death knell but to declare Christ's victory over death. He is the risen Lord, and because of Him our final enemy—death—has been defeated, and peace reigns in our hearts!

The Resurrection and the Life

*"He who believes in me will live . . .
and . . . will never die."*
JOHN 11:25–26 NIV

We have three great enemies: sin, Satan, and death. Because Christ rose from the dead, we know that sin and Satan and death have been decisively defeated. And because Christ rose from the dead, we know there is life after death and that, if we belong to Him, we need not fear death or Hell.

Jesus said, "I am the resurrection and the life. He who believes in me will live, even though he dies; and whoever lives and believes in me will never die" (John 11:25–26 NIV). He also promised, "If I go and prepare a place for you, I will come back and take you to be with me that you also may be where I am" (John 14:3 NIV).

How hopeless our lives would be if these words were not true. Every cemetery and every grave site would be a mute witness to the futility and despair of human life. But Jesus' words are true! By God's power Jesus rose from the dead and hundreds became witnesses to His resurrection (1 Corinthians 15:1–8).

What a glorious hope we have because Jesus is alive!

"Where, O Death, Is Your Victory?"

Our Savior, Jesus Christ . . . has abolished death and brought life and immortality to light through the gospel.
2 TIMOTHY 1:10

Think about the holes children make when they dig in the sand on the seashore. When the waves come in, the holes are swallowed up by the ocean. Similarly, when we know Christ, our physical death is overwhelmed by the love and grace of God. Death is swallowed up in the victory of Christ.

Death is an incident, not an end. It is a transition for a Christian, not a terminus. In death, we are freed from all that burdens us here. We lay aside the outward "tent" of our body, and we inherit "a building from God, a house not made with hands, eternal in the heavens" (2 Corinthians 5:1 NASB).

Here, our lives are filled with suffering and confusion. We experience pain and problems, and sometimes life seems to have no meaning or purpose. But the resurrection of Jesus Christ changed all that. It gives purpose and meaning to life, and life's greatest joy comes from discovering His will and fulfilling it. His resurrection also gives us hope—hope right now, and hope beyond the grave. May these truths encourage you this day!

Can We Know?

*For what I received I passed on to you as of first
importance: that Christ died for our sins according to
the Scriptures, that he was buried, that he was raised
on the third day according to the Scriptures.*

1 CORINTHIANS 15:3–4 NIV

I suppose I'd believe in life after death if I ever met someone who had gone there and then came back to tell about it," a man wrote to me once. But that is exactly what Jesus did when He died and then came back to life by the power of God.

Jesus truly died. The Roman soldiers who nailed Him to the cross attested to that fact when they took His body down and placed it in a tomb. But that was not the end of the story. . . .

Two days later the tomb was empty, and shortly afterward Jesus appeared numerous times to His followers. His resurrection proved that Jesus was who He claimed to be, the Son of God, sent from Heaven to save us from our sins. But it also proved for all time that there is life after death, and that we will go to be with Him in Heaven forever if we know Him.

Is your hope in Christ—both for this life and the life to come?

Refined and Purified

When He has tested me, I shall come forth as gold.
JOB 23:10

Affliction can be a means of refining and of purification. Just as ore must pass through the refiner's furnace before it can yield up its gold, so our lives must sometimes pass through God's furnace of affliction before they can bring forth something beautiful and useful to Him.

We might never have had the songs of Fanny Crosby had she not been afflicted with blindness. George Matheson would never have given the world his immortal song, "O Love That Will Not Let Me Go," had it not been for the pain of personal tragedy and heartache. The "Hallelujah Chorus" was written by Handel when he was poverty-stricken and suffering from a paralyzed right side and right arm.

Affliction can also make us stronger in our faith and develop our confidence in God's watchful care over us. It may also drive us back to the right path when we have wandered. David said, "Before I was afflicted I went astray, but now I keep Your word" (Psalm 119:67).

Whatever the reason, if God sends affliction your way, take it in faith as a blessing, not a curse.

The Answer to Fear

"Do not be afraid."

MATTHEW 28:10

Months after the September 11, 2001, terrorist attacks on New York and Washington, psychiatrists reported that people who lived thousands of miles away from those tragic events were still coming to them, unable to sleep and paralyzed by fear. We live in a world shaken by fear, apprehension, and anxiety.

What is the answer to this stifling fear? After Jesus had been put to death, His disciples huddled in fear behind closed doors, filled with uncertainty and despair. But suddenly they found themselves in the presence of their living Lord, and at His first words their fears disappeared: "Peace to you" (Luke 24:36). The answer to our individual fears is found in a personal faith in the living, glorified Lord.

And the answer to collective fear is a corporate faith in the living, glorified Lord. The answer to national and international tensions and fears is for the world to know Him who is alive forevermore. We do not worship a dead Christ. We worship a risen Christ, who has broken the power of sin and death and Hell and is alive forevermore. Why, then, should we fear?

Why Did He Die?

The message of the cross . . . is the power of God.
1 CORINTHIANS 1:18

We can never grasp the horror of human sin until we realize it caused the Son of God to be crucified. Not Pilate, not Judas, not the mob—but sin.

The ravages of war and poverty, the wrenching pain of loneliness and rejection, the haunting cry of the orphan and widow, the dying gasps of the world's starving— these and a thousand other tragedies all bear witness to the fact that we live in a world poisoned by sin.

And that is why Jesus died. The terrible, bitter cup of humanity's sin sent Him to the cross. Jesus prayed in those last hours, "O My Father, if it is possible, let this cup pass from Me; nevertheless, not as I will, but as You will" (Matthew 26:39). There was no other way. Why did He drink that awful cup? So you and I would not have to.

Sin is the second most powerful force in the universe, for it sent Jesus to the cross. Only one force is greater—the love of God.

The Gift of Generosity

"Give, and it will be given to you. A good measure,
pressed down, shaken together and running over, will
be poured into your lap. For with the measure you
use, it will be measured to you."

LUKE 6:38 NIV

Generosity doesn't come naturally to most of us—not the kind of generosity the Bible urges us to have. Most of us will gladly give if we think the cause is worthy and we feel we can afford it. But the Bible urges us to go beyond that: to give sacrificially to God's work.

God's work demands prayer, and dedication, and vision, and reliance on the Holy Spirit. But it also requires our financial resources. Even Jesus' little band of disciples relied on the generosity of others to carry on their work; we read of a group of godly women who "were helping to support them out of their own means" (Luke 8:3 NIV).

Never forget: everything you have has been given to you by God. Yes, you may have worked hard and become successful—but who gave you your abilities, and who put you in a society where it was possible to become prosperous? Put Christ first in everything—including your finances. Christ gave His all for you; dare you do anything less for Him?

The *M* Word

*Now about the collection for God's people. . . . On the
first day of every week, each one of you should set
aside a sum of money in keeping with his income.*
1 CORINTHIANS 16:1–2 NIV

Sadly, many people who visit churches are put off by
what may seem like constant requests for money.
But when someone complains to you about the Church
always asking for money, gently remind them of two
things.

First, invite them to consider what most churches
actually do with the money they collect. Almost without
exception they use it to reach out to others, seeking—
with God's help—to make this world a better place.
Who can object to that?

Second, encourage them to look beyond their super-
ficial impressions about Jesus, and discover what He is
really like by turning to the New Testament gospels. (I
often recommend the gospel of John as a starting point,
because it was written to help people know Jesus.)

This is basically an invitation to be honest; how
can someone who doesn't know very much about Jesus
reject Him? Once you examine who Jesus was and what
He did for you, you cannot remain neutral.

Simple but Not Always Easy

Give everyone what you owe him: If you owe taxes,
pay taxes; if revenue, then revenue.

ROMANS 13:7 NIV

Jesus stated it clearly: "You cannot serve both God and Money" (Luke 16:13 NIV). Yet too many people try.

Someone wrote to me about money he had made selling some items for cash. He didn't see any reason "to tell the government about it"—but his wife disagreed, and so did I.

First, cheating of any kind will always keep you wondering if you'll be discovered. Second, you won't like the feeling that comes with knowing you lack integrity and are dishonest.

But there is a deeper reason: as the verse above indicates, if we cheat, we are disobeying God. In His eyes, failing to pay the taxes we owe is little different from stealing from an individual. Furthermore, if we fail to pay the taxes we owe, honest citizens will have to make up the shortfall.

If cheating of any kind enters our mind, we need to ask ourselves why we would even consider it. Is money too important to us? Is greed ruling us? Whatever it is, confess it and put Christ first in your life.

Keeping Money Our Servant

"Do not worry about your life, what you will eat or what you will drink. . . . Your heavenly Father knows that you need all these things."
MATTHEW 6:25, 32

We aren't supposed to let money become the most important thing in life, but when bills mount, it's hard not to become preoccupied.

The problem is that money can all too easily become our master instead of our servant. That's why the Bible so often talks about money, warning of its dangers and urging us to put it in its rightful place. The writer of Ecclesiastes wisely observed, "Whoever loves money never has money enough; whoever loves wealth is never satisfied" (5:10 NIV).

Once we put Christ first in our life, however, we can ask Him to help us trust Him for our needs. Our Heavenly Father knows we need clothes, food, and a place to live, so we don't need to worry. That may seem impossible, but God will give us His peace as we learn to trust Him.

We also need to deal with our finances responsibly— following a realistic budget; developing a plan to pay off debt; even cutting up our credit cards if necessary.

Don't become a slave to money. Learn to trust God in everything.

Robbing God

*A poor widow came and put in two very small copper
coins. . . . Jesus said, "I tell you the truth, this poor
widow has put more into the treasury than all the
others. . . . She, out of her poverty, put in everything—
all she had to live on."*

MARK 12:42–44 NIV

A young man came to me one night and said, "Billy,
I pray, read the Bible, and go to church, but I have
no victory in my life. What can I do?"

I thought for a moment and asked, "Do you tithe?
Do you give to God's work?"

He replied, "No, I don't, but I don't make very much
money."

I said, "That's not the point. No one can rob God
and expect to experience victory in life." We can pray
all day long. We can go to church every week. We can
read our Bible through a thousand times—but if we are
robbing God, we will be miserable and spiritually dry.
There is no victory if we aren't giving a portion of our
income to the Lord.

The basis of our giving is the tithe: one-tenth of
your income is God's (Malachi 3:10). It's God's rule, and
I believe it is still valid today.

Christ in You

For to me, to live is Christ.

PHILIPPIANS 1:21

Christ once lived in history, and today He lives on in people's lives. Jesus not only lived on this Earth, but He still lives—and He will live forever.

Year after year we see thousands of men, women, and young people receive Christ as Savior throughout the world. People with problems, burdens, and sins commit their lives to Jesus, and we see a light in their eyes and a glow on their faces as they are transformed by the Spirit of God. When Christ takes up residence in their hearts, they become new creations in Him.

Today, as always, many people think they can manage without God. They may manage economically, intellectually, and even socially. But down inside they have a spiritual void that can be filled only by Jesus Christ.

Jesus not only lived in the flesh in history, but He can live right now in you: "Christ in you, the hope of glory" (Colossians 1:27). Has Christ come to live in your life? He can—and He will, as you commit your life to Him.

Heavenly News

*God both raised up the Lord and will also
raise us up by His power.*

1 CORINTHIANS 6:14

The angel who came to the garden where Jesus'
body lay rolled away the stone and permitted fresh
air and morning light to fill His tomb.

The sepulcher was no longer an empty vault or
dreary mausoleum; rather, it was a life-affirming place
that radiated the glory and power of the living God. No
longer was the tomb a dark, fearsome prison but a transformed reminder of the celestial light that sweeps aside
the shadows of death. Jesus' resurrection changed all
that—forever!

An unknown poet has said of the tomb, "'Tis now
a cell where angels used to come and go with heavenly news." No words of men or angels can adequately
describe the height and depth, the length and breadth
of the glory to which the world awakened when Jesus
came forth to life from the pall of death.

Jesus' promise has been fulfilled: "Because I live,
you will live also" (John 14:19).

The Greatest Message

I know that you seek Jesus who was crucified.
MATTHEW 28:5

On the third day after Christ's death, the Bible says, "And behold, there was a great Earthquake; for an angel of the Lord descended from heaven, and came and rolled back the stone from the door, and sat on it. His countenance was like lightning, and his clothing as white as snow. And the guards shook for fear of him, and became like dead men" (Matthew 28:2–4).

As Mary looked into the tomb, she saw "two angels in white sitting, one at the head and the other at the feet, where the body of Jesus had lain" (John 20:12). Then one of the angels who was sitting outside the tomb proclaimed the greatest message the world has ever heard: "He is not here; for He is risen" (Matthew 28:6). Those few words changed the history of the universe. Darkness and despair died; hope and anticipation were born in the hearts of men.

Because of those few words, joy and new life now dawn in the hearts of all who believe. Don't leave Jesus in the manger . . . or on the cross . . . or in the tomb. He is alive, and He wants to walk beside you every day.

A Sure Supply

My God shall supply all your need.

Philippians 4:19

One lesson that Jesus would teach us is to have confidence that God answers every true petition. Skeptics may question it, humanists may deny it, and intellectuals may ridicule it. Yet here is Christ's own promise: "If you abide in Me, and My words abide in you, you will ask what you desire, and it shall be done for you" (John 15:7).

Does this verse mean God gives us a blank check (so to speak) when we pray? Does He promise to give us anything we want if we just keep asking? No. God loves us too much to answer prayers that are foolish or might harm us. But the closer we get to Him—the more we abide in Him and the more His Word abides in us—the more we will desire what He desires, and the more our prayers will reflect His will.

The Bible promises, "No good thing does he withhold from those whose walk is blameless" (Psalm 84:11 NIV). Trust that promise with all your soul.

Facing Your Giants

David said to the Philistine, "You come to me with a sword, with a spear, and with a javelin. But I come to you in the name of the LORD."

1 SAMUEL 17:45

What giants are you facing? Peer pressure? Different ideologies and philosophies fighting for control of your life? What about social injustice, moral deterioration, or crime? Or maybe fear, joblessness, broken relationships, or family conflict?

Young David faced a giant named Goliath, a member of the Philistine nation—a bitter enemy of God's people. Goliath was more than nine feet tall and clothed with heavy armor. With a spear about the size of a tree trunk, Goliath defied the army of Israel, challenging them to send a man against him. David volunteered.

Goliath had David out-armed and out-experienced. Goliath was a great warrior; David was not. His only weapon was a slingshot—and a deep dependence on God—and God gave him victory.

Everyone has problems, but Christ wants to help—if you will let Him. No matter what giants you are facing today, put on the full armor of God (Ephesians 6:10–18) and trust Him to give you victory.

Mercy Beyond Comprehension

*The LORD your God is gracious and merciful, and will
not turn His face from you if you return to Him.*

2 CHRONICLES 30:9

Of all the people in the Bible, Manasseh may have been the most wicked. Living centuries before Christ, this king of Judah was an idolater who turned against God and worshipped every kind of pagan deity. Manasseh was guilty of immorality: he practiced every conceivable evil and perversion; he devoted himself to sorcery and witchcraft. He also was a murderer and a cruel tyrant, even sacrificing his sons to a pagan god.

So God's judgment fell: the Assyrians captured Jerusalem, and Manasseh was bound in chains and taken hundreds of miles away to Babylon. In prison, he had time to think, and he began to pray. In that dungeon, this wicked man who only deserved Hell cried out to God for forgiveness—and God answered.

The Bible teaches that God is a God of mercy. His mercy is so vast and beyond our comprehension that no matter what sin we have committed, if we truly repent, God will forgive. Be assured that there is no sin you have ever committed that the blood of Jesus Christ cannot cleanse.

Shining Lights

*"Let your light so shine before men, that they may . . .
glorify your Father in heaven."*

MATTHEW 5:16

Our Lord regarded His followers as a select company who belonged to a different world from the rest of humanity. Many of the religious people of His day were worldly and unspiritual, publicly parading their religion to impress others while privately dominated by pride, ambition, greed, and falsehood.

Jesus told His disciples they could not make their light shine by sinking to the world's low level. It was only by abiding in Christ and living under the ruling power of His Holy Spirit that they could rise above the world. Only in that way could they be salt and light to a decaying and darkened world.

Our influence on society depends on our likeness to Jesus Christ. We cannot elevate others higher than we ourselves have gone. The first-century Christians out-thought, out-lived, and out-loved their neighbors, and by their example of purity and compassion attracted countless thousands to the Christian faith.

What do others see in your life that would attract them to Christ?

A Solid Foundation

"Whoever comes to Me, and hears My sayings and does them . . . is like a man building a house, who dug deep and laid the foundation on the rock."

LUKE 6:47–48

Jesus talked about two men who were building houses. One built his house on a solid rock foundation—and when the storms came, his house stood. The other man built his house on sand—and when the storms came, his house crumbled and fell.

Many people today live in homes built on sand. Lacking the right foundation, their family is in trouble. What about you? When the floods of sorrow and the gales of adversity come, will your home stand?

Make Jesus Christ the foundation of your home—and your life. I believe that no home can stand unless the family in that home has a strong faith in Jesus. There needs to be family prayer and Bible reading, and active involvement in a church where Christ is taught and followed.

What is the foundation of your home? The rock of Christ's teaching or the sand of self-will?

God's Seven Wonders, Part I

Because your love is better than life,
my lips will glorify you.
I will praise you as long as I live.

PSALM 63:3–4 NIV

There were seven wonders of the ancient world, and from time to time we read about the seven wonders of the modern world. But God has His seven wonders too.

The first is the wonder of God's love. The Almighty God, the Creator of the whole universe, loves you and is interested in you as if you were the only person who ever lived. Even when we sin against Him, He still wants to put His arms around us and say, "I love you."

The second is the wonder of God coming to live among us. God became a man—and that man was Jesus. He took on flesh so that He might know our trials, heartaches, and temptations. He understands us.

The third is the wonder of the cross. Jesus died for you and for me. Far more than His excruciatingly painful physical death, He suffered spiritually when God laid on Him your sins and mine. He who had never known sin took the penalty for all our sin.

What wondrous love is this!

God's Seven Wonders, Part II

*"Here I am! I stand at the door and knock. If anyone
hears my voice and opens the door, I will come in and
eat with him, and he with me."*

REVELATION 3:20 NIV

The fourth of God's seven wonders is the wonder of
conversion. The word *conversion* means "to change,
to turn." You cannot convert yourself: you have to have
God help you repent. The Holy Spirit helps us say no to
sin and yes to Christ—giving us a new life.

The fifth wonder is the gift of peace and joy that
Christ gives. God's wondrous love and the gracious forgiveness He offers through Jesus Christ bring peace
and joy.

The sixth wonder is God's plan for the future. I look
forward to that day when Jesus will return. What a glorious day that will be when we see Him face-to-face!

The seventh wonder of God is your own commitment
to Jesus Christ. He has come to save you, but He won't
force you to make that commitment. Have you committed your life to Him—totally and without reserve?

Love, the incarnation, the cross, conversion, peace
and joy, God's plan, your commitment to Jesus—God
definitely is the God of wonders!

The Call to Discipleship

"Take My yoke upon you and learn from Me."
MATTHEW 11:29

A generation ago, Jim Elliot went to Ecuador to become a missionary to the Aucas. Before he was killed, he wrote, "He is no fool who gives what he cannot keep to gain what he cannot lose."

Christ calls us—just as he called Jim Elliot—to discipleship. When we come to Him, He takes away one set of burdens—the burden of sin, the burden of guilt, the burden of separation from God, the burden of hopelessness. But He also calls us to follow Him, to renounce our selfish desires, and to seek His will above all else. He calls us to "take My yoke upon you and learn from Me."

So are we simply exchanging one burden for another—the burden of sin for the burden of obedience? No! It is no burden to follow Christ. Instead, we become the bearers of joy because now we are yoked to the very Son of God. Nor is it too heavy to bear, for Christ bears it with us: "My yoke is easy and My burden is light" (Matthew 11:30).

To whom are you yoked—the world or Christ?

God Never Changes

"God is Spirit, and those who worship Him must worship in spirit and truth."

JOHN 4:24

I was reared in a small Presbyterian church in Charlotte, North Carolina. Before I was ten years of age, my mother made me memorize the "Shorter Catechism," a summary of basic Christian beliefs in the form of questions and answers. In the catechism, one question is "What is God?" The answer we learned was "God is a Spirit—infinite, eternal, and unchangeable."

Those three words beautifully describe God. He is *infinite*—not body-bound. He is *eternal*—He has no beginning and no ending. He is *unchangeable*—never changing, never capricious, never unreliable. As the Bible says, with God "there is no variation or shadow of turning" (James 1:17). He is forever self-existent.

People change, fashions change, conditions and circumstances change, but God never changes. His love never changes. His holiness never changes. His purpose never changes. His glory never changes. He is the same yesterday, today, and forever.

Can you think of any reason not to trust Him? Neither can I!

Choice, Change, Challenge

"If anyone would come after me, he must deny himself and take up his cross and follow me."
MATTHEW 16:24 NIV

What is a true Christian?

First, a Christian is a person who has made a choice. We have to choose—just as Adam and Eve did in the garden of Eden—to obey God or rebel against Him. We make that choice initially when we commit our lives to Christ, but we also make that choice day by day, moment by moment. What kind of choices are you making?

Second, a Christian is a person whose life has been changed. That transformation is the work of the Holy Spirit. The moment you receive Christ—the moment you choose Him—the Spirit of God comes to live in your heart. What changes have taken place in your life—in your thoughts, feelings, behavior, goals, relationships—since you chose to follow Jesus?

Third, a Christian is a person who has accepted a challenge. The challenge is Jesus' call to deny self—our own selfish ambitions, our own selfish sinful pleasures—and take up our cross. In what ways are you denying yourself in order to follow Jesus?

Choice, change, and challenge—these should characterize every Christian. Are they true of you?

The Hope of the Centuries

*It is good that one should hope and wait quietly
for the salvation of the LORD.*

<small>LAMENTATIONS 3:26</small>

The promised coming of Christ has been the great hope of believers down through the centuries. The ancient Nicene Creed affirms, "He shall come again with glory."

Charles Wesley wrote 7,000 hymns; 5,000 mention the coming of Christ. As the Archbishop of Canterbury crowned Queen Elizabeth II, he stated, "I give thee, O Sovereign Lady, this crown to wear until He who reserves the right to wear it shall return."

But until that time, our world remains in the grip of violence and despair. One noted columnist summed it up this way: "For us all, the world is disorderly and dangerous; ungoverned, and apparently ungovernable." Someday, however, the King will return. Someday the Heavens will shout, "The kingdoms of this world have become the kingdoms of our Lord and of His Christ, and He shall reign forever and ever!" (Revelation 11:15).

Christ alone is the answer to the burdens of our hearts and the hopelessness of our world.

The Work of Every Believer

*Yet when I preach the gospel, I cannot boast, for
I am compelled to preach. Woe to me if I do not
preach the gospel!*

1 CORINTHIANS 9:16 NIV

What is an evangelist? An evangelist is a person with a special gift and a special calling from the Holy Spirit to announce the good news of the gospel. It is a gift of God that cannot be manufactured or faked. It is also a calling from God. Understanding this will help protect us from two dangerous temptations.

First, this understanding will protect us from pride because we know that whatever gift we have and whatever opportunities may open up to us are from God. We cannot take any credit or glory for ourselves. And, second, this understanding will save us from discouragement and the temptation to give up, because we know our calling is not from man but from God.

Some are called to be evangelists—but every Christian is called to the work of evangelism, for every Christian is called to tell others about Christ and what He has done for them.

With whom will you share the good news of Christ today?

Comforting Others

Comfort each other and edify one another.

1 THESSALONIANS 5:11

It is an undeniable fact that usually those who have suffered most are best able to comfort others who are suffering. They know what it is to suffer, and they understand more than others what a suffering person is experiencing—physically, emotionally, and spiritually. They are able to empathize as well as sympathize with the afflictions of others because of what they have experienced in their own lives.

Our sufferings may be rough and hard to bear, but they teach us lessons that in turn equip and enable us to help others. Our attitude toward suffering should not be "Grit your teeth and bear it," hoping it will pass as quickly as possible. Rather, our goal should be to learn all we can from what we are called upon to endure, so that we in turn can "comfort each other and edify one another."

Your Sin Will Find You Out

*Each of you should look not only to your own
interests, but also to the interests of others.*

PHILIPPIANS 2:4 NIV

When Israel was entering the Promised Land, the two tribes of Reuben and Gad saw that the already-conquered territory on the east side of the Jordan was good for their herds and flocks. Thinking only of themselves—of their own needs and the convenience of settling the land they already stood on—rather than being concerned about Israel's inheritance as a whole, they approached Moses with a request: "Let this land be given to your servants as our possession. Do not make us cross the Jordan" (Numbers 32:5 NIV).

Moses was an old man, but his eyes blazed, his jaw set, anger came to his face. Moses said, "Shall your countrymen go to war while you sit here? . . . [If so,] you may be sure your sin will find you out" (Numbers 32:6, 23 NIV). Over the years, his words proved to be true.

That verse is God's message to any of His people who sit down in apathy and lethargy while their brothers and sisters are in need, when others are dying, and still others are spiritually lost. We can be sure that our sin will find us out.

Walk with God

My eyes shall be on the faithful of the land,
that they may dwell with me.

PSALM 101:6

Walk with God as Noah did: when the flood came, Noah was saved amidst the scorn and rejection of his neighbors. Walk with God as Moses did in the solitude of the desert: when the hour of judgment fell upon Egypt, Moses was prepared to lead his people to victory.

Walk with God as David did as a shepherd boy: when he was called to rule his people, he was prepared for the task of kingship. Walk with God as Daniel and his three young friends did in the palace of Babylon's king: when the fiery furnace and the lions' den came, God was beside them and delivered them. No, God didn't always deliver His saints from adversity or even death, nor does He today. But because they had learned to trust Him in the light, they were prepared to follow Him in the darkness.

God has not promised to deliver us from trouble, but He has promised to go with us through the trouble. "Yea, though I walk through the valley of the shadow of death, I will fear no evil; for You are with me" (Psalm 23:4).

Keep Looking Up!

"Keep watch, because you do not know on what day your Lord will come."

MATTHEW 24:42 NIV

L ooking across the centuries, the prophets declared that there would be a day when history as we know it would come to an end, with the judgment of God and the return of the Messiah.

What we are seeing today is a shuffling on the stage behind the curtain—a preparation for the day when "the kingdoms of this world have become the kingdoms of our Lord and of His Christ, and He shall reign forever, and ever" (Revelation 11:15).

The Bible is filled with promises of that coming day of glory. Its pages indicate that when Christ returns, the world will not be expecting Him. Just as the people in Noah's day did not believe that a flood was coming, multitudes today do not believe that God's judgment is coming. The flood did come, though, and so will His judgment.

Jesus calls us who know Him to wait in expectation. Our hands should be busy with His work, but our eyes should be looking up. May your watching for Jesus make you even more active in His service!

Coronation Day

Blessed is the man who endures trial, for . . .
he will receive the crown of life.

JAMES 1:12 RSV

To the Christian, death is said in the Bible to be a coronation. The picture here is that of a regal prince who, after his struggles and conquests in an alien land, returns to his native country and court to be crowned and honored for his deeds.

The Bible says we are pilgrims and strangers in a foreign land. This world is not our home; our citizenship is in Heaven. And someday all our battles on this Earth will be over, and we will enter that Heavenly home.

To the one who has been faithful, Christ will give a crown of life. Paul said, "There is laid up for me the crown of righteousness, which the Lord, the righteous Judge, will give to me on that Day, and not to me only but also to all who have loved His appearing" (2 Timothy 4:8).

When D. L. Moody was dying, he looked up to Heaven and said, "Earth is receding, heaven is opening, this is my coronation day." Never forget: if you are a Christian, you are a child of the King!

Now Is the Time

You do not know what will happen tomorrow.

JAMES 4:14

Billy Bray, a godly clergyman of another generation, sat by the bedside of a dying Christian who had been very shy about his testimony for Christ during his life. The dying man said, "If I had the power I'd shout glory to God." Billy Bray answered, "It's a pity you didn't shout glory when you had the power."

I wonder how many of us will, looking back over a lifetime of wasted opportunities and ineffective witness, weep because we did not allow God to use us as He wanted. "Night is coming, when no man can work" (John 9:4 NASB).

If ever we are to study the Scriptures, if ever we are to spend time in prayer, if ever we are to win souls for Christ, if ever we are to invest our finances for His Kingdom—it must be now.

God's Unchanging Standards

And God spoke all these words: "I am the
LORD your God, who brought you out of Egypt,
out of the land of slavery."

EXODUS 20:1–2 NIV

The Ten Commandments serve as the constitution of God's moral universe. The first four commandments show that our main priority is to love God; the other six guide our love of other people.

First, we are to serve God alone. Whatever our heart clings to is our "god," and when we cling to anything or anyone other than God, we are guilty of idolatry. God alone must be first in our heart and our life. Next, we are to avoid anything that excludes or obscures the divine nature of God. We are also to honor His name and enter His presence with reverence and respect. In addition, we are to set aside one day in seven for rest and the worship of God.

In the last six commandments, God tells us to honor and obey our parents; not to murder (literally or with our words); to be true to our marriage vows; not to steal from people or from God; not to lie or misrepresent anything; and not to covet what belongs to someone else.

What do these commandments reveal about your love for God and your love for others?

Signs of the Time

"This gospel of the kingdom will be preached in the whole world as a testimony to all nations, and then the end will come."

MATTHEW 24:14 NIV

*P*arousia, "the coming." *Epiphaneia*, "the appearing." *Apokalupsis*, "the unveiling." These three Greek words in the New Testament all refer to the return of Christ. And He will come back.

Jesus said that only the Father in Heaven knows exactly when—and this should keep us from wild speculations. But Jesus did say that we should watch for certain signs.

We should, for instance, be on guard against false Christs and false prophets. Scripture also teaches that there will be "wars and rumors of war" (Matthew 24:6), as well as unprecedented natural disasters. Christians will be persecuted because of their faith.

Another sign of Christ's return will be that once-passionate hearts will become cold toward Him. This loss of fervent love will contribute to a breakdown of morals.

Finally, the worldwide proclamation of the gospel will point to Christ's return.

Are you certain that if He came today, you are ready?

Christ Is King

Your kingdom is an everlasting kingdom.

Psalm 145:13

The government in God's Kingdom is unique. It is not a democracy where the people govern, but a "Christocracy" where Christ is the supreme authority. In a society of unredeemed people, democracy is the only fair and equitable system. But no democracy can ever be better than the people who make it up. When citizens are selfishly motivated, the government will be inequitable. When people are dishonest, the government will be the same. When everyone wants his own way, someone is going to get hurt.

But in God's Kingdom, Christ is King. He is compassionate, fair, merciful, and just. When He is sovereign in men's hearts, anguish turns to peace, hatred is transformed into love, and misunderstanding into harmony.

Is Christ the King of your motives and your attitudes?

Earnest, Focused Prayer

"When you pray, do not keep on babbling like pagans."
MATTHEW 6:7 NIV

Observe carefully the prayer life of Jesus, and notice the earnestness with which He prayed. In Gethsemane He cried out with a loud voice, and in the intensity of His supplication He fell headlong on the damp ground and pleaded before His Father until "his sweat was like drops of blood falling to the ground" (Luke 22:44 NIV). Too often—and in very sharp contrast—you and I use petty petitions, oratorical exercises, and the same words we have used for years rather than the cries of our inmost being.

Also, too often when we pray, our thoughts roam. We insult God by speaking to Him with our lips while our minds and hearts are far from Him. Suppose you were talking to a famous person. Would you let your thoughts wander for one moment? No, you would be intensely interested in everything that was said—and very careful about what you were saying. How dare we treat the King of kings with less respect!

May our prayers today—and every day—be from our hearts and with the focus of our whole being!

A Sealed Bargain

He . . . put his Spirit in our hearts as a deposit,
guaranteeing what is to come.

2 Corinthians 1:21-22 NIV

As we trust in Christ, God gives us the Spirit as a pledge or, as some translations read, an earnest guarantee. "He . . . put his Spirit in our hearts as a deposit, guaranteeing what is to come."

In the apostle Paul's day, a deposit or pledge did three things: it was a down payment that sealed a bargain, it represented an obligation to buy, and it was a sample of what was to come.

As an illustration, suppose you decided to make a down payment on a new car. What does your deposit represent? First, it seals the transaction; from now on, both you and the seller are committed. Also, it shows that you have committed yourself to pay the rest of the purchase price. Finally, it enables you to take possession of the car right now even though it still belongs to the bank.

In the same way, the Holy Spirit in our hearts is God's pledge or deposit to us—sealing His commitment to save us, guaranteeing that someday our salvation will be complete, and enabling us to experience its joys right now.

Lessons on Prayer

"If you remain in me and my words remain in you, ask whatever you wish, and it will be given you."

JOHN 15:7 NIV

Consider what Jesus teaches about prayer.

Jesus tells us to "pray for those who persecute you" (Matthew 5:44 NIV). We are to plead for our enemies—just as Jesus prayed for His crucifiers—asking God to lead them to Christ and, for His sake, to forgive them. Jesus also tells us to pray for the conversion of sinners. Prayer is key to our effort to communicate the gospel and win men and women to Christ.

Another lesson Jesus teaches is the victorious assurance that God answers every true petition (although not always the way we wish He would). We need to trust in the promise of John 15:7 and in the complementary intercession of the Holy Spirit (Romans 8:27).

We also need to remember that with God nothing is impossible. No task is too arduous, no problem too difficult, no burden too heavy for Him. Do not, however, put your will above His. Do not insist on your way. And don't expect an immediate answer to come in exactly the way, the place, and the manner that you are seeking. Rather, learn to pray as Jesus Himself prayed: "Not My will, but Yours, be done" (Luke 22:42).

Live for the Lord

My days are swifter than a weaver's shuttle.

JOB 7:6

In North Carolina, I have visited the textile mills and have watched the giant looms that turn out cloth for the nation. The shuttles move with the speed of lightning, scarcely visible to the naked eye.

Job said that our days are "swifter than a weaver's shuttle." Life passes so quickly it is almost over before we realize it. The Bible says this is the chronology of eternity. Though you live to be seventy, eighty, or ninety years old, that is but a snap of the finger compared to eternity.

Put your hand on your heart and feel it beat. It is saying, "Quick! Quick! Quick!" We have only a few brief years at the most. Let's live them for the Lord.

Kneel and See

*Far be it from me that I should sin against the LORD
in ceasing to pray for you.*

1 SAMUEL 12:23

In this world all of us have trials and tribulations, and each one is an opportunity to pray. But far too often we Christians close our conversation with someone who is struggling with, "I'll pray for you"—and, sadly, that's the last of it. We need to be true to our word; we need to live according to the golden rule and actually pray for our brothers and sisters the way we would want them to pray for us. But the blessing of such prayer isn't just for the other person. Consider this story:

In a city in Scandinavia is a famous statue of our Lord. One day a visitor standing before it was very disappointed, and he didn't hesitate to share his feelings with an attendant. "I can't see the face of the Christ," he complained.

The attendant replied, "Sir, if you want to see His face, you must kneel at His feet." The visitor knelt and he saw!

Do you want to see Jesus' face? Kneel in prayer—for others, for yourself, for the world, for His Kingdom—and be blessed.

The Secret of Purity

Who shall ascend the hill of the LORD? . . .
He who has clean hands and a pure heart.

PSALM 24:3–4 RSV

We live in the most permissive society since pagan times. Movie marquees, the covers of magazines, the Internet, billboards, television—all scream sensual messages at us. "If it feels good, do it" has become a national motto.

Yet, if you talk with people who have come to Christ out of deep sin, they will tell you that they wish they had never fallen into such sin and that they had come to Christ sooner.

Many Christian books tell of men and women who committed terrible crimes or were entangled in immorality or sensuality. We rejoice with them that Christ has redeemed and forgiven them. But how much better to have avoided such sin in the first place! God's standard has not changed: "You shall be holy, for I the LORD your God am holy" (Leviticus 19:2).

The secret of purity is God. When we are committed to Christ, we will shrink back from all that is impure. Instead, we will seek a pure heart—a heart cleansed by the Holy Spirit and the Word of God.

MAY

The Power of Prayer

I urge, then, first of all, that requests, prayers, intercession and thanksgiving be made for everyone— for kings and all those in authority, that we may live peaceful and quiet lives in all godliness and holiness.
1 TIMOTHY 2:1–2 NIV

Looking around at all the evil that happens today, we may find ourselves wondering if some people must have been born without a conscience! But the Bible teaches that God has placed within every human being some sense of right and wrong.

We can, however, ignore the voice of our conscience, and over time, become so hardened by sin that we almost can't hear its voice. This is one reason why Christians need to take a stand for what is right and not let evil go unchallenged.

But most of all, we need to pray. During this first week in May, many people will celebrate an annual Day of Prayer, praying especially for our world and its leaders—its politicians, trendsetters, media powers, athletes, and others in a position of influence. Pray that they may use their influence for good and not for evil. Remember: God is sovereign and is still at work, and He alone is our hope for a better world.

Why Pray?

"Your Father knows what you need before you ask him."

MATTHEW 6:8 NIV

If God already knows our needs, why pray? Perhaps this question has even kept you from praying—but in reality, it should make us pray more.

If you are a parent, do you discourage your children from coming to you with their requests even if you already know what they want? No, of course not. You love them, and you take delight in listening to them. Even if you say no to their requests, it's because you know better than they do what is best for them.

God, our Heavenly Father, loves us, His children— and one of our greatest privileges is coming to Him in prayer. And because He already knows our needs, we can be confident His answer will be best. If He didn't know our needs, why bother to pray? But He does, and this should give us confidence in prayer.

Thank God that He knows your needs and wants you to come to Him in prayer. Remember: His Son gave His life "that we may obtain mercy and find grace to help in time of need" (Hebrews 4:16).

Jesus' Prayer Program

He went up on the mountain by Himself to pray.
MATTHEW 14:23

It may surprise you to read this, but we were created to live a life of prayer. The problem is that sin has erected a barrier between God and us. To recover the role God intended prayer to have in our life, we would do well to follow Jesus' example: in spite of His hectic public ministry, He was never too hurried to spend hours in prayer.

By contrast, how quickly and carelessly we pray (if we pray at all). In the morning we hastily ask God for His blessing on our day, then say good-bye to Him for the rest of the day until we rush through a few closing thoughts at night. This is not what Jesus modeled. Jesus prayed deeply and repeatedly. He spent entire nights in fervent appeal to God. How different is our pattern of prayer!

One more note: our Lord frequently prayed alone, separating Himself from every Earthly distraction. I urge you to select a room or a corner in your home where you can regularly meet alone with God. That quiet, secluded, one-to-One praying can be your day's greatest blessing.

Reasons to Pray

Let us therefore come boldly to the throne of grace.

HEBREWS 4:16

Can you relate to this? "I have many people I should pray for, but I wonder if it will do any good. How can we expect God to keep track of every person on the planet?"

The real question here is "How big is God?" If God is limited—if He isn't all-powerful and all-knowing—then we would be right to think He might not answer our prayers.

But God isn't limited! He isn't like a computer without enough memory. God is infinite in His knowledge and wisdom. Since He created this universe—right down to the smallest subatomic particle—isn't He able to know every detail of what goes on in the world? Of course!

Another reason to pray is because God loves us. He is more concerned about you and about those you love than you are. As Jesus said, "Are not two sparrows sold for a penny? Yet not one of them will fall to the ground apart from the will of your Father. . . . So don't be afraid; you are worth more than many sparrows" (Matthew 10:29, 31 NIV).

So pray with confidence to your great God!

In Jesus' Name

We have peace with God through our Lord Jesus Christ, through whom also we have access by faith into this grace.

ROMANS 5:1–2

Do you know why we often close our prayers with the phrase *in Jesus' name*? Those words remind us that Jesus has opened the door to Heaven for us and that we can approach God only because of what He has done for us. But this phrase isn't a magic formula we add in order to make God answer our prayers. God answers our prayers solely because of Christ.

Does this mean God always answers our prayers the way we wish He would? No, not necessarily—and the reason is because He loves us and knows what is best for us. What if parents gave their young children everything they asked for? You know what would happen: the children not only would be spoiled, but they might end up in great danger. Wise parents know when to say no.

In a far greater way, God knows what is best for us. When you pray, therefore, seek God's will. Thank God for the privilege of prayer, and make it part of your life every day.

God's Kind of Strength

They shall walk and not faint.

ISAIAH 40:31

Never in history have the nations of the world possessed so many lethal armaments, so many ways to bring death and destruction to the human race. Some of our most brilliant minds spend their entire lives developing new and more sophisticated ways to destroy life.

But have all our weapons brought us lasting security? On the contrary. If anything, they have made the world less secure. At any one time at least thirty wars rage in various parts of the world, in addition to countless instances of civil unrest. I am reminded of the false prophets of Jeremiah's day:

"'Peace, peace,' they say, when there is no peace" (Jeremiah 8:11 NIV).

In the midst of an uncertain and threatening world, however, we can have peace. It comes from putting our trust in the living God. Isaiah's words—written in a time of great upheaval—still speak to us today: "Those who wait on the LORD shall renew their strength . . . they shall walk and not faint" (Isaiah 40:31).

Our Infinite God

Great is the LORD, and greatly to be praised.

PSALM 48:1

I grew up in the rural American South. My idea of the ocean was so small that the first time I saw the Atlantic, I couldn't comprehend how any lake could be so big! The vastness of the ocean cannot be understood until it is seen.

This is the same with God's love. It passes knowledge. Until you actually experience it, no one can describe its wonders to you. The opening lines of one of our great old hymns declare, "O the deep, deep love of Jesus / Vast, unmeasured, boundless, free! / Rolling as a mighty ocean / In its fullness over me."

Behind the love of God lies His omniscience—His ability to know and understand all. Omniscience is a quality of God that is His alone. God possesses infinite knowledge and an awareness that is uniquely His. At all times, even in the midst of any type of suffering, I can realize that He knows, loves, watches, understands, and, more than that, has a purpose.

No matter what comes your way—no matter how tempted you are to give in to despair—never forget: God's love for you can never be exhausted, for His love is beyond measure.

Walk in the Spirit

*Walk in the Spirit, and you shall not
fulfill the lust of the flesh.*

GALATIANS 5:16

To walk means to place one foot in front of the other and to go forward one step at a time. If you stop doing this, you are no longer walking. You are standing still—or worse, going backward. Walking always implies movement, progress, and direction.

This is what it means to walk with God. It means moving forward in step with Him, confident that the way He is leading is best. The problem is that we are weak. We stumble or get diverted, or we get weary and stop moving forward. But that is one reason why the Holy Spirit has been given to us. Galatians 5:16 could be paraphrased this way: "Walk by means of the Spirit."

One of the highest commendations in the Bible is found in these words about Noah: "Noah was a just man, perfect in his generations. Noah walked with God" (Genesis 6:9). Could this be said of you?

God's Perfect Plan

*Be transformed . . . that you may prove what
is that . . . perfect will of God.*

ROMANS 12:2

The Bible reveals that God has a plan for every life, and that if we live in constant fellowship with Him, He will direct and lead us in the fulfillment of this plan.

God does not reveal His plan through fortune-tellers, astrologers, soothsayers, and workers of hocus-pocus. His perfect will is reserved for those who have trusted Christ for salvation. He shares His secrets only with those who are redeemed and transformed, those who humbly seek His will for their lives.

You cannot know the will of God for your life unless you first come to the cross, confess that you are a sinner, and receive Christ as Lord and Savior. Once you do come to Him, you begin a whole new life—a life lived not for yourself but for Christ. From that moment on, God wants to show you His will. Whatever decisions you face today, commit them to God and ask Him to guide you—and He will.

Confession and Cleansing

*If we confess our sins, He is faithful and
just to forgive us our sins.*

1 JOHN 1:9

Corrie ten Boom told a story of a little girl who broke one of her mother's demitasse cups. The little girl came to her mother sobbing, "Oh, Mama, I'm so sorry I broke your beautiful cup."

The mother replied, "I know you're sorry and I forgive you. Now don't cry anymore." The mother then swept up the pieces of the broken cup and placed them in the trash can. But the little girl enjoyed the guilty feeling. She went to the trash can, picked out pieces of the cup, brought them to her mother, and sobbed, "Mother, I'm so sorry that I broke your pretty cup."

This time her mother spoke firmly to her, "Take those pieces and put them back in the trash can. Don't be silly enough to take them out again. I told you I forgave you, so don't cry anymore."

Don't keep holding on to your guilt. If you have confessed your sins to Christ, He has forgiven them and taken them away—forever.

Perfect in Weakness

When I am weak, then I am strong.
2 CORINTHIANS 12:10

God's idea of strength and man's idea of strength are opposites. The Lord told Paul, "My strength is made perfect in weakness" (2 Corinthians 12:9). Having learned this lesson, Paul could then say, "When I am weak, then I am strong" (2 Corinthians 12:10). A paradox? Not really. Only when Paul admitted his own weakness and was willing to get out of the way could God take over and work.

If we try to do God's will in our own strength, then we can take the credit for whatever gets accomplished. But that isn't God's way! When we let His strength work through us, then He alone will get the glory—and that is as it should be.

In the Old Testament God repeatedly told the leaders of Israel to reduce the size of their armies, and sometimes He announced in advance how their victory would be won. Why? So they would place their trust in Him and not in their own strength. As someone has said, "God's work, done in God's way, will never lack for God's provision."

Revive Your People, Lord

Will You not revive us again,
that Your people may rejoice in You?

PSALM 85:6

Jesus said, "Blessed are the peacemakers, for they shall be called sons of God" (Matthew 5:9), and the desire for peace is universal. But simply telling people to stop fighting and love one another isn't the solution for the tension, discord, and violence that exist around the globe. Diplomats and leaders have tried to do this for centuries, yet world history is filled with wars and conflicts.

The problem lies within the human heart; by nature we are selfish and greedy. Even leaders aren't exempt from these sins. As the Bible says, "What causes fights and quarrels among you? Don't they come from your desires that battle within you?" (James 4:1 NIV). Even when we want peace, it often eludes us because of our greed or anger or jealousy.

Only God can change the human heart, and that is why our greatest need is spiritual renewal. Pray today for our world and its leaders—and pray as well for spiritual renewal in our time.

Pray for Peace

War will continue until the end.
DANIEL 9:26 NIV

In the Bible, God calls us to work for peace and to pray for peace. But He also warns us that conflicts and wars will always be part of human society until Jesus comes at the end of history to set up His Kingdom of peace and justice. In that day all evil will be eliminated, and perfect peace will reign upon the Earth. Until that day, however, the world will always be subject to "wars and rumors of wars" (Matthew 24:6).

Why is this? Why can't we live together in peace? The reason is that our hearts are selfish and filled with anger, greed, and a lust for power. Until our hearts are changed, we will never know lasting peace.

Tragically, we are a planet in rebellion against God. That is why the world's greatest need is to turn to Christ. Only He can change us from within by His Holy Spirit.

But even when wars rage, we can have peace in our hearts as we open our lives to Christ. Ask God to give you that peace—and pray that others will know it too.

Prayers and Tears of Love

Dear friends, let us love one another,
for love comes from God.

1 JOHN 4:7 NIV

I've learned that serving the Lord requires prayer and often means tears. . . .

Any day that I leave my room without a quiet time with God, I look for the devil to hit me from every angle. Power for life, for ministry, doesn't come from our own ability; it comes from God. We need a fresh, daily anointing from the Holy Spirit, and that comes from the time we spend with God in His Word and in prayer. Are you a person of prayer?

In Boston, Massachusetts, the great soul winner John Vassar knocked on the door of a person's home and asked the woman if she knew Christ as her Savior. She replied, "It's none of your business" and slammed the door in his face. He stood on the doorstep and wept and wept, and she looked out her window and saw him weeping. The next Sunday, she was in church. She said it was because of those tears. Where are your tears?

A life fueled by prayer and characterized by His love is a life God will use.

Longing for God

My soul thirsts for God, for the living God.
PSALM 42:2

These words of the psalmist sound strange to most people today: "My soul thirsts for God, for the living God." In an age preoccupied with the things of this world, God seems almost irrelevant.

But the psalmist had discovered what most people realize sooner or later (even if they refuse to admit it): the things of this world can never satisfy the longings of our souls.

Only God can meet our deepest yearnings. As Saint Augustine said centuries ago, "You have made us for Yourself, O God, and our hearts are restless until they find their rest in You."

What crowds out a yearning for God in your life? Don't let anything—or anyone—come between you and God. Isaiah wrote, "Why do you spend money for what is not bread, and your wages for what does not satisfy?" (Isaiah 55:2).

God wants you to know Him in a personal way, and He has made this possible through Jesus Christ. He loves you, and He will give you His peace.

Loud and Clear

The mystery . . . now has been revealed to His saints.

COLOSSIANS 1:26

Radio was just coming of age when I was a boy. We would gather around a crude homemade set and twist the tuning dials. Often the only sound was the squeak and squawk of static. It wasn't very exciting, but we kept at it. We knew that somewhere out there was the unseen transmitter and that if we established contact, we could hear a voice loud and clear.

Does God speak to us? Is He trying to reach us? Yes! The problem is not with Him, but with us. Like that crude radio, we aren't attuned to Him.

We could only know God in one way: if He revealed Himself to us. And that is what He has done. He revealed Himself in the world He created, and, in a fuller way, He revealed Himself in His written Word, the Bible. Centuries ago He spoke to the prophets and the apostles, and by the inspiration of the Holy Spirit, they wrote down His Word for us.

God is trying to break through to us—but we must tune in to His Word. Are you listening?

An All-Important Appointment

If any of you lacks wisdom, he should ask God, who gives generously to all without finding fault, and it will be given to him.

JAMES 1:5 NIV

Every day, the young president of an East Coast company instructed his secretary not to disturb him because he had an important appointment.

One morning the chairman of the board arrived unannounced and said, "I want to see Mr. Jones."

The secretary answered, "I'm sorry. He cannot be disturbed. He has an important appointment."

The chairman became angry and banged open the door. Upon seeing the president of the corporation on his knees in prayer, the chairman quietly backed out of the office and softly closed the door. He asked the secretary, "Is that usual?"

When she answered, "Yes, sir. Every morning," the chairman replied, "No wonder we come to him for advice."

This company president offers each of us a good example. Do you make a regular appointment with God each day—and do you keep it? And when you meet with your Father, is a request for wisdom for your day part of the conversation?

God's Secret Agents

He will give his angels charge of you
to guard you in all your ways.

PSALM 91:11 RSV

A secret agent is one who seeks to protect his country, his king, or his president against evil forces that are opposed to the one he serves. The American Secret Service is charged with protecting the president of the United States. They do an excellent job, but even they will tell you that someone who is fiercely determined to assassinate the president could be successful.

God has His own secret agents—the angels. Unseen and unrecognized by the world, they never fail in their appointed tasks. Much has been written recently about angels—often not based on the Bible but on popular legends. But angels are real, and God has commanded them to watch over us. Only in eternity will we know how many accidents they prevented or how often they kept Satan's malicious spirits at bay. In the meantime, we can take comfort in their presence and thank God for the love He expresses for us through their service.

In the Presence of Christ

The upright shall dwell in Your presence.
PSALM 140:13

What would you do if you were about to meet the Queen of England? I'm sure you would go out of your way to dress correctly and to be properly briefed so you didn't say the wrong thing or act in an improper way.

Someday, you and I will meet a far greater Sovereign: the King of the universe. His dazzling glory far exceeds that of any Earthly monarch, and in His presence we can only bow in humble worship and praise. Our cry will be that of Revelation: "You are worthy, O Lord, to receive glory and honor and power" (4:11).

Are you prepared for that day when you will meet the King of kings face-to-face? No one knows the day or the hour when life will end. The time for you to prepare is now, by committing your life to Christ and beginning to live as a child of the King.

History-Changing Prayer

*[Hezekiah prayed,] "O LORD our God, deliver us from
[the enemy's] hand, so that all kingdoms on earth
may know that you alone, O LORD, are God." . . .
That night the angel of the LORD went out
and put to death a hundred and eighty-five
thousand men in the Assyrian camp.*

2 KINGS 19:19, 35 NIV

As someone has said, "Prayer is the highest use to which speech can be put." But today we often regard prayer as merely an honored tradition or a polite formality. But prayer—sincere, believing prayer—is so much more.

Cover to cover, the Bible tells of people whose prayers turned the tide of history. Hezekiah prayed, and God spared his nation when the Assyrians attacked. Elijah prayed, and God sent fire to confound the false prophets. Elisha prayed, and the son of the Shunammite woman was raised from the dead. Jesus prayed, and Lazarus came forth from the tomb. Paul prayed, and new churches were born. The early Church prayed, and Peter was delivered from prison.

We can change the course of events if we go to our knees in believing prayer. What will you pray about tonight?

A Step in the Process

Blessed is the man whom You instruct, O Lord.
Psalm 94:12

A child develops muscles through exercise. Only when our muscles encounter resistance do they become stronger.

In the same way, the Bible tells us that we only become stronger spiritually through exercise—through using our spiritual muscles to meet the challenges of life. This is especially true when we face suffering and affliction, for they are one way God makes us strong. One reason God allows suffering to come to His people, the Bible says, is to discipline, chasten, and mold us.

In the last essay he wrote before he died, the great Christian writer C. S. Lewis said, "We have no right to happiness; only an obligation to do our duty." Sometimes our God-given duty will include suffering. When it does, ask God to teach you through it. Remember the psalmist's words I quoted above: "Blessed is the man whom You instruct, O Lord."

Keep at It!

*"Shall God not avenge His own elect who cry out day
and night to Him?"*

LUKE 18:7

Almost every week I get at least one letter from someone who has been praying for years for a family member, friend, neighbor, or coworker who doesn't know Christ. In many cases that person has eventually turned to Christ, and his or her life has been changed. But what if the person writing to me had stopped praying?

Whenever we pray, we need to remember that God's ways and God's timing aren't always the same as ours. In fact, His time frame rarely matches ours.

We also need to remember that God is able to do what we can't do. Only He can convict nonbelievers of their sins; only He can convince them of the truth of the gospel. That is why no one is hopeless, for God can break through even the hardest heart. "Is not My word . . . like a hammer that breaks the rock in pieces?" (Jeremiah 23:29).

For whom are you praying? Keep at it!

One More Time!

"[My word] will not return to me empty,
but will accomplish what I desire
and achieve the purpose for which I sent it."

Isaiah 55:11 niv

I remember hearing a professor say that during His Earthly ministry, Jesus probably repeated Himself more than five hundred times.

During college I had a professor who deliberately repeated himself three times. He said that the people in the first two or three rows will get the message the first time. The second time the people in the middle of the lecture hall will get it. The third time the people in the back will get it. And the ones in the front row will never forget it.

We need to keep that fact of human nature in mind as we share God's love with the people He puts in our path. We need to repeat ourselves—to repeat our acts of service, our deeds of love, and, yes, our words of truth. The Bible says, "Let us not become weary in doing good, for at the proper time we will reap a harvest if we do not give up" (Galatians 6:9 niv).

Let us saturate ourselves in the Word of God and in prayer. Then we will be equipped to share His truth—and to repeat it again and again!

A New Creation

If anyone is in Christ, there is a new creation:
everything old has passed away.

2 CORINTHIANS 5:17 NRSV

I once heard a carpenter say that it is always better, and usually more economical, to construct a new house than to patch up an old one. This is even truer in the spiritual realm.

The old nature with its deceitfulness, its depravity, and its wickedness must give way to a new nature. And this is exactly what God stands ready to do. God says, "I will give you a new heart and put a new spirit within you" (Ezekiel 36:26).

What a challenge! It is much more difficult to change our dispositions than it is our apparel. As a matter of fact, it is utterly impossible for us to change our dispositions in our own strength.

But God can! "If anyone is in Christ, there is a new creation." God doesn't just want to patch us up. He wants to remake us completely into the likeness of Christ! He wants to come into our lives and begin to change us from within. Have you asked Him to do that? He will!

Flee!

Flee these things and pursue righteousness, godliness, faith, love, patience, gentleness.

1 TIMOTHY 6:11

God intends for us to have victory over sin, and when we don't, it's not because God's power has failed. By His Holy Spirit, He is able to give us the power to live just as good a life as Paul or Timothy lived. However, we need to do our part and, by prayer, appropriate the Holy Spirit's power.

We also need to flee these things that God has labeled wrong. We need to flee pride—that tendency to think of ourselves more highly than we ought— and instead live with humility. We need to flee envy and jealousy. We need to avoid causing strife, and the anger, bad temper, irritability, and self-centeredness that prompt it. We need to avoid abusive language and instead develop a Spirit-controlled tongue. We are also to flee lust, the love of money, and evil thoughts about other people.

And you and I can do all this by the power of God's Spirit. Don't depend on yourself and your ability to fight sin, but ask God to fill you with His Spirit—and He will.

Ambassadors Under Authority

We are ambassadors for Christ, as though God
were pleading through us.

2 CORINTHIANS 5:20

What is an ambassador? He is a representative and servant of his government in a foreign land. He is not free to set his own policies or develop his own message, but must carry out the will of the government he represents. In other words, he is a person under authority.

In the same way, we are called to live under the authority of Jesus Christ and the authority of the Scriptures. We are servants. We must live under the authority of the Word of God. We are called not to do our will, but Christ's.

The world today is looking for holy men and women who live under the authority of the Word of God. Unbelievers will not listen to what we say unless we back it up with the way we live. Are you a faithful ambassador for Christ to those around you?

Living a Peaceable Life

*Lead a quiet and peaceable life in all
godliness and reverence.*

1 TIMOTHY 2:2

As Christians, we aren't to isolate ourselves from the world in which we live. We are part of society, and we share in its difficulties, problems, and hopes.

The Bible has much to say about our social responsibility. The Old Testament prophets condemned those who ignored the poor and exploited the weak. Not that it is easy. As Christians, we know human society is affected by sin, and any effort to improve society will always be incomplete and imperfect. We will never build a Utopia on Earth.

But we must do all we can to alleviate suffering and to strike at the root causes of injustice, racial prejudice, hunger, and violence. We are to work for a peaceable life and human dignity for others. Why? Because God loves this suffering world. Jesus saw the crowds and "was moved with compassion" (Matthew 9:36).

Christ is concerned about the whole person—including the society in which that person lives. Do we share His concern?

God's Unchanging Word

*All Scripture is God-breathed and is useful
for teaching, rebuking, correcting and
training in righteousness.*

2 TIMOTHY 3:16 NIV

Early in my life I had some doubts about whether or not the Bible was really God's Word. But one night in 1949, I knelt before a stump in the woods of Forest Home, California, opened my Bible, and said, "O God, there are many things in this Book I do not understand. But by faith I accept it—from Genesis to Revelation—as Your Word."

By God's grace that settled the issue for me once and for all. From that moment on, I have never had a single doubt that the Bible is God's Word. When I quote Scripture, I know I am quoting the very Word of God.

This confidence in God's Word not only gives authority to one's ministry; it provides a solid foundation for one's life. We who trust in God's Word aren't living according to what someone says about the Bible or some human philosophy. We are basing our faith, our ministry, even our life itself on God's unchanging truth as it is presented in His unchanging Word. Is God's Word the foundation of your life?

God's Work

As many as are led by the Spirit of God,
these are sons of God.

ROMANS 8:14

The first key for usefulness in God's Kingdom is humility. Pride cuts us off from God (and from other people) and deceives us into thinking we can do God's work without God's power. When we rely on the Holy Spirit, however, He sanctifies us and empowers us so we can be effective tools in God's hands.

But there is a second key, and that is faith—faith that God is sovereign and that He is at work even if we can't see it. Habakkuk complained to God that evil people were winning the day. But God replied, "I will work a work in your days which you would not believe, though it were told you" (Habakkuk 1:5).

God is at work in the midst of the problems, pessimism, and frustrations of our day. He alone is sovereign, and that is why we can trust Him even when the way seems dark.

A Great Gift

*The kingdom of God is . . . righteousness and
peace and joy in the Holy Spirit.*

ROMANS 14:17

To the great gift of forgiveness God adds the great gift of the Holy Spirit. He is the source of power who meets our need to escape from the miserable weakness that grips us. He gives us the power to be truly good, as we yield ourselves to Him.

If we are to live a life of sanity in our modern world, if we wish to be men and women who can live victoriously, we need the two-sided gift God has offered us: first, the work of the Son of God *for* us; second, the work of the Spirit of God *in* us. In this way God has answered humanity's two great cries: the cry for forgiveness and the cry for goodness.

As a friend of mine has said, "I need Jesus Christ for my eternal life, and the Holy Spirit of God for my internal life." He might have added, "so I can live my external life to the fullest."

Confidence and Peace

You will keep him in perfect peace,
whose mind is stayed on You.

ISAIAH 26:3

Peace carries with it the idea of unity, completeness, rest, ease, and security. Many times when I meet Jewish friends I greet them with "*Shalom,*" the Hebrew word for "peace." And often when I greet my Arab friends I use a similar term that they use for "peace," "*Salam.*"

Notice the key phrase in that verse: "whose mind is stayed on You." When troubles hit, our minds naturally focus on them. When suffering comes, all we can think about is the pain. It takes a deliberate act of the will to turn away from the problem and focus our minds on God.

When our minds are stayed on God, we won't be worried about the future, because we know it is in His hands. We won't tremble over what might happen, because our lives are built upon the solid rock of Christ.

When you and I yield to worry, we deny our Guide the right to lead us forward in confidence and peace. Don't cause Him to grieve over you by indulging in worry, but trust everything into His all-loving care.

Heart Medicine

"For God so loved the world that he gave his one and only Son, that whoever believes in him shall not perish but have eternal life."

JOHN 3:16 NIV

One time I was preaching in Africa to a small group of tribal people. I had been told that they had heard very little about the gospel, and I wanted to bring a basic, straightforward gospel message they could understand. So I preached on John 3:16 as simply as I knew how. Trying to explain John 3:16, I used every illustration I could think of that would help make the message clear. Afterward—by the work of the Spirit—several people indicated that they wanted to receive Christ.

The next Sunday, I was to preach at the parish church of Great St. Mary's at Cambridge University in England, and I thought, *I'm going to try something. I am going to preach the same simple sermon at Cambridge that I preached to the people in Africa.* And I did. That Sunday many students in the congregation came to know Christ as Lord and Savior.

Human hearts are the same the world over—in rebellion against God, suffering from the disease of sin, and dying . . . until they discover the simple yet profound truth of God's love for us in Jesus Christ.

Salt and Light

"You are the salt of the earth. . . . You are
the light of the world."
MATTHEW 5:13–14

Many people doubt that there are any answers to life's basic questions. What is the purpose of life? What happens after I die? Is there any hope for the world today?

However, the human mind—like nature itself—abhors a vacuum. If our minds and hearts are not filled with God's truth, something else will take its place: cynicism, occultism, false religions and philosophies, drugs—the list is endless.

Already a terrifying spiritual and moral tide of evil has loosed our society from its spiritual moorings. Ideas that could easily destroy our freedoms are rushing into the vacuum that results when societies turn from the moral truths found in Scripture. Moral and spiritual chaos is the inevitable result.

May we who know God's truth stay committed to the principles outlined in His Word. Above all, may we be salt and light in this world, proclaiming God's righteousness and love to a confused and dying world.

Crying Out

When [blind Bartimaeus] heard that it was Jesus
of Nazareth, he began to cry out and say, "Jesus,
Son of David, have mercy on me!"

MARK 10:47

Blind Bartimaeus probably never expected to be able to see—and then Jesus Christ came to town.

When He did, Bartimaeus cried out, and he cried out for the right thing: he cried for mercy. He needed other things, but what he—like you and I—needed most of all was God's mercy.

Bartimaeus also cried out to the right Person. He cried to the Lord Jesus Christ, the only One in all the world who could help him. And Jesus is there for us: "Salvation is found in no one else, for there is no other name under heaven given to men by which we must be saved" (Acts 4:12 NIV).

Third, Bartimaeus cried out at the right time. Suppose Bartimaeus had said, "I'm going to find out what other people think about Him, or perhaps I'll wait until He comes to Jericho again." But Jesus never returned to Jericho.

The Bible says, "Now is the time of God's favor, now is the day of salvation" (2 Corinthians 6:2 NIV). What do you need to cry out to Jesus about?

Holy Spirit Within Us

"When [the Holy Spirit] has come, He will convict the world of sin, and of righteousness, and of judgment."
JOHN 16:8

The Holy Spirit is God Himself, as He comes to live within us. But why has He come?

First, the Holy Spirit comes to convict us of our sin. He makes us admit to ourselves that we are sinners. We cannot come to Christ.unless the Holy Spirit convicts us of our sin. He also convinces us of the truth about Christ as the Savior.

In addition, the Holy Spirit gives us new life. When we give our lives to Jesus and trust Him as our Savior and Lord, the Spirit renews our souls and brings the life of God into us. We have joy and peace, and we have a new direction to our lives because the Spirit of God has imparted to us the very life of God.

The Bible also teaches that the Holy Spirit produces fruit in our lives. Our thoughts, words, actions, motives—all that we are and all that we do—begin to reflect the Spirit's fruit of "love, joy, peace, patience, kindness, goodness, faithfulness, gentleness and self-control" (Galatians 5:22–23 NIV). This fruit comes as we yield ourselves to the Spirit.

How yielded is your life today?

Witness to the World

*Rejoice with those who rejoice, and
weep with those who weep.*

ROMANS 12:15

Jesus ate with publicans and sinners; nearly everyone He associated with was an outcast. But His relationship with them was not purely social; it was redemptive.

We must not get our worlds mixed up at this point. God meant that we are not to mingle with the world and be polluted by the world, but we are to witness to the world. We are to "weep with those who weep," suffer with those who suffer, and identify ourselves with the poor, the sick, and those needy in body, mind, and spirit. How else can we reach them for Christ?

We are to love those who are involved in the world without being contaminated, influenced, or swayed by them. We can do this only through a close walk with Christ. Like Him, we are to be in the world, but not of the world.

It is good for a ship to be in the sea, but bad when the sea gets into the ship.

The Fact of Christ's Return

"I will come back and take you to be with me."
JOHN 14:3 NIV

C S. Lewis identified three reasons why people don't want to believe in the return of Christ.

First, they claim that Jesus' return did not take place as the early Church hoped—so it must be a myth. This argument is not new; in his second letter the apostle Peter put it this way: "In the last days scoffers will come, scoffing and following their own evil desires. They will say, 'Where is this "coming" he promised? Ever since our fathers died, everything goes on as it has since the beginning of creation'" (2 Peter 3:3–4 NIV).

Second, if we believe humanity is constantly progressing, we will never see the need for the return of Christ. Why do we need Christ to come back if we can reach perfection on our own?

Third, the teaching of Christ's return cuts across the plans and dreams of millions of people. They want to eat, drink, and be merry, and Christ's return would interrupt what they are doing—and they don't want that.

But Jesus will return despite these denials. Are you ready?

When Christ Returns

They will beat their swords into plowshares
and their spears into pruning hooks.
Nation will not take up sword against nation,
nor will they train for war anymore.

MICAH 4:3 NIV

First, the sobering news.

When Jesus returns, a judgment will be held. Every person outside of Christ will give an account not only of the things done and the things said, but also an account of all their thoughts and motives.

Now for the glorious news. When Jesus returns, all evil will be destroyed. There will be worldwide justice, complete safety, and total security. There will be no more war. Jesus Christ will rule as King of kings and Lord of lords, and "his kingdom will never end" (Luke 1:33 NIV).

And under His rule there will be universal joy: "Everlasting joy will crown their heads. Gladness and joy will overtake them, and sorrow and sighing will flee away" (Isaiah 51:11 NIV). Everlasting joy—think of it!

So, with joyful anticipation, "[we wait] for the blessed hope and glorious appearing of our great God and Savior Jesus Christ!" (Titus 2:13). Is your hope in Him?

Discover God's Grace

We conducted ourselves in the world . . .
by the grace of God.
2 CORINTHIANS 1:12

Is God's grace really sufficient in times of trouble? Can it sustain us in the midst of life's storms?

Yes—but to be honest, sometimes it's hard for us to rely on God's grace instead of ourselves. We think we have to have control of our lives, and we believe the responsibility for shaping our future is in our hands.

When troubles come, therefore, we resist them instead of depending on God to see us through. Alexander Maclaren, the distinguished British preacher of another generation, once wrote, "What disturbs us in this world is not trouble, but our opposition to trouble."

Put God to the test when troubles come. He won't let you down. In the midst of a painful illness, Paul begged God to intervene and take it away. But God replied, "My grace is sufficient for you" (2 Corinthians 12:9). It was sufficient for Paul, and it will be for you.

God's Formula of Grace

It is by grace you have been saved, through faith—and
this not from yourselves, it is the gift of God.

EPHESIANS 2:8 NIV

Astronomers tell us that every star moves with precision along its celestial path. To ignore the detailed rules of the universe would spell ruin to a star. The laws of nature are fixed, and for a star to ignore those laws would be folly—if it were even possible.

If the laws in God's material realm are so fixed and exact, would He be haphazard in the spiritual realm, where the eternal destinies of billions of people are at stake? No! Just as God has equations and rules in the material realm, He also has equations and rules in the spiritual realm. For instance, the Bible says, "The wages of sin is death" (Romans 6:23). This is God's formula: when a person sins, he or she will pay for it—in this life and in the life to come.

The formula continues, though, and it is the way of God's grace—Jesus' death on the cross for our sins. We cannot be saved by our own good works, but only through faith in the One who took our sins upon Himself and died in our place. That is grace!

A Home in Heaven

> *"If I go and prepare a place for you, I will come
> again and receive you to Myself."*
> JOHN 14:3

During Christ's ministry on Earth, He had no permanent home. He once said, "Foxes have holes and birds of the air have nests, but the Son of Man has no place to lay his head" (Matthew 8:20 NIV).

What a contrast to the Heavenly home He left in order to come to Earth. From all eternity His dwelling place had been filled with unimaginable glory and splendor. And yet, the Bible says, He "emptied himself . . . being born in human likeness" (Philippians 2:7 NRSV). Out of love for you and me, He left Heaven's glory for Earth's misery.

But the story doesn't end there. Now He has returned to Heaven—and someday we will join Him. Think of it: He wants to share Heaven's glory with us!

One evening, a little girl was taking a walk with her father. Looking up at the stars she exclaimed, "Daddy, if the wrong side of Heaven is so beautiful, what must the right side be like!"

Two Sets of Books

If anyone's name was not found written in the book of
life, he was thrown into the lake of fire.

REVELATION 20:15 NIV

These are sobering words—the most sobering words imaginable.

The Bible says that in Heaven there are two sets of books. One set records every detail of our lives: everything we have done since the day we were born. All of that will be held against us at judgment.

But Scripture tells us there is another book in Heaven: the Book of Life. When we come to Christ—when we receive Him, when we come to the cross where He died for us, when we believe that He is risen and we receive Him into our lives—our names are blotted out of the first set of books. God no longer even remembers our sins because they have been blotted out by the blood of Christ, shed on the cross for us.

The moment our names are blotted out of the first set of books, God writes them in the Book of Life. Only those whose names are recorded there will enter the Kingdom of Heaven.

Is your name written in the Book of Life? Make sure by opening your heart to Christ and committing your life to Him without reserve.

Fear Not!

There is no fear in love; but perfect love casts out fear.
1 JOHN 4:18

The world of Jesus' day was filled with fear. The Romans feared rebellion, and their subjects feared Rome's power. The Sadducees feared the Pharisees, and both were suspicious of the publicans. The hearts of people everywhere were filled with fear and distrust. Life was precarious, and above all, people feared death.

The world lives with fear even today. What is your fear? Do you fear the future? Do you fear life's burdens that sometimes seem almost overwhelming? Do you fear death? Most of us fear everything except God—yet it is God whom we should fear most of all!

Jesus can put an end to fear for all who trust in Him. "Do not fear, little flock" is a phrase typical of His teaching and preaching (Luke 12:32). He is the answer to any fear you have. After all, God's power is greater than the powers of evil, and "neither death nor life, neither angels nor demons, neither the present nor the future . . . nor anything else in all creation, will be able to separate us from the love of God that is in Christ Jesus our Lord" (Romans 8:38–39 NIV).

The Greatest Security

*He who dwells in the secret place of the Most High
shall abide under the shadow of the Almighty.*

PSALM 91:1

Someone has said that the only certainty in life is uncertainty—and it is true. Governments collapse, stock markets plummet, wars destroy, disasters strike, relationships end. As the writer of Hebrews put it, "Here we have no continuing city" (13:14).

Yet deep in the human heart is a yearning for security—a yearning that will not go away. We know we need a solid foundation to life, a foundation that cannot be shaken. Where will it be found?

Only God never changes. His love does not change, and neither do His promises. That is why we can look to Him for the security and stability we all seek. King David knew the secret: "He who dwells in the secret place of the Most High shall abide under the shadow of the Almighty."

Salvation is not an occasional, vague feeling of God's presence. It is actually dwelling with God, secure in His presence forever. Is your security in Christ?

In Giving, We Receive

"Love one another as I have loved you."
JOHN 15:12

Saint Francis of Assisi had discovered the secret of happiness when he prayed:

O Divine Master, grant that I may not so much seek
To be consoled as to console,
To be understood as to understand,
To be loved as to love;
For it is in giving that we receive;
It is in pardoning that we are pardoned;
It is in dying that we are born to eternal life!

Tears shed for self are tears of weakness, but tears of love shed for others are a sign of strength. I am not as sensitive as I ought to be until I am able to "weep o'er the erring one and lift up the fallen." And until I have learned the value of compassionately sharing others' sorrow, distress, and misfortune, I cannot know real happiness.

The opposite of love isn't hate. It's selfishness. Will you ask the Holy Spirit to free your life from selfishness and fill you instead with His love?

A Positive Influence

Do not be conformed to this world,
but be transformed.

ROMANS 12:2

I have found that the casual Christian has little or no influence for good upon others. Only the Christian who refuses to compromise in matters of honesty, integrity, and morality is bearing an effective witness for Christ.

Casual, worldly Christians are prepared to do as the world does and will condone practices that are dishonest and unethical because they are afraid of the world's displeasure. They ignore the Bible's clear command: "Do not be conformed to this world."

Only by a life of obedience to the voice of the Spirit, by a daily dying to self, by a full dedication to Christ and constant fellowship with Him are we enabled to live a godly life and have a positive influence on this ungodly world. Is the world changing you . . . or are you changing the world?

Choose to Love

I have set before you life and death . . .
therefore choose life.

DEUTERONOMY 30:19

I f God were to remove all evil from our world (but somehow leave human beings on the planet), it would mean that the essence of "humanness" would be destroyed. We would become robots.

Let me explain what I mean by this. If God eliminated evil by programming us to perform only good acts, we would lose this distinguishing mark—the ability to make choices. We would no longer be free moral agents. We would be reduced to the status of robots.

Let's take this a step further. Robots do not love. God created us with the capacity to love. Love is based upon one's right to choose to love. We cannot force others to love us. We can make them serve us or obey us. But true love is founded upon one's freedom to choose to respond.

Given the choice, I would rather be responsible for my actions than be a robot without responsibility! Are you using your ability to make decisions wisely—and using it for God?

Victory over Sin

In all these things we are more than
conquerors through Him who loved us.

ROMANS 8:37

We sing "Onward, Christian soldiers, marching as to war," but so often when Satan mounts an attack against us we behave as if we were prisoners of war or, worse, conscientious objectors! But as Christians, we don't have to live defeated lives. God wants us to live victorious lives—lives that are constantly conquering sin.

There is only one way to have victory over sin. That is to walk so closely with Christ that sin no longer dominates your life. It becomes the exception rather than the rule.

Why does a close walk with Christ make the difference? Simply this: The closer we are to Christ, the farther we are from Satan. The Bible says, "Resist the devil and he will flee from you. Draw near to God and He will draw near to you" (James 4:7–8). Is the devil farther away from you today than he was a week ago?

Relinquish Control

This is God,
our God forever and ever;
He will be our guide
even to death.

PSALM 48:14

The story is told of a little girl whose father was an airline pilot. As they crossed the Atlantic, a storm came up. The flight attendant awakened the little girl and told her to fasten her seat belt because they were in some turbulent weather. The little girl opened her eyes, saw the lightning flashing around the plane, and asked, "Is Daddy at the controls?" The flight attendant replied, "Yes, your father is in the cockpit." The little girl smiled, closed her eyes, and went back to sleep.

God is at the controls of our lives. Or, rather, He wants to be at the controls. But He gives us the freedom to pilot ourselves as we wish. The problem is that we often crash, much as we would if we took the controls of an airplane we had not been taught to fly.

God knows us. He knows our strengths and weaknesses, and He knows what is best for us. If we will only relinquish the control of our lives to Him, He will see us safely home.

Our Hope of Heaven

*God made him who had no sin to be sin for us, so that
in him we might become the righteousness of God.*

2 CORINTHIANS 5:21 NIV

You'll never be good enough to go to Heaven.

That statement may shock you, but I hope you
keep reading because it is true. The reason is because
God is absolutely holy and pure—and because of that,
He cannot tolerate sin. To put it another way, even one
sin would be enough to keep you out of Heaven. The
Bible is clear: "Nothing impure will ever enter [Heaven],
nor will anyone who does what is shameful or deceitful" (Revelation 21:27 NIV).

Does that mean there is no hope? No! Because of
Jesus, you and I have hope. God loves us and wants
us to be with Him in Heaven forever. To make that
possible, He sent Christ into the world. Jesus, who was
God in human flesh, was without sin—but on the cross
all our sins were transferred to Him, and He died in our
place. We deserve to die for our sins, but Christ took our
death and our Hell. Now we can be forgiven! Now we
can enter Heaven!

God Wins!

> *Blessed is the one who reads the words of this prophecy, and blessed are those who hear it and take to heart what is written in it, because the time is near.*
>
> REVELATION 1:3 NIV

God gave us the book of Revelation to encourage us and show us there is hope for the future—and the reason is because the future is in His hands.

Look at it this way: if you only read the daily headlines, you'd probably conclude that the world is caught in a never-ending cycle of war, crime, and violence; it would be easy to become cynical and discouraged. Like the writer of Ecclesiastes, you would be tempted to ask in despair, "What does man gain from all his labor at which he toils under the sun?" (1:3 NIV).

But Revelation gives us a different picture. Someday, it says, Jesus will triumph over all the forces of death and Hell and Satan. Someday the Heavenly hosts will sing, "The kingdom of the world has become the kingdom of our Lord and of his Christ, and he will reign for ever and ever" (Revelation 11:15 NIV). All evil and death will be destroyed, and His victory over sin and Satan will be complete.

No matter what you are facing today, you can have hope—because of Christ.

Deflect Despair

[God] gives us the victory through our Lord Jesus Christ.

1 CORINTHIANS 15:57 NIV

There is a story about Martin Luther going through a period of discouragement and depression. For days, his long face darkened the family table and dampened the family's home life. One day his wife came to the breakfast table all dressed in black, as if she were going to a funeral. When Martin asked her who had died, she replied, "Martin, the way you've been behaving lately, I thought God had died, so I came prepared to attend His funeral."

Her gentle but effective rebuke drove straight to Luther's heart, and as a result the great Reformer resolved to never again allow worldly cares, resentment, depression, discouragement, or frustration to defeat him. By God's grace, he vowed, he would submit his life to the Savior and reflect His grace in a spirit of rejoicing, whatever came.

When was the last time you praised God in the midst of despair? Don't wait until you feel like it, or you'll never do it. Do it, and then you'll feel like it!

A Reason to Do Right

Nothing in all creation is hidden from God's sight.
Hebrews 4:13 niv

Do people who have died and gone to Heaven know what happens on Earth? The Bible doesn't give us an absolutely clear answer about this, but it does hint that they may be aware of what takes place here on Earth.

The writer of Hebrews reminds us of some great Old Testament heroes who lived for God, often despite great opposition (Hebrews 11). Then he concludes, "Since we are surrounded by such a great cloud of witnesses, let us throw off everything that hinders and the sin that so easily entangles, and let us run with perseverance the race marked out for us" (12:1 niv).

Here the writer paints a picture of a stadium filled with spectators, perhaps watching us as we live out our lives and cheering us on as we stretch toward the finish line. So perhaps those who have entered Heaven are watching us, even now.

What we do know for sure is that God sees us—and that should be enough to encourage us to live for Christ and do what is right.

One Way

*"I am the way, the truth, and the life. No one
comes to the Father except through Me."*

JOHN 14:6

An old saying declares: "All roads lead to Rome."
Perhaps it was true in the ancient world, but
today you can get lost anywhere! The road you are on
may lead in exactly the opposite direction from your
goal. The only sure way to reach your destination is to
consult a good road map or ask someone who knows
the way.

Not all roads lead to God, as some suggest. The reason? There is a roadblock that keeps man from reaching
God. The roadblock of sin. But God has provided a
map—the Bible—and a Guide who knows the way and
can give us directions—Jesus Christ.

Jesus did not say, "I am one of many roads to God."
What He said was, "I am the way." That wasn't arrogance, or narrow-mindedness, or a lack of compassion.
It is truth: only Christ came from Heaven to pay the
price for our sins. Follow Christ and never be lost!

From Trial to Triumph

Walk in wisdom . . . redeeming the time.
Colossians 4:5

The master musician knows that suffering precedes glory and acclaim. He knows the hours, days, and months of grueling practice and self-sacrifice that precede the one hour of perfect rendition when his efforts are applauded.

The master craftsman knows that years of work, sacrifice, and suffering as an apprentice precede his being promoted to the master of his trade.

The student knows that years of study, self-denial, and commitment precede the triumphant day of graduation with honors.

Astronauts spend years training for a flight that can be as short as a few days.

The Bible teaches that sacrifice and discipline are necessary if we are to be faithful servants of Christ. Paul wrote, "I discipline my body and bring it into subjection, lest, when I have preached to others, I myself should become disqualified" (1 Corinthians 9:27).

Discipline your time . . . discipline your eyes . . . discipline your mind . . . discipline your body . . . all for the sake of Christ.

Mysterious Evil

"In this world you will have trouble. But take heart! I have overcome the world!"

JOHN 16:33 NIV

I have to admit that I do not know why some people suffer more than others do. There is a mystery to evil that we will never fully understand this side of eternity; the Bible speaks of "the mystery of iniquity" (2 Thessalonians 2:7 KJV).

But I do know this: We live in a world that is in the grip of evil, and in this present age God's plans are often blocked by Satan's supernatural power. This world is not the way God meant it to be; it is in the grip of "spiritual forces of evil in the Heavenly realms" (Ephesians 6:12 NIV).

In light of that truth, we must not blame God for everything that happens in our lives, especially the bad things. Instead, we need to remember that God has already entered the battle against evil, and someday His victory will be complete. In His death and resurrection, Jesus Christ confronted Satan—and won! That is our hope—and that is our comfort.

Learning from Bad Examples

These things happened to them as examples and were written down as warnings for us.

1 CORINTHIANS 10:11 NIV

I find it very encouraging that God included real-life, flesh-and-blood, sinful people in His Word. David committed adultery, Abraham lied about his wife—the list goes on and on. Why are they in the Bible? So we will learn from their wrongdoings.

One lesson is that sin always has consequences. Take David. He was a great leader and a good man in many ways. But over the years he became complacent, and instead of carrying out his responsibilities, he fell into immorality (2 Samuel 11–12).

And consider the tragic consequences of his sin. Not only did the child born of that illicit union die, but David committed other sins—lying, murder—in a vain attempt to cover up his adultery. Furthermore, his influence for good was lost, and his latter years as king were marked by rebellion and tragedy.

God has much to teach us from the examples of His people who failed. But most of all His Word points us to Christ, who alone can forgive us and set our feet on the right path.

Not the Right Ticket

"There is none righteous, no, not one."

ROMANS 3:10

D o you know people who are trusting in their good deeds to get into Heaven? If so, you might want to ask them this important question: "By what standard do you think God will judge you?"

Their reply might run something like this: "I'm a good person. I may not be perfect, but I've always tried to do what's right. Isn't that what God expects?"

But God's standard is higher than that; His standard is nothing less than perfection. That means we can't make it into Heaven on our own, for no matter how good we are, we still aren't perfect. Even the best person sins in words and actions, as well as in thoughts and motives. God's standard is perfection, and even one sin will keep us out of Heaven.

So if you know people who think good deeds are their ticket to Heaven, urge them not to gamble with their soul. Instead, urge them to repent of their pride and trust Jesus alone for their salvation.

Loving People into the Kingdom

*Let your conversation be always full of grace,
seasoned with salt, so that you may know how to
answer everyone.*

Colossians 4:6 niv

Have you noticed that you can seldom argue a person into the Kingdom of God? That's because the real reason for disbelief in God usually has nothing to do with logic.

Instead, the real reason usually has to do with a person's emotions and will. In other words, people don't believe in God because they don't want to believe—and they don't want to believe because they want to run their own lives. If they admit that God exists, they know they'd have to humble themselves before Him and yield control of their lives to Him. They don't want to do that.

We must do our best to answer—with gentleness and respect—any question we're asked, even if we think it isn't sincere or is only meant to put us on the spot. But the most important thing we can do is to show by our life and love that Jesus is real. Our actions often speak far louder than our words. Do others see Christ in you, both in what you say and in what you do?

Hope for the Home

He sets the poor on high . . .
and makes their families like a flock.

PSALM 107:41

One of the primary reasons for the breakdown of the home is that we have forgotten God's commands about marriage.

God gave marriage to us, and His standards have not changed. Jesus said, "A man shall leave his father and mother and be joined to his wife. . . . Therefore what God has joined together, let not man separate" (Matthew 19:5–6).

Divorce was not part of God's original design. The Bible declares, "The LORD God of Israel says that He hates divorce" (Malachi 2:16). Marriage is a symbol of the unity between Christ and His Church—a unity that should never be torn.

No marriage is beyond repair with God's help. But we must humble ourselves and put aside our pride and self-will. We must put others ahead of ourselves.

If you have experienced divorce, God can forgive the past, heal the present, and give you hope for the future. But if you are married, treasure your spouse as a gift from God and yield your marriage to Christ.

Transforming Power

They saw what seemed to be tongues of fire. . . . All of them were filled with the Holy Spirit.

ACTS 2:3–4 NIV

Within fifty days of Jesus' death and the apparent collapse of His cause, the city of Jerusalem rang with the cries of those who boldly declared that God had raised Jesus from the dead and that they were eyewitnesses to that truth. Hundreds had seen the resurrected Jesus!

As the Holy Spirit descended on the day of Pentecost, cowards became courageous confessors. Humble fishermen became heralds of the King. Something had utterly transformed their lives.

On that day of Pentecost, the resurrection was the keynote of Peter's sermon, causing three thousand people to confess Jesus as Lord (Acts 2:14–41). The earthshaking fact that God had raised Jesus from the dead was the axle and wheels of the early Christian Church.

What difference will the resurrection and the Holy Spirit's power make in your life today?

Jesus Will Answer

*He will give his angels charge of you
to guard you in all your ways.*

PSALM 91:11 RSV

Once a poor Chinese woman went up to the foothills to cut grass. Her baby was tied to her back, and a little child walked beside her.

Just as she reached the top of a hill, she heard a roar. Frightened, she turned and saw a mother tigress springing at her, followed by her two cubs.

The illiterate Chinese woman had never attended school or church, but a missionary once told her about Jesus, "who is able to help you when you are in trouble." As the tiger's claws tore into her arm, the woman cried out, "O Jesus, help me!" The tiger, instead of attacking again, suddenly turned and ran away.

What "beasts" are attacking you? Chances are you will never be attacked by a wild tiger, but you will be attacked by doubts, fears, worry, loneliness, or despair.

Cry out to Jesus and He will answer you just as surely as He heard and answered the Chinese woman's desperate cry.

JUNE

Give Your Fears to Jesus

"I know the plans I have for you . . . plans to prosper you and not to harm you, plans to give you hope and a future."
JEREMIAH 29:11 NIV

What are you afraid of?

A young person I know would like to get married, but she is afraid of getting into a serious relationship because her parents went through a bitter divorce. She is afraid her marriage will also fail.

Intellectually, she knows that just because her parents failed in their marriage doesn't mean she is also destined to fail. In fact, she knows she can learn from their mistakes and be better prepared for marriage than they were.

Emotionally, however, this woman feels trapped by fears and insecurities that are constantly telling her she will always be a failure. But it isn't necessarily true. Our emotions can lie to us, and we need to counter our emotions with truth.

And the greatest truth you can use to counteract your fears is the truth that God loves you and His plans for you are good. So give your fears—and every aspect of your life—to Christ. Then let the truth of His Word, the Bible, take root in your soul every day. Trust your future to Him who knows your needs and loves you deeply.

His Most Precious Blood

Jesus Christ . . . loved us and washed us from
our sins in His own blood.

<small>REVELATION 1:5</small>

When J. P. Morgan, the multimillionaire, died, it was found that his will consisted of about ten thousand words and thirty-seven articles. He made many transactions, some involving large sums of money.

But we are left in no doubt as to what he considered his most important transaction: "I commit my soul into the hands of my Savior, in full confidence that, having redeemed and washed it in His most precious blood, He will present it faultless before my heavenly Father; and I entreat my children to maintain and defend, at all hazard and at any cost of personal sacrifice, the blessed doctrine of the complete atonement for sin through the blood of Jesus Christ, once offered, and through that alone."

In the matter of his soul's eternal blessing, J. P. Morgan's vast wealth was powerless. He was just as dependent on God's mercy as was the dying thief at Calvary. No matter who you are or what you have done, only Christ can save you, for only "the blood of Jesus Christ . . . cleanses . . . from all sin" (1 John 1:7).

Lots of Questions

"Take My yoke upon you and learn from Me."
MATTHEW 11:29

Have you ever known someone who had lots of questions about God and the Bible? No matter how many you answered, they always had more!

Our faith can stand up to any question, but sometimes people ask questions—and keep asking questions—just to avoid facing their own spiritual needs and acknowledging who Jesus really is. Their questions may only be an excuse to keep from turning their life over to Christ.

In that situation, consider asking this question: "If I could answer every question you have, would you be willing to repent of your sins and commit your life to Jesus?" If they are honest, their answer may be no—but even if it is, let them know you still care about them and want to be their friend. But don't hesitate to warn them that someday they "will give an account to Him who is ready to judge the living and the dead" (1 Peter 4:5).

In addition, make sure your friends know what the gospel is. Many people really don't understand it—although they think they do. Never give up hoping that someday they will give their life to Jesus.

And of course pray for them—only God can change hearts.

Ask and Receive

"Whatever things you ask when you pray, believe that you receive them, and you will have them."

MARK 11:24

Someone has said that before our prayers can mean anything to God, they must first mean something to us. Mindlessly repeating a prayer we memorized in childhood or vaguely asking God to bless everyone, everywhere—that isn't authentic prayer. Prayer is speaking to God about the deepest concerns of our hearts.

What is the source of true prayer? It is a heart attuned to God. It is a life lived in loving obedience to the Father. The Bible says, "And whatever we ask we receive from Him, because we keep His commandments and do those things that are pleasing in His sight" (1 John 3:22).

God delights in the prayers of His children—prayers that express our love for Him, prayers that share our deepest burdens with Him. Don't pray casually or thoughtlessly, but "come boldly to the throne of grace, that [you] may obtain mercy and find grace to help in time of need" (Hebrews 4:16).

Living a Holy Life

"Lay up for yourselves treasures in heaven."
MATTHEW 6:20

An old man, a great man of God, lay on his death-bed. He summoned his grandson to come to his side. Calling the boy's name, he said, "I don't know what type of work I will be doing in heaven, but if it's allowed, I'm going to ask the Lord Jesus to let me help build your mansion. You be sure you send up plenty of the right materials."

Living a life of purity and love, leading others to Christ as we share our faith, doing good works in Christ's name—all of these things are materials that may be sent on ahead. These can never be touched by the fluctuations in the Earthly economy, by natural disaster, or by thievery.

What kind of materials are you sending up to Heaven?

God's Old Testament

Man shall not live by bread alone; but man lives by
every word that proceeds from the mouth of the LORD.

DEUTERONOMY 8:3

The Old Testament may not seem relevant to us today—but God has much to teach us through its pages.

After all, Jesus knew and often quoted the Old Testament. One reason the Old Testament is so important, He declared, is because it points to His coming as the promised Messiah.

The detailed instructions that governed the Old Testament sacrificial system no longer strictly apply to us because they have been fulfilled in Christ's sacrifice of Himself on the cross. Yet they still have much to teach us about the holiness of God and the seriousness of sin.

The book of Psalms is the Bible's hymnbook. It shows you what it means to walk with God in prayer and praise. The prophets and historical sections show how God dealt with His people in times past—and how He wants to deal with us today. Remember: "All Scripture is given by inspiration of God, and is profitable for doctrine, for reproof, for correction, for instruction in righteousness" (2 Timothy 3:16).

What to Do with Anger

The tongue is a fire, a world of iniquity.
JAMES 3:6

Have you ever been falsely accused of something? Even when it was later proven false, did you suspect that some people still wondered if it was true? Did that unfounded accusation damage your reputation?

That kind of experience vividly demonstrates the dangerous power of a lying tongue. And when the lie is about us, the temptation is to strike back and hurt the person who hurt us, perhaps by telling lies. But in the long run, doing so only damages our own credibility and makes people even more suspicious of us.

Anger and bitterness—whatever the cause—only end up hurting us. So, whenever a situation causes you to be angry, turn that anger over to Christ. Ask Him to forgive your anger, help you get rid of it, and enable you to forgive the person who hurt you.

Remember that Jesus was falsely accused of sin. Rather than strike back at His accusers, He willingly went to the cross so that we could be forgiven for all our sins—including our sins committed in anger.

Rest for the Weary

"Come to Me . . . and I will give you rest."
MATTHEW 11:28

We forget that Jesus was human as well as divine. He had calluses on His hands. If the chisel slipped and cut His finger, His blood was red and warm like ours. He knew what it meant to work long hours, to come in at night tired and weary.

That is one of the reasons Jesus could say with such appeal, "Come to Me, all you who labor and are heavy laden, and I will give you rest" (Matthew 11:28). When we are exhausted and hurting, we can take comfort from the fact that Jesus knows what it is to be exhausted and hurting.

But the greatest work Jesus did was not in the carpenter's shop, nor at the marriage feast in Cana where He turned the water into wine. The greatest work Jesus did was not when He made the blind to see, the deaf to hear, the dumb to speak, nor even the dead to rise.

What was Jesus' greatest work?

His greatest work was what He accomplished through the cross and resurrection. There the burden of our sins was placed on Him, and there He won our salvation. And that is why we can come by faith to Him, and He will give us rest.

The Basics

May we know what this new doctrine is of which you speak?
ACTS 17:19

Paul's preaching in Athens attracted great curiosity, and when a well-known group of intellectuals invited him to speak to them, he readily accepted and in his address covered three important points.

First, Paul talked about the one true God, the Creator who is the holy, unchangeable God of love. Calling their attention to an altar he had seen dedicated "To an Unknown God," Paul pointed them to the God who made them and sustained them—who can be known and seeks our fellowship.

Paul also talked about the need to repent and the coming judgment. Repentance means recognizing and accepting God's holiness, our sinfulness, and Jesus' sacrificial death for us.

Finally Paul talked about the resurrection, which gives us hope for the future. There will be a glorious and eternal tomorrow for those who have trusted Christ!

Most in Athens rejected Paul's message, but some believed and became followers of Jesus. Have you committed your life to Christ, and are you seeking to tell others about Him?

More Attached to God

God is our refuge and strength,
an ever-present help in trouble.

Psalm 46:1 niv

Back in the nineteenth century, a young Irishman named Joseph Scriven was deeply in love with a young woman, and their marriage plans had been made. The night before their wedding, however, she drowned in a tragic accident. For months Scriven was bitter and in utter despair.

At last he turned to Christ and, through His grace, found peace and comfort. Out of this experience Scriven wrote the familiar hymn that has brought consolation to millions of aching hearts: "What a friend we have in Jesus / All our sins and griefs to bear!"

Sometimes our way lies in the sunlight. It was so for Joseph Scriven as he approached his wedding day. But like him, we may find that our path also leads through the dark shadows of loss, disappointment, and sorrow.

Yet even sorrows turn to blessings when they make us less attached to the Earth and more attached to God. Then more than ever we discover that Jesus truly is our friend—"All our sins and griefs to bear!"

Take the Leap

By my God I can leap over a wall.
PSALM 18:29

The Bible confronts us with our moral independence within ourselves and our spiritual dependence upon God.

In the picturesque words of Psalm 18, David says, "By my God I can leap over a wall." We can jump over some barriers in life by our own will and our own efforts; God has not left us completely powerless. But some walls are so high we need more.

The psalmist knew such walls. They could be leaped only with the help of God. When we try to jump over them by ourselves, we repeatedly fall short. But with God's help, we can scale them.

What walls do you need to jump over? A habit you cannot break? An emotion that defeats you? An attitude that separates you from others? A heart beset with doubt or discouragement or fear? Whatever it is, with God's help, you can leap over that wall.

Our Timeless God

Before the mountains were born
or you brought forth the earth and the world,
from everlasting to everlasting you are God.

PSALM 90:2 NIV

An eight-year-old once asked me, "How old is God?" I told him he'd asked a very good question and said I was glad he wanted to know more about God.

Then I told this child that God is timeless: He has always existed. God has no beginning, and He has no end. He was never young, and He will never grow old.

I know that statement was hard for him to understand, because everything around us grows old or wears out. Perhaps, I told him, you have a grandfather or a grandmother; you probably think of them as old. At one time, however, they were just as young as you are. Now the years have passed, and they have grown old. But God isn't like that. He doesn't change, nor does He grow old and weak.

Why is this important? Because this means you can trust God with your life. He won't die or grow weak or forgetful; He loves you, and He is always there to take care of you. That's an important truth, whatever our age!

The Seal of the Spirit

> *Having believed, you were marked in him with a seal, the promised Holy Spirit.*
>
> EPHESIANS 1:13 NIV

God places a seal on us when we receive Christ. And that seal is a person—the Holy Spirit. By the Spirit's presence God gives us security and establishes His ownership over us.

The Spirit is also God's pledge. He not only seals the arrangement, but He represents God's commitment to see us through. And fellowship with the Spirit is a sample of what we can expect when we come into our inheritance in Heaven.

Finally, the Spirit witnesses to us, by the Scriptures and within our hearts, that Christ died for us and that, by faith in Him, we have become God's children.

What a wonderful thing to know the Holy Spirit has been given to us as a seal, a pledge, and a witness! May each of these give us new assurance of God's unchanging love for us, and give us confidence as we seek to live for Him.

God's Grace

Your eyes are too pure to look on evil;
you cannot tolerate wrong.

HABAKKUK 1:13 NIV

What do pastors mean when they talk about "the grace of God"? It refers to much more than His kindness and mercy, although those traits are certainly evidence of His grace.

Grace means "undeserved favor or goodness." God doesn't owe us anything—yet in His grace, He still gives us good things. We don't even deserve the next breath we take, but God in His grace grants it. Most of all, we don't deserve to go to Heaven, but in His grace God has provided the way: He sent Jesus Christ to die for our sins.

Remember: by nature we have no right to expect anything from God except His judgment. We are sinners, and sin is rebellion against God. We don't like to admit this. We like to think we aren't so bad after all, and God ought to overlook our sins. But that's just not true.

Thank God for His saving grace, extended to you in Jesus Christ. Then seek—by His power—to glorify Him in your life.

A Clear Conscience

I myself always strive to have a conscience
without offense toward God and men.
ACTS 24:16

Benjamin Franklin composed this little rhyme: "Keep conscience clear, then never fear." George Bernard Shaw, the great Irish writer, said, "Better keep yourself clean and bright; you are the window through which you must see the world."

If conscience was such a vital concept to these secular writers, how much more concerned should we as Christians be that our consciences are "without offense toward God and men"? Without a conscience, we would be like rudderless ships at sea, or missiles without a guidance system.

God has given our conscience to us. Its very presence is a reflection of God in the human soul. Sin, however, can dull or even distort our conscience, silencing its voice and leading us astray. But God's Word can purify and sharpen our conscience—and when that happens, "He leads [us] in paths of righteousness for His name's sake" (Psalm 23:3). Is this happening in your life?

Confidence About the Future

*"Trust in God; trust also in me. . . . I am going
there to prepare a place for you."*
JOHN 14:1–2 NIV

Almost since the dawn of the human race, people
have tried to discern the future. The horoscopes
published in many daily newspapers are evidence that
it still goes on today.

As a Christian, though, I believe that only God
knows the future and that we are to look to Him—not to
the stars or the tea leaves or the lines on the palm of our
hand—to find confidence for the future. Some of these
attempts to learn what the future holds are merely foolish or useless, but others involve occult practices that
can bring people into contact with spiritual forces that
are not from God but from Satan.

This is one reason why the Bible strongly urges us
to avoid any practice that may be linked with the occult.
Astrology can never give you the answers to life's deepest questions—especially where you will spend eternity.
Committing your life to Christ means having the joyous
confidence that your future is securely in His hands.
Tomorrow and forever.

In the Time of Trouble

Cast your burden on the LORD,
and He shall sustain you.
PSALM 55:22

Years ago I came across this oft-quoted prayer: "God, grant me the serenity to accept things I cannot change, the courage to change the things I can, and wisdom to know the difference." This prayer expresses an important thought, one we should all pray—and live.

Some things in life cannot be changed—and some can. Some things God has given to us as fixed realities that we must accept. And some things He would have us not accept, but (with His help) work to change. If we fail to do both of these—to accept some things and work to change others—we will end up burdened with worry, undeserved guilt, and frustration.

Someone once said, "Worry is the interest paid on trouble before it comes due." Instead, God would have us learn to trust Him. "Cast your burden on the LORD, and He shall sustain you."

Faith in the Darkness

I do believe; help me overcome my unbelief!

MARK 9:24 NIV

Evil is real, and at one time or another most of us have wondered why God doesn't just reach down and stop it. Sometimes He does—but not always, and the Bible says evil is a mystery that we won't fully understand until we get to Heaven. In the meantime, God calls us to trust Him and have confidence in His love, no matter the circumstances.

Maybe someone you love has cancer, or just lost a job, or is dealing with a prodigal child. . . . The list of the ways that evil intersects our daily life goes on and on. Bitterness and anger can result, but don't let those emotions drive a wedge between you and God. That gains you nothing and, in the long run, will only destroy you.

Instead, let your attitude be that of the psalmist: "As for me, it is good to be near God. I have made the Sovereign LORD my refuge" (73:28 NIV). Ask God to help you trust Him even when the way is dark.

God's Good Promise

Blessed be the LORD. . . . There has not failed one word of all His good promise.

1 KINGS 8:56

When we purchase something of great value—a house, for example—we are usually required to put down a deposit to indicate our sincerity and to promise that our intentions are serious. That deposit is a form of insurance, a guarantee that adds substance to our word.

God has made some incredible promises to us—promises that stagger our imaginations. He has promised that we might have a relationship with Him through His Son. He has promised never to leave us or forsake us and to be with us always. He has promised to take us to Heaven when we die. The Bible is full of God's promises.

Someone might ask, "What insurance do we have that God is serious? How do we know His promises can be trusted?" God's deposit is the most precious investment anyone could make: His Son, who by His death and resurrection purchased our salvation. Not only is Jesus Christ a sufficient "down payment" on God's promises, He is, in fact, payment in full!

Jesus' Question for You

"Who do you say that I am?"

MATTHEW 16:15

Some years ago, C. S. Lewis pointed out that there are only four possible conclusions you can reach about Jesus. Either He was a liar, or He was self-deceived, or He was insane—or He was in fact who He claimed to be: the Son of God.

Which was He? The only logical conclusion is that Jesus was the Son of God. A liar couldn't have taught the lofty moral principles He did. A self-deceived person couldn't have performed the miracles He did. A lunatic couldn't have held up under pressure the way Jesus did. After closely observing His life every day, His disciples reached their conclusion: "You are the Christ, the Son of the living God" (Matthew 16:16).

But there is an even more compelling reason to believe that Jesus was who He claimed to be: His resurrection from the dead. In all of human history, only one person came back from the grave: Jesus Christ "was declared with power to be the Son of God by his resurrection from the dead" (Romans 1:4 NIV). Who do you say He is?

The Privilege of Prayer

"Ask, and you will receive, that your joy may be full."
JOHN 16:24

What a privilege is ours—the privilege of prayer! Just think of it: you and I have the incredible privilege of approaching the God of the universe, "the High and Lofty One who inhabits eternity, whose name is Holy" (Isaiah 57:15)! We can only do this because Jesus Christ has opened the way.

We are to pray in times of adversity, lest we become faithless and unbelieving.

We are to pray in times of prosperity, lest we become boastful and proud.

We are to pray in times of danger, lest we become fearful and doubting.

We are to pray in times of security, lest we become self-sufficient.

Pray, believing in the promise of God's Word that "if we ask anything according to His will, He hears us" (1 John 5:14).

Whitewashed Tombs

Rid yourselves of all malice and all deceit, hypocrisy,
envy, and slander of every kind.

1 PETER 2:1 NIV

Unfortunately, sometimes those of us who are Christians are the worst advertisements for our faith. We keep sinning even after we name Jesus as our Savior and Lord, and we often appear to others as insincere and hypocritical. And all too often, we are.

Some of Jesus' strongest words were reserved for hypocrites—for people who claimed to believe in God, yet were insincere and only used their religion to try to impress others. Jesus called those people "whitewashed tombs, which look beautiful on the outside but on the inside are full of dead men's bones" (Matthew 23:27). What an indictment!

Ask God to reveal any hypocrisy in your life, any inconsistency between what you profess and what you practice. Then ask God to bring you so close to Christ that you won't have any desire to live an inconsistent, deceitful life. Not only will you be a better person, but God will begin to use you to point others to Christ and His transforming love.

Overflowing Joy

But the fruit of the Spirit is . . . joy.
GALATIANS 5:22

The word *joy* has all but disappeared from our current Christian vocabulary. One reason is because we have confused joy with happiness, and have come to believe it is found in pleasure, security, and prosperity. In doing this, however, we have believed a lie that Satan is constantly telling the world to believe.

But James did not say, "Count it all joy when you fall into an easy chair." He said, "Count it all joy when you fall into various trials" (James 1:2).

Joy is not the same as happiness—although they may overlap. Happiness depends on circumstances; joy depends on God. Happiness vanishes when life turns painful; joy keeps going and may even grow.

Joy comes from a living, vital relationship with God. It comes from knowing this world is only temporary and that someday we will be with God forever. It comes from the fact that, although we do not yet see God, we "believe in him and are filled with an inexpressible and glorious joy" (1 Peter 1:8 NIV). It comes from a life of submission to the Holy Spirit—regardless of circumstances.

God's Truth, Your Life

*But you are a chosen people . . . that you may
declare the praises of him who called you out of
darkness into his wonderful light.*

1 PETER 2:9 NIV

I have found that people who say, "You can't trust
what the Bible says" often have never actually read
it for themselves. Instead, they are only using this as an
excuse to avoid God.

The real issue for them isn't the trustworthiness
of the Bible but their determination to keep God away.
Down inside, they sense that if they took God seriously
and gave their life to Christ, they would have to change
their way of living—and they don't want to do that.

So don't be afraid to challenge your nonbelieving
friends to read the gospels and learn about Jesus for
themselves. God's Word can break down their barriers
and bring them to Himself.

Also pray for them. You can't change their hearts
and minds—but God can. Ask Him to awaken your
friends to their need for Christ.

Finally, be a good witness by the way you live. Let
these friends know you really care. Let them see Jesus'
love and peace and joy in your life. The way we live is
often more convincing than the words we say.

A Beacon of Hope

"If I go and prepare a place for you, I will come again. . . ."
JOHN 14:3

In his remarkable book *Christian Behavior*, C. S. Lewis said, "Hope is one of the theological virtues." He meant that a continual looking forward to the eternal world is not, as some people think, a form of escapism or wishful thinking, but one of the things a Christian is meant to do.

This does not mean we are to leave the present world as it is. If you read history, you will find that the Christians who did the most for the present world were those who thought the most of the next. It is only since Christians have largely ceased to think of the next world that they have become so ineffective in this one. "Aim at heaven," said Lewis, "and you will get earth thrown in. Aim at earth, and you will get neither."

In the midst of the pessimism, gloom, and frustration of the present hour there is one bright beacon of hope—and that is the promise of Jesus Christ, "If I go and prepare a place for you, I will come again and receive you to Myself" (John 14:3).

Learning from Death

*To everything there is a season . . . a time to be born
and a time to die.*

ECCLESIASTES 3:1–2

Have you ever watched a loved one struggle with pain, growing disability, and approaching death? Perhaps you asked yourself, "Why doesn't God just let her die?"

I don't have a complete answer for you. We live in a fallen, sin-scarred world, and much of what happens falls far short of God's original plan.

But I do know this: even when we can't understand why God allows things like this to happen, He still can be trusted to do what is right. God is sovereign, and He knows what is best—for you, for the person who is suffering, and for all those affected by their suffering. In God's time, He will take the suffering saint to be with Him.

When someone is suffering or dying, we should ask God to teach us whatever lessons He has for us in this experience. Sometimes, I believe, God allows a loved one to linger because family members need to come together and be reconciled to each other. God also may use situations like this to teach us how to love others who are in need and to remind us of the brevity of life.

Power for Problems

I can do all things through Christ who strengthens me.

Philippians 4:13

A friend told me of a nonbeliever who came to him in the midst of a troubled day. Knowing my friend was a Christian, the man asked, "If I get born again, will all of my problems go away?"

"No," said my friend, "but you will have the power to deal with them."

God will give us wisdom and courage. He will surround us with brothers and sisters in Christ to help carry our burdens, and He will even provide us with insight and practical assistance.

Satan will always try to discourage those who belong to Christ. When problems persist, he may even whisper, "See, God doesn't care about you!" But with the Holy Spirit's help, we can combat the evil one and contradict his lies.

If God dismissed all our problems with a single stroke, we would be left defenseless, unequipped to meet the inevitable attacks of the Enemy of our souls. But in the midst of life's problems, God supplies everything we need to see us through.

Before It's Too Late

Now instead you ought to forgive and comfort him, so that he will not be overwhelmed by excessive sorrow.

2 CORINTHIANS 2:7 NIV

The situation was heartbreaking. The father had abused his children and abandoned the family. Years later, when he was sick, he wrote to his children asking to see them, asking for their forgiveness. . . .

Situations like this make Jesus' command to forgive seem impossible to obey. But when the guilty party is near the end of life—and especially if that person has requested reconciliation—we need to prayerfully consider honoring the request. Although we may not realize it at the time, someday we will regret never being reconciled to the family member or friend who hurt us.

Forgiveness isn't easy. In fact, often we can't forgive the person who hurt us deeply without God's help. But is it impossible for God to overcome those hurts and heal the wounds? No, of course not.

Remember what it cost Christ to forgive you—and then ask Him to help you forgive others. What the person did was wrong, and you may still bear the emotional scars. But God doesn't want you to carry those hurts forever.

Whom do you need to forgive before it's too late?

Let Go

Draw near to God and He will draw near to you.
JAMES 4:8

One day a little child was playing with a valuable vase. He put his hand into it and could not take it out. His father, too, tried his best to get the little boy's hand out, but all in vain. They were thinking of breaking the vase when the father said, "Now, my son, make one more try. Open your hand and hold your fingers out straight as you see me doing and then pull."

To the father's astonishment the little fellow said, "Oh no, Daddy! I couldn't put my fingers out like that because if I did I would drop my penny."

Smile if you will, but thousands of us are like that little boy. We are so busy holding on to the world's worthless trifles that we cannot accept God's freedom.

What "trifle" is keeping you from God? A sin you won't let go of? An unworthy goal you are determined to reach? A dishonorable relationship you won't give up? I beg you to drop that trifle in your heart. Surrender! Let go and let God have His way in your life.

What God Hates

To fear the LᴏRD is to hate evil;
I hate pride and arrogance,
evil behavior and perverse speech.

Pʀᴏᴠᴇʀʙѕ 8:13 ɴɪᴠ

From our human standpoint some sins—sins like murder, assault, or stealing—are worse than others. But the Bible doesn't tell us which sin is worst in God's eyes, and the reason is because God hates all sin. God is absolutely pure and holy; even the smallest sin is evil in His sight.

I'm afraid we have largely lost sight of the holiness and purity of God today. This is one reason why we tolerate sin so easily and casually dismiss so many sins as minor or insignificant. It is also the reason why we ignore sin in our lives and neglect to repent of it.

We need a new vision of who God is and who we are as sinners in His sight. No matter how good we think we are, God's judgment still stands: "There is none who does good, no, not one" (Romans 3:12).

But God loves us despite our sin, and He yearns to forgive us and welcome us into His family forever. Don't excuse your sin or tolerate it any longer, but repent of it and, with God's help, begin following Christ every day.

Nearer than You Think

His angels . . . keep you in all your ways.
PSALM 91:11

Occasionally I see reports of happenings that cannot be humanly explained—of visitors unexpectedly appearing to assist in times of crisis or warn of impending danger. These can only be explained as the intervention of God's angels.

In the Bible, angels occasionally assumed visible form—at the birth of Jesus, for example. But usually angels go about their business unseen and unrecognized. They never draw attention to themselves, but point us instead to Christ.

C. S. Lewis once said that we tend to make one of two errors about Satan: we either make too little of him, or we make too much.

The same could be said of angels. Don't make too little of them. God has given "His angels charge over you, to keep you in all your ways" (Psalm 91:11). On the other hand, don't worship them or become preoccupied with them. Instead, thank God for His angels and rejoice in their unseen watchfulness over you.

God's True Purposes

"Whatever you ask in My name, that I will do."
JOHN 14:13

Prayer links us with God's true purposes, for us and for the world. It not only brings the blessings of God's will to our own personal lives, but it also brings us the added blessing of being in step with God's plan.

Prayer also—in ways we will never fully understand this side of eternity—makes us partners with God in what He is doing in the world. God works through our prayers!

The model prayer Jesus gave us concludes with "thine is the kingdom, and the power, and the glory, for ever" (Matthew 6:13 KJV). Remember that we must seek God's glory in our prayers and not just our own selfish desires. If we are to have our prayers answered, we must be willing to give God the glory when He acts—no matter what the result. Our Lord said to His disciples, "Whatever you ask in My name, that I will do, that the Father may be glorified in the Son" (John 14:13).

The Spirit of Antichrist

As you have heard that the Antichrist is coming, even now many antichrists have come.

1 JOHN 2:18

One of the characteristics of the Antichrist who will come in the last days is that he will be "a deceiver" (2 John 1:7) who turns many away from God by his lies and apparent miracles.

His very name—Antichrist—clearly indicates his character as well as his mission: he will be sent into the world as Satan's representative to oppose God at every turn. The Bible calls him "the man of lawlessness . . . [who] will exalt himself over everything that is called God or is worshipped . . . proclaiming himself to be God" (2 Thessalonians 2:3–4 NIV).

Is the Antichrist alive today? No one can say for sure. But the Bible tells us a very important truth: the spirit of the Antichrist has often been among us. Satan is always at work to oppose God's work, and some people deliberately take their stand with Satan, not God.

What does all this mean? It means we must be sure of our own commitment to Christ. If our lives are not built on Christ's truth, we can easily be led astray. Don't let this happen to you!

Evil Hearts

The hearts of men, moreover, are full of evil and there
is madness in their hearts while they live.

ECCLESIASTES 9:3 NIV

As the headlines any day of the week indicate, terrible things happen in our world—wars, conflicts, terrorist attacks, injustice, and so forth. Why? Because the human heart is capable of incredible evil.

We like to pretend this isn't the case; we may even think that the more civilized or educated we are, the less likely we will be to do something evil. But that isn't necessarily so. Even people who are decent and respectable on the surface may be harboring deep hatred and anger in their hearts.

Only Jesus can cleanse us from the moral and spiritual filth we have allowed to accumulate in our hearts. When we go to Him, God not only forgives us of our sins, but He comes to live within us by His Holy Spirit. God's promise is for all who turn in faith to Christ: "I will give you a new heart" (Ezekiel 36:26).

Are you, day by day, seeking Jesus' help to do His will? And are you praying that He will restrain evil and hasten the coming of His Kingdom?

True Beauty

Your beauty should not come from outward adornment.

1 PETER 3:3 NIV

Our world bombards us with messages about what is beautiful and handsome. It sets standards for our physical appearance and our material success that penetrate our minds and shape our personalities and our goals—often without us even realizing it. It's difficult to ignore these loud and ever-present voices as they speak to us from magazines, television, movies, the Internet, and advertising. The problem is, these messages will lead us astray.

To cope with all this, first ask God to help you be content with the way you are. God made you, and it's wrong for you to think He made a mistake. God loves you just as you are!

Second, focus on what the Bible calls true beauty—the beauty of a godly character, "the unfading beauty of a gentle and quiet spirit, which is of great worth in God's sight" (1 Peter 3:4 NIV).

Take care of your body; the Bible calls it a "temple of the Holy Spirit" (1 Corinthians 6:19). But most of all, take care of your soul by feeding on the Word of God and letting His Spirit transform you from within.

White As Snow

Wash me, and I shall be whiter than snow.

PSALM 51:7

Snow is so white that one can see almost anything that is dropped on it, even at great distances. We can take the whitest object we can find, like newly washed clothing, but when we place it next to snow, it still looks dirty by comparison.

Our lives are like that. At times, we may think of ourselves as morally good and decent; we are content that we are "not like other men" (Luke 18:11). But compared to God's purity, we are defiled and filthy.

In spite of our sins and uncleanness, God still loves us. And because He loves us, He decided to provide for us a purity we could never attain on our own. That is why He gave His Son, Jesus Christ, to die for us on the cross. Only when our sins have been washed in the blood of Jesus Christ will we appear as white as snow in the eyes of God. Thank God today that you are now "whiter than snow," because "you were washed . . . in the name of the Lord Jesus and by the Spirit of our God" (1 Corinthians 6:11)!

Sincere Devotion

The fruit of the Spirit is love, joy, peace . . .
gentleness, self-control.
GALATIANS 5:22–23

We should seek to produce the fruit of the Spirit in our lives. Or to put it more accurately, we should allow the Holy Spirit to produce His fruit in our lives.

You say, "I am powerless to produce such fruit. You don't know how weak and self-centered I am. It would be utterly impossible for me to do so!"

With that I agree! That is, we can't produce this fruit in our own strength. When the Spirit of God dwells in us and has control of our lives, He will produce that fruit. Our responsibility is to cultivate the soil of our hearts through sincere devotion and surrender, so He might find favorable ground to produce His fruit.

I might have a fruit tree in my yard, but if the soil isn't enriched and the bugs carefully destroyed, it will not yield a full crop. What keeps the Holy Spirit from producing His fruit in your life?

Attention!

No man knows when his hour will come:
As fish are caught in a cruel net . . .
so men are trapped by evil times
that fall unexpectedly upon them.

ECCLESIASTES 9:12 NIV

Has God ever tried to get your attention? Sometimes a narrow escape in a car accident or a false-positive test for cancer or a major surgery can make us realize that we aren't ready to die—and make us wonder if God is trying to get our attention.

Perhaps, for instance, God is trying to tell you that you are on the wrong road. You may have chosen a self-centered, self-indulgent path—but where does it lead? Jesus warned, "Wide is the gate and broad is the road that leads to destruction, and many enter through it" (Matthew 7:13 NIV).

Or God may be warning you that life is short; you cannot count on having time to turn to Him later on. If you are going to turn to Christ, the time is now.

Above all, God wants to tell you that He loves you. He loves you so much that He gave His Son to die on the cross for you. When we know Christ, we have joy and peace, because we know our future is secure—and someday we will be with Him forever.

The Brevity of Life

> *What is your life? You are a mist that appears*
> *for a little while and then vanishes.*
> JAMES 4:14 NIV

Several years ago a university student asked me what had been my biggest surprise in life. Immediately, I replied, "The brevity of life." Almost before we know it, the years have passed and life is almost over.

On one hand, life's brevity should challenge us. If ever we are to live for Christ and share Him with others, it must be now. Jesus said, "The night is coming when no one can work" (John 9:4).

But life's brevity should also comfort us. Life is short—and before us is eternity! When sufferings overwhelm us or difficulties assail us, we know they will soon be over. Paul wrote, "Our light affliction, which is but for a moment, is working for us a far more exceeding and eternal weight of glory. . . . For the things which are seen are temporary" (2 Corinthians 4:17–18).

Don't live as if this life will continue forever. It won't. Live instead with eternity in view!

Heaven or Hell?

"In hell, where he was in torment, he looked up and . . . called to him, 'Father Abraham, have pity on me . . . because I am in agony in this fire.'"

LUKE 16:23–24

It isn't fashionable today to talk about Hell—but the Bible is clear: God created us with a soul or a spirit that will live forever—and when we die, we will continue to exist—either in the place the Bible calls Heaven or in the place it calls Hell.

Hell, the Bible says, is reserved for those who reject God and turn their backs on Him. If you want nothing to do with Him in this life, then you will have nothing to do with Him in the next life.

And let me be as clear as possible: you don't want to go to Hell. The Bible speaks of Hell as a place of "darkness [where] there will be weeping and gnashing of teeth" (Matthew 25:30). Hell is a place of absolute loneliness and hopelessness.

But the good news is that God doesn't want you to go there! Jesus paid the price for your sins; He took upon Himself the death and Hell we deserve, through His death on the cross. Trust Jesus as your Lord and Savior, and thank Him that you will spend all eternity with Him in Heaven.

Free but Not Cheap

"If anyone desires to come after Me, let him . . . take up his cross, and follow Me."

MATTHEW 16:24

During the early years of the twentieth century, Bill Borden turned his back on one of America's great family fortunes to become a missionary to China. He only got as far as Egypt where, still in his twenties, he died of typhoid fever. Before his death he wrote, "No reserves, no retreats, no regrets!"

Discipleship is always costly. No, it may not cost us our lives. But it will cost us. It will cost us our plans, our wills, our selfish desires. Jesus' standard has not changed: "If anyone desires to come after Me, let him deny himself, and take up his cross, and follow Me" (Matthew 16:24). Instead of controlling our lives, we turn them over to Christ as Lord.

Someone has said, "Salvation is free but not cheap." It cost Jesus His life, and it will cost us as well. But could anything be greater? Could anything be more fulfilling?

Follow Christ, and at life's end you will be able to say, "No regrets!"

The Only Spiritual Reality

"No one has ever seen God, but God the One and Only,
who is at the Father's side, has made him known."

JOHN 1:18 NIV

Many today sense there must be something more to life than material things, and they are searching for a deeper spiritual reality. Often, however, their search takes them down paths that will not lead them to the living God.

If you know people like that, urge them to put aside whatever prejudices they may have against Jesus Christ and encourage them to seek God with an open heart and mind. God hasn't left us in the dark: He has revealed Himself to us through His Word and His Son.

Remember: God took upon Himself human flesh and became a man—a fact that should stagger our imagination. If we want to know what God is like, we only need to look at Jesus, for He was God in human flesh.

Pray for people you know who are seeking God, that they won't be deceived or led down a path that will only take them away from God. And ask God to use you to point them to Jesus' love and truth. Only Christ can meet the deepest hunger of our souls.

The Cure for Spiritual Cancer

Now in Christ Jesus you who once were far off have been brought near by the blood of Christ.

EPHESIANS 2:13

Suppose you had a deadly form of cancer, and one day you discovered a cure for it. Wouldn't you want other people who had that same disease to know what you had learned? Wouldn't you try to point them to the same discovery you had made? I'm sure you would; it would be monstrous to do otherwise.

The Bible teaches that we all have a spiritual cancer—a deadly spiritual disease called sin. Not only does it cripple us right now morally and spiritually, but it will also destroy us in the future and keep us from the blessings God has for us in Heaven.

Is there any answer to this spiritual cancer? Yes! The answer is Christ, who came "to reconcile to himself all things . . . by making peace through his blood, shed on the cross" (Colossians 1:20 NIV).

Show that you care about your friends by letting them know that you've found the cure for our spiritual cancer. Who in your life needs to know that good news today?

Our Omnipotent Helper

*"The Spirit of truth who proceeds from the
Father, He will testify of Me."*

JOHN 15:26

God the Holy Spirit is equal with the Son and with the Father in every respect. Although the doctrine of the Trinity is difficult for us to understand, the Bible teaches that He is coequal with God the Father and coequal with God the Son.

The Bible also teaches that the Holy Spirit is a person. He is never to be referred to as "it." He is not an impersonal power or force, nor is He just a divine influence or agent. He is a mighty person, the Holy Spirit of God.

The Bible tells us as well that the Holy Spirit is omnipotent. That means He has all power. The Bible also tells us that He is omnipresent. That means He is everywhere at the same time.

What should this mean to me? With the seventeenth-century Anglican bishop Jeremy Taylor, I can say, "It is impossible for that man to despair who remembers that his Helper is omnipotent."

Sufficient Grace

My grace is sufficient for you.
2 CORINTHIANS 12:9

The prayer of Jesus in the Garden of Gethsemane is perhaps the greatest, most moving prayer ever uttered. In it our Lord asked that the cup of crucifixion, which was about to be thrust upon Him, might be taken away. But then, in the very next breath He said, "Nevertheless, not as I will, but as You will" (Matthew 26:39). What a prayer! What strength! What power!

When the apostle Paul asked God to remove his "thorn in the flesh," God did not remove it, saying instead, "My grace is sufficient for you" (2 Corinthians 12:9). Rather than complain or become angry at God, Paul joyfully submitted to God's will. He discovered that God's grace truly was sufficient, even in the midst of pain.

Christ desires to be with you in whatever crisis you may find yourself. Call upon His name. See if He will not do as He promised He would. He may not make your problems go away, but He will give you the power to deal with them and to overcome them by His grace.

Loving and Just

The LORD our God is righteous in everything he does.

DANIEL 9:14 NIV

The Bible tells us that God is loving and merciful—and this is absolutely true. That truth, however, makes some people wonder how He could send anyone to Hell.

But do you honestly think God ought to excuse people like Hitler or Stalin, and tell them He doesn't really care that they killed tens of millions of innocent people? Do you really think God should welcome them into Heaven in spite of their relentless evil? I doubt if you do.

Sins like murder and rape and violence are an offense to our holy and pure God—as is every sin. God can't simply ignore evil or pretend it doesn't exist; to do so would be unjust. If someone hates God and chooses to do evil, God should not overlook that lifelong rebellion. The Bible is very clear: "He has set a day when he will judge the world with justice" (Acts 17:31 NIV).

Those of us who name Jesus as Savior and Lord, however, have trusted Him for our eternal salvation. And we know that someday evil will be destroyed and Christ will reign forever.

Changed for Life

We . . . are being transformed into the same image from glory to glory.

2 CORINTHIANS 3:18

You can scrub a pig, sprinkle Chanel No. 5 on it, put a ribbon around its neck, and take it into your living room. But when you turn it loose, it will jump into the first mud puddle it sees because its nature has never been changed. It is still a pig.

We constantly try to reform ourselves. Stores are filled with self-help books claiming to hold the secret to personal reformation. But such efforts are only temporary at best. A deeper transformation is needed—a transformation of the heart.

And it is possible! The Bible teaches that when we come to Christ, we are spiritually born again. God's Spirit comes to live within us and change us. Our motives change, our objectives change, our dispositions change, our eternal destiny changes.

No, it doesn't happen all at once. We will spend the rest of our lives learning what it means to follow Christ. But it begins now, as we open our hearts to Him. Is your life "being transformed . . . from glory to glory"?

Be Alert!

"Therefore keep watch because you do not know when the owner of the house will come back—whether in the evening, or at midnight, or when the rooster crows, or at dawn."

MARK 13:35 NIV

A re we living in the end times? Will Jesus return soon? The world does seem to be getting worse, and this should remind us that someday Christ will come again to bring an end to this present world.

Jesus taught that certain events or signs would point to His coming, and we certainly see many of these today. Jesus warned, for instance, that before He comes again "you will hear of wars and rumors of wars . . . famines, pestilences, and earthquakes in various places . . . false prophets will rise up and deceive many" (Matthew 24:6–7, 11). Satan will thrash about in one last burst of evil, hoping to capture as many souls as possible before his inevitable end.

So is Christ's coming near? It may well be—although the Bible warns us not to make precise predictions. But we must be alert and ready for His coming by being certain of our commitment to Christ and approaching every day as if it were our last.

Be a Blessing

*Bear one another's burdens, and so fulfill the
law of Christ.*

GALATIANS 6:2

Sadly, we often don't realize how heavy another person's burden is until we walk along a similar path.
Most of us are insensitive to the sufferings of others until
we experience them ourselves. We become wrapped up
in our own circumstances, and we overlook the needs
of those around us—even members of our own family.
But this isn't God's plan. We are to show our love by
bearing one another's burdens.

We can't change the past; it may be too late to apologize to someone for our thoughtlessness. But we don't
need to carry around a burden of guilt over this. When
Jesus died on the cross, He died for every sin you ever
committed, including this one. If you confess your sin,
He will cleanse you (1 John 1:9).

We can't change the past—but we can change our
behavior now. Ask God to help you be a burden-bearer
to those around you. Ask Him to show you how and to
whom you can be a blessing and an encouragement.
Whose burden will you help shoulder today?

Making Good Decisions

Then the king . . . rejected the advice of the elders.

2 CHRONICLES 10:13

Tragically, many people are the victims of their own bad decisions. Faced with choices every day, they turn their backs on what is right or what is best and decide instead on what is wrong or what will bring them harm. Only afterward do they realize that bad decisions always result in bad consequences.

King Rehoboam stubbornly rejected the wise advice of his nation's elders and instead followed those who told him only what he wanted to hear. As a result, conflict broke out and the nation divided. The Bible warns, "Whatever a man sows, that he will also reap" (Galatians 6:7).

Life is filled with decisions—some minor, but some life changing. How will you make them? The most important thing I can tell you is this: Seek God's will in every decision. Pray. Turn to the Scriptures. Seek the advice of godly friends. Ask the Holy Spirit to guide you. God loves you, and His way is always best.

Listening and . . .

There is a time for everything . . .
a time to be silent and a time to speak.
ECCLESIASTES 3:1, 7

When we are hurting, we value the presence of a friend who will just listen. But when someone we know is hurting, we often are tempted to do anything but listen. We chatter away and give unwanted advice to them, instead of just letting them share their burden with us.

But remember: sometimes the best thing we can do is listen quietly when friends have a problem, letting them share their feelings and assuring them that we care, even if we don't have any answers. In the midst of his suffering, Job cried out to those who were constantly giving him advice, "Oh, that you would be silent!" (Job 13:5).

In addition to listening, pray for your hurting friends—and let them know you are praying. And when you do talk with them, encourage them and urge them to commit their problem—and their entire life—into Jesus' hands. God can work in unexpected ways to bring good out of bad.

When your friends are hurting, ask God to help you be an encourager and a burden-bearer—for Jesus' sake.

What God Calls Wisdom

*He Himself is our peace, who . . . has broken
down the middle wall of separation.*

Some time ago, a university professor was quoted as saying, "There are two things that will never be solved—the problems of race and war." Perhaps he was right; only time will tell.

Admittedly, however, the Bible gives us little reason for optimism about any lasting solution to these problems. The reason? Both racism and war have their origin in the pride and covetousness of the human heart. Until our hearts are changed, we will fall back into the same destructive sins.

That doesn't mean we throw up our hands in despair and refuse to do anything about war or racism—not at all! The Bible calls Christ the "Prince of Peace" (Isaiah 9:6). He shattered the prejudices of His day by reaching out to those of another race, and He expects no less of us.

The object of the cross is not only pardon for our sins; it is also a changed life. Ask God to help you be an instrument of His love to those around you.

God Will Forgive

Cleanse me with hyssop, and I will be clean;
wash me, and I will be whiter than snow.

Psalm 51:7 niv

Do you believe that God can't forgive you for something you've done, even a long time ago? If so, know that those thoughts are actually from your Enemy, Satan. He will do almost anything to make us think God hates us and won't forgive us. One of his favorite tricks is to encourage us to keep dredging up the sins of the past, and he uses our memory of them to condemn us and tell us how terrible we are. That is why the Bible calls Satan "the accuser of our brethren" (Revelation 12:10). But his accusations are false!

Here is the truth: if you have honestly turned to Jesus and asked Him to forgive you, then you are forgiven—totally and absolutely. When Jesus died on the cross, every sin you ever committed—every one—was placed on Him. He died to pay the penalty for all your sins.

So don't believe your emotions and don't let the memories of the past defeat you. The Bible says, "The blood of Jesus Christ His Son cleanses us from all sin" (1 John 1:7). That is God's promise to you—and God cannot lie.

Truly Trusting

*Blessed is the man
who makes the Lord his trust.*

PSALM 40:4 NIV

Some years ago, someone gave my little boy a dollar. He brought it to me and said, "Daddy, keep this for me." But in a few minutes he came back and said, "Daddy, I'd better keep my own dollar." He tucked it in his pocket and went out to play. In a few minutes he came back with tears in his eyes, saying, "Daddy, I lost my dollar. Help me find it."

How often we commit our burdens to the Lord and then fail to trust Him by taking matters into our own hands. Then, when we have messed things up, we pray, "Oh, Lord, help me! I'm in trouble."

The choice is yours. Do you want to trust your life in God's "pocket" or keep it in your own? The Bible's promise is true: "Blessed is the man who makes the Lord his trust."

Never Too Late

Humble yourselves in the sight of the
Lord, and He will lift you up.

JAMES 4:10

He and his brother were in prison awaiting trial for selling drugs. In his letter he said, "We both know we've messed up our lives and . . . hurt our parents a lot." It was my privilege to reassure him that it is never too late to get back on God's path, the path his Christian parents had raised him to know. Nor is it ever too late for you to honestly face your sins and turn to Jesus in repentance and faith.

One reason this young man's parents are hurting is because they love him, yet he rejected them by his actions. In a far greater way, God loves each one of us, and yet we hurt Him deeply when we turn our backs on Him. But He loves us despite our sin, and He stands ready to forgive us. Forgiveness is not something we deserve; it only comes as a gift of God's grace.

I told this young man something you, too, may need to hear: don't let another day go by without Christ. No matter what the future holds, you will never be alone when Jesus lives within.

The Transfer Is Complete

*He made Him . . . to be sin for us, that we might
become the righteousness of God in Him.*

2 CORINTHIANS 5:21

When we come to Christ, the Bible says He imparts His righteousness to us. Once we were sinners in God's eyes; now He sees us as righteous because of Christ.

How could this happen? In ourselves we aren't righteous. As the Bible says, "There is none righteous, no, not one" (Romans 3:10). But when we accept Christ, the filthy rags of our sin are replaced by the glorious robe of Christ's righteousness. Our sins were transferred to Him—and His righteousness was transferred to us.

Did we deserve it? No. Did we earn it? No. It is all because of grace—all because of God's undeserved favor toward us in Christ. We can never win God's favor by our deeds, no matter how good we are. Only Christ can save us. Thank God that you now stand before Him, clothed in the perfect righteousness of Christ!

Hope for the Future

[Jesus] is able to save completely those who come to God through him, because he always lives to intercede for them.

HEBREWS 7:25 NIV

Sometimes life brings us to the point where we don't see much hope for the future. If you're there right now—whatever the situation, whatever the reason—let me assure you that God cares and that, because of Him, your future can be different.

Committing our lives to Christ or renewing our commitment to Him doesn't mean all our problems will suddenly vanish. We can't undo the past, and when we have made unwise decisions, we often have to live with the consequences. But isn't it better to face the future with God than without Him? God loves you, and even when life is dark and uncertain, that truth will bring you encouragement and strength.

Jesus knows what you are going through, and—as the verse above says—He is praying for you. So commit your problems and your future into His hands. Ask Him to help you make wise decisions about your future and to follow Him every day. Then "the God of hope [will] fill you with all joy and peace in believing" (Romans 15:13).

Keep Heaven in View

We are afflicted in every way, but not crushed.

2 CORINTHIANS 4:8 NRSV

I have found in my travels that those who keep Heaven in view remain serene and cheerful in the darkest day. If the glories of Heaven were more real to us, if we lived less for material things and more for things eternal and spiritual, we would be less easily disturbed by this present life.

This is not escapism, as some would argue. If anything, a firm faith in the future should make us more responsible in the present. All around us are people who never give a moment's thought to Heaven or eternity. How will they learn of the future if we don't tell them in the present? The real escapism, I would contend, is refusing to face the future that God has prepared for us.

In these days of darkness and upheaval and uncertainty, the trusting and forward-looking Christian remains optimistic and joyful, knowing that Christ someday must rule and that "if we endure, we shall also reign with Him" (2 Timothy 2:12).

Right and Wrong

Everyone did what was right in his own eyes.

JUDGES 21:25

Is our society today any different from the ancient society reflected in this verse? Sadly, not different enough. Too many people today feel that the old moral standards are useless and out of date, and they ought to be free to make up their own minds about what is right and what is wrong.

I wonder if we have honestly faced the logical result of this belief. What is actually being said is that there is no such thing as right or wrong, so we should be free to decide how we want to behave. But aren't things like racism and injustice and genocide always wrong? Shouldn't we always condemn as immoral a tyrant who allows millions of children to die of starvation?

The moral standards God has given us are always best—for society and for us as individuals. The reason is because He created us, He loves us, and He knows what is best for us. Don't be misled by those who deny God's moral standards. His way is always best.

Peace, Perfect Peace

"Peace I leave with you, My peace I give to you."

JOHN 14:27

Worry," says Vance Havner, "is like sitting in a rocking chair. It will give you something to do, but it won't get you anywhere." Worry and anxiety have hounded the human race since the beginning of time, and modern man with all his innovations has not found the cure for the plague of worry.

What is the answer? Imagine in your mind a ferocious ocean storm beating against a rocky shore. The lightning flashes, the thunder roars, the waves lash the rocks. But then imagine that you see a crevice in the rocky cliff—and inside is a little bird, its head serenely tucked under its wing, fast asleep. It knows the rock will protect it, and thus it sleeps in peace.

God promised Moses, "I will put you in the cleft of the rock, and will cover you with My hand" (Exodus 33:22). That is God's promise to us. Christ is our Rock, and we are secure in His hands forever. The storm rages, but our hearts are at rest.

JULY

The Call of Christ

The wisdom of this world is foolishness with God.

1 CORINTHIANS 3:19

Some may contend that the way for the Church to make the world a better place is to become like it. But whenever the Church does this, it ends up compromising its spiritual authority and losing its influence. Instead of changing the world, the world changes it.

God doesn't want us to isolate ourselves. In praying for His disciples, Jesus said, "As You sent Me into the world, I also have sent them into the world" (John 17:18). If we isolate ourselves from others, we have no impact and demonstrate a lack of love.

But neither does God want us to become like the unbelieving world. We are to be separate, refusing to adopt its motives, attitudes, and patterns of behavior. The Bible warns, "All that is in the world—the lust of the flesh, the lust of the eyes, and the pride of life—is not of the Father but is of the world" (1 John 2:16). Let Christ fill your life, and there won't be room for the world.

The Light of Salvation

Whoever confesses that Jesus is the Son of God,
God abides in him.

1 JOHN 4:15

Only when we comprehend the great price God was willing to pay for our redemption do we begin to realize that something is horribly wrong with the human race. It must have a Savior, or it is doomed!

Sin cost God His very best. Is it any wonder the angels veiled their faces and were silent in their consternation as they witnessed the outworking of God's plan? How inconceivable it must have seemed to them, when they considered the fearful depravity of sin, that Jesus should shoulder it all.

But they were soon to unveil their faces and offer their praises again. A light was kindled that day at Calvary—"the light of the gospel of the glory of Christ, who is the image of God" (2 Corinthians 4:4). The cross blazed with the glory of God as the most terrible darkness was shattered by the light of salvation. Satan's depraved legions were defeated; they could no longer keep humanity in darkness and defeat.

Has the light of the gospel shone in your heart? And is it shining through you to others?

A Clean Slate

Create in me a clean heart, O God,
And renew a steadfast spirit within me.
PSALM 51:10

Did you ever have the experience in school of erasing an entire blackboard? When the slate has been wiped clean, it is as if nothing at all had ever been written on it.

This is what God does for us when we come to Him, confessing our sin and trusting Christ as our Savior and Lord. First John 1:9 says, "If we confess our sins He is faithful and just to forgive us our sins and to cleanse us from all unrighteousness." Note what He promises to do: forgive and cleanse. The slate is wiped clean! Only God can do that. We can't do it ourselves.

How many times in your life have you wished you could start all over again with a clean slate, with a new life? Resolve right now to allow God to wipe your slate clean by confessing your sins and letting Him give you a brand-new start.

The Business of Our Lives

The proverbs of Solomon . . .
for acquiring a disciplined and prudent life,
doing what is right and just and fair.

PROVERBS 1:1, 3 NIV

The great eighteenth-century American preacher Jonathan Edwards wrote this about the Puritans who settled in America: "The practice of religion is not only their business at certain seasons, but the business of their lives."

The Puritans ordered their personal life, worship, church, business affairs, political views, even recreation according to the Bible's commandments. What a contrast to the permissiveness of our day!

Millions today want instant gratification. The whole world seems bent on pleasure, and there is an alarming preoccupation with self. When nations or individuals live only for pleasure, they begin to die morally and spiritually, oblivious to God's will and scornful of His judgment.

The Puritans knew that the life of faith is a struggle. Still, they persevered.

Like these spiritual forefathers, may it be said of us that our faith is "the business of [our] lives."

Strengthening Our Nation—One Child at a Time

Teach [God's words] to your children, talking about them when you sit at home and when you walk along the road, when you lie down and when you get up.

DEUTERONOMY 11:19 NIV

Abraham Lincoln once said, "The strength of a nation lies in the people—in the homes of the people."

The home today is disintegrating. There is concern, deep concern, for what our children are being taught or not being taught, whether at home or at school or in the media. They are no longer being taught what is right and wrong—and they are floundering. They don't know which way to turn.

I don't believe that young people today can live clean, pure lives without the help of God. The peer pressure is too great, and the temptations they see in the movies and on television and hear in their music are too much. Only Christ can protect them. Only Christ can give them the power to say no.

Who in your home . . . in your neighborhood . . . in your life . . . would God have you prayerfully and carefully teach His truth and His way? Start today.

Our Greatest Need

O Lord, revive thy work in the midst of the years.

HABAKKUK 3:2 KJV

I once asked a university professor what he thought our greatest need was. He said, "I may surprise you, because I'm not a religious man, but I believe that the greatest need that we have at this hour is a spiritual awakening that will restore individual and collective morals and integrity throughout the nation."

How do we achieve such a renewal? First, there must be prayer—the kind that springs from a deep-seated heart-yearning for revival. We do not need pious platitudes and religious mouthings—but earnest, fervent prayer.

Second, we Christians must forsake our sins, both individually and corporately. We must forsake our pettiness, our peevishness, our littleness, and our conflicts, as well as our evil ways.

Third, God must become real to us. Let the Bible's truth soak deeply into your heart and mind every day. Then you will rediscover that God is holy, righteous, absolute, personal, loving, and merciful—and this reality will be transferred into action, and revival can come. It has worked before in history. It will work again.

Praying for Your Nation

"If My people . . . pray and seek My face . . .
I will hear from heaven."
2 CHRONICLES 7:14

A great crisis in American history came at the Constitutional Convention called in Philadelphia to ratify a constitution for the new country that was being born. The delegates got angry with one another, and because they couldn't resolve their conflicts or agree on anything, they picked up their hats and coats and started to leave. Suddenly, Benjamin Franklin spoke up.

"What a minute, gentlemen," he is reported to have said. "This country was conceived in faith in God. Many of us here believe in prayer. Let us get upon our knees and pray to Almighty God and see whether God shall give to us the answer to our dilemma."

Upon their knees those men went, and out of that prayer meeting came the immortal Constitution of the United States of America.

What dilemma in your nation—or in your life—is compelling you to get down on your knees and seek God's answer?

A Statue of Liberty

"If the Son makes you free, you shall be free indeed."

JOHN 8:36

During the national observance of the hundredth anniversary of the Statue of Liberty in New York Harbor, I was struck by the great emphasis on the number of immigrants who had often left everything behind. Coming to America with nothing but the clothes on their backs, they risked their lives for something they valued more highly than everything they had left behind: freedom. They did not take their adopted country's hard-won freedom for granted—and neither must we.

Their experience is a picture of what we must do when we come to Christ. We must forsake our allegiance to this world, leave behind all that it offers, and become citizens of a new kingdom—the Kingdom of God. His statue of liberty is the cross.

The statue in New York Harbor lifts her lamp "beside the golden door." The statue of liberty on that hill outside Jerusalem lights the way into eternal life.

The Battle Rages

> *For our struggle is not against flesh and blood, but against the rulers, against the authorities, against the powers of this dark world and against the spiritual forces of evil in the heavenly realms.*

EPHESIANS 6:12 NIV

When we were in Romania, we visited a beautiful area known as Moldavia.

The bishop took us around Moldavia and showed us famous churches with paintings from scripture on them. In the past, before most people could read, they drew scenes from the Bible on the church walls and used those paintings to teach God's Word and His truth.

I will never forget one picture of a stairway to Heaven, with pilgrims going up the ladder. Below them are devils trying to pull them down into the flames of Hell. At the top of the picture, Jesus stands, waiting in Heaven for the faithful, and above the pilgrims are angels helping them along. That scene shows the great battle between good and evil, between God and Satan, that still rages today.

Today—and every day—put on the full armor of God to fight Satan's attacks, so you can and "be strong in the Lord" (Ephesians 6:10).

The Knowledge of God

*Oh, the depth of the riches both of the
wisdom and knowledge of God!*

ROMANS 11:33

It was the mystery of lightning (so the story goes) that
prompted Benjamin Franklin to attach a key to the
tail of a kite during a thunderstorm to prove the relationship between lightning and electricity. We have
always tried to understand the world around us; it is
one of the things that sets us apart from the animals.

Some of the mysteries of the past have been figured
out by science. Others still puzzle us. This fact remains:
all of the garnered wisdom of the ages is only a scratch
on the surface of humanity's search for the knowledge
of the universe.

This inability to comprehend fully the mysteries of
God's creation does not in any way cast doubt on the
Christian faith. On the contrary, it enhances our belief.
We do not understand the intricate patterns of the stars
in their courses, but we know that He who created them
does and that, just as surely as He guides them, He is
charting a safe course for us.

The next time you look into the heavens at night,
remember the words of the psalmist: "The heavens
declare the glory of God" (19:1).

Virtues for Living

Add to your faith goodness; and to goodness,
knowledge; and to knowledge, self-control; and to
self-control, perseverance; and to perseverance,
godliness; and to godliness, brotherly kindness; and to
brotherly kindness, love.

2 PETER 1:5–7 NIV

Loving God with our whole hearts, and loving our neighbor as ourselves—this is our primary calling as Christians.

Yet love is only one of the virtues God wants us to have. If we ignore the other virtues—such as joy, peace, patience, kindness, goodness, gentleness, and self-control (Galatians 5:22–23)—our life will be unbalanced and incomplete.

Why are these virtues so important? These virtues were part of Christ's character—and God's will is that we would become more like Christ. Furthermore, the apostle Peter said, "If you possess these qualities in increasing measure, they will keep you from being ineffective and unproductive" (2 Peter 1:8 NIV).

Ask God to show you if any of these virtues are missing in your life—and then open your heart and mind to Christ's transforming power and love.

A Glorious Grandstand

Since we are surrounded by so great a cloud of
witnesses, let us lay aside every weight.

HEBREWS 12:1

If the angels rejoice over one sinner who repents (Luke 15:10), then the angelic hosts are numbered among the spectators in the Heavenly grandstands. They are included among those who are referred to as "so great a cloud of witnesses" (Hebrews 12:1); and they never miss any of the details of our Earthly pilgrimages.

Nor does our God—Father, Son, and Holy Spirit—overlook what goes on here. As the Bible says, "All things are . . . open to the eyes of Him to whom we must give account" (Hebrews 4:13).

In his book *Though I Walk Through the Valley*, Dr. Vance Havner tells of an old preacher who worked into the night on a sermon for his small congregation. His wife inquired why he spent so much time on a message he would give to so few. To this the minister replied, "You forget, my dear, how large my audience will be!" Dr. Havner adds, "Nothing is trivial here if heaven looks on. We shall play a better game if, 'seeing we are encompassed,' we remember who is in the grandstand!"

The Day Is at Hand

Put on the armor of light.
Romans 13:12 nasb

I once read about a sundial on which was inscribed the cryptic message, "It is later than you think." Travelers would often pause to meditate on the meaning of that phrase. Its author undoubtedly wanted to remind others of the shortness and uncertainty of life.

We Christians have a sundial—the Word of God. From Genesis to Revelation it bears its warning: "It is later than you think." Writing to the Christians of his day, Paul said, "It is already the hour for you to awaken from sleep; for now salvation is nearer to us than when we believed. The night is almost gone, and the day is at hand. Let us therefore lay aside the deeds of darkness and put on the armor of light" (Romans 13:11–12 nasb).

Learn to live each day as if it were your last. Someday, it will be.

A Gospel of Crisis

Multitudes, multitudes
in the valley of decision!
For the day of the LORD is near
in the valley of decision.

JOEL 3:14

Christianity is a gospel of crisis. It is the gospel of good news, to be sure—the news that God has a plan for your life, that God loves you, that He is a God of mercy, that He will forgive, lead, and bless you if you confess and forsake your sins and trust Jesus Christ as your personal Savior and Lord.

But as far as the unbelieving world's understanding is concerned, Christianity is a gospel of crisis: it boldly proclaims that this world's days are numbered. Every cemetery testifies that our days on this planet are indeed numbered. The Bible teaches that life is only a vapor that appears for a moment and then vanishes (James 4:14).

There is another sense, however, in which the world-system will end: the end of history will come, and the end of a world that has been dominated by evil. Jesus will come again and set up His Kingdom of righteousness and social justice, and hatred, greed, jealousy, war, and death will no longer exist. Are you ready for that day?

Join me in praying, "Come quickly, Lord Jesus!"

God Feels What We Feel

*Through the LORD's mercies we are not consumed,
because His compassions fail not.*

LAMENTATIONS 3:22

When I was a small boy, I thought of God as an old man with a long white beard. After all, hadn't Michelangelo and other artists painted Him that way? Perhaps in my childish mind, I thought He resembled an old man in other ways also—somewhat feeble and harmless, not quite in touch with me and my problems.

Later, as I read the Bible, I realized that God is a spirit. He does not have a body, nor is He confined to one place as a physical being would be. At the same time, He has the attributes of a person: He thinks, He speaks, He communicates, He loves, He becomes angry, He grieves. Because God is a person, He feels what we feel.

No matter what we face, God understands what we are going through. He even understands our temptations, for Christ "has been tempted in every way, just as we are—yet was without sin" (Hebrews 4:15 NIV). And that is why you can bring anything—*anything*—to Him in prayer, confident that He will understand.

Whom Will You Serve?

*"These people come near to me with their mouth
and honor me with their lips,
but their hearts are far from me."*

<small>ISAIAH 29:13 NIV</small>

Do you serve God only with your lips? You profess God, you profess Christ, you go to church, you give to the church, perhaps you teach Sunday school or serve on the church board. But deep in your heart are you totally surrendered and committed to Christ?

Outwardly the Israelites in Joshua's day were followers of God—but in their hearts they were idolaters. Joshua told them that this hypocrisy could not continue. They were to decide whether they wanted to serve the true and living God or serve their idols. It was Israel's day of decision. They were to go on record—either for God or against Him.

Regardless of the decision his fellow Hebrews would make, Joshua declared, "As for me and my household, we will serve the LORD" (Joshua 24:15 NIV).

Likewise, we must decide whom we will serve. Will we forsake everything false and turn wholeheartedly to Jesus?

Will you decide to serve the true and living God? If so, what idols must you first forsake?

An Experience with God

I heard the voice of the Lord, saying: "Whom shall I send, and who will go for Us?"
Then I said, "Here am I! Send me."
ISAIAH 6:8

I think Isaiah 6 is one of the most unforgettable chapters in the Bible, for there we find Isaiah's intimate account of his experience with God.

First, Isaiah comprehended who God is. The ultimate experience of life is knowing God, and Isaiah came to know God in His righteousness and holiness.

Second, when Isaiah saw who God really is, his response was a deep conviction of his own sinfulness. Anyone who has genuinely seen God is deeply convicted of his or her own sin.

Isaiah's conviction about his sin led to confession, and then came cleansing as God touched a coal to Isaiah's lips, symbolizing the purging of his sin. Eight hundred years later Jesus would die on the cross so our sins could be washed away by His cleansing blood.

Finally came the challenge: we who see God as He is, are to see the world as He sees it—and then step out in faith to make difference.

What part of Isaiah's experience do you stand in need of today?

A Thirst for Righteousness

*"Blessed are those who hunger and
thirst for righteousness."*

MATTHEW 5:6

God is the only source of true happiness, because He alone offers those intangibles that we mistakenly believe can be found on Earth: contentment, security, peace, and hope for the future. None of these can be found in a job, a human relationship, money, power, or position. They are God's alone to give.

How hard it is for us to believe this, however! This is understandable if we haven't given our lives to Christ; then, the Bible says, our spiritual eyes are blind, unable to see God's truth until the Holy Spirit opens them. But blindness can happen to believers also when we fall into the pattern of the world, vainly pursuing happiness in the same ways the world does.

That is why the Lord Jesus, in His Sermon on the Mount, told us where ultimate happiness lies: "Blessed are those who hunger and thirst for righteousness, for they shall be filled" (Matthew 5:6). This is God's promise—and it is true.

Riches or righteousness? Which is your goal?

Pulling Out the Weeds

Let the word of Christ dwell in you richly.
COLOSSIANS 3:16

Have you ever had a weed in your yard that you chopped down and thought was gone—only to have it spring up again? Its roots, you discovered, were still alive, and they might even have spread.

Sinful thoughts can be like that. When we come to Christ, He begins to change our thinking, and new thoughts begin to take root in our mind—thoughts about God's love for us and His will for our life. But those old thoughts haven't been completely killed, and sometimes they suddenly spring to the surface. When they do, Satan will try to deceive us into thinking that we aren't new creations in Jesus after all, because we have failed Him.

Don't be surprised when old ways of thinking crop up—but don't let them linger. When they come, immediately turn to God and ask Him to help you get rid of them, just as you pull weeds out of your garden.

Most of all, let the Word of God fill you and renew your mind every day. When our minds are on Christ, Satan has little room to maneuver.

Peacemakers

"Blessed are the peacemakers,
for they shall be called sons of God."

MATTHEW 5:9

To have peace with God and to have the peace of God in our hearts is not enough. This vertical relationship must have a horizontal outworking, or our faith is in vain. Jesus said that we were to love the Lord with all our hearts and our neighbors as ourselves.

This dual love for God and others is like the positive and negative poles of a battery: unless both connections are made, we have no power. A personal faith is normally useless unless it has a social application. (A notable exception would seem to be the thief on the cross, who repented only moments before his death—and yet countless people have been touched over the centuries by his example of faith.)

If we have peace with God and the peace of God, we will become peacemakers. We will not only strive to be at peace with our neighbors, but we will be leading them to discover the source of true peace in Christ. Is the peace of Christ in your life overflowing to others?

I Am the Truth

*"You shall know the truth, and the truth
shall make you free."*
JOHN 8:32

Many today say there is no such thing as absolute truth. From philosophers to pop musicians, the word goes out that truth is only what you want it to be, and what is true for you isn't necessarily true for anyone else.

But Jesus Christ is absolute truth. Dozens of times He declares, "I tell you the truth." In one of His boldest and most uncompromising statements, He affirmed, "I am the way, the truth, and the life" (John 14:6). The apostle John stated, "Grace and truth came through Jesus Christ" (John 1:17). James said that God "chose to give us birth through the word of truth" (James 1:18 NIV).

Do not be misled by the moral and spiritual relativity of our age. God has revealed His truth to us—in His written Word, the Bible, and in the living Word, Jesus Christ. And because Jesus is absolute truth, you can depend on Him absolutely!

Blessed Assurance

[God] has also set eternity in the hearts of men.

ECCLESIASTES 3:11 NIV

How do we know that Heaven even exists? How do we know it isn't just a myth, a product of our imaginations?

Let me give you two reasons why we can know Heaven exists (although I could give other reasons). First, I am convinced Heaven exists because God has put the hope of Heaven within our hearts. That hope is almost universal, and it is part of every religion. The Bible says that this hope comes from God: He wants us to know that death is not the end and that we were meant to live forever with Him. As the verse above says, God placed within our hearts a yearning for Heaven.

The main reason I know Heaven exists, however, is the death and resurrection of Jesus. When He died on the cross, He erased the only thing that can keep us out of Heaven: our sin. When He rose from the dead, He guaranteed for all time that there is life after death and that Heaven is real. Jesus said, "I am going there to prepare a place for you" (John 14:2 NIV).

By a simple prayer of faith, ask Jesus to forgive your sins and come into your life. Then thank Him that someday you will go to be with Him in Heaven forever.

Pray for the Persecuted

Remember those in prison as if you were their fellow prisoners, and those who are mistreated as if you yourselves were suffering.

HEBREWS 13:3 NIV

F ew things touch my heart more than the news that some of my brothers and sisters in Christ are being persecuted, tortured, and killed for their love of Jesus.

It has been estimated that more Christians have been killed for their faith during the last one hundred years than in all the other centuries since the time of Christ combined. One reason is the great expansion of Christianity in the last few centuries—often into places of great unbelief and hostility. Another reason is the rise of militantly antireligious political systems.

Even where persecution isn't an issue, an upsurge in secularism and religious intolerance is apparent, and religion has been scorned and removed from public life. The Crucified One warned us: we who choose to follow Him would do so at the risk of rejection and persecution.

Thank God for whatever measure of religious freedom you enjoy—and pray today for those suffering for their faith in Christ.

Crucified with Christ

Be imitators of God as dear children.

EPHESIANS 5:1

The story is told of a man who glanced at the obituary column in his local newspaper. To his surprise he saw his own name, indicating that he had just died. At first he laughed about it. But soon the telephone began to ring. Stunned friends and acquaintances called to inquire and to offer their sympathy.

Finally, in irritation, he called the newspaper editor and angrily reported that, even though he had been reported dead in the obituary column, he was very much alive. The editor was apologetic and embarrassed. Then, in a flash of inspiration, he said, "Don't worry, sir! I'll make it right tomorrow—I'll put your name in the births column."

This may sound like merely a humorous incident, but it is also a spiritual parable. Not until we have allowed our old selves to be nailed to the cross and die can our new selves be born again and emerge to grow up into the likeness of Christ. The Bible is marvelously true: "You He made alive, who were dead in trespasses and sins. . . . Therefore be imitators of God as dear children" (Ephesians 2:1; 5:1).

God Promises Protection

"I will never leave you nor forsake you."
HEBREWS 13:5

Never doubt that you are in the midst of a battle—a spiritual battle with Satan, who will do everything he can to discourage and defeat you. Never underestimate his determination or misunderstand his intentions.

God wants to teach us how to defend ourselves against sin and Satan. Satan, the ultimate bully, attacks us at our weakest points and wants to defeat us so that we will not be effective for God.

God offers spiritual training to build us up inside in much the same way that physical exercise can build us up on the outside. He has also provided all the resources we need to defend ourselves and keep Satan at bay. These include the Bible, prayer, faith, righteous living, and the Holy Spirit within us.

But, like physical training, we must be diligent in their application. God has not promised to shield us from trouble, but He has promised to protect us in the midst of trouble. Most of all, never forget that because of Christ's death and resurrection, Satan is already a defeated foe—and someday the war will be over.

Wisdom—or Self-Centeredness?

*"Greater love has no one than this, that he lay
down his life for his friends."*

Has an unbeliever ever accused you of being a hypocrite because you didn't show them Christian love? We need to take such accusations seriously in case we have been at fault. But not every accusation like this is justified; sometimes the accuser is just being selfish, demanding, and unrealistic.

We aren't hypocritical just because we don't meet a person's every demand. Would we really be helping them if we met their every demand, no matter how selfish? We might just be encouraging greater self-centeredness on their part. Sometimes love says no because that is what is best for the other person.

If you can fulfill someone's request, however, do so even if it involves sacrifice on your part. The Bible says, "Let us not love with words or tongue but with actions and in truth" (1 John 3:18 NIV). This is the kind of love God showed us when He sent His Son into the world to die for our sins.

May you always be an example to others of Jesus' selfless love—and may He grant you wisdom to know what that will mean in every situation.

Making Us Like Christ

*We also rejoice in our sufferings, because we know
that suffering produces perseverance; perseverance,
character; and character, hope.*

ROMANS 5:3–4 NIV

God can take anything that happens to us—even
bad things—and use it to shape us and make us
into a better, more Christlike person—if we will let Him.

This doesn't mean God necessarily causes everything that happens to us; sometimes He only allows
things to happen. Often, for instance, bad things happen to us because we made bad decisions—decisions
that were the opposite of God's will for us. When that's
the case, we can't blame God for the consequences.

Sometimes we don't know why God allows bad
things to happen to us. Even then, however, God can
use them to teach us and make us into better people.
Disappointments and tragedies, for example, can teach
us to turn in trust to God for the hope and comfort we
need. These experiences can also teach us patience and
make us more sensitive to others who are suffering.

Are you passing through a difficult time today? Ask
God to use it to increase your faith and make you more
like Christ.

Beyond the Starry Sky

We are looking for the city that is to come.

HEBREWS 13:14 NRSV

P aul looked forward to death with great anticipation. He said, "For to me, to live is Christ and to die is gain" (Philippians 1:21 NIV). Death for him was not an enemy to be feared, but a reality to be welcomed in God's time. For Paul, death was the joyous gateway to new life—the life of Heaven.

Without the resurrection of Christ, we could have no hope for the future. The Bible promises that someday we are going to stand face-to-face with the resurrected Christ. All our questions will be answered, and all our sorrows and fears will vanish. An old gospel hymn puts it well:

> *Face to face with Christ, my Savior,*
> *Face to face, what will it be,*
> *When with rapture I behold Him,*
> *Jesus Christ, who died for me?*
> *Face to face I shall behold Him,*
> *Far beyond the starry sky;*
> *Face to face in all His glory*
> *I shall see Him by and by!*
>
> —CARRIE E. BRECK

The Blessing of Burdens

The LORD has comforted his people,
and will have compassion on his suffering ones.
ISAIAH 49:13 NRSV

C omfort and prosperity have never enriched the world as much as adversity. Out of pain and problems have come the sweetest songs, the most poignant poems, the most gripping stories, the most inspiring lives.

Yet it is hard to think about this when troubles overwhelm us or uncertainty and fear grip our hearts. Our problems are real, and it is difficult in the heat of the moment to think of anything else.

Our oldest daughter married a Swiss, and they often spend the summer in Switzerland. Sometimes when we have visited them, we have soared above the countryside on chairlifts high in the Alps. Looking down we can see almost a carpet of wildflowers, some of the most beautiful in the world. Only a few months before, those plants were buried under heavy snow. Yet that snow prepared the way for their growth—providing them with water and even insulating them from the winter winds. Our burdens can be like that snow, preparing the way for something beautiful once the winter is past.

Time for a U-Turn?

There is a way that seems right to a man,
but in the end it leads to death.

PROVERBS 16:25 NIV

Are you walking on a path that you are realizing is not God's best for you? Do you need to make a complete U-turn, but are struggling to find the courage to do so? For example, is it time to end a wrong relationship, cast off a habit that isn't healthy, or leave behind an undisciplined life that always seems to put God in second place?

Whatever situation has you feeling stuck, know that there is no shortcut or easy way out. You need to make the right decision—firmly and decisively—and then stick with it with God's help. You may need to get family members or friends to pray for you and support you.

There is no time like the present to begin building— or rebuilding—your life on the foundation of Christ and His will for you. He loves you, and He knows what is best for you. Don't be satisfied with anything less than His will for you—for His will is always best.

Which Road?

*"Small is the gate and narrow the road that
leads to life, and only a few find it."*
MATTHEW 7:14 NIV

You may not be old enough to remember July 16,
1969, but on that historic day, American astronauts
astonished the world with their spectacularly successful first visit to the moon. They were able to succeed
because they steered the Apollo 11 craft along a very
narrow trajectory through space. No deviation was permitted, and flight corrections were made periodically
throughout the historic voyage.

Now suppose the NASA control center in Houston
had received word from Apollo 11 that the astronauts
were off-course and replied, "Oh, that's all right. A
number of roads lead to the moon. Just keep going the
way you are going." You and I know they would have
kept going—but they would never have come back.

People today don't like the word *narrow*, but Jesus
clearly said there are two roads to the future for all of
us: the path to Hell and destruction is broad, but the
way to Heaven is narrow. Which road are you on? Is a
course correction necessary?

Only One Way

Whoever desires, let him take the water of life freely.

REVELATION 22:17

A driver stopped to ask the way to a certain street. When told, he asked doubtfully, "Is that the best way?" The man replied, "That is the only way."

There is only one way of salvation—and that is Christ. Jesus said, "No one comes to the Father except through Me" (John 14:6). Peter declared, "There is no other name under heaven given among men by which we must be saved" (Acts 4:12).

Is this arrogance or intolerance? No—and Christians must never be guilty of those attitudes. We are saved solely by God's grace; we do not deserve it. But Christ was God's appointed means of salvation. Only Christ died for our sins; only Christ rose from the dead.

God's offer of forgiveness and new life still stands. If you have never done so, turn to Christ today. And if you do know Him, pray today for someone you know who does not yet believe, and ask God to help you tell that person of His salvation.

Committed Love

Perfect love casts out fear.
1 JOHN 4:18 NIV

When I understand something of Christ's love for me as a sinner, I respond with love for Christ—and that love includes feelings and emotions.

But emotions come and go, and we must not allow them to mislead us. God loves me, whether I feel it or not. Christians who gauge their relationship with Christ only by their feelings seldom have a stable spiritual life.

What makes the difference? It can be summarized in one word: *commitment*. Feelings come and go, but commitment stays. We who have committed our lives to Christ may feel joy, gratitude, love, and so on. But even when we don't have those feelings, our commitment keeps us true to Christ.

This commitment not only keeps us faithful to Christ when we don't feel like it, but it also keeps away negative emotions such as doubt and fear. John Witherspoon, the only cleric to sign the Declaration of Independence, once said, "It is only the fear of God that can deliver us from the fear of man."

Giving with Joy

*Each man should give what he has decided in his
heart to give, not reluctantly or under compulsion,
for God loves a cheerful giver.*

2 CORINTHIANS 9:7 NIV

Why give to God's work? After all (perhaps you've said to yourself), what good can my little amount do, when the needs are so great? Why bother to give?

But God looks at our finances differently. First, He knows that our giving is a measure of something far more important: the depth of our commitment to Jesus Christ. And it isn't a question of how much we give, but what our attitude is as we give. Do we give reluctantly, under compulsion, or perhaps to impress other people? If so, our giving strongly suggests that we love ourselves more than we love Christ. Don't let this be true of you.

But God also is able to take what we give and use it in ways we could never imagine. That extra dollar might keep a starving child alive one more day or bring the gospel to someone who would otherwise never hear of Jesus. Give prayerfully . . . give joyfully . . . and ask God to use your gifts to help others in the name of Jesus.

Trusting in God's Love

From everlasting to everlasting
*the L*ORD*'s love is with those who fear him.*
PSALM 103:17 NIV

Most of us are pretty good at worrying, aren't we? When worries come, however, I've found it helpful to counter them with the Bible's promises about God's steadfast love. He loves us and, no matter what happens to us, He never abandons us. We know this because Jesus Christ demonstrated God's love for us by giving His life for our salvation.

Does this mean that things will never go wrong or that we'll never have any problems? Absolutely not! But it does mean that nothing we experience ever catches God by surprise or is too big for Him to handle. Even when our day seems dark, God never leaves us, nor does He allow anything to come our way that can overwhelm us.

Make it a practice to thank God every day for the blessings you have. Thank Him each day for His love. Worries flee before a spirit of gratitude. Then, when problems do come, commit them in faith to God. Since God takes care of the smallest birds, Jesus said, can't we trust Him to take care of us? "Are you not much more valuable than they?" (Matthew 6:26 NIV).

Return to Me

The way of the LORD is strength for the upright.

PROVERBS 10:29

Because God is the giver and source of life, He has a legitimate claim upon our lives. He is our Heavenly Father, and He has the right to expect us to be His loyal and loving children. Because I am His child, He also longs to have fellowship with me.

The story of the prodigal son (which you can read in Luke 15:11–32) is a revelation of God's desire for human fellowship. He yearns over His children who have wandered far from Him and longs for them to come home and be near to Him.

All through the Bible we see God's patience and perseverance as He pursues misguided and obstinate men and women—men and women who were born to a high destiny as His sons and daughters, but who strayed from His side. From Genesis to Revelation God is constantly saying, "Return to Me."

No matter how far you have strayed, God still loves you, and He wants to welcome you home—forever.

Our Perfect Parent

So [Joseph] got up, took the child and his mother and
went to the land of Israel . . . and he went and lived in
a town called Nazareth.

MATTHEW 2:21, 23 NIV

I find it significant that God placed the young Jesus in a family. God knew that, with Mary and Joseph's love and guidance, His Son would grow "in wisdom and stature, and in favor with God and men" (Luke 2:52).

Twenty-one centuries later, this should happen in our families also. Parents are given the privilege—and responsibility—of teaching their children about God and helping them become wise in His ways. Yet we parents often fall short of God's design. When that happens, our children may grow angry and bitter, lashing out at us for the hurts we supposedly caused.

Did you allow anger and bitterness—even over things that happened many years ago—to poison your relationship with your parents? Don't let your parents' failures—real or imagined—hold you in their grip any longer. Instead, ask God to help you forgive the past. Then ask Christ to change you into the person He wants you to be. And if you are a parent, ask God to help you be a loving and wise guide for your children and to build your family on Christ and His will.

The Final Word

Forever, O LORD,
Your word is settled in heaven.

PSALM 119:89

As we survey the world with Bible in hand, we know we do not worship an absentee God. He is standing in the shadows of history, still working to bring His plans to completion.

Therefore we are not disturbed by the pictures of chaos, violence, bloodshed, and war that fill our television screens and flood our newspapers. We know these are the consequences of humanity's evil and sin, caused by our rebellion against God. Every headline, every news report confirms what the prophet Jeremiah said centuries ago: "The heart is deceitful above all things, and desperately wicked; who can know it?" (Jeremiah 17:9).

But never forget: God will speak history's final word. Every day, the world moves closer to the time when Christ will return, Satan will be defeated, and God's perfect plan will be fulfilled.

No matter how foreboding the future, the Christian knows the end of the story—and it is glorious! Don't lose heart. The best is yet to be!

Valuable to God

He who trusts in his riches will fall,
But the righteous will flourish like foliage.

PROVERBS 11:28

A certain rich man died and the question was asked at his funeral, "How much did he leave?"

"He left it all," came the reply.

Often I hear someone introduced this way: "This is Bob, and he works for . . . ," as if where a person works or what a person does determines his or her value. (I have noticed it is usually only the well-to-do or those who are thought of as "successful" who are introduced this way.)

Yet God does not judge us by our success. He loves each person the same. Your value and mine do not come from what we do, the clothes we wear, the house we live in, or the type of car we drive. Our value comes from the fact that God made us, God loves us, and Christ died for us. Our value comes from the fact that He adopted us into His family, and we are now His children forever.

Don't depend on possessions or position for your identity. Get your identity from Christ, for you are of infinite worth to Him!

Life-Changing Love

*If you confess with your mouth, "Jesus is Lord,"
and believe in your heart that God raised him
from the dead, you will be saved.*

One heartbreaking question I'm sometimes asked goes like this: "I've asked Christ to come into my life dozens of times, but He hasn't. Does God hate me?" Perhaps you have felt like this.

But the Bible's teaching is clear: God does not hate you. God loves you, and He wants to be part of your life even more than you want Him to! From beginning to end, the Bible proclaims this simple truth: God loves you.

Why, then, hasn't God apparently come into your life? The key word is *apparently*. If you have confessed your sin and acknowledged that Jesus is your Lord, who died on the cross for you and rose again to give you eternal life, then God has promised to forgive you and save you. God does not lie, and He has promised that if we truly commit our life to Christ, He will save us and come into our life. Salvation is God's gift to you—a gift paid for by Christ's sacrifice of Himself for you.

You may not feel any different, but you will be different because Christ now lives within you. Don't go by your feelings, but by the fact of God's promises to you.

Victory in Jesus

Thanks be to God, who gives us the victory through our Lord Jesus Christ.

1 CORINTHIANS 15:57 NRSV

Haydn, the great musician, was once asked why his church music was so cheerful. He replied, "When I think upon God, my heart is so full of joy that the notes dance and leap, as it were, from my pen, and since God has given me a cheerful heart, it will be pardoned me that I serve Him with a cheerful spirit."

Haydn had discovered the secret to lasting joy: "I think on God." Looking at our circumstances won't bring us lasting joy. It may even make us depressed or angry. But when we "think on God"—when we turn our minds and hearts to His power and His love for us—we can't help but be joyful. Paul said, "Set your mind on things above, not on things on the earth" (Colossians 3:2). Discouragement flees in the face of joy.

Every day brings battles and temptations. But the strength we need for conquering them comes from Christ. We can do like the little girl who said that when the devil came knocking with a temptation, she just sent Jesus to the door!

Meeting the Challenge

How can a young man keep his way pure?
By living according to your word.

PSALM 119:9 NIV

Young men aren't the only ones who find it challenging to live a pure life. All believers are called to be holy in mind, body, and spirit (1 Peter 1:15), and it certainly isn't easy. Advertisements and entertainment have become so saturated with sexual themes and images that it is difficult to avoid them. Greed, self-gratification, and the lust for power seem to drive our culture. We have become like the people of Jeremiah's day: "They have no shame at all; they do not even know how to blush" (Jeremiah 8:12 NIV).

If we are to be pure and holy, we must first commit ourselves—mind, body, and spirit—completely to Christ. We can't hold back any area of our life from Him. Second, we must avoid situations that might encourage impure thoughts or actions. And, third, we must fill our mind and heart with Christ by feeding our souls on a daily diet of prayer and God's Word. With God's help, we can keep our way pure by living according to His Word. Is this your goal?

Look to God

"Lift up your heads, because your redemption draws near."

<small>Luke 21:28</small>

If you've ever flown in an airplane, you know that your perspective of the Earth is far different from what it was when you were on the ground. Pictures of the Earth that have been taken from the moon and from space show an Earth that looks much different from what we see down here.

This is the kind of perspective God wants to give us concerning our lives. As we look to God instead of to ourselves and our circumstances, our perspective changes.

Don't get bogged down in the circumstances of life. At the moment we see only our immediate problems and burdens, but God sees the whole. He sees not only the present but the future as well. He wants to lift us above ourselves. He wants us to see everything in light of His plans. The psalmist said, "The Lord will perfect that which concerns me" (138:8).

Don't get bogged down. Keep your eyes on God, for He sees the whole picture and knows what is best for you. You can trust Him, because He loves you.

Serving God

*Be very careful to . . . serve him with all your
heart and all your soul.*

JOSHUA 22:5 NIV

What comes to mind when you hear the phrase *serving God*?

Maybe you think of missionaries or pastors. Maybe you think of qualifications like seminary training, a holy life, or a solid knowledge of God's Word. Or maybe you think of people who are younger and healthier than you or older and more experienced than you as the people God can use most effectively.

But listen: God wants to use you right where you are. Every day you probably come in contact with people who will never enter a church, talk with a pastor, or open a Bible—and God wants to use you to point them to Christ. You may be the bridge that God uses to bring them to Himself.

Be alert for opportunities to share the good news of Christ's love with others—even today. Never underestimate what God can do through even your smallest effort to reach out to others in the name of Jesus.

Nothing Is Too Hard!

*Sovereign LORD, you have made the heavens
and the earth by your great power. . . . Nothing
is too hard for you.*

JEREMIAH 32:17 NIV

Are there some things God cannot do? The answer may surprise you: yes, there are some things that God can't do.

God cannot, for instance, tell a lie or go back on His promises. Neither can He do something evil or have an impure thought. Why? Because God cannot do anything that is contrary to His basic character. Remember: God is not some vague force like gravity or electricity. He is a person, and He is holy and perfect in His character.

But the Bible's focus is on what God can do. Not only is He perfect, but He is also absolutely sovereign and all-powerful. And because of that—as Jeremiah wrote—nothing is too hard for Him. If He could bring Jesus back from the dead, can't He also help you overcome whatever situation you are facing today?

Put whatever burden you are carrying into His hands because He loves you, and nothing is too hard for Him.

A Solid Foundation

The LORD is my rock and my fortress and my deliverer.

2 SAMUEL 22:2

My children used to sing a song in Sunday school classes: "The wise man built his house upon the rock." A wise man does build his house upon the Rock—the Lord Jesus Christ and His Word—for nothing built of or on any other substance will stand the test of time.

In big cities I often see wrecking balls destroying old structures to make way for new ones. Some of these "old structures" in America are less than a hundred years old. In Europe, buildings several centuries old are common. But even these buildings will eventually be destroyed by a natural disaster, if not by man.

Only what is built on the solid foundation of Christ will last. Jesus said, "Everyone who hears these words of mine and puts them into practice is like a wise man who built his house on the rock" (Matthew 7:24 NIV). Are you listening to God's Word and putting it into practice every day?

Hope for Today, Hope for Eternity

I desire to depart and be with Christ,
which is better by far.

PHILIPPIANS 1:23 NIV

Her pain was more than physical. Over the years the crippling arthritis had taken its toll on her emotions as well, and now she was praying that God would take her to Heaven. Was this prayer, she asked me timidly, wrong or even sinful?

First of all, I reminded her, it is not a sin to long for Heaven. If we know Jesus, we know that in Heaven all our burdens and pain will be lifted forever. It is, as the apostle Paul stated, "better by far" to be in Heaven with Jesus than to be suffering on this sin-filled Earth.

At the same time, though, God has a purpose in keeping us here until He finally takes us home. He has things to teach us about Himself, and He can still use us to bless others. Only eternity will reveal the powerful ways God used the prayers and the witness of men and women who could no longer do everything they once did, but who still trusted God to use them.

Keep your eyes on eternity—but also seek Christ's will for you right now, no matter what you are facing.

A Gentle Kindness

The Lord's servant must not be quarrelsome
but kindly to everyone.

2 TIMOTHY 2:24 NRSV

Jesus was a gentle and compassionate person. When He came into the world, there were few hospitals, few places of refuge for the poor, few homes for orphans. There were no hospitals to treat the mentally ill, no shelters for the homeless. In comparison to today, it was a cruel world.

Christ changed all that. He healed the sick, fed the hungry, and opened the eyes of the blind. He commanded His disciples, "Love your neighbor as yourself" (Matthew 19:19) and taught them to observe what we have come to call the golden rule: "In everything, do to others what you would have them do to you" (Matthew 7:12 NIV). Wherever true Christianity has gone, Jesus' followers have performed acts of kindness, love, and gentleness.

Do others see Christ's gentleness and compassion in you?

Overcoming Tribulation

*"You will have tribulation; but be of good
cheer, I have overcome the world."*

JOHN 16:33

When trials come, we sometimes act as if God is on vacation. We question God: *Why is this happening to me? What did I do to deserve this? Why am I going through this difficult circumstance? What's wrong with You, God?!*

But such complaining is shortsighted and wrong. God is far higher than we are, so who are we to say He is wrong or tell Him what He ought to be doing? As God reminded Job, "Where were you when I laid the foundations of the earth?" (Job 38:4). Such complaining also shows a lack of faith: we are doubting God's wisdom and His love for us.

Read the promises of Scripture for the answer. Jesus said, "In the world you will have tribulation." He didn't say that you could have tribulation or that if you aren't a good person, tribulation will come your way. Jesus flatly stated you will have tribulation. It is as certain as growing older.

But the wonderful promise of Christ is that while you will have trials and tribulations, "Be of good cheer. I have overcome the world."

Easier Said than Done

*If it is possible, as far as it depends on you,
live at peace with everyone.*

ROMANS 12:18 NIV

God's will is for us to live at peace with everyone, but sometimes the door to a broken relationship seems closed forever. The marriage has died, or the children are rejecting you. Your father abandoned your family, or your disapproving mother has cut off all contact. A business partner has turned away in anger, or a former friend wants nothing to do with you.

If someone rejects us and absolutely refuses to have anything to do with us, we can't force that person to change. But we can—and should—do everything we can to keep the door open to a possible reconciliation. We shouldn't strike back or condemn; instead, we should let them know we still care and that we hope someday his or her attitude will change. And if we were at fault—even in small ways—we need to admit it and ask for forgiveness.

We also should pray. We can't change the person we're estranged from, but God can. Even when the door seems firmly closed, God is able to open it. Do all you can to restore that broken relationship—and trust God for the outcome.

Joy on the Journey

*The joy of the L*ORD *is your strength.*

NEHEMIAH 8:10

Some people have a warped idea of the Christian life. Seeing talented, successful Christians, they attempt to imitate them. But when they discover that their own gifts are different or their contributions are more modest (or even invisible), they collapse in discouragement and overlook genuine opportunities that are open to them. They have forgotten that they are here to serve Christ, not themselves.

Be like the apostle Paul and say, "None of these things move me" (Acts 20:24). Few men suffered as Paul did, yet he learned how to live above his circumstances—even in a prison cell. You can do the same. The key is to realize you are here to serve Christ, not yourself.

God does not promise us an easy life, free of troubles, trials, difficulties, and temptations. He never promises that life will be perfect. He does not call His children to a playground, but to a battleground. In the midst of it all, when we serve Christ, we truly discover that "the joy of the LORD is [our] strength."

God's Household

*[You are] fellow citizens with God's people and
members of God's household.*

EPHESIANS 2:19 NIV

S omeone once described a church as a group of por-
cupines in a snowstorm: we need each other to keep
warm, but the closer we get, the more we poke each
other—and the more uncomfortable we become.

But of course, it shouldn't be that way. A church
should be a place of warmth and fellowship, a place
where even the newest member or latest visitor feels
welcome and at home. Is this true in your church?
Simply attending a worship service doesn't automatically mean closer relationships with others.

If you are an old-timer in your church, go out of your
way to welcome visitors and new members. And if you
are a visitor or new member, make a special effort to
get to know people. What Bible classes are held? Does a
group of people your age meet regularly? Don't depend
only on one worship service a week to help you meet
people or grow closer to Christ.

If this step sounds a little daunting, remember that
your best Friend of all—Jesus Christ—will be with you
each step of the way.

Committing Your Life to Jesus

Salvation is found in no one else, for there is no other name under heaven given to men by which we must be saved.

Acts 4:12 niv

Suppose you are riding down a road and you come to a deep gorge. The bridge has been washed away, and jumping across the gorge is not an option. Seemingly, you have no hope of reaching your destination.

But then you notice another bridge some distance away. You watch people cross it to the other side. It certainly seems sturdy.

What would you have to do to get across? First, believe that the bridge will hold you. Then, commit yourself to it: put your full weight on it and walk across it.

This illustrates what it means to commit your life to Jesus Christ. By His death and resurrection, Jesus bridged the gap between us and God—a gap caused by sin. But simply believing intellectually that He has done this is not enough. Like that bridge across the gorge, we must trust Him and commit our lives to Him. And when we do, we will discover that He can be trusted to save us, because He truly is the bridge between us and God.

Have you committed your life in faith and trust to Jesus Christ as your "bridge" and your Savior?

A Victorious Christian

The Spirit also helps in our weaknesses.

ROMANS 8:26

We need to rely constantly on the Holy Spirit. We need to remember that Christ dwells in us through the Holy Spirit. Our bodies are the dwelling place of the third person of the Trinity.

Why don't we rely on Him as we should? We don't realize how weak we are. We don't realize how strong our Enemy is. We may even doubt if God is really going to help us. Or we think we can do it all ourselves—or that we must.

But we should ask God to take over in our lives. We should tell Him how weak, helpless, unstable, and unreliable we are. It is important that we stand aside and let Him take over in all our choices and decisions. We know that the Holy Spirit prays for us (Romans 8:26), and what a comfort that should be to the weakest of us.

A victorious Christian is one who, in spite of worries, inner conflicts, and tensions, is confident that God is in control and will be victorious in the end. Whatever our difficulties, whatever our circumstances, we must remember, as Corrie ten Boom used to say, "Jesus is victor!"

When God Calls

> *[God] said to [Paul], "My grace is sufficient for you,*
> *for my power is made perfect in weakness."*
> 2 CORINTHIANS 12:9 NIV

God says the same thing to you that He said to Paul when He calls you into service for His Kingdom.

Perhaps you are asked to teach a Sunday school class. You feel inadequate, unsure that you know enough about the Bible. When an invitation like this comes, pray. Ask God if He wants you to accept this responsibility even if you don't feel qualified or prepared. If God wants you to serve in this position, He will make it clear to you.

Once you accept the invitation to serve, know that as you turn to God and rely on Him, He will empower and guide you. Do all you need to do to be ready to serve in whatever capacity God calls you—and realize that the knowledge of God's Word is an essential tool for any aspect of Kingdom work.

Don't be afraid to take a step of faith in response to God's call to serve. It is a wondrous thing to have God's power be made perfect in our weakness as He uses us for His eternal work.

Guiding Light

Choose this day whom you will serve.

JOSHUA 24:15 NRSV

Repeatedly in the Bible, both nations and individuals had to make decisions affecting their futures—and so do we. Sometimes they made wrong choices and suffered the consequences as a result.

When we face decisions, we need to remember that God hasn't left us in the dark, nor is He uninterested. God loves us, and He wants what is best for us. He has a perfect path in life for us, and He wants us to choose it instead of the wrong paths Satan would tempt us to follow.

Even when our way seems unclear, God gives us light. He gives us His Word, the Bible—and many of our decisions would be much easier if we only knew its moral and spiritual principles. He also gives us wisdom (sometimes through other people) to understand our situation, and He gives us the Holy Spirit to guide us.

Never make a decision without committing it to God and seeking His will. He promises to guide you—and He will.

Simple Trust

Trust in the Lord with all your heart,
And lean not on your own understanding.

PROVERBS 3:5

There will always be secrets and motives of God that lie beyond our grasp. God knows everything; we do not. Only in Heaven will we understand God's ways more fully. As Paul said, "Now I know in part, but then I shall know just as I also am known" (1 Corinthians 13:12).

But based upon what we do know about God's character, demonstrated supremely in the cross, we can trust that God is doing what is best for us. God says in His Word, "I know the plans I have for you . . . plans to prosper you and not to harm you, plans to give you hope and a future" (Jeremiah 29:11 NIV).

As Corrie ten Boom once explained, "Picture a piece of embroidery placed between you and God, with the right side up toward God. Man sees the loose, frayed ends; but God sees the pattern."

God is in control. Whatever comes into our lives, we can confidently say, "We know that all things work together for good to those who love God, to those who are the called according to His purpose" (Romans 8:28).

Louder than Words

I urge you to live a life worthy of the calling you have received.

EPHESIANS 4:1 NIV

Someone has wisely observed that the only Bible some people will ever read is the one they see demonstrated in the life of a Christian.

In other words, the way we live often speaks far louder than our words. People may tell us they don't believe the Bible—but they can't deny its power as they see it change our life, guide our decisions, and influence how we live.

What do people see when they look at you? Do they see someone whose life reflects Christ? Do they see in you the Christlike traits of love, joy, peace, patience, kindness, goodness, faithfulness, gentleness, and self-control (Galatians 5:22–23)?

Ask God to rule in your heart and to remake you from within into the person He wants you to be. Then ask Him to help you be sensitive to those around you who may be successful on the outside, but inwardly are empty and confused, so that by your life and your words they may discover the joy and peace that come from knowing Christ.

The Light of Life

Your faith and hope are in God.

1 PETER 1:21 NIV

We get so used to this world that we lose sight of the next. We get so used to the darkness and chaos of this world's suffering and violence that we lose sight of the brightness of Him who alone could say, "I am the light of the world. He who follows Me shall not walk in darkness, but have the light of life" (John 8:12).

He alone is "the Lamb of God who takes away the sin of the world!" (John 1:29). He alone is the Hope of the hopeless, the Savior of the lost, the Guide of the wandering. He alone is "the radiance of God's glory and the exact representation of his being, sustaining all things by his powerful word" (Hebrews 1:3 NIV).

Today world leaders struggle with almost insurmountable problems—and they always will. But in the midst of this world's persistent darkness, never lose sight of Jesus. He alone is the hope of the world—and He is your hope as well.

Fully Man—and Fully God

*The Son is the radiance of God's glory and the
exact representation of his being.*

HEBREWS 1:3 NIV

T he Bible's message is centered in Jesus Christ,
God's one and only Son—who He is and what He
has done for us by His death and resurrection. When
we read its pages, we discover that Jesus was not only a
great man, but He was God in human flesh, "the exact
representation of [God's] being."

Why is this important? Because only a divine Savior
can save us from our sins. We cannot save ourselves;
even one sin, the Bible teaches, would be enough to keep
us out of Heaven. Nor can a Savior who is less than God
save us, for only God can forgive sin and make us part of
His family forever. This is why "salvation is found in no
one else, for there is no other name under heaven given
to men by which we must be saved" (Acts 4:12 NIV).

Tonight—even as you close this book—pause and
thank God for coming to Earth in the person of Jesus
Christ, His Son. And thank Him that, because of Jesus,
we know God loves us and that someday we will be with
Him and see Him in all His glory.

Effective Prayer

"Before they call, I will answer;
And while they are still speaking, I will hear."

Isaiah 65:24

John Knox spent much time in prayer, and the Church in Scotland burst into new life. John Wesley prayed long and often, and the Methodist movement was born. Martin Luther prayed earnestly, and the Reformation exploded across Europe.

Why was prayer so important to these spiritual giants of the past? Because they knew they were up against almost overwhelming forces of spiritual opposition. They knew the urgency of the gospel message, and they understood that prayer is an essential weapon in advancing the gospel to the ends of the Earth. Like Paul, they knew that "the weapons of our warfare are not carnal but mighty in God for pulling down strongholds" (2 Corinthians 10:4). Is our situation any different today?

God desires that we Christians be concerned and burdened for a lost world. If we pray this kind of prayer, an era of peace may come to the world and wickedness may be turned back. "The effective, fervent prayer of a righteous man avails much" (James 5:16).

When Judgment Comes

For it is time for judgment to begin with the family of
God; and if it begins with us, what will the outcome
be for those who do not obey the gospel of God?

1 PETER 4:17 NIV

Does God's judgment happen only after we die? Or does it take place now, before we die?

The answer is both. Someday we each will die and stand before God to give an account of our lives—and if we have ignored God and turned away from His offer of salvation, we can only expect His judgment. The Bible is clear: "Man is destined to die once, and after that to face judgment" (Hebrews 9:27 NIV). Those are sobering words that we ignore at our peril.

But the Bible warns us that God also brings judgment upon us in this life. The Bible says, "You may be sure that your sin will find you out" (Numbers 32:23 NIV). The headlines are filled with people who thought they could sin and get away with it—only to have their sin come out in the open and bring their lives crashing down.

Don't ever take God's judgment lightly—and don't ever take sin lightly. God doesn't take them lightly. The proof is that they cost His dear Son His life.

AUGUST

Prayer Releases God's Power

Pray without ceasing.
1 THESSALONIANS 5:17

How many times have you heard someone say, "All I can do is pray"?

All I can do is pray?! You might as well say to a starving man, "All I can do is offer you food," or to a sick person, "All I can do is give you medicine that will make you well," or to a poor child, "All I can do is buy the toy you most want for your birthday."

Praying unlocks the doors of Heaven and releases the power of God. James 4:2 says, "You do not have because you do not ask." The Bible says, "Be anxious for nothing, but in everything by prayer and supplication, with thanksgiving, let your requests be made known to God" (Philippians 4:6).

And we are to let God know not only our needs but also the needs of others. So often our prayers focus only on ourselves. But God wants to use us, through our prayers, to touch the lives of other people as well. For whom should you be praying this day?

Freely and Fully Forgiven

As far as the east is from the west,
so far has He removed our transgressions from us.

PSALM 103:12

If you could know beyond a shadow of a doubt that God had completely forgiven you, what reason would you have to keep feeling guilty? Absolutely none.

Well, God offers you exactly that: complete and total forgiveness, no matter what you have done. Jesus willingly took your sins and mine upon Himself, and He paid the penalty we deserved. The Bible puts it this way: "For God made Christ, who never sinned, to be the offering for our sin, so that we could be made right with God through Christ" (2 Corinthians 5:21 NLT).

We don't need to wonder if we've been forgiven; we don't need to carry around a burden of guilt. If memories from the past return, immediately remind yourself of the truth of 1 John 1:9—"If we confess our sins, he is faithful and just and will forgive us our sins and purify us from all unrighteousness" (NIV). Then thank God for forgiving you, freely and fully, because of Christ's sacrifice for you.

Growing Through Fellowship

For we are members of [Christ's] body.

EPHESIANS 5:30

The only thing that counts as far as our salvation is concerned is our relationship to Jesus Christ. If you have acknowledged your sinfulness and truly trusted Christ to save you, then nothing can take away your salvation.

If we are committed to Jesus, however, God also wants us to become part of a fellowship of believers. God wants us to grow in our faith, and one of the ways we do this is through our fellowship with other believers. The Bible says, "As iron sharpens iron, so one man sharpens another" (Proverbs 27:17 NIV). It also says, "Let us not give up meeting together . . . but let us encourage one another" (Hebrews 10:25 NIV).

Ask God to lead you to a church—to a body of believers—where you can grow spiritually. God will use the preaching of His Word and the congregation's worship to encourage and strengthen you. Also get involved in other activities in your church—a Bible study, a prayer group, or a service project. God will use them to help you grow in your faith—and He also will use you to help others.

Choose Life

I have set before you life and death . . .
therefore choose life.
DEUTERONOMY 30:19

Before the space shuttle program, American ships and helicopters would recover astronauts whose tiny space capsules had parachuted into the enormous sea. The astronauts would be lifted out of their capsule into a helicopter, which would then fly them to the safety of the ship.

I often thought, as I watched these scenes on television, how like God this operation was. God hovers over the entire world, seeking to pluck from sin those immortal souls in danger of drowning in Hell. He tosses out a line to all those who are in trouble. Some grab on to God's line and freely receive the gift of His Son, Jesus Christ. They are pulled to safety and, eventually, taken to Heaven.

But others ignore the line or even knock it away, believing they are not really in peril or that they can make it to safety on their own. Tragically, they are lost not because God has rejected them, but because they have rejected God.

Don't make the wrong choice!

Our Sovereign God

Do you show contempt for the riches of his kindness, tolerance and patience, not realizing that God's kindness leads you toward repentance?

ROMANS 2:4 NIV

Has it ever bothered you that some people who turn their backs on God seem to go through life without ever having anything bad happen to them? Life is so easy for them that they can't see any reason to bother with God.

But we don't know their hearts. Deep inside they may actually be very insecure and fearful—and they may not even be able to admit it to themselves.

We also need to remember that God sees the whole picture, while we see only a little part. God knows what He is doing, and He can be trusted to do what is right according to His perfect plan.

Sadly, these people will one day die and face judgment. God's goodness to them should have caused them to turn to Him in thankfulness and trust, but instead they ignored His blessings and lived only for themselves. How tragic!

Ask God to use you to point others to Christ—even those who seemingly have no interest in Him.

Christ—Our Example

He learned obedience by the things
which He suffered.

HEBREWS 5:8

The main reason Jesus died on the cross was to save us from our sins. But the New Testament also stresses the importance of His suffering as an example for us.

The Greek word for *example* comes from ancient school life. It refers to something written down by a teacher so it could be followed and copied exactly by a child learning to write. Christ is our copybook. We look to Him as our teacher: His suffering gave us an example to follow, so we can learn how suffering is to be borne.

How did Jesus bear it? By not giving in to despair or doubt. By looking beyond His suffering and seeing the glory that was to come. By remembering that the Father was with Him and would use His suffering for good. We can do the same.

The author of Hebrews wrote, "Consider him who endured such opposition from sinful men, so that you will not grow weary and lose heart" (12:3 NIV). Yes, consider Him.

Patience and Perfection

The testing of your faith produces patience.
JAMES 1:3

Patience isn't easy for most of us. If a plane is delayed a few minutes or something doesn't happen exactly when or how we expected it to, we get impatient and frustrated. I have heard of people who quit going to a particular church because the preacher didn't stop exactly on time! James said, "Be *patient*, then, brothers, until the Lord's coming. See how the farmer waits for the land to yield its valuable crop and how *patient* he is for the autumn and spring rains. You too, be *patient* and stand firm, because the Lord's coming is near" (James 5:7–8 NIV, italics mine).

Patience is not simply teeth-clenched endurance. It is an attitude of expectation. The farmer patiently watches his barren ground because he knows there will be results. He has patience as he labors because there will be products of his labor.

So it is in the spiritual realm. God knows the final product of what is happening to us, so He would have us link patience to our faith. Ask God for the gift of patience—and then use it.

Satan's Persistence

*The devil . . . was thrown into the lake of burning
sulfur . . . tormented day and night for ever and ever.*
REVELATION 20:10 NIV

God—who cannot lie—assures us that this is what awaits Satan. So why doesn't the Enemy just give up and stop bothering us?

Perhaps he still expects to win. After all, Satan totally rejects everything about God—including His promises. Even in the garden of Eden, Satan rejected God's words and branded God a liar (Genesis 3:1–4). Perhaps Satan still rejects everything God says, even what He says about his own destiny.

But Satan also persists because he has one main goal: to block God's work in any way he can. As long as he is active, people will be deceived into following his way instead of God's way. Even believers can be diverted from God's plan for their life and be content with a lukewarm faith that makes little impact on others.

Yes, someday Satan will be defeated—but in the meantime, we must be on our guard, because he "prowls around like a roaring lion looking for someone to devour" (1 Peter 5:8 NIV). Don't be his next victim!

Peace on Earth?

He Himself is our peace.

EPHESIANS 2:14

For as long as I can remember there have been innovative ideas for bringing peace to this Earth. Organizations have been created, much money and time have been spent, treaties have been signed, books have been written—all in an effort to find a formula that would bring peace on Earth and goodwill to men.

World War I was called "the war to end all wars," but it wasn't. Whether nations fight one another or not, there is warfare in the home: warfare between husband and wife, between parents and children, between brothers and sisters, between neighbors, between boss and employee.

What can be done? It sounds almost simplistic to say we need to turn to God, but that is the only lasting solution. Only God can remove the poisons of greed and hatred and jealousy in our hearts, and replace them with contentment and compassion and forgiveness. Only He can subdue the violence and anger that rage within us, and replace them with His peace and love.

Whatever wars rage in your life, lay them at the foot of the cross and ask Jesus to give you His peace.

A Child's Faith

*"Let the little children come to me, and do
not hinder them, for the kingdom of God
belongs to such as these."*

MARK 10:14 NIV

Young children can ask the most amazing questions about God and Heaven! And when they do, we shouldn't ignore them or act like their questions aren't important—because they are.

When children ask you about God, do your best to answer simply and honestly in terms they can understand. They don't need deep and complicated answers, but just because they can't understand everything about God doesn't mean they can't understand something about Him. I don't understand electricity, but that doesn't mean I can't turn on a light switch.

Ask God to give you patience also; children have a way of asking questions until we adults run out of answers! Be thankful for their interest in spiritual things, and do all you can to let them know that God is important to you. They can begin to sense Jesus' love for them through your love and your words.

Jesus told His disciples to let the children come to Him, and He continues to open His arms to them twenty-one centuries later. So should we.

Making Godly Decisions

In all your ways acknowledge [God],
and he will make your paths straight.

PROVERBS 3:6 NIV

A re you facing a significant decision? Then look again at these words in Proverbs 3:6. Implicit in this verse is the truth that God knows what is best for us and that He wants to guide us so we will make right, God-honoring decisions.

When you face a decision about your future, seek God's will above all else. Make your decision a matter of prayer, and ask Him to guide you. If we are truly open to His will, He will direct us.

Does this mean we should just wait around until God gives us some kind of miraculous sign or deep inner conviction? No, not necessarily. God wants us to be practical. Do research if you need to; understand yourself and your gifts; seek the advice of others. Make your decision in light of God's Word: God never leads us to do anything that is contrary to the Bible.

Remember, too, that God often guides us only one step at a time—but that is all we need to know. So don't be anxious. Trust God to guide you, and He will.

Pray About Your Problems

Don't worry about anything; instead,
pray about everything.

PHILIPPIANS 4:6 TLB

What do you do when you have a problem? Do you worry? Most of us do. But does worrying solve the problem? No, it does not. So if worry doesn't solve the problem, why worry?

The Bible's account about Hezekiah gives us an idea for problem solving: "Hezekiah received the letter from the hand of the messengers, and read it; and Hezekiah went up to the house of the LORD, and spread it before the LORD. Then Hezekiah prayed before the LORD" (2 Kings 19:14–15).

Instead of turning to God as a first resource, we so often turn to Him as a last resort. Follow Hezekiah's formula. Turn to God first with your problems, for only He is capable of handling them in a way that will be in your best interest—and according to His perfect will.

A Happy Home

Children are a gift from the LORD;
they are a reward from him.
PSALM 127:3 NLT

Today there are more pressures on the home than perhaps at any other time in the history of the human race.

By necessity or by desire, more women are working today than ever before. Many feel guilty about leaving their children in the care of others or having them return to an empty home while they are at work. But many women (and men too) still devote more attention to their working life than they do to their family life. Is it any wonder, then, that so many homes are in trouble?

What achievement in life is equal to a happy home and children who grow up to praise their parents? Every material goal, even if it is met, will pass away. But the heritage of godly children is timeless.

Our primary responsibility is to be sure our children grow up in homes where God is honored and the love of Christ reigns. Do your children sense that Christ is at the center of your home?

A Glimpse of Heaven

Though the doors were locked, Jesus came
and stood among them.

JOHN 20:26 NIV

There is much about Heaven we don't know; God hasn't chosen to reveal everything to us. But we do know Heaven will be far more glorious than anything we can imagine.

One truth God has revealed to us, however, is one we sometimes overlook: in Heaven we will have new bodies—bodies that will be free from the pain and death of this present world. They will be like Christ's body after His resurrection: somewhat like our present bodies, yet free from the limitations we now experience. Someday, the Bible says, Christ "will transform our lowly bodies so that they will be like his glorious body" (Philippians 3:21 NIV).

Can you imagine this? I can't—not fully. But this verse reminds us that God cares about our physical bodies—and so should we. It tells us, too, that someday all evil and sin will be destroyed, and we will be part of "a new heaven and a new earth, the home of righteousness" (2 Peter 3:13 NIV). Is your hope in Christ and the glorious future He has prepared for us?

Sovereign over All

It is God who works in you to will and to act according to his good purpose.

PHILIPPIANS 2:13 NIV

Is everything that happens to us already determined by God? Or do we have the ability to carry out plans on our own, regardless of what God hoped would happen? You have probably wondered about this question yourself.

Theologians have disagreed for centuries: some stress God's absolute control over everything, and others emphasize our freedom to act on our own. The reason they haven't agreed is because the Bible teaches both God's sovereignty and our human responsibility. To us this sounds like a contradiction—one I don't believe we'll fully understand until we get to Heaven. Until that day, we need to hold firmly to both truths: God is in control of everything, but we also are responsible for our actions.

Why is this important? In the verse above Paul stressed that God is working behind the scenes to accomplish His purposes. What if He weren't? What if it were all left up to us? What hope would we have then? But God *is* at work—even if we can't fully understand it now. Be comforted by this truth today.

The Problem of Suffering

I have kept His way and not turned aside.

JOB 23:11

Some scholars think Job may be the oldest book in the Bible. Whether that is true or not, it certainly deals with one of humanity's oldest questions: Why does God allow suffering?

It isn't an easy issue, because it goes to the heart of our deepest questions about God. After all, the argument runs, how could a loving and gracious God allow suffering? To put it another way: if God lets us suffer, He must not love us. But that conclusion is false. God does love us, and the proof is the suffering He allowed His Son to endure on the cross.

What, then, is the answer to this age-old question? The key is to understand the character of God. That is what Job discovered. No, God never gave him a logical, complete rationale for his suffering. But through his experience, Job came to realize that God could be trusted because He is merciful and loving. And you can trust God too—not because He always gives us all the answers, but simply because He is God.

The Promise of Prayer

*"Whatever you ask the Father in My name
He will give you."*
JOHN 16:23

One of the most amazing things in all the Scriptures is how much time Jesus spent in prayer. He had only three years of public ministry, yet He was never too hurried to spend hours in prayer. He prayed before every difficult task confronting Him. He prayed with regularity—not a day began or closed in which He did not unfold His soul before His Father.

How quickly and carelessly, by contrast, we pray. Snatches of memorized verses are hastily spoken in the morning; then we say good-bye to God for the rest of the day, until we rush through a few closing petitions at night.

And yet, in light of the wonderful promise God gives to those of us who pray, why would we not make prayer time a higher priority? Remember God's Word in John 16:23, and be prepared to discover a whole new dimension to prayer as you explore God's promise to those who pray with faith and humility toward His will.

Our Furious Foe

But mark this: There will be terrible times in the last days . . . evil men and imposters will go from bad to worse, deceiving and being deceived.

2 TIMOTHY 3:1, 13 NIV

Is the world getting worse? Is the devil working more furiously today than ever before?

To many observers this certainly seems to be the case. Take the record of the last century: two world wars and other conflicts that killed more people than all previous wars combined; six million Jews mercilessly killed in the Holocaust; millions more innocent civilians slaughtered by evil atheistic despots; more Christians martyred for their faith than at any other time in history.

In the verse above, Paul called the final days before Jesus' return "terrible times"; Jesus Himself declared that we "will hear of wars and rumors of wars. . . . Nation will rise against nation" (Matthew 24:6–7).

Why will it be like this? The reason, the Bible says, is because Satan will lash out in one final burst of fury, seeking with all his might to block Christ's victory.

Does this alarm you? Don't let it—because Christ, not Satan, will be victorious. In the meantime, "be joyful in hope, patient in affliction, faithful in prayer" (Romans 12:12 NIV).

Trust and Toil

> *As the body without the spirit is dead, so faith*
> *without works is dead also.*
>
> JAMES 2:26

The Scriptures teach that a Christian is one who trusts Christ as Savior and obeys Him as Lord. That is the essence of Christian discipleship: believing and following.

The New Testament makes no separation between belief and obedience. They are linked together as one, because if you truly believe, you will truly follow. Trust makes us part of God's Kingdom, but our love for Him and obedience to His will are the badges of our citizenship in that Kingdom.

That is why the Christian life is a happy blend of trust and toil, resting and striving, receiving and doing. God does His part, and we must do ours. A farmer's crop is a gift from God—but it also requires hard work. God may give a person the gift of music—but it takes practice and discipline to make it come alive.

Is any area of your life "off-limits" to Christ? Believe—and obey.

The Promise of Blessing

Blessed are they whose ways are blameless,
who walk according to the law of the LORD.

PSALM 119:1 NIV

These words from the psalmist's pen present a view of life that is the exact opposite of what the world around us promotes through advertising, the media, entertainment, and the lifestyles of the rich and famous. "Live for yourself," the world proclaims. "Have a good time; indulge your senses; pursue every pleasure; strive for success. And if you do," these voices add, "then you'll be happy and blessed."

But God calls us to another way—His way. Blessing, He says, comes only from following Him. No other way can deliver what it promises; in fact, every other way delivers exactly the opposite of what it promises. Some of the most miserable people I have ever known were highly successful in the eyes of the world. But down inside, they were restless and spiritually empty.

Have you fallen into the world's trap, following its self-indulgent goals and driven by its self-centered motives? It can happen without you even being aware of it. Keep Christ first in your life, and make it your goal to live according to His Word.

Swimming Upstream

Everyone who wants to live a godly life in
Christ Jesus will be persecuted.
2 TIMOTHY 3:12 NIV

The apostle Paul knew what it meant to be persecuted. A quick survey of Acts reveals that he and his companions encountered opposition almost everywhere they went. His brief notes in 2 Corinthians 11:23–33 catalog an even larger number of persecutions.

Millions of Christians experience this same reality every day. Faithfulness to Christ can mean rejection by their families, loss of their jobs, social ostracism, injustice, violence, even imprisonment or death. We may never meet them this side of eternity, but their commitment and courage should challenge and inspire us all. Pray for them and learn from their example.

We may not face the same situation they do—but every believer knows what it is to swim upstream against the current of an unbelieving world—of the friend or relative who mocks you, the business associate who scorns your integrity, the indifference of those around you to moral and spiritual values. But don't let them sway you. Be faithful to Christ, who, for your sake, "endured the cross, scorning its shame" (Hebrews 12:2 NIV).

God, Our Father

*"I will be a Father to you,
and you shall be My sons and daughters."*

2 Corinthians 6:18

In the familiar story of the prodigal son (Luke 15:11–32), the young man was not satisfied to be in his father's house with all of his needs met. He wanted more. He believed the lie that something more exciting was in store for him away from his father.

Isn't this how we sometimes behave? We think that God is holding out on us, that there is something better than a close relationship with our Heavenly Father, that the world offers us more excitement and greater fulfillment than God does.

But it isn't true. By thinking this way and then acting on it—whether or not we go as far away as the prodigal—we create our own desperate circumstances. Then we turn back to God, crying out for deliverance and forgiveness.

Fortunately, our Heavenly Father always hears our cries. Full repentance is always answered by full forgiveness. But wouldn't it have been far better to have avoided the sin in the first place? Don't ever, ever think that Satan's way is better than God's way. It never is.

The Deeper Problem

"For from within, out of men's hearts, come evil
thoughts, sexual immorality, theft, murder, adultery,
greed, malice, deceit, lewdness, envy, slander,
arrogance and folly."

MARK 7:21–22 NIV

F ew words of Jesus were less likely to win Him the affection of those who opposed Him. Jesus cut through their veneer of righteousness to reveal the pride and evil that actually motivated them—and every human being.

That is why, over twenty centuries later, our world is still filled with conflict and war, turmoil and insecurity. The basic problem is in our hearts—and the reason is that we are alienated from our Creator. Instead of giving God His rightful place at the center of our lives, we have substituted the god of self. Only Christ can change our hearts—and, through us, begin to change our world.

God wants us to fight evil—poverty, war, injustice, famine, sickness, disease—wherever we find it. But our greatest need is for repentance and spiritual renewal.

Pray for renewal—beginning with you.

The Hope of Heaven

Precious in the sight of the LORD
Is the death of His saints.
PSALM 116:15

Death is the one experience through which all will pass. We may meet it with resignation, denial, or even without a moment's thought—but come it will.

But death for the believer is distinctly different from what it is for the unbeliever. For us, it isn't something to be feared or shunned, for we know death is but the shadowed threshold to the palace of God. No wonder Paul declared, "I desire to depart and be with Christ, which is better by far" (Philippians 1:23 NIV).

Sometimes God gives His departing saints glimpses of Heaven (partly, I believe, to encourage those of us who remain). Just before dying, my grandmother sat up in bed, smiled, and said, "I see Jesus, and He has His hand outstretched to me. And there is Ben, and he has both of his eyes and both of his legs." (Ben, my grandfather, had lost an eye and a leg at Gettysburg.)

Are you looking forward to that day when you will go to be with Christ, "which is better by far"?

Everlasting Love

"I have loved you with an everlasting love;
Therefore with lovingkindness I have drawn you."
JEREMIAH 31:3

Who can describe or measure the love of God? Our Bible is a revelation of the fact that God is love. When we preach His justice, it is justice tempered with love. When we preach His righteousness, it is righteousness founded on love. When we preach atonement for sin, it is atonement necessitated because of love, provided by love, finished by love.

When we preach the resurrection of Christ, we are preaching the miracle of love. When we preach the abiding presence of Christ, we are preaching the power of love. When we preach the return of Christ, we are preaching the fulfillment of love.

No matter what sin we have committed, no matter how black, dirty, shameful, or terrible it may be, God loves us. We may be at the very gate of Hell itself, but God loves us with an everlasting love. The proof? Jesus Christ, God's only Son, went to the cross for us. "For God so loved the world that He gave His only begotten Son, that whoever believes in Him should not perish but have everlasting life" (John 3:16).

The Only Sin That Can't Be Forgiven

"I tell you the truth, all the sins and blasphemies of men will be forgiven them. But whoever blasphemes against the Holy Spirit will never be forgiven; he is guilty of an eternal sin."

MARK 3:28–29 NIV

I suppose I've been asked it almost more than any other question over the years: "What is the unforgivable sin?"

But notice what Jesus first said: "All the sins and blasphemies of men will be forgiven them." Think of just a few of the people Jesus forgave during His ministry: the woman caught in adultery; the murderer who was executed with Him; Peter, who denied Him three times; the deranged, demon-possessed man in Gerasene. Or think of Saul of Tarsus, violently attacking Christians and determined to stamp out the Church. If God could forgive them, can't He forgive anyone, no matter what they have done? Can't He even forgive you?

The only sin God cannot forgive is the sin of rejecting Christ. Turn to Him in repentance and faith, and He will forgive.

The Work of Angels

Bless the LORD, you His angels,
who excel in strength, who do His word.

PSALM 103:20

It's natural to concentrate on what the angels do for us, these beings who are "sent to serve those who will inherit salvation" (Hebrews 1:14 NIV).

But the Bible indicates that angels do much more than this. Especially, we are told, the angels unite in constant praise to God, giving glory to His name and rejoicing in His holiness and perfection.

God gave Isaiah a vision of Heaven, where the angelic hosts proclaim, "Holy, holy, holy is the LORD of hosts; the whole earth is full of His glory!" (Isaiah 6:3). John saw "many angels around the throne . . . saying with a loud voice: 'Worthy is the Lamb who was slain!'" (Revelation 5:11–12). Jesus said there is "rejoicing in the presence of the angels of God over one sinner who repents" (Luke 15:10 NIV).

Are these angels not examples to us? Shouldn't rejoicing and praise be hallmarks of our lives? Praise banishes darkness and brings us closer to God. Martin Luther once said, "Come, let us sing a psalm and drive away the devil!"

The One Who Made It All

In the beginning God created the
heavens and the earth.

Genesis 1:1

What image, if any, comes into your mind when you think of God? A kindly old grandfather? A stern policeman or harsh judge? Or even a vague, impersonal power or force?

Look again at that first sentence in the Bible: "In the beginning God created the heavens and the earth." Can you even begin to comprehend the power it took to bring into being the billions of stars that astronomers are still discovering with their telescopes? Can you even begin to comprehend the wisdom it took to develop the complex laws that would govern the whole creation, from the smallest subatomic particle to the swirling galaxies of outer space? As the Bible says, "Since the creation of the world God's invisible qualities—his eternal power and divine nature—have been clearly seen, being understood from what has been made" (Romans 1:20 NIV).

Don't ever underestimate God's power—and don't ever underestimate His love. And because of His power and love, He is worthy of our trust and our worship.

Full Surrender

"Whoever loses his life for My sake . . . will save it."
MARK 8:35

A police sergeant once asked me the secret of victorious Christian living. I told him there is no magic formula. But if any one word could describe it, it would be *surrender.*

You may ask, "How can I surrender my life?" It is surrendered in the same way that salvation comes to the sinner. There needs to be confession of sin and a complete yielding of every area of our lives, personalities, and wills to Jesus Christ—plus faith that Christ will accept that commitment.

It's not enough for us to be confirmed or to make a decision for Christ at an altar. We cannot walk successfully in the glow of that experience for the rest of our lives. Again and again, we need to renew those vows and covenants with the Lord. We need to take inventory and have regular spiritual checkups.

Jesus said, "If anyone desires to come after Me, let him deny himself, and take up his cross daily, and follow Me" (Luke 9:23). Daily surrender—that's the key to daily victory.

The Hardest Commandment

"Love your neighbor as yourself."

LEVITICUS 19:18

Why is it easier to see someone else's faults than to see our own?

I can think of several reasons—but one of the strongest is because we naturally love ourselves more than we love other people. And because we love ourselves, we don't like to criticize ourselves or admit our faults. That can be painful, and we don't like pain.

But the Bible tells us to love others as much as we love ourselves. Jesus, in fact, taught that this commandment—along with the commandment to love God above all else—summarizes God's law (Luke 10:27).

How can we truly love others? First, we ask God to help us see them through His eyes. He knows their faults far better than we do—but He still loves them, just as He loves us, in spite of our faults. Then, we ask God to replace our selfishness with His love—the self-giving love that sent His Son to the cross for us. Finally, we demonstrate our love with a kind word, a helping hand, a prayer for salvation.

The Cure for Loneliness

*The Lord God said, "It is not good that
man should be alone."*

Genesis 2:18

"My husband died two years ago," her letter said, "and I'm so lonely I don't care if I die. It's like a searing pain that just won't go away." Her letter reflects something we all know: loneliness is one of the most painful experiences many of us will ever face.

The Bible says we weren't meant to be alone. Even in the garden of Eden—long before sin entered the world— God knew that Adam needed someone with whom he could share his life, so God created Eve.

When loneliness afflicts you, remember two truths. First, we are never alone when we know Christ. You can't see Him, but He is more real than the chair you are sitting in, and He is with you. Take comfort in His promise: "Never will I leave you; never will I forsake you" (Hebrews 13:5 niv).

Second, learn to reach out to others. All around you are people who are lonely. Ask God to help you be a friend to someone who is going through hard times. Whom will you reach out to today?

Fervent Prayer

*"If My people . . . will . . . pray and seek My
face, . . . I will hear from heaven."*

From one end of the Bible to the other, there are stories of those whose prayers were answered—men and women who turned the tide of history by prayer, who fervently prayed and saw God answer.

Elijah prayed, and God sent fire from Heaven to consume the offering on the altar he had built in the presence of God's enemies. Elisha prayed, and the son of the Shunammite woman was raised from the dead. Hannah prayed, and God gave her a son, Samuel, who would bless God's people for decades.

Paul prayed, and dozens of churches were born in Asia Minor and Europe. Peter prayed, and Dorcas was raised to life, adding years of service for Jesus Christ.

These believers' prayers were the natural outflow of their deep inner faith. Their prayers were part of a greater whole: godly lives lived for God's glory. As the seventeenth-century theologian John Owen said, "He who prays as he ought, will endeavor to live as he prays."

Two Paths, Two Destinations

"Wide is the gate and broad is the road that leads to destruction, and many enter through it."

MATTHEW 7:13 NIV

Advertisers know that we're more likely to buy a product if they can convince us that everyone else uses it. "If everyone else is using it, then it must be good, and I ought to buy it"—or so they hope we'll say to ourselves.

And, on a far more serious matter, this is what Satan hopes you will say to yourself. "Look at the way most people are living," he whispers in our ears. "They're having a good time—enjoying life, living for themselves, absorbed in the moment, not bothering about God or eternity. Follow them! That's the path to real life!" But it is a lie. Jesus warned that the world's way will only lead to destruction and Hell.

Jesus calls us to take another path—His path. Yes, it may be harder, and far fewer take it. But it alone offers us the true peace and joy that can only come from knowing God. And Jesus' path alone leads to eternal life and Heaven. On which path are you? Don't let another day go by without Christ.

Teacher and Lord

*"You call Me Teacher and Lord, and you
say well, for so I am."*

JOHN 13:13

I wonder if you've ever thought about the incredible number of messages that rain down on us every day: television ads, e-mails, phone calls, magazines, junk mail, videos, billboards, conversations. The list is almost endless.

How many of those shape our thinking? How many of them subtly convince us that the road to happiness is really paved with possessions, or beauty, or money, or fame, or any of a hundred other things? How many of them persuade us that the most important thing in life is financial success, or the esteem of others, or power, or sex? It's hard to resist the cumulative impact of so many messages.

But God says our thinking must be shaped by His truth. What this world calls valuable, God calls worthless. What this world scorns, God exalts. "My thoughts are not your thoughts, nor are your ways My ways" (Isaiah 55:8).

Jesus said, "You call Me Teacher and Lord, and you say well, for so I am." Is He your Teacher and Lord—or is the world?

Daily Living by Faith

*This righteousness from God comes through
faith in Jesus Christ to all who believe.*
ROMANS 3:22 NIV

Have you ever stopped to think about all the things you accept by faith every day? By faith we assume the other driver will stop at his red light. By faith we assume the pharmacist filled the prescription correctly. By faith you assumed that when you put your feet on the floor this morning, it wouldn't collapse. Faith is a much greater part of life than most of us realize.

A skeptic may protest that these are things we can see and touch, whereas God is not. But look at the world around you, with all of its beauty and complexity. Isn't it more logical to believe in an all-powerful and all-wise Creator, than to think the universe happened by chance?

The real foundation of our faith is Jesus Christ: He was God in human flesh, and He proved it by dying and then coming back from the grave. If you want to know not only if God exists but what He is like, look at Jesus Christ—and then put your faith and confidence in Him.

Hope for the Heart

My heart is glad, and . . .
My flesh also will rest in hope.

PSALM 16:9

Perhaps the greatest psychological, spiritual, and medical need that all people have is the need for hope. Dr. McNair Wilson, the famous cardiologist, remarked in his autobiography, *Doctor's Progress*, "Hope is the medicine I use more than any other—hope can cure nearly anything."

Years ago Dr. Harold Wolff, professor of medicine at Cornell University Medical College and associate professor of psychiatry, said, "Hope, like faith and a purpose in life, is medicinal. This is not a statement of belief, but a conclusion proved by meticulously controlled scientific experiment."

When hope dies, despair will overwhelm. Hope is both biologically and psychologically vital. Men and women must have hope, and true hope comes only from Christ. He gives us hope for the future as we turn in faith to Him—hope for eternity and hope for right now.

Loving Compassion

In this is love, not that we loved God,
but that He loved us.
1 JOHN 4:10

The supreme happiness of life," Victor Hugo said, "is the conviction that we are loved." "Love is the first requirement for mental health," declared Sigmund Freud.

Unfortunately, many people go through life feeling unloved—and unlovable. Perhaps they were constantly criticized or ignored as children, or their family was torn by conflict. Perhaps they made bad choices about important issues in life—which only confirmed their belief that they were unworthy of love. This may be your experience.

But listen: I have good news! No matter the reason, your feelings aren't telling you the truth! God loves you, and if you begin to see yourself the way God sees you, your attitudes will begin to change. If He didn't love you, would Christ have been willing to die for you? But He did! The Bible says, "By this we know love, because He laid down His life for us" (1 John 3:16).

God loves you. Hammer that truth into your heart and mind every day. It will make all the difference.

The Man Who Was God

[Paul was called to preach] the gospel [God] promised
beforehand through his prophets in the Holy
Scriptures regarding his Son . . . who through the
Spirit of holiness was declared with power to be the
Son of God by his resurrection from the dead:
Jesus Christ our Lord.

ROMANS 1:2–4 NIV

Most people will readily admit that Jesus was a great man. But why have Christians always insisted that He was more than a man—that He was also divine?

One reason is that Jesus Himself claimed He was divine. "I and the Father are one," He stated (John 10:30 NIV).

In addition, the gospel writers repeatedly pointed out the way Jesus fulfilled the Old Testament's prophecies concerning the Messiah. But Jesus' divinity was demonstrated most clearly by His resurrection from the dead and His ascension into Heaven.

What difference does Jesus' divinity make? Only a sinless, divine Savior could save us, for only He could become the perfect and final sacrifice for our sins. Pause right now and thank Him for leaving Heaven's glory and coming to Earth for you.

Just a Bunch of Hypocrites

"If you love me, you will obey what I command."
JOHN 14:15 NIV

You know it as well as I do: the most common charge leveled against the Christian faith is that Christians are "just a bunch of hypocrites." Sadly, those who make such a charge often have someone in mind who claimed to be a Christian, but didn't act like it.

What these accusers may not know, however, is that some of Jesus' strongest words were reserved for hypocrites—for people who claimed to believe in God and follow His laws, but in reality lived only for themselves. Jesus compared them to "whitewashed tombs, which look beautiful on the outside but on the inside are full of dead men's bones and everything unclean" (Matthew 23:27 NIV).

None of us is perfect; even the most dedicated Christian falls short. And when we do, we need to confess our failing and seek God's help to live in better obedience to His commands. But hypocrisy—living a deliberate lie—is another matter. Be on guard; don't let hypocrisy take root in your soul. Instead, make sure of your commitment to Christ and walk close to Him every day.

Facing Rejection

He is despised and rejected by men,
A Man of sorrows and acquainted with grief.

ISAIAH 53:3

Throughout His Earthly life, Jesus was constantly exposed to personal criticism and rejection. At the beginning of His ministry, His own townsfolk in Nazareth tried to hurl Him down from the brow of a hill (Luke 4:29). Religious and political leaders constantly argued with Him and conspired to kill Him. Eventually, Jesus was arrested and brought to trial before Pilate and Herod. Even though He was guiltless of the accusations, He was denounced as an enemy of God and man and sentenced to death.

How did Jesus respond to this criticism and rejection? First, with steadfastness. He did not tone down His message, nor did He stop doing what He knew was right. Second, with strength. Ahead of Him was the cross, but He did not lose courage or shrink from what He knew was God's will. Third, with submission. When Herod prodded Jesus to defend Himself, "He answered him nothing" (Luke 23:9). Only one thing mattered: fulfilling God's purpose for His life.

How will you meet criticism?

Shining in a Dark World

[Be] blameless and pure, children of God without fault in a crooked and depraved generation, in which you shine like stars in the universe as you hold out the word of life.

PHILIPPIANS 2:15–16 NIV

I have enough problems of my own," a man said to me once. "I'm a Christian, but I just haven't got the time or the energy to worry about anyone else's problems."

I could understand his attitude. When we have problems, they have a way of blocking out everything and everyone else. And it's not necessarily wrong to give attention to our own problems and—with God's help—to overcome them if we can. But when our problems deafen us to the hurts of others or when they make us fail to reach out to someone we could help, then we have become part of the darkness instead of shining like stars and holding out the word of life as we should.

Do you remember the good Samaritan? No doubt he was preoccupied with his journey, but he still stopped and took care of the man who had been left for dead (Luke 10:25–37). Ask God to free you from whatever preoccupies you today, so you can be a light for Christ in the midst of this dark world.

The Way of Meekness

"Blessed are the meek,
for they shall inherit the earth."

MATTHEW 5:5

No person is meek by nature. We insist on our own way, and if anyone blocks our path, we react with hurt, anger, resentment, and even revenge.

Moses was meek, but he was not meek by nature. God worked meekness into his life over a forty-year period.

Peter was certainly not meek by nature. He was impetuous, saying and doing the first thing that came into his mind. But, little by little, the Holy Spirit of God transformed Peter after the resurrection of Jesus.

Before his conversion, Paul was not meek. His job was to persecute Christians! Yet Paul wrote to the church at Galatia, "The fruit of the Spirit is . . . gentleness, goodness . . . meekness" (Galatians 5:22–23 KJV).

It is our human nature to be proud and self-assertive, not meek. Only the Spirit of God can transform our lives through the new birth experience and then make us over again into the image of Christ. He is our example of true meekness.

Hidden Weakness

Blessed is he who has regard for the weak.
PSALM 41:1 NIV

Weakness in others takes all kinds of forms—and some of them are easy to overlook.

Sometimes, of course, a person's weakness is obvious: a chronic illness, a physical disability, a destructive habit or addiction. Sometimes it is less obvious (but no less real): a tendency to make bad decisions, a personality trait that alienates others, a destructive habit no one knows about. And then there are the weaknesses we may never detect because the person has successfully hidden them from others—and even from himself. Often those who seem to be the strongest on the outside are the weakest on the inside.

But God sees our weaknesses, and He sees the weaknesses in others as well. And just as He wants to help us deal with our own weaknesses, so He wants to use us to help others deal with theirs. Ask God to make you sensitive to those around you who are weak—whatever their weakness may be—and to help them, both in practical ways and by pointing them to Christ and His transforming power and love.

The Reality of Heaven

God will wipe away every tear from their eyes.

REVELATION 7:17

In the midst of his suffering, Job said, "Man is born to trouble as surely as sparks fly upward" (Job 5:7 NIV). It is true. I have never met a person who did not have troubles of some kind. Fear and sickness rob us of happiness; broken relationships and shattered dreams destroy our peace.

But one of God's greatest promises is that all of these will be forgotten in Heaven, where "there shall be no more death, nor sorrow, nor crying. There shall be no more pain, for the former things have passed away" (Revelation 21:4).

This is the supreme reality of Heaven. Throughout eternity there will be an intimate relationship between Christ and His Church. He will be the Lamb who is on the throne, and He shall lead His people to fountains of living waters.

When we have this great certainty and assurance, the future holds no terrors we cannot face. Beyond any crisis lies Heaven. Thus we Christians should never be filled with fear, discouragement, or despondency. Ahead of us is Heaven!

Truly Transformed

Present your bodies a living sacrifice. . . . And do
not be conformed to this world.
ROMANS 12:1–2

Others can't see what goes on inside of you—your thoughts and emotions, your dreams and motives. Nor can they see your inner commitment to Christ.

All they can see is your body, and they will judge what is on the inside of you by what they see happening on the outside. A frown signals concern or disapproval; a smile signals gratitude or welcome; a clenched fist signals hostility or anger.

Do you see why Paul tells us to "present [our] bodies a living sacrifice"? The reason is simple: the way we use our bodies will signal to others what we really are on the inside. We may claim to follow Christ, but if our actions tell a different story, people have a right to question our claim. Our dress, our speech, our habits—all should honor Christ. We are to be "blameless and pure, children of God without fault in a crooked and depraved generation" (Philippians 2:15 NIV).

Do your outer actions reflect your inner commitment to Christ?

Our Sure Foundation

"My Father, who has given them to me, is greater than all; no one can snatch them out of my Father's hand."

JOHN 10:29 NIV

If you asked Christians if they knew beyond a shadow of doubt they would go to Heaven when they die, many would admit they weren't sure. Yet God wants us to be sure—and we can be, once we understand what Jesus Christ did for us.

The problem is that down inside, many of us still feel our salvation must be up to us, and we can only go to Heaven if we are good enough. But how do you know when you are good enough? The answer is—you don't. And that's why many Christians lack assurance of their salvation.

The key is to understand that Christ took away all our sins—not part of them, but all of them. No matter how good we are, we can't save ourselves because God's standard is perfection. But Christ, who was without sin, did for us what we could never do for ourselves: He took all our sins upon Himself, and He took the death and Hell we deserve. Depend solely on Christ for your salvation. He paid the price—and now you owe nothing!

Turning It Aside

A gentle answer turns away wrath,
but a harsh word stirs up anger.
PROVERBS 15:1 NIV

What a different world this would be if we only learned to heed this advice!

Behind these words in Proverbs is a profound truth: our tongues have enormous power—both for good and for evil. The apostle James put it this way: "The tongue also is a fire, a world of evil among the parts of the body. . . . With the tongue we praise our Lord and Father, and with it we curse men, who have been made in God's likeness" (James 3:6, 9 NIV).

Commit your tongue to God. Beyond that, commit your whole inner being to Christ, and ask Him to cleanse you of anger and hate and to fill you instead with His love and patience. After all, our words are an expression of our inner hearts and minds, and only Christ can change those. So when someone tries to provoke you to anger or deals with you in a way that makes you want to strike back, don't take the bait. Instead, immediately ask God to remind you that "a gentle answer turns away wrath."

Pure in Heart

"Blessed are the pure in heart,
for they shall see God."

MATTHEW 5:8

Why does Jesus say we should be "pure in heart"? The reason is because our heart—our inner being—is the root of all our actions. From our hearts come our motives, our desires, our goals, our emotions. If our hearts aren't right, our actions won't be either.

Jesus put it this way: "From within, out of the heart of men, proceed evil thoughts, adulteries, fornications, murders, thefts, covetousness, wickedness, deceit, lewdness, an evil eye, blasphemy, pride, foolishness" (Mark 7:21–22).

But God wants to give us a pure heart—and He will. He does this first of all when we turn to Christ in repentance and faith, for "the blood of Jesus Christ His Son cleanses us from all sin" (1 John 1:7). But God also purifies our hearts day by day as we submit to the Holy Spirit and—with His help—flee from evil and seek what is good. "Blessed are the pure in heart."

A Tough Truth

Do not be deceived. . . . A man reaps what he sows.
GALATIANS 6:7 NIV

One of life's hardest lessons is that we cannot turn back the clock and change something we've already done. When we make a wrong decision or act foolishly, we have to live with the consequences, bitter as they may be. In biblical terms, we must reap what we have sown.

Then why bother to ask for God's forgiveness? If nothing is going to change and if we still must face the consequences of our sin, why seek God's forgiveness?

One reason is that it is the only way to deal with our guilt. Down inside, we feel unclean and ashamed for what we've done—but when we turn to Christ and seek His forgiveness, that burden of guilt is lifted. When we seek forgiveness, the Bible says, "The blood of Jesus . . . purifies us from all sin" (1 John 1:7 NIV).

But we also need God's forgiveness to keep from becoming spiritually hardened. Unconfessed sin leads inevitably to spiritual coldness. Does any sin in your life need to be brought to God for forgiveness?

He Still Sustains Us

The eternal God is your refuge.

DEUTERONOMY 33:27

When we hear the word *suffering*, we usually think of physical pain. But psychological suffering is just as real—and sometimes more devastating.

It may be an inner grief or sorrow you cannot express, even to your dearest friend or spouse. It may sap your strength or paralyze you with anxiety. It may harm your relationships or grip you so tightly that it becomes a serious psychological illness.

Paul knew what it was to experience psychological suffering. He told the Corinthians he had written them "out of much affliction and anguish of heart" (2 Corinthians 2:4). In the Garden of Gethsemane, Jesus, "being in agony, . . . prayed more earnestly" (Luke 22:44). After denying his Lord three times, Peter "went out and wept bitterly" (Luke 22:62).

But when such times come (and they come to us all) God still loves us. He does not abandon us. Remember: "The eternal God is your refuge, and underneath are the everlasting arms" (Deuteronomy 33:27).

He Has Always Known You

> *"Before I formed you in the womb I knew you,*
> *before you were born I set you apart;*
> *I appointed you as a prophet to the nations."*
>
> JEREMIAH 1:5 NIV

Think of it: God not only knows what is going on in your life right now, but He knew all about you even before you were born. In fact, He gave you life and put you on this Earth. You are not here by accident; you are here by His design!

The same is true of every human being. Every single person on this Earth (even those not yet born) is important in the eyes of God. Don't ever scorn people who are different from you or ignore them when they suffer. God calls them valuable—so valuable that His Son gave His life for them. Human life is sacred, and we must never lose sight of that fact.

But look again at what God said to Jeremiah. Not only did God know him and put him on Earth—He put Jeremiah here for a purpose: "I set you apart; I appointed you as a prophet." The same is true of you. Have you asked God to show you His purpose in putting you here? Are you seeking to fulfill it?

God Is Our Strength

The LORD is my light and my salvation;
Whom shall I fear?

PSALM 27:1

It is a fact: the Lord is my light and my salvation. So why should I be afraid? Since the Lord fears nothing, why should we fear?

The Scriptures also declare that God is a "very present help in trouble" (Psalm 46:1). If we can't trust the all-powerful, all-knowing, all-loving God of the universe to help us, where can we turn? But we can trust Him!

God is able, indeed He is anxious, to deliver us from all sorts of trouble. He wants to give us strength to overcome the temptation to the sin that separates Him from those He loves. He wants to give us the courage to confront our problems instead of avoiding them or denying them, and then He will provide the practical wisdom and help we need to deal with them.

What do you fear today? Failure? Rejection? An illness or physical danger? The uncertainty of the future? Whatever it is, ask God to help you turn it over to Him. "The LORD is my light and my salvation; whom shall I fear?"

In His Hands

No man has power over the wind to contain it;
so no one has power over the day of his death.

ECCLESIASTES 8:8 NIV

Ultimately, our lives are in God's hands. Even the next breath you take is a gift from Him. If He were to withdraw His hand from you, your life would end, despite the most strenuous efforts of your doctors. The psalmist said it well: "When you take away their breath, they die and return to the dust" (104:29 NIV).

What difference should this make? First, it should remind us of our dependence on God. All too often we assume that our lives and our futures are in our hands. But they aren't; they are in His hands. He gave us life, and someday He will bring our time on Earth to an end.

But this should also remind us that each day is a gift from God—a gift to be used wisely, joyfully, and for His glory. And this gift of life should remind us of an even greater gift—the gift of eternal life in Christ. Thank God for the gift of today and for the gift of eternal life that awaits us in Heaven.

The Divine Fire

"I will give them a new heart and a new mind."

EZEKIEL 11:19 TEV

When a person comes in contact with the living God, he or she can never be the same again. This divine fire either draws or drives, saves or destroys, helps or hinders. Accepted and utilized, it becomes a boon and a blessing. Rejected, it becomes a bane and a curse.

One dying thief was drawn to the warmth of the Savior; he responded in faith and was saved. The other dying thief turned away and rejected God's compassion; he was lost forever.

God takes the weak and makes them strong. He takes the vile and makes them clean. He takes the worthless and makes them worthwhile. He takes the sinful and makes them pure.

With this in mind, Ezekiel spoke on behalf of the Lord, saying, "I will give them a new heart and a new mind. I will take away their stubborn heart of stone and will give them an obedient heart" (Ezekiel 11:19 TEV).

No, you will never be the same once you know Christ. What difference did He make in your life today?

An Attitude of Gratitude

Let the peace of Christ rule in your hearts. . . .
And be thankful.

Colossians 3:15 niv

T hankfulness isn't our usual response when something goes wrong. We may have a hundred good things for which to be thankful, but let one bad thing happen, and it's all we think about!

But the Bible says, "In everything give thanks" (1 Thessalonians 5:18). No matter what happens, we are to give thanks. So cultivate a spirit of thanksgiving in your life. Thank God for every blessing He gives you. Thank Him for Christ and what He has done for you. Even when things go wrong, thank God that they aren't worse and that you are still in His hands.

Having an attitude of thankfulness in all of life's circumstances will help you react as Matthew Henry did when he was mugged. He wrote in his diary, "Let me be thankful first because I was never robbed before; second, although they took my purse, they did not take my life; third, because although they took my all, it was not much; and fourth, because it was I who was robbed, not I who robbed."

I wonder if I could be that thankful!

When Faith Is Tested

Consider it pure joy, my brothers, whenever you
face trials of many kinds, because you know that the
testing of your faith develops perseverance.

JAMES 1:2–3 NIV

James reminded us that difficulties and trials can take many different forms. It may be a soured relationship, a financial reversal, an unexpected illness, a sudden disability, or the death of a loved one. For others, trials may take the form of mockery or even persecution for their faith.

It's natural for us to shrink back from any kind of trial. We all wish we could be free of problems and instead live a life of peace and serenity all our days. But life isn't like this, and we all know that our situation can radically change even in a matter of seconds. The real question is how we will react. Will we react with anger or despair? Will we lash out with hatred or seek revenge? Or will we turn to God in faith and seek His help?

Trials will either make you turn away from God or drive you toward Him. When we choose the latter, our faith will grow stronger—and we will be better equipped to meet the next challenge that comes our way.

Perfect Peace

The love of God has been poured out in our hearts by the Holy Spirit who was given to us.

ROMANS 5:5

Years ago when I traveled to Europe to preach, I liked to travel by sea. I enjoyed the five days of relative quiet on the ship.

On one of my voyages, Captain Anderson of the United States took me down to see the ship's gyroscope. He said, "When the sea is rough, the gyroscope helps keep the ship on an even keel. Though the waves may reach tremendous proportions, the gyroscope helps stabilize the vessel and maintain a high degree of equilibrium."

As I listened, I thought how like the gyroscope is the Holy Spirit in our hearts. Let the storms of life break over our heads. Let Satan come in like a flood. Let the waves of sorrow, suffering, temptation, and testing be unleashed upon us. The Holy Spirit will keep our souls on an even keel and in perfect peace. He comforts us with God's abiding presence and assures us that God's promises are true.

Words That Hurt

*They sharpen their tongues like swords
and aim their words like deadly arrows.*

PSALM 64:3

We've all been hurt by the words of others. Often—perhaps more often than we realize—what was said was simply spoken thoughtlessly or carelessly. But sometimes words were meant to sting—and they did.

Either way, when others criticize us or say something hurtful or insensitive, our first reaction should be to ask ourselves if there is any truth in what they say. If so, we need to be honest with ourselves and ask God to help us correct whatever may need correcting. But even if those words were spoken maliciously, we need to turn our hurts over to God and ask Him to help us respond with forgiveness and grace.

In addition, if we're honest, we have to admit that we sometimes hurt others with our words. Don't excuse it or ignore it, but admit it and seek forgiveness—both from God and from the person you have hurt. Then make the psalmist's prayer yours: "Set a guard over my mouth, O LORD; keep watch over the door of my lips" (141:3 NIV).

Our Way or God's Way?

We all, like sheep, have gone astray,
each of us has turned to his own way.
ISAIAH 53:6 NIV

L ife is full of decisions. Some of them are minor and relatively insignificant, but others are major. Even if we don't realize it at the time, they can have enormous consequences.

Does God care about the decisions we make? Of course He does—and the reason is because He loves us, and He wants what is best for us. When we go down a wrong path in life, God grieves over our foolishness, because He knows we are hurting ourselves. He also knows that making poor decisions is our natural tendency, because we—like sheep—easily wander and stray from the only Shepherd who can guide us and keep us safe.

What decisions are you facing? Don't rely only on your own wisdom or even on the wisdom of others. Instead, ask God to guide you and show you His will. Remember: His way is always best—always. God's promise is for you: "I will instruct you and teach you in the way you should go" (Psalm 32:8 NIV).

Diamonds in the Dark

Blessed is the man who fears the LORD,
Who delights greatly in His commandments.

PSALM 112:1

We Christians should stand out like sparkling diamonds against a dark velvet background. We should be more wholesome than anyone else. We should be poised, cultured, courteous, gracious—but firm in the things we do and do not do. We should laugh and be radiant; but we should refuse to allow the unbelieving world to pull us down to its level.

Christ meant for His followers to be different—and if we are truly following Him, we will be. But merely being different is not enough. We are to be the cleanest, the most holy, the kindest, the most unselfish, the friendliest, the most courteous, the most industrious, the most thoughtful, the truest, and the most loving people on Earth. The Bible says, "Those who are wise will shine like the brightness of the heavens, and those who lead many to righteousness, like the stars for ever and ever" (Daniel 12:3 NIV).

Dr. Albert Schweitzer, the great missionary doctor and statesman, once said, "To be glad instruments of God's love in this imperfect world is the service to which man is called."

Using Our Skills

*Every skilled person to whom the L*ord *has given*
skill and ability . . . [is] to do the work just as the
L*ord has commanded.*

Exodus 36:1 niv

We sometimes forget that for most of His life Jesus was a carpenter, working with His hands among His neighbors in the town of Nazareth. "Isn't this the carpenter?" some of His critics asked scornfully, implying that no mere carpenter could possibly be the promised Messiah (Mark 6:3 niv).

Do you tend to downplay the work you do? "I'm only a housewife." "I'm just a plumber." "I simply teach school." "I'm merely a clerk in a grocery store." "I make my living as an accountant." But if God gave you that skill and you are where He wants you to be, then your work is valuable and significant in His sight.

Here's another thought for you to ponder. What kind of a carpenter do you suppose Jesus was? Did the doors fall off His cabinets? Do you suppose He took shortcuts or did just barely enough to get by? No, of course not. The Bible says, "Whatever you do, work at it with all your heart, as working for the Lord, not for men" (Colossians 3:23 niv). And we can be sure Jesus did exactly that.

Rest for God's People

There remains therefore a rest for the people of God.

We are the most entertained generation in history. Television sets pull in thousands of channels. Professional sports teams and pop music groups take in (and spend) billions of dollars. Millions of people own second and third homes for vacations. Our children are upset if they don't get the latest computer games for Christmas.

I believe this frantic search for entertainment is a symptom of something deeper. Some have suggested we are the most bored generation in history, and perhaps they are right. But I'm convinced that down inside is an empty place in our hearts—a restlessness, a desire for inner peace and tranquility that will not go away. The irony is, the more we try to satisfy it, the less content we become.

Only Christ can fill that empty space in our hearts, and He will do so as we open our lives to Him. But God's Word also points us to the future—to Heaven, where our restless hearts will be at peace. "There remains therefore a rest for the people of God."

SEPTEMBER

A Time Apart

The eyes of the LORD are on the righteous,
And His ears are open to their prayers.
1 PETER 3:12

Many people want to work *for* God, but they don't want to spend time *with* God. They are content with busyness instead of calmness, instead of walking quietly in the presence of a Friend.

God calls us to work for Him because there is no place in Christian life for laziness or a lack of diligence. But God also calls us to be with Him: "Come with me by yourselves to a quiet place" (Mark 6:31 NIV).

Jesus, we read, "having risen a long while before daylight . . . went out and departed to a solitary place; and there He prayed" (Mark 1:35). If the Son of God needed time alone with His Father, how much more do we?

It is not easy to shut out the world, set aside a few minutes by yourself, and spend time in God's Word and prayer. But it is essential if we are to grow in our relationship with God and be strengthened for the battles ahead. Don't delay. Begin now to spend time alone with God every day.

Under the Spotlight

Search me, O God, and know my heart;
test me and know my anxious thoughts.
See if there is any offensive way in me.

PSALM 139:23–24 NIV

Have you ever stopped to think how difficult it must have been for David to pray this prayer? We don't know if he penned these words before or after his terrible sin with Bathsheba (2 Samuel 11–12). But either way, David knew he was capable of terrible sin and that often his first impulse when he sinned was to deny it or try to hide it from God. To ask God to search out the darkest, most secret corners of our minds and hearts takes courage.

And yet what happens if we aren't willing to do this? Then the sins we know about remain unconfessed, and our fellowship with God remains cold and distant. Perhaps more important, the hidden sins we may not even realize we have—sins like pride, suppressed anger, withheld love, jealousy, a secret yearning for recognition—remain firmly in place, manipulating us and eventually destroying us.

So have the courage to pray this prayer. And whatever God reveals to you, confess it, repent of it, and ask Christ to replace it with His purity and love.

Our Stubborn Wills

Repent therefore and be converted.
ACTS 3:19

Becoming a Christian is a once-for-all event when we repent of our sins and cast ourselves on Christ alone for our salvation. When we are converted, God takes us "out of darkness into His marvelous light" (1 Peter 2:9).

But *being* a Christian is a daily, ongoing experience. It is a lifelong process of daily repentance and faith, of turning from sin and seeking to live for Christ by the power of the Holy Spirit. That is where our wills come in. Although we have been converted and God has come to live in us, our old nature is still alive and kicking. Our stubborn wills still demand to put self first instead of Christ. It isn't easy to bring our stubborn wills into submission to Christ, but when we do, it is as if a misplaced vertebra has snapped back into place. Instead of the stress and tension of a life out of harmony with God, we discover the serenity of His presence.

Who will control your will today? You—or Christ?

His Grand Design

And they sang [to Jesus] a new song:
"You are worthy . . . because you were slain,
and with your blood you purchased men for God
from every tribe and language and people and nation."

REVELATION 5:9 NIV

Never forget: Jesus Christ died to save people from even the most remote corners of the world—people you and I will never know during our lifetimes, but people we will be with in Heaven forever. "For God so loved the world that he gave his one and only Son . . ." (John 3:16 NIV). God's plan is universal! No tribe, no language group, no nation is beyond the scope of His love.

The same should be true of us. Jesus' words to His disciples have never been rescinded: "You will receive power when the Holy Spirit comes on you; and you will be my witnesses . . . to the ends of the earth" (Acts 1:8 NIV).

Not everyone is called of God to be a missionary or evangelist. But if you know Christ, you are a partner in His grand design to call men and women from every part of the world to Himself. By your prayers, your giving, your faithful witness, and your service, you can have an impact for the gospel far beyond your homeland. How will you respond?

Back from the Brink

Remember this: Whoever turns a sinner from the error of his way will save him from death and cover over a multitude of sins.

JAMES 5:20 NIV

How do you react when you see someone whose lifestyle is inevitably going to destroy them? Do you shake your head in disgust? Or simply ignore that person? Or do you secretly congratulate yourself that you aren't as bad off as they are?

Or do you ask God to use you to help them?

Think of all the people Jesus dealt with during His ministry. Some were society's rejects— lepers, the woman caught in adultery, despised Samaritans, the criminals on the cross. Others were powerful and sophisticated— Nicodemus, Pilate, the Pharisees. They covered the whole social spectrum—but they all needed the Savior; they were all headed toward death and eternity; they were all the objects of His love.

Not everyone Jesus tried to turn back from the brink of destruction responded—nor will they always respond to us. But that didn't keep Jesus from trying—nor should we be discouraged. Whom would God have you reach out and try to help in the name of Christ today?

We Need Mercy

The LORD is good;
His mercy is everlasting.

PSALM 100:5

Many Christians do not see God in all of His wholeness. We glibly quote John 3:16—but we forget this verse: "He who does not believe has been judged already" (v. 18 NASB).

Yes, God is loving and compassionate, but He is also absolutely holy and pure. He is the holy Judge who will someday bring His full wrath to bear on those who refuse to repent.

All too often we are more afraid of physical pain than of moral wrong. The cross is the proof that holiness is a principle for which God would die. God cannot clear the guilty until atonement is made. But that is what happened at the cross.

So do not take sin lightly. Do not tolerate sin in your life, saying, "Oh well, God will forgive me anyway." Sin is an offense to Almighty God. He will have mercy on us when we repent, but He also is the Judge, and "everything is uncovered and laid bare before the eyes of him to whom we must give account" (Hebrews 4:13 NIV).

Shaping the Future

> *Impress [these commandments] on your*
> *children. Talk about them when you sit at home*
> *and when you walk along the road, when you*
> *lie down and when you get up.*
> DEUTERONOMY 6:7 NIV

Parenting may be the hardest job you will ever undertake. If your parenting days are ahead of you, brace yourself! And if they are mostly behind you, then you know what I mean. (I say "mostly" because parenting is never completely finished.)

One of your goals as a parent is to work yourself out of a job. Someday your children will leave home, and a major part of your responsibility is to prepare them for that day. From teaching them to brush their teeth and tie their shoes to helping with their homework and encouraging them to make wise decisions, your goal is to prepare them for the day when you won't be there.

But what about their spiritual foundations? Have your children learned from you what it means to walk with Christ every day? Have you taught them to pray, to love the Bible, and to live by its truths? Have you encouraged them to give their lives to Jesus Christ? Don't leave it until it's too late, but begin now to help them build the moral and spiritual foundations they need for life.

God Is at Work

There is laid up for me the crown of righteousness.
2 TIMOTHY 4:8

Many people are asking, "Where is history heading?" A careful student of the Bible will see that God is in control. Amidst the world's confusion, God's omnipotent hand moves, working out His unchanging plan and purpose.

Not that we always see His hand at work. As poet and hymn writer William Cowper put it, "God moves in a mysterious way, His wonders to perform." God is not absent. By His providence He sustains us, and behind the scenes He is working out His divine purpose.

What is that purpose? Paul put it this way: "That . . . He might gather together in one all things in Christ, both which are in heaven and which are on earth" (Ephesians 1:10). Someday Satan's rule will be ended, and Christ will reign as Lord over all creation. Someday all the sin and rebellion of this corrupted universe will be destroyed, and Christ's Kingdom of righteousness and peace will rule forever.

So don't be discouraged by what you see in the headlines every day. God is at work, and someday Christ will rule.

Strength in Weakness

For when I am weak, then I am strong.
2 CORINTHIANS 12:10

L ook carefully at these words written by the apostle Paul. Don't they seem like a contradiction? After all, how can you be strong if you are weak?

But it isn't a contradiction—not in God's eyes. Paul was stating a very important truth: When we attempt to do God's work in our own strength instead of God's strength, we will fail. Only when we acknowledge our weakness and look to the Holy Spirit for the wisdom and strength we need will God bless our efforts.

Perhaps you teach a class of young people in your church . . . or someone has come to you with a problem . . . or you are thinking of volunteering for a summer mission project . . . or your children are beginning to ask questions about God. How will you do what needs to be done? Yes, you'll study and work diligently; trusting God for the outcome doesn't mean we sit back and do nothing. But only God can work in the hearts of those you are seeking to help. Confess your weakness to Him and trust Him to work through you—today and always.

Home at Last

"Behold, I make all things new."
REVELATION 21:5

Heaven is a place so beautiful that when the apostle John caught a glimpse of it, the only thing to which he could liken it was a young woman on the crowning day of her life: her wedding day. He said that the holy city was like "a bride beautifully dressed for her husband" (Revelation 21:2 NIV).

Artists have tried to paint pictures of Heaven, but even the most impressive image falls far short of the reality. Under the inspiration of the Holy Spirit, John could only hint at the splendor we shall see someday: "[The holy city] shone with the glory of God, and its brilliance was like that of a very precious jewel, like a jasper, clear as crystal" (Revelation 21:11 NIV).

Yet the Bible's emphasis is not on Heaven's beauty, but on Heaven's joy. The Bible teaches that Heaven will be a home that is happy because there will be nothing in it to hinder happiness. "There shall by no means enter it anything that defiles. . . . But the throne of God and of the Lamb shall be in it" (Revelation 21:27; 22:3).

What joy we will experience when we are home at last in the presence of our Lord!

Compassion and Love

*Beloved, if God so loved us, we also
ought to love one another.*
1 JOHN 4:11

Charles Allen once made this statement: "Some people seem to have such a passion for righteousness that they have no room left for compassion for those who have failed."

I pray that would never be true of Christians today. God, our Father, has shown us such great kindness and gentle mercy. May we ever reach out to the lost in compassion and love to bring them gently to Jesus Christ, who "when He saw the multitudes . . . was moved with compassion for them, because they were weary and scattered, like sheep having no shepherd" (Matthew 9:36).

Let me share these lines from an unknown poet:

Just to be tender, just to be true,
Just to be glad the whole day through,
Just to be merciful, just to be mild,
Just to be trustful as a child:
Just to be gentle and kind and sweet,
Just to be helpful with willing feet . . .
Just to let love be our daily key,
That is God's will for you and me.

Perfection . . . Someday

*Not that I have already obtained all this, or have
already been made perfect, but I press on to take
hold of that for which Christ Jesus took hold of me.
Brothers, I do not consider myself yet to have taken
hold of it. But one thing I do: Forgetting what is
behind and straining toward what is ahead.*

PHILIPPIANS 3:12–13 NIV

We will never be completely free from sin in this
life. Although Jesus Christ came to live within
us by His Spirit when we gave our lives to Him, our old
sinful nature still resides within us, and as long as we
live, it will keep trying to assert itself.

But that must not keep us from battling sin and
embracing righteousness. God's will is that we would
become more and more like Christ in our purity, love,
and service. The Bible says, "Do not conform any longer
to the pattern of this world, but be transformed by the
renewing of your mind" (Romans 12:2 NIV).

Someday we will enter God's presence forever—and
when we do, not even a hint of sin will remain. But until
that day, make it your goal to become more like Christ
by refusing to let sin have its way, and pursuing instead
that which is pure and good in the sight of God.

A Firm Place

*I waited patiently for the L*ORD*;*
he turned to me and heard my cry.
He lifted me out of the slimy pit,
out of the mud and mire;
he set my feet on a rock.

PSALM 40:1–2 NIV

We don't know exactly what "slimy pit" David had been experiencing before he wrote this psalm—but it doesn't really matter, because life for any of us has its share of slimy pits. For many it's the mud and mire of sin, of a life that has no place for God and desperately pursues happiness in ways that can never satisfy. Or we may find ourselves mired in the pit of a broken marriage, or a lost job, or sickness, or a thousand other pits of confusion or despair.

David said he "waited patiently" for God to act—and sometimes that's hard for us to do. But in time God did answer, and He lifted David out of the mire and put his feet on a rock—a picture of what happens when we give our lives to Jesus Christ. He alone is the solid, unshakable rock on which to build our lives (Matthew 7:24–27).

If you're in a pit right now, don't give up. Instead, turn to Christ and find in Him the solid foundation you need.

God Hates Sin

I acknowledged my sin to You,
And my iniquity I have not hidden.

PSALM 32:5

We live in an age when sin is winked at and God is treated as indulgent, tolerant of those who break His commandments. People today find it difficult to believe that God hates anything, including sin. The image many people have of Him is of a rather senile old grandfather who shakes his head in amusement when his grandchildren misbehave.

But I will tell you that God is very aware of sin, though some may pretend it doesn't exist. God hates sin. Why? Because He loves us, and He knows the terrible devastation sin brings to us.

Sin is like a deadly cancer, inexorably leaving suffering and death in its wake. Left unforgiven, sin also sends men and women into an eternity apart from God—into Hell. God hates sin, because He hates what it does to us! Confess your sin today. Don't wait. Receive God's forgiveness and restoration so that you might be of use to Him and enjoy His love forever.

Complete Consecration

"Whoever desires to come after Me, let him deny himself."
MARK 8:34

Today Christ is calling Christians to cleansing—to dedication—to consecration—to full surrender. If you are a Christian and have been suffering defeat or living outside the will of God, I beg you to surrender every area of your life to Christ.

Only surrendered Christians will make an impact on our world. The world does not need any more lukewarm Christians, lazy Christians, quarrelsome Christians, doubting Christians, or prideful Christians. The Bible says, "A double minded man is unstable in all his ways" (James 1:8 KJV). What keeps you from fully surrendering your life to the King of kings and the Lord of lords?

Your response will make the difference between success and failure in your spiritual life. It will make the difference between your needing help and your being able to help others. Total surrender of your life to Jesus will revolutionize your habits, your prayer life, your Bible reading, your giving, your testimony, and your church relationships. This is the Christian's hour of decision!

While He Is Near

Seek the LORD while he may be found;
call on him while he is near.

ISAIAH 55:6 NIV

Some people claim to be disappointed with God: "If He really cared about me, I wouldn't have so many problems. But since He doesn't do anything about them, why should I bother with Him?" As a result, they go through life without ever knowing God or giving Him His rightful place.

What is the problem? Almost always, I've discovered, these people have made no effort to seek God or find His answers to their problems. Instead of actively seeking Him, they passively expect Him to come to their aid without any effort on their part. They ignore Jesus' words: "Ask, and it will be given to you; seek, and you will find" (Matthew 7:7).

If you have never trusted Christ for your salvation, don't sit back and wait for a better time to accept Him; that moment may never come. And if you do know Christ but are struggling with some problem or decision, don't try to solve it on your own. Commit it to God and seek His will without delay.

Peace in the Storm

May the God of hope fill you with all joy and peace.
ROMANS 15:13

A wonderful old hymn says, "He gives us peace in the midst of a storm."

In life we face all kinds of storms—financial worries, problems in our marriage or family, illness, the betrayal of a friend, and so forth. And we face other kinds of storms that also threaten to engulf us—storms of materialism, storms of secularism, storms of moral degeneracy, storms of injustice, terrorism, and war.

Do you remember the violent storm that came upon Jesus and His disciples one night on the Sea of Galilee? His disciples grew panicky—but Jesus stayed fast asleep. He was at peace because He knew God was in control. He was at peace also because He was sovereign over the storm, and He knew it would vanish at His words: "Peace, be still!" (Mark 4:39).

Jesus' words still calm the turmoil in our lives. Is some storm making you fearful today? Stay close to Jesus, for His Word brings peace.

Renewing Power

*He who was seated on the throne said, "I am
making everything new!"*
REVELATION 21:5 NIV

Think of all the advancements in medicine, commu-
nications, and technology the human race has made
in the last century or so. We should be grateful that God
has given us the ability to make this kind of progress.

But now also think of the tragic fact that these
same centuries have seen the most devastating wars
in human history. In spite of our accomplishments, we
humans are still a painful mixture of good and bad, love
and hate, joy and sorrow. We have the ability to reach
the moon, but we can also destroy millions with the
touch of a button.

Even those of us who have committed our lives to
Jesus Christ often do things we don't want to do, and
we don't do the things we ought to do (Romans 7:19–
20). That's why we need to open our hearts continually
to Christ and allow Him to take away our sin and self-
centeredness. Only He can make us new; only He can
change our hearts and make us more like Himself.

Don't be satisfied to remain the same person you
have always been, but open your heart and life to
Christ's transforming power.

When Troubles Come

Is any one of you in trouble? He should pray. . . . The prayer of a righteous man is powerful and effective.
JAMES 5:13, 16 NIV

You've probably had your doctor take a little rubber hammer and tap you on the knees—and if your reflexes are good, your lower legs responded with a gentle kick. That reflexive action occurs automatically, and it's the same every time that nerve gets hit.

But how do you respond when troubles hit you? What is your automatic reflexive action then? Panic? Anger? Depression? Confusion? All of these?

In the verses, James reminds us what our reflexive action should be: turning to God in prayer. Why? For one thing, prayer is an acknowledgment of our helplessness. You will never pray if you think you can solve everything on your own or if you are too proud to ask God for help. Pride leads to prayerlessness.

But prayer is also an acknowledgment of God's power and love. We aren't trying to manipulate God when we pray—but we are looking to Him to bless us and help us according to His perfect will. When troubles come, may prayer be your automatic response.

Reach for His Hand

*The LORD, He is the One who goes
before you. He will be with you.*

DEUTERONOMY 31:8

Many years ago, when I was going through a dark period, I prayed and prayed, but the Heavens seemed to be made of brass. I felt as though God had disappeared and I was alone with my trial and burden. It was a dark night for my soul.

I wrote my mother about the experience and will never forget her reply: "Son, there are many times when God withdraws to test your faith. He wants you to trust Him in the darkness. Now, son, reach up by faith in the fog, and you will find that His hand will be there." In tears I knelt by my bed and experienced an overwhelming sense of God's presence.

Whether or not we feel God's presence when our way seems dark, by faith we know He is there. You can stake your life on His promise: "I will never leave you nor forsake you" (Hebrews 13:5).

Things That Cannot Be Shaken

We are receiving a kingdom which cannot be shaken.
HEBREWS 12:28

T he date of September 11 will be engraved on the memories of people everywhere for generations to come. On that terrible day when terrorists commandeered several passenger planes and killed thousands of innocent people in New York and Washington, we saw the true depths of evil in the human heart, as well as the uncertainty and fragility of life itself.

What lessons would God teach us from such an appalling tragedy? I confess I don't know the full answer. But I do know that many people faced the shallowness and emptiness of their lives for the first time, and they turned to God as a result. Millions came together to pray.

Another lesson God would teach us all is that our only lasting hope is in Him. Life has always been uncertain; September 11 only made that uncertainty more obvious. Where will you turn for your security? Put your life in Christ's hands, for only He offers us "a kingdom which cannot be shaken."

In Life's Dark Hours

God is our refuge and strength,
an ever-present help in trouble.
Therefore we will not fear, though the earth give way
and the mountains fall into the heart of the sea.

PSALM 46:1–2

The horror of what took place on September 11, 2001, will remain stamped on our memories for generations to come. Who will ever forget the sight of those hijacked airplanes slamming into the twin towers of the World Trade Center and the side of the Pentagon? Who will forget the courageous men and women who stopped another plane from reaching its destination, or the brave emergency personnel who lost their lives in the line of duty?

I have asked myself hundreds of times why God sometimes allows evil to flourish—and I don't have the answer. But evil is real, and we ignore it at our peril. Evil is so real that it cost God's Son His life.

But I do know this: even in life's darkest hours, "God is our refuge and strength." Not money, not military might, not diplomacy, not human cleverness—but God. As you reflect on what happened on that September 11, God can be your refuge and strength as you open your heart to Jesus Christ.

Choosing the Best

As we have opportunity, let us do good to all people.
GALATIANS 6:10 NIV

D o you sometimes feel frustrated because you can't solve all the problems you see around you? It's easy to feel helpless when you read about a famine or natural disaster in some foreign land that threatens the lives of millions. It's easy to feel helpless when you read about the dropout rate in your local school system or the number of people who are homeless or hungry in your community.

No, you can't solve everything—but don't let that keep you from obeying the Bible's injunction to do good to everyone you can as God gives you opportunity. It may be by supporting the work your church is doing in your community, or by sending money to an international Christian humanitarian aid organization. Or it may be by helping a single parent who lives near you, or by tutoring in a local school, or by simply being a friend to someone who is going through hard times.

Jesus said, "Whatever you did for one of the least of these brothers of mine, you did for me" (Matthew 25:40 NIV).

Angels Watching

We should live soberly, righteously, and
godly in the present age.

TITUS 2:12

God's command to live a righteous and godly life should sober us, for the Bible tells us that our lives are Heaven's primary concern. Paul said, "I solemnly charge you in the presence of God and of Christ Jesus and of the chosen angels that you guard and keep [these rules]" (1 Timothy 5:21 AMP).

Think of it: even the angels of Heaven are constantly watching how we as Christians live! Is it merely curiosity on their part, idly wondering if we will fail or prove faithful? No. The angels know the hour is urgent and that what we do is important. Eternal issues are at stake, and we are in the midst of a cosmic struggle.

Don't think it doesn't matter how you live; it does! It matters to God, it matters to His holy angels, and it matters to those around you. Jesus said, "Let your light so shine before men, that they may see your good works and glorify your Father in heaven" (Matthew 5:16).

Abundant Pardon

Blessed is he whose transgression is forgiven,
whose sin is covered.

PSALM 32:1

The story is told about a sensitive boy in the eighteenth century who joined the British Army, but when the shots began to fly, he deserted. Years later he became a great astronomer, even discovering a new planet. King George sent for him. He went, fearful the king would order his execution for being a deserter. Instead, the astronomer was given an envelope, and inside was a royal pardon. The king said, "Now we can talk, and you shall come up and live at Windsor Castle." The astronomer was Sir William Herschel.

Herschel was guilty of desertion and deserved condemnation. But King George had mercy on him and even made him a member of the royal household. This is what God promises us. We are guilty and helpless. But God loves us, and "he saved us, not because of righteous things we had done, but because of his mercy" (Titus 3:5 NIV). Never forget that "God did not send His Son into the world to condemn the world, but that the world through Him might be saved" (John 3:17).

When Hope Seems Impossible

Why are you downcast, O my soul?
Why so disturbed within me?
Put your hope in God.

PSALM 42:5 NIV

How can we have hope when there isn't any reason to have hope?

Some people, I've found, are just naturally optimistic; no matter what happens to them, they almost always react with a brave smile and a positive outlook. "We must keep up our hopes," they say—even when they have no reason to hope. Unfortunately, their hope is little more than wishful thinking.

And that isn't the kind of hope the Bible urges us to have. The Bible tells us to find our hope in God—not in our circumstances, or our natural optimism (or pessimism), or our family or friends—but in God.

How is this possible? It happens when we realize how much God loves us. His love is so deep that He was willing to give His Son's life for us. And it happens when we realize that this life is not all, but ahead of us is Heaven. Is your hope in Jesus—both for this life and the life to come?

The Proper Proportion

Do not love the world or the things in the world.
1 JOHN 2:15

Christians are warned not to love the world—but what is worldliness? Some have misunderstood it.

Worldliness is an attitude, a spirit, an atmosphere that permeates the whole of human society. It is an attitude that puts self first and ignores God and His commandments. Its horizon is this present world, and it never gives a thought to God or to eternity. Worldliness exhibits itself in a thousand different ways—in habits, in selfish pleasures, in a grasping for material things, in driving ambition, in exalting oneself at the expense of others.

We must avoid everything God has labeled sinful; of that there can be no doubt. But some elements of daily life aren't necessarily sinful in themselves; they only become sinful if they are abused. Pleasure isn't always wrong—unless it is abused. Ambition is an essential part of true character—but, abused, it can destroy us.

Be on guard, lest a spirit of worldliness creep into your life. The Bible warns, "Do not love the world or the things in the world."

Seeing Through God's Eyes

So from now on we regard no one from
a worldly point of view.

2 CORINTHIANS 5:16 NIV

When we first meet the apostle Paul in the Bible, he was called Saul—and his mission in life was to stamp out the Christian faith: "Saul was still breathing out murderous threats against the Lord's disciples" (Acts 9:1). But all that changed when Saul met the risen Lord Jesus on the road to Damascus. From that moment on, the persecutor became the proclaimer, fearlessly spreading the gospel throughout the Roman Empire.

What made Paul change? First, he became absolutely convinced that the gospel was true and that Jesus Christ was no imposter; He was the risen Son of God, sent from Heaven to save us from our sins. How could Paul remain silent in the face of this profound truth?

But there was another reason for Paul's change: he began to see people the way God sees them. He now saw them in their lostness and confusion—and he saw them as people for whom Christ died.

What difference does the truth of the gospel make to you? And are you asking God to help you see others through His eyes?

God Values Faith

How precious also are Your thoughts to me, O God!
How great is the sum of them!
PSALM 139:17

How happy would parents be if their child constantly questioned them about whether his or her needs would be met? The parents would feel frustrated and sad, perhaps even angry that the child did not trust them.

The Bible has scores of references telling us how much it pleases God for us to trust Him for our every need. The Roman soldier expressed great faith when he told Jesus just to "say the word" and his servant would be healed (Matthew 8:8). Jesus told His disciples, "Look at the birds . . . they neither sow nor reap nor gather into barns; yet your heavenly Father feeds them. Are you not of more value than they?" (6:26).

God values our trust in Him above every other character quality. And how do we strengthen our trust in God? By spending time in God's presence, by praying, by worshipping, and by reading His Word. We develop trust also as we step out in faith and discover that God really can be trusted. Are you trusting God for every need in your life?

Shaping the Next Generation

*Fathers, do not embitter your children, or
they will become discouraged.*

COLOSSIANS 3:21 NIV

His marriage is over, so after years of tension and coldness between the young man and his parents, he is back living with them while he tries to sort out his future. "I'm glad he came home," his father said to a friend of mine. "I'm afraid we didn't treat him the way we should have when he was a boy, and it's hurt him."

As they grow older, our children become responsible for the decisions they make in life; parents shouldn't take upon themselves all the blame if those decisions are bad. But our failures as parents do have an impact on our children, making them more prone to foolish or evil ways. Harsh, unreasonable discipline—neglect—favoritism—failure to express love—being too busy to give them any attention—failing to teach them the difference between right and wrong—all these and more can "embitter your children" so that "they will become discouraged."

Don't let this happen in your family. And if it has, ask God to forgive you and help you reverse the damage as much as possible.

Kept by the Spirit

We know that He abides in us, by the Spirit whom He has given us.

1 JOHN 3:24

A boat doesn't sink because it is in the water; it sinks because the water gets into it.

In the same way, Christians don't fail to live as they should because they are in the world; they fail because the world gets into them. We don't fail to produce the fruit of the Holy Spirit because we live in a sea of corruption; we fail because the sea of corruption has gotten into us.

It can happen almost without our realizing it. At one time we were dedicated to Christ, surrendered to the will of God. But little by little, the chilling waters of the world crept in. We became preoccupied with the things of this world rather than the things of Christt.

Most oceangoing ships have pumps running constantly, sucking out any water that might have leaked into the hull. Similarly, we need to keep the pumps of repentance running. We need to plug the holes with the truth of God's Word. Don't let the world sink your ship!

Beauty Out of Ashes

The LORD has anointed me . . .
to bestow on them a crown of beauty
instead of ashes.

ISAIAH 61:1, 3 NIV

One of the Bible's greatest truths is that our lives can be different. No matter what our past has been, Christ stands ready to forgive and cleanse us—and to make us new. The Bible says, "If anyone is in Christ, he is a new creation; the old has gone, the new has come!" (2 Corinthians 5:17 NIV).

When Isaiah wrote about beauty coming forth from ashes, he was probably thinking of Jerusalem, the once-proud city now shattered and burned at the hand of a brutal enemy. Some seven hundred years later, Jesus applied this passage from Isaiah to the ministry God had given Him.

Only Christ can bring hope to lives that have been turned into ashes by the assaults of Satan. And Jesus doesn't merely restore us to what we once were; He gives us "a crown of beauty"—the beauty of forgiveness, and the beauty of hope and joy and peace. Who around you is experiencing the ashes of a shattered life? Pray for them and ask God to use you to point them to Christ.

Perfect Peace

May the God of hope fill you with all joy and peace.
Romans 15:13 niv

I know that modern living taxes the faith of the strongest Christians, but none of us should doubt the ability of God to give us grace sufficient for our trials, even amid the stresses of this new century. We Christians are to trust that God is still on the throne. He is a sovereign God, working out things according to His own plan.

Some section hands on a British railroad found a thrush's nest under the rail and the hen peacefully sitting on the eggs, undisturbed by the roar of the fast trains above and around her. What a picture of perfect trust! The Bible says, "You will keep him in perfect peace, whose mind is stayed on You" (Isaiah 26:3).

Believe me, God's grace is more than adequate for these times. Even as I grow older, I am still learning, day by day, to keep my mind centered on Christ. When I do, the worries and anxieties and concerns of the world pass away, and nothing but "perfect peace" is left in my heart.

Love in Action

This is how God showed his love among us: He
sent his one and only Son into the world that
we might live through him.

1 JOHN 4:9 NIV

Love isn't just a feeling; love must be expressed in action. If it isn't, we don't have any reason to believe that love to be genuine, no matter how much that person claims it is.

Likewise, God's love is not just a vague feeling or sentimental emotion hidden in His heart. God's love is real—and we know it because He demonstrated it to us. He put His love into action! Do you want to know if God loves you? Here is the proof: Jesus Christ left Heaven's glory and came down to this sin-infested Earth to die for you. Paul put it this way: "Very rarely will anyone die for a righteous man, though for a good man someone might possibly dare to die. But God demonstrates his own love for us in this: While we were still sinners, Christ died for us" (Romans 5:7–8 NIV).

Have you been tempted to doubt God's love for you? Don't doubt it any longer, but look instead at Christ and the cross. There you will see God's love poured out for you.

Why, God? Why?

> *If only my anguish could be weighed*
> *and all my misery be placed on the scales!*
> *It would surely outweigh the sand of the seas.*
>
> JOB 6:2–3 NIV

Have you ever cried out as Job did here, weighed down beyond measure with heartache, grief, and anger, and demanding to know why God let it happen—but not receiving an answer?

If so, let me assure you first of all that God isn't upset or angry at you; He understands your heartaches and weaknesses. As the psalmist said, "He knows how we are formed, he remembers that we are dust" (103:14 NIV).

In reality, however, we often don't know why God permits certain things to happen to us. We do know that evil is real: we live in a world that is ravaged by sickness and death and sorrow—a world that isn't the way God intended it to be. Someday Christ's victory will be complete, and all this will be changed—but not yet. In the meantime, put your faith and hope in Christ. He knows what it is to suffer: He went to the cross for us. And because He did, we have hope even in the midst of life's darkest hours.

Pray Without Ceasing

Men always ought to pray and not lose heart.

LUKE 18:1

A prayer does not have to be eloquent or contain the language and terms of a theologian. In fact, sometimes our simplest, most heartfelt prayers are the most pleasing to God.

When you made your decision for Christ, you became a child of God, adopted by Him into His family forever. Now you have the wonderful privilege of going directly into God's presence and addressing Him as your Father. In the beginning you may not be fluent, but it's important to begin. My wife has a notebook she kept of our children as they were beginning to talk. She treasures these first attempts, mistakes and all. She said, "I wouldn't take anything for that book."

When Paul said we should "pray without ceasing" (1 Thessalonians 5:17), he chose a term used in his day to describe a persistent cough. Repeatedly, throughout our day, we should be turning quickly to God to praise and thank Him, and to ask for His help. God is interested in everything we do, and nothing is too great or too insignificant to share with Him.

Like the Tossing Sea

But the wicked are like the tossing sea,
which cannot rest,
whose waves cast up mire and mud.
"There is no peace," says my God, "for the wicked."
ISAIAH 57:20–21 NIV

You probably know people who are like this, or you may have been one of them yourself: they have no stability in their lives, and are constantly pursuing one goal after another, one relationship after another, one pleasure after another. Yet they never find the happiness they seek.

The reason? They have left God out of their lives—and without Him, they have no purpose or direction, no ultimate sense of right and wrong. A life without God is like a boat without an rudder.

But God didn't intend for our lives to be this way. When we come to know Christ, He brings calm to our chaos and direction to our drifting. It doesn't necessarily happen overnight—but as we learn to live by the principles He has given us in His Word, we leave the past behind and discover the peace He alone can give. Thank God for doing this in your life—and pray for your friends who do not yet know Christ, that they may find in Him the stability and peace they seek.

Christ Is Coming Again

Looking for the blessed hope and glorious appearing of our . . . Savior Jesus Christ.

TITUS 2:13

One of the best ways to get rid of discouragement is to remember that Christ is coming again. What is happening in your life right now is not going to last forever!

The most thrilling, glorious truth in all the world is the second coming of Jesus Christ. When we look about today and see pessimism on every side, we should remember that the Bible is the only book in the world that reliably predicts the future. It says the consummation of all things shall be the coming again of Jesus Christ to this Earth.

This truth gives us hope—but it should also make us sober and more diligent. After all, we do not know exactly when Christ will return. Jesus Himself said, "Of that day and hour no one knows, not even the angels of heaven, but My Father only" (Matthew 24:36). Believing in the return of Christ doesn't make us less concerned about this world; it makes us more concerned, because we know time may be short. Now is the time to live for Christ and witness for Him.

The Staff of Life

Your word I have hidden in my heart,
That I might not sin against you.

PSALM 119:11

The Bible isn't just another great book. It is God's Word, given by God to tell us about Himself.

Peter declared, "We did not follow cunningly devised fables . . . for prophecy never came by the will of man, but holy men of God spoke as they were moved by the Holy Spirit" (2 Peter 1:16, 21). Paul stressed, "All Scripture is given by inspiration of God, and is profitable for doctrine, for reproof, for correction, for instruction in righteousness" (2 Timothy 3:16).

I have known many outstanding leaders who made the Bible their guide. Businessman Herbert J. Taylor, former president of Rotary International, told me he began each day by reading the Sermon on the Mount aloud.

Let the Bible be your firm foundation. Let it be the staff of life that nourishes your soul. Let it be the sword of the Spirit that cuts away sin. Many years ago I heard these words: "Sin will keep you from God's Word—or God's Word will keep you from sin!"

Adopted into His Family

He chose us in him before the creation of the world . . .
to be adopted as his sons through Jesus Christ, in
accordance with his pleasure and will.

EPHESIANS 1:4–5 NIV

From time to time someone writes me who was adopted as a child and is now haunted by the idea that they had been rejected by their birth parents, and, therefore, they must have been unloved and unlovable. These feelings have oppressed them most of their lives.

What they have forgotten—and what I always try to point out to them—is that they weren't unloved and unwanted by their adoptive parents—not at all. That couple had a choice in the matter—and they deliberately chose to bring this child into their family. The truth is, they are loved, and they are wanted.

In an even greater way, God loves us so much that He chose to make us part of His family. Jesus' death and resurrection accomplished many things for us— forgiveness, new life, even an eternal destiny. But something else took place when you accepted Christ: you were adopted into His family forever. God loves you that much!

God of All Comfort

Because he himself suffered when he was tempted, he is able to help those who are being tempted.

HEBREWS 2:18 NIV

Once when I was in my late teens, I was in love with a girl. It might have been puppy love, but it was real to me, the puppy! We became tentatively engaged to be married even though we were both much too young. However, she felt that the Lord was leading her to another young man—one of my best friends.

I suffered a broken heart, and I remember going to a clergyman friend of mine to seek his help. He pointed me to 2 Corinthians 1:3–4: "Blessed be the God and Father of our Lord Jesus Christ . . . who comforts us in all our tribulation, that we may be able to comfort those who are in any trouble, with the comfort with which we ourselves are comforted by God."

From those words of the apostle I gained comfort. But there is more to it than that. This passage from Paul suggests a new insight into suffering: not only are we comforted in our trials, but our trials can equip us to comfort others. Has God taught you something through your trials that could help someone else in your life?

Faith Versus Feelings

*Now faith is being sure of what we hope for and
certain of what we do not see.*

HEBREWS 11:1 NIV

This verse introduces one of the Bible's great chapters—what someone has called "The Bible's Hall of Fame." Beginning in Genesis—with Abel, Enoch, Noah, and Abraham—and continuing through the Old Testament, the author spotlights spiritual heroes who stayed faithful to God in the face of almost overwhelming odds.

Why did they remain faithful? One reason is because their faith was in God and His promises, not in their feelings. These great men and women of faith faced discouragement and doubt just as we do. But they trusted God, not their emotions—and we should do the same.

Emotions aren't wrong; God gave them to us, and they are an important part of life. But our feelings go up and down—and if our faith is based merely on our feelings, it, too, will go up and down. Only when we build our lives on Christ will our faith be stable and strong. Don't let your feelings mislead you, but base your faith solely on Christ and what He did for us through His death and resurrection.

Jesus As Lord

"Why do you call me, 'Lord, Lord,' and do not do what I say?"

LUKE 6:46 NIV

Jesus demands to be Master and Lord of every part of your life.

Is He Lord of your mind, of what you think, read, and believe? Of what you dream about, meditate on, and entertain yourself with?

Is Jesus the Master and Lord of your body? Are you presenting it to Christ as a living sacrifice? Do your eyes belong to Christ? What about your ears? Your mouth? Your hands? Your feet? Your sexual urges? Our eyes can be covetous and never satisfied. Our tongues can do unspeakable harm. Our hands can do the work of the devil. Our feet can take us where we shouldn't go. And our sexuality can get us in trouble before we know it.

Is Jesus the Master and Lord of your social life—your friendships, your relationships, your amusements? Always ask yourself these questions when making plans: "Can I ask God's blessing on this? Can I do this to the glory of God? Or will this be a stumbling block to me or to someone else?"

Searching for Hope

*"In the world you will have tribulation; but be of
good cheer, I have overcome the world."*

JOHN 16:33

Once when I referred to the future that God is
planning, a university student asked me, "Isn't
this a form of escapism?" I said, "In a sense, yes; and
before the devil gets through with this world, we are all
going to be looking for exit signs!"

As Christians we look beyond this world to God's
promise of "new heavens and a new earth in which
righteousness dwells" (2 Peter 3:13). But in the meantime, the world remains mired in the same heartaches
and injustices it has suffered since the Fall—and Jesus
said we shouldn't be surprised: "In the world you will
have tribulation."

Some people mistakenly think that if they become
Christians, God will take away all their problems. It just
isn't so. Sin still dwells within us, and Satan is still at
work.

But that isn't the full story! Jesus added, "Be of good
cheer, I have overcome the world." Notice that He not
only *will* overcome the world—He already *has*!

Which Wing?

> *What good is it, my brothers, if a man claims to have faith but has no deeds? . . . Faith by itself, if it is not accompanied by action, is dead.*
>
> JAMES 2:14, 17 NIV

Which wing of an airplane is more important? Obviously both are equally necessary, and therefore both are equally important.

Which is more important: what we believe about God or what kind of life we live? Again, both are equally necessary, and therefore both are equally important.

In fact, the Bible says that if we claim to believe in Christ but our faith doesn't impact the way we live, then our faith isn't genuine. That is the exact point James was making in the verses above as he warned us about the dangers of a shallow belief in Christ.

At the same time, don't lose sight of the fact that we are saved solely by our faith in Christ, not by our good deeds. Only Christ can save us, for only He is the sinless Son of God who took all our sins upon Himself when He died on the cross for us. As the Bible says, "By grace you have been saved through faith" (Ephesians 2:8).

What impact will your faith make on your life today?

God's Word

*Desire the pure milk of the word, that
you may grow thereby.*

1 PETER 2:2

Just as our bodies need food, so our souls need spiritual food. Without it we become malnourished and weak, susceptible to every temptation and unable to do the work God calls us to do.

Where do we find this spiritual food? In the Bible, God's Word. The Bible reveals Christ, the Bread of Life and the Water of Life. If we fail to partake of this spiritual nourishment, we will lose our spiritual vitality.

People in some parts of our world do not enjoy the freedom we have to read the Bible. But most of us cannot hide behind that excuse. The problem for most of us is not getting a Bible, but using a Bible—actually picking it up and reading it.

Don't be content to skim through a chapter merely to satisfy your conscience or some long-established habit. Rather, read the Bible as if your life depended on it. Meditate on it, memorize it, and hide it in your heart so it permeates your whole being. A small portion well digested is of far greater spiritual value than a lengthy passage hurriedly scanned.

God in Human Flesh

[Jesus] is the image of the invisible God.
COLOSSIANS 1:15

The incarnation—God's taking upon Himself our humanity and becoming a man—is an amazing truth, and one that gives us a solid foundation for our faith.

Both Jesus and the very first Christians clearly asserted that He was fully divine, and over the centuries this truth has remained central to the Christian faith. Long before Jesus' miraculous birth, the Old Testament foretold that God would enter this world in human form (Matthew 1:23). When confronted by those who questioned His divinity, Jesus responded, "I and the Father are one" (John 10:30 NIV). The consistent witness of the apostles was that "the Son is the radiance of God's glory and the exact representation of his being" (Hebrews 1:3 NIV). When Thomas—unconvinced at first that Jesus had been raised from the dead—met the risen Savior, he immediately exclaimed, "My Lord and my God!" (John 20:28 NIV).

Spend a few minutes marveling over this wondrous truth—and thank God for demonstrating His great love for us by taking upon Himself our human flesh.

God's Revelation

Forever, O Lord,
Your word is settled in heaven.

PSALM 119:89

What does *revelation* mean? It means that something that has been hidden is now made known.

Some people see God as hidden and unknown. Such a view assumes God doesn't want to be known or even that God is incapable of being known because He is just a vague, impersonal force like gravity.

But God has revealed Himself. He is not hidden! He has spoken to us, and if we will listen, we can not only discover what He is like, but we can also come to know Him in a personal way.

God has two textbooks. One is the textbook of nature. By looking at the world, we can learn something about its Creator.

The other is the textbook of revelation, the Bible. It is more than an ancient record of events; it is God's Word, given to us by the inspiration of the Holy Spirit to guide our lives. God has spoken—and He still speaks. Are you listening?

Whom Do We Blame?

Each one is tempted when, by his own evil desire, he is dragged away and enticed. Then, after desire has conceived, it gives birth to sin.

JAMES 1:14–15 NIV

Is Satan always to blame when things go wrong in our lives? Or are we sometimes responsible?

On one hand, the Bible makes it clear that Satan is real and that he is ultimately behind all the evil that goes on in the world. Before he rebelled against God (long before the human race was created), the world was perfect; sin and evil didn't exist. But now we live in a fallen, twisted, sin-infested world—and Satan is the reason.

On the other hand, Satan is not all-powerful, nor does he directly cause every bad thing that happens to us. Sometimes we don't know the cause—but often we alone are responsible, because we have turned our backs on God and deliberately followed our own sinful desires instead of His will. When we do this, we pay the consequences; as the Bible warns, "God cannot be mocked. A man reaps what he sows" (Galatians 6:7 NIV).

But remember: by His death and resurrection, Jesus triumphed over all the forces of evil—those in our heart and those in the world. Turn to Him for the strength you need to resist temptation and follow Him.

Treasure That Lasts

"Lay up for yourselves treasures in heaven."

MATTHEW 6:20

Some time ago two old friends were dying. One was rich, and the other poor. The rich man was outside of Christ, but the poor man was a strong believer. One day the rich man was talking to another of his friends. "When I die," he said, "I shall have to leave my riches. When he dies, he will go to his riches."

In just a couple of sentences, the rich man summed up the contrast between the poor man and himself. The man worth everything, in reality, had nothing; the man with nothing, in reality, had everything.

These two men are a vivid illustration of what Jesus said to His disciples: "Do not lay up for yourselves treasures on earth . . . but lay up for yourselves treasures in heaven. . . . For where your treasure is, there your heart will be also" (Matthew 6:19–21).

Does that mean we must renounce everything we own? No, not unless God clearly commands us to do so. But it does mean that we should commit everything we have—including our lives—to Christ and choose to put His will above everything else.

Free of Pride

Patience is better than pride.

ECCLESIASTES 7:8 NIV

He had dropped out of church when he didn't agree with a building project that was being planned. After his wife died, however, he found himself wishing he had never left; his loneliness was almost more than he could bear. But would he have the courage to swallow his pride and go back to church? Finally he did, and his only regret was that he hadn't done it sooner.

Maybe this reminds you of a situation in your life. Do you need to swallow your pride? Do you need to apologize or admit you were wrong about something? Do you need to work to restore your relationship with a brother or sister in Christ—especially if you were the one at fault? Or, like this widower, do you need to get back into a fellowship of believers?

If so, confess your pride and seek God's wisdom and strength for the future. Let go of your pride—and then patiently wait to see how God will work to restore your heart and change your life.

Faith in God

Faith is the substance of things hoped for.

HEBREWS 11:1

Faith must have an object. We don't simply have faith; we have faith in something or someone. Faith in "faith" is meaningless.

For the Christian, there is only one object for faith: the living God. Anything less is insubstantial, unreal, even deceptive. Our faith is in the God who created this world and who came down to Earth in the person of His Son, Jesus Christ. We put our faith in Christ because He alone is the Savior. The Bible says, "Through Him [you] believe in God, who raised Him from the dead and gave Him glory, so that your faith and hope are in God" (1 Peter 1:21).

People today put their faith in all kinds of ideas and beliefs, from astrology and alleged spirit guides to science and humanism. But only Christ reveals God to us, and only He can bridge the gap between us and God—the gap caused by sin. Do not be deceived or misled. Only Christ is worthy of your faith.

Spiritual Food

Your word is a lamp to my feet
and a light for my path.
PSALM 119:105 NIV

I recently heard from a dear woman in the Lord. Listen to what she wrote: "I am eighty-four, and almost all my life I read the Bible every day. But now my vision is getting very bad, and the doctor says I'll probably be blind soon. I miss seeing the way I once did, but most of all I miss reading my Bible. Please tell people to read the Bible while they can, because it truly does give light for my path."

She had learned a vital lesson: nothing will help us grow spiritually more than spending time alone with God every day, reading His Word and praying. I know our lives are busy today, but time alone with God is essential to our spiritual welfare. Most of us wouldn't think of missing a meal, yet we miss our spiritual meals when we neglect God's Word—and we end up spiritually weak.

Many years ago I heard a speaker say something I have never forgotten: "Either sin will keep you from God's Word, or God's Word will keep you from sin." Even five minutes alone with God each day can renew and strengthen your soul.

Our Great Assurance

Let us draw near with a true heart in
full assurance of faith.

HEBREWS 10:22

Disregard your feelings when you come to Christ. You aren't saved by your feelings; you are saved by Christ. Feelings come and go, but Christ remains.

Only the facts matter—the fact that Jesus Christ died for your sins and rose again; the fact that if you have committed your life to Him, He has promised to forgive you and save you. The Bible says, "God has given us eternal life, and this life is in His Son. He who has the Son has life" (1 John 5:11–12).

That is God's promise to you—and He cannot lie. Your feelings will lie to you, and Satan may even use them to convince you that God has abandoned you or that you have lost your salvation. But remember: "There is no truth in [Satan]. When he lies, he speaks his native language, for he is a liar and the father of lies" (John 8:44 NIV).

How wonderful to know our faith is based on God's truth, and not our feelings!

Pure Spiritual Milk

*Like newborn babies, crave pure spiritual milk, so
that by it you may grow up in your salvation.*

1 PETER 2:2 NIV

Birth is only the beginning for a newborn baby; that child isn't meant to be a baby forever, but to grow and become strong and eventually reach adulthood. The same is true for us. When we first come to Christ, we are "spiritual newborns"—but we aren't meant to remain that way. God's plan is for us to grow strong in our faith and become mature in our understanding of His will.

We must take steps to grow spiritually strong, and we do this by consuming the "pure spiritual milk" God has provided for us. And what is that milk? First, God has given us the Bible; through it we learn about Him and His will for our lives. God has also given us the privilege of prayer and fellowship with other believers. If any of those—God's Word, prayer, fellowship—is missing, our growth will be stunted.

Are you growing in your faith? If not, why not? Make God's "pure spiritual milk" part of your soul's diet every day.

To Die Is Gain

To me, to live is Christ and to die is gain.

PHILIPPIANS 1:21 NIV

Most of us know what it means to be stunned by the sudden passing of a dedicated friend, a godly pastor, a devout missionary, or a saintly mother. We have stood at the open grave with hot tears running down our cheeks and asked in utter bewilderment, "Why, O God? Why?" We know the impact these people made, and we can't help but think of the good they might have continued to do had they lived longer.

The death of the righteous is no accident. Do you think that God—whose watchful vigil notes the sparrow's fall and who knows the number of hairs on our heads—would turn His back on one of His children in the hour of peril? With Him there are no accidents, no tragedies, and no catastrophes as far as His children are concerned.

It was Sir Walter Scott who asked, "Is death the last sleep? No, it is the final awakening." That is true for every believer in Christ. Even when grief overwhelms us or confusion assails us, we still can trust God's all-knowing love.

Safe and Secure

*He became the author of eternal salvation to
all who obey Him.*

HEBREWS 5:9

With the exception of Jesus, probably no one in the Bible endured more scorn than Noah. Told to build an ark to escape God's judgment, "Noah did; according to all that God commanded him" (Genesis 6:22).

Can you imagine what his neighbors said? Can you picture them shaking their heads and laughing, calling him a fool and murmuring he must be out of his mind? Can you envision them angrily rejecting his warnings of coming judgment and returning to their idolatrous ways?

When the flood came, only Noah and his family were saved. For those who scorned his pleas, it was too late.

You and I are called to proclaim a message that often seems foolish to an unbelieving world—the message of the cross. Will everyone accept it? No. Will some mock us? Yes. But never stop sharing the gospel, for it is still "the power of God for the salvation of everyone who believes" (Romans 1:16 NIV).

Perfection Lost

God saw all that he had made, and it was very good.

GENESIS 1:31 NIV

I could hear the puzzlement in her question: "Why would God say the world is good when so much of it is obviously imperfect or even evil?"

After God created the world, He said it was perfect, because He had made it exactly the way He wanted it to be. But notice that He pronounced His creation "very good" before Satan tempted Adam and Eve, before the world was invaded by sin.

The world was indeed a perfect place before Adam and Eve chose to believe Satan's lies instead of God's truth. Adam and Eve had everything they needed, and they walked in perfect harmony with God—until they turned their backs on Him. Suddenly sin—like a deadly cancer—took root in the human heart, and even the plants and animals became ravaged by sin and death.

The Bible tells us, however, that this sin-sick, fallen world won't last forever. At the end of time, God will intervene, and the new Heaven and new Earth He will create will be free from all evil and pain. Come quickly, Lord Jesus!

Dispel Discouragement

Wait on the LORD;
Be of good courage,
And He shall strengthen your heart.

PSALM 27:14

The root of discouragement is unbelief. Perhaps you are discouraged because you think you aren't making enough money, and you aren't convinced that God can supply your needs. Or you are frustrated in your job, and you refuse to believe God can help you be content. Or maybe you are worried about health problems, and you don't even stop to consider that your life is in God's hands.

Discouragement is a large cloud that, like all clouds, obscures the warmth and joy of the sun. In the case of spiritual discouragement, the cloud eclipses the Son of God, the Lord Jesus, in our lives. Discouragement is Satan's device to thwart the work of God in our lives. Discouragement blinds our eyes to the mercy of God and makes us perceive only the unfavorable circumstances.

There is only one way to dispel discouragement, and it is not by our own strength or ingenuity. It is by turning in faith to God, believing that He loves us and is in control. The Bible says, "Wait on the LORD . . . and He shall strengthen your heart."

Learning from Their Example

*Now these things occurred as examples to keep us
from setting our hearts on evil things as they did.*

1 CORINTHIANS 10:6 NIV

Sometimes people ask me why they should bother reading the Old Testament. After all, they say, didn't Christ, by His death, fulfill all the detailed sacrificial laws we find there? And besides, what can we possibly learn from people who lived so long ago?

But the Old Testament is just as much God's Word as the New Testament, and God has much to teach us in its pages. "All scripture is given by inspiration of God, and is profitable" (2 Timothy 3:16 KJV). One of the most important things God wants to teach us from the Old Testament is how *not* to live.

The Old Testament tells us about some of God's greatest servants—Joseph, Moses, Jeremiah, and others—and God has much to teach us from their example. But the Old Testament is also filled with the accounts of men and women who failed God. How did it happen? What were the consequences? They, too, are examples, warning us of what happens when we turn aside from following Christ. Learn from them how not to live.

OCTOBER

Opened Eyes

*God opened [Hagar's] eyes and she saw a well of
water.... [And] God was with the boy as he grew up.*
GENESIS 21:19–20 NIV

Hagar was a single parent, and she almost gave in to despair. Perhaps you are in that situation also, or you may know of someone who is.

Hagar was Sarah's handmaiden (or personal attendant), and after Sarah mistakenly tried to fulfill God's promise of a son by giving Hagar to her husband, Abraham, Hagar became the mother of Ishmael. Forced to flee into the desert with her son, Hagar ran out of water and felt the end had come. But God had not abandoned her, and we read that He helped her see a well of water He had provided. It had been there all along, but Hagar only saw it with God's help.

Being a single parent is very difficult. But God knows your situation just as He knew Hagar's, and perhaps He wants to show you a well He has already prepared—something or someone to refresh and help you.

Don't give in to despair or self-pity, but look to Jesus Christ every day for the hope and strength you need. He loves you and your children, and He will not abandon you.

Triumph over Tragedy

*Every good gift and every perfect gift is from above,
and comes down from the Father of lights.*

The key to understanding tragedy is to understand its source. Death and pain and every other tragedy came into this world because of sin. When Adam and Eve sinned in the garden of Eden, they weren't just doing something God had told them not to do. It was a blatant, open act of rebellion—in thought, word, and deed—against the God who had made them and had supplied their every need. It was saying God was a liar and believing Satan instead. It was yielding to the temptation to "be like God" (Genesis 3:5).

Every graveyard, every hospital, every prison, every courtroom is a witness to the terrible legacy of that rebellion. No, I don't fully understand why God allows evil to happen. But evil happens because we are sinful people living in an evil world. Never underestimate the devastating effects of sin.

What was sin's greatest tragedy? It was the cross—for had it not been for sin, Jesus would never have had to die. But Christ triumphed over tragedy—and so can we, because of Him.

Christ Won for You

While we were still sinners, Christ died for us.
ROMANS 5:8

One of the hardest truths for some people to accept is that there is absolutely nothing they can do to win their salvation.

No matter how generous or how honest or how compassionate they are—it is never enough. God is holy, and His standard is perfection. If we think we are good enough, that thought simply proves our pride.

Only when we see ourselves as God sees us—sinners, guilty before Him—will we realize our need of a Savior. C. H. Spurgeon said, "The first link between my soul and Christ is not my goodness but my badness, not my merit but my misery, not my riches but my need."

But the amazing thing is this: in spite of our sin, God still loves us. He loves us so much that Christ died on the cross for us. All we can do is believe and receive—believe Christ died for us and by faith receive Him into our lives. No, you can't win your salvation—but Christ has already won it for you!

The Gospel Is Complete

*Dear friends . . . [I] urge you to contend for the faith
that was once for all entrusted to the saints.*

JUDE V. 3 NIV

Is the gospel of Jesus Christ complete? Or do we need something else in addition to what the Bible tells us?

Perhaps you've had people come to your door asking to speak to you about the beliefs of their particular religious group. If you invited them in, however, it wasn't long before you realized they were convinced that their group—and only their group—has the full truth about God and salvation. And if you probed further, you discovered that they were convinced that the Bible's message of salvation through faith in Christ is not enough; the message in the books "discovered" or written by their founder is also necessary.

But Jesus Christ is all we need. He alone was the Son of God, sent from Heaven as God's final sacrifice for our sins. Cults deny this—but the Bible is clear: "Salvation is found in no one else, for there is no other name under heaven given to men by which we must be saved" (Acts 4:12 NIV). Thank God for this truth!

Answered Prayer

Let us . . . come boldly to the throne of grace,
that we may obtain mercy.

HEBREWS 4:16

Frequently people say to me, "God answered my prayer!" Usually they mean God granted them whatever they had requested, either for themselves or for others.

God always answers the prayers of His children—but His answer isn't always yes. Sometimes His answer is no, or "Wait"—and they are answers just as much as yes.

Think of Paul, pleading with God to remove his "thorn in the flesh" (probably a painful illness). God's answer was no (2 Corinthians 12:7–10). God had something better in mind for Paul—a path leading him into deeper dependence on God and His grace. Or think of Jesus, praying as He faced the agony of the cross: "If it is possible, let this cup pass from Me" (Matthew 26:39). Again God's answer was no—because there was no other way for our salvation to be won.

God knows far better than we do what is best for us. Thank God even when He says no or "Wait." His answer is always perfect.

Anger's Cruel Harvest

*As churning the milk produces butter,
and as twisting the nose produces blood,
so stirring up anger produces strife.*

PROVERBS 30:33 NIV

Have you ever asked yourself why God takes anger so seriously and urges us to cast it out of our lives? One reason is because of what it does to other people. When we lash out at people in anger, we hurt them and create conflict with them, and that is wrong. God loves them just as much as He loves us, and when our anger hurts someone, we are harming someone God loves.

God also hates our anger because of what it does to us. Our anger cuts us off from others; no one likes to be around someone who may explode at any moment. Anger also hurts us by turning us into resentful, bitter, unloving people. Most of all, anger cuts us off from God, because anger makes us preoccupied with our own problems rather than with God's will for our lives.

Commit your anger to God and seek His forgiveness. Then ask Him to fill you with His patience and love. "The fruit of the Spirit is . . . patience" (Galatians 5:22 NIV).

God's Plans Are Best

As for God, His way is perfect.
PSALM 18:30

Things didn't always work out the way Paul planned. Expecting to preach in Asia Minor, he was "forbidden by the Holy Spirit" (Acts 16:6). Looking forward to instructing the new converts in Philippi, Paul and his companion instead found themselves thrown into prison (vv. 11–24). Encouraged by the response to the gospel in Thessalonica, he was suddenly assailed by a mob and accused of having "turned the world upside down" (17:6). As a result he was forced to flee.

But in every instance God was in control. Paul was forbidden to preach in Asia Minor—because God was opening the door to Europe. Paul found himself in jail—and as a result the Philippian jailer and his family were converted. Paul had to flee Thessalonica—and Berea, the next town, "received the word with all readiness" (v. 11).

Things don't always work out the way we plan. But if we commit our way to God and walk in obedience to Him, we discover His plans are always better.

We Will Be Whole

The body that is sown [in death] is perishable, it is raised imperishable; it is sown in dishonor, it is raised in glory; it is sown in weakness, it is raised in power.

1 CORINTHIANS 15:42–43 NIV

Almost nothing is more painful than losing someone we deeply love.

"We were convinced God was going to heal my husband of his cancer, but He didn't," a woman wrote me recently. "Why didn't God answer us?"

I had to confess to her that I didn't know why God hadn't restored her husband to health. I assured her, however, that God knew what she was going through, that He still loved her, and that He was with her. He truly is the One "who comforts the downcast" (2 Corinthians 7:6).

But I also pointed out that even if God didn't answer her prayers the way she hoped He would, He did not ignore them. In fact, He answered her prayers in a far greater way than she realized—because now her husband is in Heaven, and all his sickness and pain are over. He has been healed! In the midst of our tears there still can be joy, because we know that those who die in the Lord are now with Christ, "which is better by far" (Philippians 1:23 NIV).

No Other Gods

"You cannot serve God and mammon."
LUKE 16:13

The Bible strictly forbids idolatry. One of the Ten Commandments declares, "You shall not make for yourself a carved image . . . you shall not bow down to them nor serve them" (Exodus 20:4–5).

But almost anything can become an idol—something we worship and serve in place of God. It might be success, or pleasure, or possessions, or money, or anything else we let control our lives. These things aren't necessarily wrong in themselves, but they become idols when we make them the focus of our lives.

The Bible rejects idols for at least two reasons. First, idols are false. They cannot save us or change our lives for the better. Second, idols cut us off from God. We substitute them for God—and, as a result, we turn our backs on Him. We never come to know Him and love Him as we should.

Has any idol taken God's rightful place in your life? Don't let it happen. God has commanded, "You shall have no other gods before Me" (Exodus 20:3).

Returning to God

This is what the LORD Almighty says: "Return to me,"
declares the LORD Almighty, "and I will return to you."

ZECHARIAH 1:3 NIV

We don't use the word *backsliding* as much as we used to—but the reality is still with us: a seemingly sincere Christian begins to "slide backward" in their faith, returning to their old ways and acting as if Jesus no longer means anything to them.

Why does this happen? Sometimes their faith wasn't real; they had never committed their lives to Jesus Christ in the first place. The writer of Hebrews warned, "See to it, brothers, that none of you has a sinful, unbelieving heart that turns away from the living God" (Hebrews 3:12 NIV).

But backsliding also happens to believers—and when it does, Satan rejoices. Perhaps old habits overwhelm them; perhaps they cave in to the pressure of the crowd; perhaps temptation lures them into sin. Whatever the reason, a backsliding Christian compromises their faith and causes unbelievers to mock the gospel.

The good news is that God loves even the backslider and stands ready to forgive. Guard against sliding backward in your faith—but if you do, don't stay that way. Return to God—and He will return to you.

Strangers in the World

I urge you, as aliens and strangers in the world,
to abstain from sinful desires.
1 PETER 2:11 NIV

People from other countries are rarely shown the welcome mat. They are often accepted reluctantly, and they may even find themselves victims of discrimination, rejection, or intolerance.

The Bible says that we Christians are "aliens and strangers in the world." Our citizenship is in Heaven, which is our real home. As long as we live on Earth, we don't quite fit in. Our customs are different, our goals are different, our ways of living are different, and our concerns are different.

And as Christ's followers (instead of followers of this world), we may find ourselves scorned, rejected, or even persecuted. If so, we shouldn't be surprised. Jesus warned, "If they persecuted Me, they will also persecute you" (John 15:20).

But never forget: you are a citizen of the Kingdom of God. And someday you will be home in Heaven!

Yes and No

Love the brotherhood of believers.

1 Peter 2:17 NIV

Someone has wisely observed that if we ever found a perfect church, it would be imperfect the minute we joined it! We Christians aren't perfect, and we don't become perfect when we join together in a church.

All the same, can a person be a Christian without going to church? Is a walk through the woods or a relaxing game of golf as spiritually uplifting as a service of worship? The answer is . . . both yes and no. Yes, when you come to Christ and commit your life to Him, God accepts you as an individual, just as you are. And sometimes He draws us closer to Himself when we reflect on His beauty or enjoy His good gifts.

But when you come to Christ, you also become part of His family. Every true Christian is now your brother or sister—and we need each other. Don't use your church's imperfections as an excuse to stay away. Instead, ask God to use the preaching of His Word and your fellowship with others to make you more like Christ.

Yielded to God

Know ye not, that to whom ye yield yourselves
servants to obey, his servants ye are?

ROMANS 6:16 KJV

Eric Liddell, the missionary and great runner whose story is told in the film *Chariots of Fire*, has been described as "ridiculously humble in victory, utterly generous in defeat." That's a good definition of what it means to be meek. Eric Liddell was fiercely competitive, determined to use his God-given abilities to the fullest. But his meekness, kindness, and gentle spirit won the admiration even of those he defeated.

Meekness involves being yielded. The word *yield* has two meanings. The first is negative, and the second is positive. On one hand, it means "to relinquish, to abandon"; on the other hand, it also means "to give." This second definition is in line with Jesus' words: "He who loses [or gives] his life . . . will find it" (Matthew 10:39).

Those who submit to the will of God do not fight back at life. They learn the secret of yielding—of relinquishing and abandoning—their own lives and wills to Christ. And then He gives back to them a life that is far richer and fuller than anything they could ever have imagined.

Always Relevant

Prophecy never had its origin in the will of man,
but men spoke from God as they were carried
along by the Holy Spirit.

2 PETER 1:21 NIV

The Bible is a remarkable book for many reasons, but the most important of all is that it is God's Word. It isn't just an ancient collection of human wisdom; it was written by people who were "carried along by the Holy Spirit." God gave Scripture to us so we could come to know Him and His will for our lives.

Don't dismiss the Bible because it was written thousands of years ago. God has not changed, human nature has not changed, and neither has our need for Christ and His salvation. From Genesis through Revelation, the Bible points us to Jesus Christ, who was God in human flesh, sent from Heaven to save us from our sins. It also points us to God's perfect will for our lives.

Let the Bible's truth become part of your life every day.

God's Constant Love and Compassion

Because of the LORD's great love we are not consumed,
for his compassions never fail.

LAMENTATIONS 3:22 NIV

Have you ever had someone you loved do something that embarrassed or hurt you? Probably. But did you stop loving that person? No! You might have been disappointed, but you kept on loving them.

In a far greater way, God still loves us even when we disappoint Him or do something wrong. He loves us in the good times, but He also loves us when things aren't going our way and we begin to doubt Him. God's love for us is constant—in the good times and the bad, "for his compassions never fail."

Think about Peter for a moment. He was one of Jesus' closest disciples, yet after Jesus was arrested, Peter denied even knowing Him (Luke 22:54–62). But Jesus forgave Peter when he repented and returned to Him, and Peter became one of the most powerful preachers of the gospel in that generation.

Difficult times come to us all. Will you let them drive you away from God—or draw you closer to Him in trust and faith? The time to decide is now.

God's Message

"He who hears My word, and believes Him
who sent Me, has eternal life."
JOHN 5:24 NASB

I know little about nuclear fission or uranium and other elements used in making nuclear explosives. Yet I believe in the atomic bomb, and so do you. But how can we believe that it exists, if we don't understand it or have any scientific knowledge about the way it works?

The answer is obvious. Others understand nuclear fission even if we don't, and others have seen what happens when a nuclear reaction takes place even if we haven't. We read what they say, and we accept it as the testimony of reliable witnesses.

I spend much of my time perusing the pages of a certain book—the Bible. In it I discover that centuries ago God acted and spoke, and reliable witnesses recorded it all. God even guided them as they wrote, so now I read the very words of God Himself.

I may not understand *everything* there is to know about God, but I know Him and trust Him because of what I read of Him in the Bible. Most of all, I know He came down to Earth in the person of His Son, and "grace and truth came through Jesus Christ" (John 1:17).

Surrounded with Song

You shall surround me with songs of deliverance.
PSALM 32:7

Someone has said that when faith is strong, troubles become trifles.

That doesn't mean our troubles aren't real, or that we act as if they didn't exist. God takes them seriously—so seriously that He sent Jesus Christ into the world to deal with their root cause, which is sin.

But just as Jesus triumphed over death, so He helps us triumph over trouble. Even in the midst of troubles, Jesus is able to "turn their mourning to joy" (Jeremiah 31:13).

How does it happen? By looking in faith to God and reminding ourselves that He has not abandoned us and that God has plans for our future. God can even give us an optimistic spirit—somewhat like the Englishman I heard about during World War II who stood looking at the deep hole in the ground where his bombed-out home had once stood. "I always did want a basement, I did," he said. "Now I can jolly well build another house like I always wanted!"

Angels Watching over Us

*Are not all angels ministering spirits sent to serve
those who will inherit salvation?*

Hebrews 1:14 niv

Her car accident was serious; she felt she had been almost miraculously delivered from death. "It's almost as if an angel intervened to protect me," she wrote. "Do angels still do things like that?"

The answer is yes; angels are just as active today as they were in Bible times. Angels are spiritual beings that seldom assume physical form, which is why we don't see them and why we are largely unaware of their presence. But I am convinced that when we get to Heaven, we will be amazed to discover how often God's angels intervened to help or protect us. The Bible says that God "will command his angels concerning you to guard you in all your ways" (Psalm 91:11 niv).

If you have ever had an experience similar to this woman's, I hope you didn't consider it merely a lucky escape—because it wasn't. God protected and preserved you. Don't miss whatever lessons He wants to teach you from that experience. And thank Him for both His protection and His lessons!

Unity's Witness

"May they be brought to complete unity to let the world know that you sent me and have loved them even as you have loved me."

JOHN 17:23 NIV

It is unfortunate when Christians can't get along or even refuse to have anything to do with one another. Not only does this harm our witness to an unbelieving world, but it turns us away from God's priorities for us.

No church has cornered the market on God's truth, and in my travels around the world, I have found sincere believers in virtually every church and denomination imaginable. I know the issues are complex and won't be solved this side of eternity, but that is no excuse for lovelessness and conflict.

Shortly before His death on the cross, Jesus prayed for unity among those who would come to believe in Him. When the world sees Christians fighting, it wonders if the gospel is really true. Only Satan wins when sincere Christians reject one another.

So do what you can to live at peace with your fellow believers—and join your Lord in praying for the unity of Christ's people, so "that the world may believe" (John 17:21).

The Clouds of Life

The LORD went before them by day in a pillar of cloud to lead the way.

EXODUS 13:21

C louds will come. They are part of life. But by God's grace we need not be depressed by them. Just as clouds can protect us from the brightness of the sun, life's clouds can reveal the glory of God, and from their lofty height God speaks to us.

Like the children of Israel, we are travelers to the Promised Land. As they traveled through the wilderness, the Bible says, "The LORD went before them by day in a pillar of cloud to lead the way."

Perhaps like them, you are passing through a wilderness right now. It may be the wilderness of a broken marriage, or a financial reversal, or a major disappointment, or a threatening illness. It may even be a wilderness of doubt or sin.

But God is with you in the wilderness, and He goes before you to encourage and guide you. He brought the children of Israel through the desert wilderness—and He will bring you through yours as well, as you look in faith to Him. Never forget: "He is the living God, and steadfast forever" (Daniel 6:26).

A Spiritual Virus

What kind of people ought you to be? You
ought to live holy and godly lives.

2 PETER 3:11 NIV

Do you remember the last time you had the flu? You probably felt terrible—and with good reason. That flu virus had invaded your whole body, and it made you weak all over. That is what sin is like. Sin is like a spiritual virus that has invaded our lives, making us morally and spiritually weak, and we will never be completely free of it this side of eternity. The only sinless person who ever lived was Jesus Christ.

Why can't we be sinless in this life? Why can't we become perfect? One reason is because sin has weakened us so much that we don't have the strength to overcome its power. Sin is like a deadly disease that infects every part of us: our body, our mind, our emotions, our relationships, our motives—everything.

But when we come to Christ, another spiritual power takes up residence within us: the Holy Spirit. So take sin seriously; be on guard against it, resist its tug, and fight its power. But most of all, take the Holy Spirit seriously; call on Him to help you overcome sin's power and live a holy and godly life.

Redeemed by Love

You were redeemed . . . with the precious blood of Christ.

1 PETER 1:18–19 NIV

The word *redeem* means "to buy back"—to recover by paying a price. The word *redeemed* can be illustrated by the ancient world through the position of a slave who had been captured in battle or enticed into serving one who was not his legal master. His real master, intent on recovering his slave's service and love, would buy him back—redeem him from the enemy—at great personal cost.

That is what God did for us. Captured by Satan and enticed into his service, we were slaves of sin, without any hope of deliverance. But God still loved us, and He was determined to restore us to His household. By His death on the cross, Jesus paid the price for our deliverance, a price far greater than our true value. He did it solely because He loved us. Now we have been redeemed!

Sin's Magnetism

*Flee the evil desires of youth, and pursue
righteousness, faith, love and peace.*
2 TIMOTHY 2:22 NIV

Did you ever play with magnets when you were a child? If you had two of them, you probably remember that the closer they got to each other, the harder it was to pull them apart.

Temptation is something like that. The more you dwell on it and the closer you get to it, the stronger its attraction becomes. In fact, if you don't look out, it will become almost impossible for you to pull away from it. Don't let that happen.

Why do I mention this? Because the first step you need to take to gain victory over sin is to flee from whatever tempts you. Don't play with it or toy with it in your mind; get as far from it as possible. I have known of people who had to change jobs to keep away from something (or someone) that was tempting them to do wrong! But it was the only way to avoid giving in to temptation and sinning.

What step do you need to take to overcome temptation in your life?

Determined Disciples

"If you abide in My word, you are My disciples indeed."

JOHN 8:31

A disciple in Jesus' time was someone who followed a teacher or philosopher. A disciple was both a learner and a follower, believing the teacher's message and then putting it into practice.

Jesus gave the word *disciple* added meaning, however, because His disciples also went out to tell others about Him. A disciple of Jesus, therefore, is someone who has committed his or her life to Jesus and who seeks each day to learn, to follow, and to share Him with others. Does this describe you?

No, the first disciples weren't perfect, and neither are we. Like them, we need to learn more, follow more, and share more. But all of us who belong to Christ are called to be disciples. Unlike the original disciples, we can't physically spend time with Jesus, but we can learn from Him by reading His Word. We can follow Him by obeying His will. And we can share Him with a world that desperately needs to be saved.

An Altered Attitude

Return to the LORD your God,
For He is gracious and merciful.
JOEL 2:13

From time to time I have had people pour out their heart to me because their sins had been discovered and they were in serious trouble. They wept bitterly because they had devastated their marriage or ruined their reputation.

But later someone would tell me they were back in the same situation. They had not learned from their experience, and seemed determined to bring even more chaos into their lives.

What was the problem? The problem was lack of repentance. Their tears were tears of self-pity, not of repentance. True repentance involves a turning from sin—a conscious, deliberate decision to leave sin behind—and a conscious, deliberate turning to God, with a commitment to follow His will.

Repentance is only one part of our response to Christ (and even the strength to repent comes from God). But it is an essential part, for without it we cannot claim Christ is our Lord. The Bible says, "Godly sorrow brings repentance that leads to salvation and leaves no regret" (2 Corinthians 7:10 NIV).

Faith Building

*I pray that out of his glorious riches
he may strengthen you.*

EPHESIANS 3:16 NIV

How can your faith become stronger?

First, be sure of your commitment to Christ. Have you acknowledged your sins to God and put your faith and trust in Jesus Christ as your Savior and Lord? Sometimes a person's faith is weak because he or she has never clearly taken this step of commitment. If you haven't done this—or if you aren't sure—ask Christ to come into your life today—and He will.

Second, build your faith on the truths of God's Word. The Bible is spiritual "food" given to us by God to strengthen our faith. In the Scriptures, we learn of God's love for us, and also how He wants us to live. Without a firm knowledge of God's Word, our faith will always be vague and uncertain.

Finally, draw strength from other believers. You need to hear God's Word as it is preached and taught. Bible studies, prayer groups, and other programs can also help you grow stronger in your faith.

Don't stand still in your faith. Use the resources God has given you to move forward in confidence and joy.

Triumph Through Trust

Neither death nor life . . . nor things present nor things to come . . . shall be able to separate us from the love of God.

ROMANS 8:38–39

There are two ways to respond to adversity: with discouragement or with trust.

The problem with giving in to discouragement is that it only makes things worse, for with discouragement may come bitterness, anger, jealousy, revenge, and so forth. We may even try to escape through drugs or alcohol. But do any of these solve the problem? No!

God has a better way—the way of trust. Sometimes He may show us that we were in the wrong. When that is the case, we need to confess it, repent, and seek His forgiveness. Sometimes, however, we can only accept what is happening and ask God to help us endure it and triumph over it.

Turning to God's Word will also encourage us; many of the psalms, for example, were written in the midst of suffering and adversity. Follow the psalmist's example and praise God right in the midst of your adversity: "Bless the LORD, O my soul, and forget not all His benefits" (103:2).

An Upside-Down World

God is not ashamed to be called their God.

HEBREWS 11:16

We live in an upside-down world. People hate when they should love, quarrel when they should be friendly, fight when they should be peaceful, wound when they should heal, steal when they should share, do wrong when they should do right.

I once saw a toy clown with a weight in its head. No matter how it was placed, it invariably assumed an upside-down position. It could be placed on its feet or on its side and when let go it flipped back on its head.

The clown illustrates why the disciples seemed to be misfits to the world. To an upside-down nonbeliever, a right-side-up follower of Christ seems upside down. To the nonbeliever, the true Christian is an oddity and an abnormality.

Yet this isn't the whole picture, for all around us are people who sense something is wrong with their topsy-turvy lives, and they yearn to be right side up. Will you pray for them? Ask God to help you point them to life's only solid foundation—Jesus Christ.

When Temptation Knocks

Jesus said to him, "Away from me, Satan! For it is written: 'Worship the Lord your God, and serve him only.'" Then the devil left him.

Matthew 4:10–11 niv

How do you know if the devil is tempting you to do something wrong, or if it's only your own desires?

In truth, we don't always know when the devil is tempting us directly or only working in the background. But the basic issue is the same: we are being tempted to turn our backs on God.

The devil is the source of all temptation (Matthew 4:3). But he is able to succeed only because we let him— and we let him because of our own weakness.

This is one reason why we need Christ. He can give us the strength, by the power of His Spirit, to resist temptation. In His encounter with the devil at the beginning of His ministry, Jesus pointed the way to victory: using the truth of God's Word to counteract Satan's lies. Three times Satan attacked Jesus with almost-overwhelming temptations—and three times Jesus replied with scripture.

A friend of mine says, "When the devil comes knocking, I just send Jesus to the door." Try that next time!

Hope from God's Word

The grass withers, the flower fades,
but the word of our God stands forever.

ISAIAH 40:8

A missionary in China, imprisoned by the Japanese during World War II, managed to take a forbidden gospel of John with her into her cell. She carefully hid it, and each night when she went to bed, she pulled the covers over her head and memorized one verse. She did this until the day she was freed.

When the prisoners were released, most of them shuffled out, but the missionary was so chipper someone said she must have been brainwashed. A *Life* magazine reporter who had interviewed her said, "She's been brainwashed for sure. God washed her brain."

I urge you not only to read God's Word but to memorize it. You may find it hard at first, but as you repeat a verse or a group of verses over and over to yourself, you will find they begin to take root in your soul. The psalmist declared, "Your word I have hidden in my heart, that I might not sin against You" (119:11). Then when adversity or troubles arise, those verses will come back and give you hope.

Is God's Word stored up in your heart and mind for the future?

Love and Marriage

He who loves his wife loves himself.

Ephesians 5:28

There are three elements to a successful marriage. The first is love—not just an emotional feeling or a physical attraction, but a deep commitment to put the other person first. The apostle Paul defined *love* beautifully in 1 Corinthians 13. Read it and you will know how God defines *love*. Men are to love their wives as Christ loved the Church. What woman wouldn't respond to such a selfless expression of love?

Maturity is the second ingredient in a successful marriage. Too many are getting a divorce at the first sign of trouble. Maturity means a willingness to act responsibly and not take the easy way out.

Third, faith must be an ingredient for a marriage to be successful. Marriage is difficult, but without Christ at the center of a marriage and a home, it becomes even more difficult. Put differently, it takes three to make a great marriage: you, your spouse, and Christ. I have seldom seen a marriage fail when the husband and wife pray and worship God together.

Pray with Confidence

*This is the confidence we have in approaching God: that
if we ask anything according to his will, he hears us.*

1 JOHN 5:14 NIV

The frustration and discouragement in his letter were unmistakable: "I know I ought to pray, but sometimes I feel like my prayers aren't getting above the ceiling. Is there a secret to praying?"

Prayer is not something mysterious or secret; prayer is simply talking to God. And God wants you to talk to Him! He loves you, and He has promised to hear you when you pray.

Prayer is possible because Jesus Christ removed the barrier between God and us, a barrier caused by our sins. Sin separates us from God, and because of that, we had no right to come to Him in prayer. But Jesus removed that barrier when He died on the cross for us. When we commit our lives to Christ, God gives us the privilege of approaching "the throne of grace with confidence, so that we may receive mercy and find grace to help us in our time of need" (Hebrews 4:16 NIV).

If you find prayer awkward or intimidating, remember this: God promises to hear you—and He cannot lie. Trust that promise and learn to bring every concern to Him in prayer.

God Wants Our Fellowship

Come near to God and he will come near to you.

JAMES 4:8 NIV

What a blessed promise and provision this is! It means each of us can come close to God, with the assurance He will come close to us—so close that we become conscious of His presence. This is the greatest experience we can know.

But for most of us, this isn't easy. Life presents us with too many distractions, and the last thing we have time for is to be alone with God. Children, work, television, the Internet, even church activities drain away our time.

Maybe you will have to readjust your priorities. Maybe you will have to say no to certain activities or demands. Whatever it takes, make time to be alone with God.

Remember: He wants your fellowship, and He has done everything to make it a possibility. He has forgiven your sins at the cost of His own dear Son. He has given you His Word and the priceless privilege of prayer and worship.

He will come near to you if only you will come near to Him.

The Riches of the Old Testament

Turn my heart toward your statutes
and not toward selfish gain.
Turn my eyes away from worthless things;
preserve my life according to your word.

PSALM 119:36–37 NIV

Sadly, many people find the Old Testament confusing and hard to understand. Some even wonder if it has any value to those of us living on this side of the cross.

But remember: the Old Testament is God's Word just as much as the New Testament is, and God wants to teach and encourage us through it.

The Old Testament helps us understand how we should live. For example, we can learn much from studying the lives of its main characters—including their failures.

Don't worry about the parts you don't understand. Instead, ask God to help you learn from the parts you can understand. If you have never really studied the Old Testament, begin with the book of Psalms—the hymnbook of the Old Testament—or Proverbs, the Old Testament's guide to practical living.

Thank God for the entire Bible—and make reading it a part of your life every day.

Teacher and Guide

"When He, the Spirit of truth, has come,
He will guide you into all truth."
JOHN 16:13

The moment you receive Jesus Christ as Savior and Lord, the Holy Spirit takes up residence in your heart. Right now He lives within you! The Bible says, "If anyone does not have the Spirit of Christ, he is not His" (Romans 8:9).

The Holy Spirit helps us in life's struggles, and we must never forget that. But the Holy Spirit also plays two other important roles we must not overlook.

First, He convicts us of sin. The Bible says, "He will convict the world of sin, and of righteousness, and of judgment" (John 16:8). While this verse focuses on His convicting power among unbelievers, the Holy Spirit also convicts believers when we sin.

The second role of the Holy Spirit is as a teacher. The Bible says, "He will guide you into all truth." Just as surely as the Holy Spirit inspired the writers of the Bible, so He will instruct us as we meditate on God's Word.

Are you a willing student of the Holy Spirit?

Black Sheep

"I have loved you with an everlasting love."

JEREMIAH 31:3

Did your family have a black sheep—someone who disgraced the family or behaved in a disreputable way? Were you even considered your family's black sheep?

Well, the Bible tells us that God loves black sheep! Think of Jacob, for example, who cheated his brother Esau out of his rightful inheritance and his father's blessing. Remember Manasseh, who rebelled against his godly father, King Hezekiah. Yet, in time, God humbled both Jacob and Manasseh, and they became His servants.

No matter who we are and what we have done (or haven't done), God still loves us—even the black sheep. In fact, all of us who call Earth our home are black sheep in God's eyes, for we all have sinned and rebelled against God. But He has not rejected us even if we have rejected Him.

Never doubt the depths of God's love. Even if you had been the only black sheep who needed to be brought back into the fold of God, Jesus Christ still would have died for you. Let Him welcome you home today.

Moved with Compassion

You, O Lord, are a God full of compassion . . .
abundant in mercy and truth.

PSALM 86:15

The word *compassion* comes from two Latin words meaning "to suffer with." What better picture to describe God's compassion for us?

Suffering is the common lot of the human race. We see pictures on television of people ravaged by war or famine, and our hearts are touched (as they should be). But all around us are people who suffer in others ways: loneliness, fear, rejection, disability, grief, poverty, discrimination, addiction, or a multitude of other problems.

But God has compassion on us—He suffers with us. He knows what we are going through, and He cares. The greatest act of compassion in the history of the human race was the cross, for there Christ suffered for us. He endured sin's penalty so we would not have to endure it ourselves.

Now Jesus calls us to have compassion on others— to suffer with them and to point them to the One who suffered for them.

Speak the Truth—Always

*Each of you must put off falsehood and speak
truthfully to his neighbor.*
EPHESIANS 4:25 NIV

W hy is it wrong to tell a lie, even if it doesn't seem
to hurt anyone?

One reason—and one that we should take very seriously—is because God commands us to tell the truth.
One of the Ten Commandments states clearly, "You
shall not give false testimony against your neighbor"
(Exodus 20:16 NIV).

But another reason is because a lie always—without
exception—hurts someone. How do you know, for instance, what impact your untruthful words might have
on someone's reputation? The answer is, you don't. And
do you honestly want your children to grow up thinking
it doesn't matter whether or not they tell the truth? Do
you honestly want your unbelieving friends to conclude
that Christ doesn't mean anything to you?

Most of all, a lie always hurts the one who tells it. It
makes them less concerned about God's truth. In addition, others will eventually realize that they can't be
trusted.

Don't compromise on the truth. Instead, commit
every part of your life to Christ, including your speech.

"Come Home"

Our citizenship is in heaven, from which we also eagerly wait for the Savior.

PHILIPPIANS 3:20

Once there was a widow and her son who lived in a miserable attic. Years before, she had married against her parents' wishes and had gone with her husband to live in a foreign land.

He had proved irresponsible and unfaithful, and after a few years, he died without having made any provision for her and the child. It was with the utmost difficulty that she managed to scrape together the bare necessities of life.

One day the postman knocked at the attic door. The mother recognized the handwriting on the letter he brought and, with trembling fingers, broke the seal. There was a check and a slip of paper with just two words: "Come home."

Someday all who know Christ will have a similar experience. We do not know when the call will come. It may be when we are in the midst of our work. It may be after weeks or months of illness. But someday a loving hand will be laid upon our shoulder and this brief message will be given: "Come home."

The Purpose of the Stars

The heavens declare the glory of God;
the skies proclaim the work of his hands.

PSALM 19:1 NIV

I f God created the stars," she wrote me, "isn't it reasonable to believe that He wants to send us messages through them? Why shouldn't Christians practice astrology, since millions of people do?"

One reason Christians shouldn't practice astrology is, quite simply, because the Bible tells us not to. Astrology and other forms of fortune-telling were very common in the ancient world, but the Bible writers called them "detestable practices" (Deuteronomy 18:12 NIV).

Why is this? First, they knew that God did not create the stars to give us insights into the future, but to witness to His power and glory. "The heavens declare the glory of God," the psalmist wrote.

Second, Christians don't follow astrology because we don't need to. God tells us everything we need to know about the future in His Word. Of course, the Bible doesn't tell us what will happen next week or next year; if it did, we would never learn to trust God or seek His guidance. But the Bible does tell us that the future is in God's hands and someday Christ will come again. And that is really all we need to know.

Heart Conditions

"The heart is deceitful above all things
and beyond cure.
Who can understand it?"

JEREMIAH 17:9 NIV

Our hearts are sinful. All the things happening in the world that discourage us and cause despair come from the human heart.

Our hearts, Jesus said, are a storehouse of evil (Mark 7:21). Fornication, murder, theft, covetousness, wickedness, deceit, blasphemy, pride—all these come from the heart.

Our hearts are far from God (Matthew 15:8). Many of us go to church and outwardly live a good life, but we are living for ourselves instead of Christ. Even hearts redeemed by Christ's love can be unbelieving, blind, proud, rebellious, idolatrous, and cold toward God.

Jesus died on the cross to show us the seriousness of our heart condition. He came to cleanse our hearts, to give us a heart-softening picture of God's divine and infinite love, and to woo us to Himself when the world tempts us to stray. Turn to the Great Physician for healing—whatever your current heart condition.

It Was Love

"I have loved you with an everlasting love;
therefore with lovingkindness I have drawn you."

JEREMIAH 31:3

Many people have difficulty believing God is a God of love. "How could He be," they ask, "when the world is filled with so much suffering and evil?" It is not an easy issue—but if you really want to know the reality of God's love, look at the cross.

It was love, divine love, that made Christ endure the cross, despising the shame.

It was love that restrained Him when He was falsely accused of blasphemy and led to Golgotha to die with common thieves. He raised not a hand against His enemies. It was love that kept Him from calling legions of angels to come to His defense.

It was love that made Him, in a moment of agonizing pain, pause and give hope to a repentant sinner who cried, "Lord, remember me when You come into Your kingdom" (Luke 23:42).

It was love that caused Jesus to lift His voice and pray, "Father, forgive them, for they do not know what they do" (Luke 23:34).

Does God love us? Yes—and the proof is the cross.

A Clear Conscience

The blood of Christ . . . [will] cleanse our consciences.
HEBREWS 9:14 NIV

Each of us has a conscience that sits as a judge over our every thought, word, and deed. Our conscience can be sensitive, undeveloped, or distorted, depending upon the way we have used or abused it.

The human conscience is defiled by sin, says the Bible—and that is one reason it is not a reliable guide by itself. Our conscience needs to be cleansed by the purifying work of the Holy Spirit, and honed and sharpened by the truth of the Word of God. For Satan can twist our consciences if they are not yielded to Christ, convincing us that wrong is really right.

But in spite of its frailty, our conscience is still important, and God still uses it to warn us of danger. All of us have experienced the backlash of guilt after a transgression.

Is God speaking to you about something that is not right in your life? Something you may be doing although you know it dishonors Christ? Don't ignore that voice. Face your sin, confess it, put it right, and never touch it again.

The God of the Bible

Jesus Christ is the same yesterday,
today, and forever.

HEBREWS 13:8

Too many people talk about God being a God of wrath in the Old Testament and a God of love and peace in the New Testament. But God is the same throughout the Bible.

It is true that the Old Testament tells us God is holy and pure, and He punishes those who rebel against Him. But the New Testament tells us the same thing. In fact, some of the strongest warnings about judgment in the Bible come from the lips of Jesus (Matthew 7:14).

In the same way, the New Testament certainly stresses God's love and mercy. In fact, it gives us the greatest proof that God loves us: Jesus laid down His life for our salvation (1 John 3:16). But the Old Testament also tells us repeatedly about God's love for us: "I have loved you with an everlasting love; I have drawn you with lovingkindness" (Jeremiah 31:3 NIV).

Still not convinced? Then consider this an invitation to open the pages of the Bible for yourself. You'll be blessed as you get to know God more fully—in all of His righteousness and love.

Here for a Reason

"Seek the peace and prosperity of the city to which I have carried you. . . . Pray to the LORD for it."

JEREMIAH 29:7 NIV

You aren't where you are by accident; you are there by God's design. Your country, your city, your family, your job or school—God put you there, and He never does anything without a reason. You are where you are by God's sovereign design, and He wants to use you right where you are.

Jeremiah and his fellow countrymen had every reason not to seek the peace and prosperity of the places where they were living. They were no longer in their homeland; a vicious enemy had conquered their nation and forcibly taken them away into exile. Why help an enemy prosper there? And yet that is what God ordered them to do.

This world is not our final home. Because of what Christ has done for us we have "an inheritance that can never perish, spoil or fade—kept in heaven for [us]" (1 Peter 1:4 NIV). But in the meantime God calls us to be instruments of His love and justice in an unbelieving world. Ask God to use you for His glory right where He has placed you.

Resting Faith

The testing of your faith produces patience.

JAMES 1:3

Dwight L. Moody was fond of pointing out that there are three kinds of faith in Jesus Christ: struggling faith, which is like a man floundering and fearful in deep water; clinging faith, which is like a man hanging to the side of a boat; and resting faith, which finds a man safe inside the boat and secure enough to reach out his hand to help someone else.

Notice that each man had faith. Each knew the boat was his only hope. But only one had a resting faith. Only one had discovered he could actually be in the boat—where all he had to do was rest.

This is the kind of faith God wants us to have—a faith that trusts Him totally. But sometimes we discover its reality only after we have endured a struggling or clinging faith. Sometimes we only realize we can get in the boat when the storm rages and we cry out to God with new faith. Then our Savior graciously extends His hand and says, "Come to Me . . . and I will give you rest" (Matthew 11:28).

Who Is Boss?

Whatever you do, work at it with all your heart,
as working for the Lord, not for men.
COLOSSIANS 3:23 NIV

Even the most interesting job has its moments of routine or drudgery; even the most fascinating and fulfilling position requires contact with difficult and demanding people. No job is perfect, and no position can insulate us completely from life's tensions and conflicts. With some jobs the stress is almost constant—and, after a time, it takes its toll.

The Bible tells us two important truths about our work. First, it acknowledges that work—is work! After Adam and Eve sinned, God cast them out of Eden and declared that "by the sweat of your brow you will eat your food" (Genesis 3:19 NIV). But the Bible also tells us that God has given our work to us and that it has dignity and value in His eyes. It should in our eyes as well.

Whatever your job—no matter how difficult or enjoyable it is—"work at it with all your heart, as working for the Lord, not for men." It will make all the difference—in your attitude and your output.

Doing God's Will

[Do] the will of God from the heart.

EPHESIANS 6:6

We are admonished to seek out the will of the Lord. In Ephesians 5:17 we read, "Do not be unwise, but understand what the will of the Lord is."

Some people, however, misunderstand the will of God. They think it must be a harsh, joyless thing, intended to make us miserable. But listen: God's will comes from God's love.

If you love someone, will you want to make that person miserable? Will you go out of your way to punish them if they don't do exactly what you tell them to? No, of course not—not if you really love them.

The same is true with God. God loves you, and because He loves you, He cares about what happens to you. He loves you too much to let you wander aimlessly through life, without meaning or purpose. The Bible says, "You will show me the path of life; in Your presence is fullness of joy" (Psalm 16:11).

Covet God's will for your life more than anything else. To know God's will—and to do it—brings life's greatest joy.

Fit for the Battle

Put on the full armor of God so that you can take your stand against the devil's schemes.

EPHESIANS 6:11 NIV

Don't doubt for a moment the devil's existence, and don't doubt for a moment that he is your Enemy. Forget the cute cartoon images of an impish figure with a pitchfork and a red suit. Satan is absolutely malicious and evil, and he has great influence over this world. The Bible says, "Your enemy the devil prowls around like a roaring lion looking for someone to devour" (1 Peter 5:8 NIV). Satan is strong, and he is determined to make you stumble. He is also clever and scheming, bent on deceiving and outmaneuvering us at every turn.

But we are not defenseless! God has provided us with all the armor we need—armor so strong that Satan and his servants cannot penetrate it. Truth, righteousness, peace, faith, salvation, the Word of God, prayer—every one of these has a role in defeating our adversary. (You can read Paul's full description in Ephesians 6:10–18.)

What pieces of God's armor are missing in your life? Don't let another day go by without putting on "the full armor of God."

One Sure Guide

Your word is a lamp to my feet
And a light to my path.

PSALM 119:105

As Christians, we have only one authority, one compass: the Word of God.

In the midst of a thousand different voices, all claiming authority and clamoring for our allegiance, only one Voice will tell us the truth. That Voice? The written Word of God, given to us by God to tell us what we are to believe and how we are to live. As the psalmist said, "The entrance of Your words gives light" (119:130).

In a letter to a friend, Abraham Lincoln said, "I am profitably engaged in reading the Bible. Take all of this Book upon reason that you can and the balance upon faith, and you will live and die a better man."

Coleridge said he believed the Bible to be the Word of God because, as he put it, "It finds me."

"If you want encouragement," John Bunyan wrote, "entertain the promises."

Martin Luther said, "In Scriptures, even the little daisy becomes a meadow."

The Bible is our one sure guide in an unsure world. Is it your guide?

How to Grow Your Faith

*Faith comes from hearing the message, and the
message is heard through the word of Christ.*
Romans 10:17 niv

Would you like to grow weak? It's not difficult, you know; all you have to do is stop eating and exercising. And yet no one in their right mind would willingly do this.

Why, then, do we fail to see the connection between the weakness of our faith and our lack of spiritual food and exercise? Faith doesn't grow automatically; it requires spiritual food as nourishment. Faith also requires exercise—the practice of seeing God work as we put our faith into action. If we don't feed and exercise our souls, we shouldn't be surprised when our faith grows weaker and weaker. But it doesn't need to be this way—and it mustn't be this way. Christ's work is too important and too demanding for it to be carried out by spiritual weaklings.

What is the main food God has given to strengthen us? It is the Bible, the Word of God. Jesus prayed, "Sanctify them by the truth; your word is truth" (John 17:17 niv). Read God's Word. Study it. Meditate on it. Listen to it preached and taught. And then watch your faith grow.

The Ark of Salvation

*By faith Noah . . . became an heir of the
righteousness which comes by faith.*

<small>HEBREWS 11:7 RSV</small>

God warned the people of Noah's day, "My Spirit shall not strive with man forever" (Genesis 6:3). They laughed at Noah, mocked his words, and went about their usual business and pleasures without ever dreaming he might be right. God was speaking—but they ignored Him. Eventually, God's patience gave out—and by then it was too late.

Outside the Ark, men and women struggled for their lives, clutching pieces of driftwood until the pitiless hand of death reached up and drew them down beneath those cruel waves. All were lost. Every soul outside the ark perished. They had had their chance, but they had tossed it away.

You cannot come to Christ unless the Spirit of God brings you. But what if you ignore His warnings? Then you are in the gravest danger, for someday God will no longer be calling to you. Then it will be too late. Come to Christ while there is still time. Christ, God's greater Ark, stands ready to welcome you to safety today.

Are you in the Ark?

October 27 – Morning

God Is Never Late

The LORD is your keeper;
the LORD is your shade at your right hand.
PSALM 121:5

In order for a plant to grow and bear fruit, its seed must first be put in the ground, where is dies. In order for spiritual fruit to appear in our lives, we must first be planted in the Word of God and then die to self. In the face of chastening, adversity, discipline, and affliction, God's Word nourishes our lives, and fruit begins to appear. But it doesn't happen overnight. It takes time and patience.

Joseph would never have been of use to God had he not been sold into slavery by brothers who hated him and then wrongly accused by Potiphar, who put him in prison. Even after he had told Pharaoh's cupbearer he would be restored to the king's court and asked him to tell Pharaoh of his unjust imprisonment, Joseph had to wait two more years to be released from prison.

As we wait upon the Lord, He may sometimes seem slow in coming to help us, but He never comes too late. His timing is always perfect.

Loving with God's Love

*Love is patient, love is kind. . . . It is not rude,
it is not self-seeking, it is not easily angered, it
keeps no record of wrongs.*

1 CORINTHIANS 13:4–5 NIV

I can't live with him, but I can't seem to live without him either," her letter said. She had moved out three times but kept coming back. With minor variations, her story is repeated thousands of times every day.

Every marriage is different, and we mustn't over-simplify or overlook the uniqueness of every relationship. But what is the fundamental problem? Why can't spouses seem to get along?

Let me answer by asking another question: What is the opposite of love? It isn't hate (although it may take that form). The opposite of love is selfishness. When a husband and wife are concerned only about their own individual desires, the stage is set for conflict.

The Bible gives us another way—the way of Christ. True love, it says, is self-giving, not self-seeking. True love puts the needs of others first. This is what Christ did when He left Heaven's glory and came down to Earth for us. Begin a new page in your marriage by asking Christ to become the center of your life—and your marriage.

Coming in Glory

"At that time men will see the Son of Man coming in clouds with great power and glory."

MARK 13:26 NIV

Jesus' first coming passed almost unnoticed: He was born in a small, out-of-the-way town and laid in a manger with only animals and humble shepherds to greet Him that first night. Even at the height of His ministry, Jesus could say, "Foxes have holes and birds of the air have nests, but the Son of Man has no place to lay his head" (Luke 9:58 NIV).

How different Jesus' second coming will be! Then "every eye will see Him" (Revelation 1:7), and He will come with glory and power to establish His Kingdom of perfect justice and righteousness. No one will be able to dismiss Him as insignificant or unimportant; all will acknowledge Him as King of kings and Lord of lords.

Does the thought of His return fill you with concern, or even terror? It shouldn't—not if you have trusted Him as your Lord and Savior and put your life into His hands. If that's the case, Jesus' return should fill you with expectancy and joy and worship. Make sure you are ready and then pray for His quick return.

Citizens of Heaven

"Because I live, you will live also."

JOHN 14:19

People spend billions of dollars every year on cosmetics, health spas, physical fitness machines, and concoctions claiming to make them live longer or look younger. But age will overtake even the most beautiful or physically fit people in the world, and eventually they will die—as will we.

But someday we who know Christ will have perfect bodies that will never age or experience pain. Someday our dead bodies will be "raised in glory" (1 Corinthians 15:43), and we will be like Christ in His resurrection body.

Can I imagine what that will be like? Not fully. But I do know this: the resurrected body of Jesus is the pattern or design for our new bodies. "For our citizenship is in heaven, from which we also eagerly wait for the Savior, the Lord Jesus Christ, who will transform our lowly body that it may be conformed to His glorious body" (Philippians 3:20–21).

What a future we have in Christ!

Seeds of Doubt

> [Satan] said to the woman, "Did God really say, 'You must not eat from any tree in the garden'?"
>
> GENESIS 3:1 NIV

The devil is a master at making us question God and His Word. God's command to Adam and Eve had been crystal clear: they could eat of every tree in the Garden—except one. If they ate of it, death would come upon them. But now Satan raises the question: "Did God really say . . . ?" It is the first question in the Bible, and it's significant that it comes from the mouth of the one whose primary goal is to turn us away from God.

But notice: Satan misquoted God! What he said wasn't what God had told them—as Eve points out in her reply. Twisting Scripture, taking a verse out of context, deceiving us into thinking God is mean-spirited—these are some of Satan's favorite tricks.

Eve's mistake was in prolonging the conversation—and eventually being deceived by the Deceiver. The Enemy's promise—that she would become like God if she ate from the forbidden tree—was a lie. Don't let Satan sow seeds of doubt in your soul. Stand firmly on the truth of God's Word.

Finding Fulfillment

"Let your soul delight itself in abundance."

ISAIAH 55:2

When Satan tried to trap Jesus at the beginning of His ministry, he used the same temptations he uses today.

One trap was the lure of things. Jesus had fasted for forty days, and Satan tried to take advantage of His hunger by urging Him to use His supernatural power to turn stones into bread. But Jesus replied, "Man shall not live by bread alone, but by every word that proceeds from the mouth of God" (Matthew 4:4).

Bread is important, but it isn't all-important, as Satan was suggesting. Pleasure and recreation have their place, but they mustn't have first place. Money is necessary, but money must serve us; we are not to serve it.

Isaiah said, "Listen carefully to Me . . . and let your soul delight itself in abundance" (Isaiah 55:2). Yes, delight in abundance—the abundance God gives you, both material and spiritual. Especially delight in the abundance of joy that comes from His presence. Satan will always offer you substitutes. Refuse them!

Satan's Broken Promises

"You belong to your father, the devil. . . . He is a liar and the father of lies."

JOHN 8:44 NIV

Although many prisoners find hope in Jesus, this letter was from one who was still skeptical: "Can you give me even one reason to give my life to Jesus? It won't get me out of prison any quicker, and no one here would believe me anyway if I said I gave my life to God."

The best reason to give your life to Jesus Christ, I told the prisoner, is because you need Him. You need Him for this life, and you need Him for the life to come. So far in life—whether you realize it or not—you have been following the devil. He promised to give you happiness and peace. But has he kept his promise? No, not at all—nor will he ever keep it. The Enemy also promises that you don't need to worry about what will happen to you when you die—which is another lie.

But Christ does not lie—neither to this prisoner nor to you. You can depend on His promises—and the greatest promise of all is God's promise of new life in Christ. No matter what you have done, God can forgive you and give you the power to start life again. Begin today by committing your life and your future to Jesus Christ.

The Highest Calling

"Whoever of you does not forsake all that he has cannot be My disciple."

LUKE 14:33

When the Standard Oil Company was looking for a representative in the Far East, they approached a missionary and offered him $10,000. He turned down the offer. They raised it to $25,000, and he turned it down again. They raised it to $50,000, and he rejected it once more.

"What's wrong?" they asked.

He replied, "Your price is all right, but your job is too small." God had called him to be a missionary, and anything else was not worthy of his consideration.

What should we be for Jesus Christ? Most Christians are not called to be missionaries or preachers, but they are called to follow Christ. They are called to be faithful wherever He puts them—in the school, in the home, in the factory or office, in the neighborhood and nation. They are called to be controlled by the Spirit and to bear the fruit of the Spirit. They are called to be Christ's ambassadors wherever God puts them.

Nothing less than God's call is worthy of our consideration.

Stand Strong!

Submit yourselves, then, to God. Resist the devil, and he will flee from you. Come near to God and he will come near to you.

JAMES 4:7–8 NIV

Whenever God is at work, you can be sure Satan will counterattack. His goal has always been to try to stop whatever God is doing.

The Bible doesn't tell us in detail about Satan and how he works. After all, our focus should be on God, not on Satan. (If we concentrate on Satan, we'll become overly fearful or overly fascinated—and both are wrong.)

But the Bible does tell us two important truths about Satan (whose name means "adversary"). First, he is real, and he will do everything he can to draw us away from Christ. He tempts us to do wrong, but most of all he tempts us to turn away from God. Second, Satan is a defeated foe. By His death and resurrection, Jesus conquered Satan, so by the power of His Holy Spirit in us, we can stand against him.

Don't be deceived by Satan and his lies. Stay close to Christ—because the closer you are to Him, the farther away you are from the devil.

Prayer Partners with God

The Spirit Himself makes intercession for us with
groanings which cannot be uttered.

ROMANS 8:26

Have you ever faced a situation that was so over-whelming or confusing that you didn't even know how to pray about it? Have you ever been so overcome with grief or burdened by heartache you couldn't put your emotions into words, much less pray about them?

What a comfort these words are: "The Spirit helps us in our weakness. We do not know what we ought to pray for, but the Spirit himself intercedes for us . . . in accordance with God's will" (Romans 8:26–27 NIV).

Think of it! Even when we don't know how to pray, the Spirit knows our needs, and He brings the deepest cries of our hearts before the throne of God. In ways we will never understand on this side of eternity, God the Holy Spirit pleads for us before God the Father.

Turn to God in every situation—even when you don't feel like it. The Spirit is interceding for you, in accordance with God's will.

NOVEMBER

Families of Faith

Through wisdom a house is built,
And by understanding it is established.

PROVERBS 24:3

The family is the most important institution in the world. It was God's idea in the first place. It was not the invention of sociologists or economists or government bureaucrats who decided it would make society operate more smoothly. Families existed before cities and governments, before written language, nations, temples, and churches.

In the home, character and integrity are formed, values are made clear, and goals are set. These last a lifetime. And if they aren't formed correctly, that, too, will result in patterns—bad patterns—that last a lifetime, if God doesn't intervene.

Today, Satan is attacking the family as never before. But what are our defenses against such attacks? As always, our best defense is the Word of God. Read the Bible together as a family. Have family devotions. Pray for one another daily by name. Be on guard against the forces that tend to pull families apart today. And most of all, commit your marriage to Christ, and make Him the center of your home—and your life.

Now Is the Time

*Man is destined to die once, and after
that to face judgment.*

HEBREWS 9:27 NIV

Many today find the idea of reincarnation attractive—the belief that after we die we come back to Earth again and again. Some of these people have been influenced by other religions; others simply like the thought of enjoying life's pleasures indefinitely.

The Bible, however, is clear: reincarnation is not true, and the life we are leading now is the only one we will ever live. Once we die, we go into eternity—either to Heaven to be with God forever or to that place the Bible calls Hell, where we will be eternally separated from God and His blessings.

What difference should this make? First, it gives urgency to our lives right now. If you are ever going to trust Christ for your salvation—if you are ever going to live for Him—the time is now. The Bible says, "Now is the time of God's favor, now is the day of salvation" (2 Corinthians 6:2 NIV).

Second, it should give us a greater burden for those who don't know Christ. With whom should you be sharing Christ today?

Living by God's Standards

"I tell you the truth, until heaven and earth disappear, not the smallest letter, not the least stroke of a pen, will by any means disappear from the Law."
MATTHEW 5:18 NIV

God's moral standards do not change. What He decreed in the Ten Commandments thousands of years ago is still in force. Not murdering, committing adultery, stealing, lying, coveting—these commandments will be in force until the end of time (Exodus 20:1–17).

Why don't God's standards change according to the fashions and whims of the times? One reason is because God is absolutely pure—and these standards are a reflection of His righteous character. And because His character does not change, neither do His moral standards. "I the LORD do not change" (Malachi 3:6 NIV).

But God has given us these standards for another reason: He loves us, and He wants what is best for us. What happens when an individual or a society ignores these basic moral laws? What happens when lying and stealing and immorality and murder become the norm? Chaos. Thank God that He cares about us so much that He has told us how to live. Ask Him to help you obey.

Being Honest with God

I loathe my very life;
therefore I will give free rein to my complaint
and speak out in the bitterness of my soul.

JOB 10:1 NIV

You can understand Job's bitterness; he had lost everything—family, possessions, health, even his friends. But the hardest blow of all was that he couldn't understand why the God he had worshipped and served so faithfully had done this to him.

Have you ever felt this way? Life can be hard, leaving us confused or even angry and bitter. And like Job, you may have told God exactly how you felt. And why not? He already knew your mind and heart, and He doesn't want you to pretend that everything is all right when it isn't. God didn't chastise Job for his honesty; He understood Job's heartache, just as He understands ours. And God still loved Job, just as He still loves us.

But Job didn't just keep complaining (as we're prone to do). Instead, he turned toward God in faith, and in time, God gave him comfort and peace. Not all of Job's questions were answered—but he realized that God can be trusted even when we don't understand. May this be true of you.

True Happiness

*Happy is the man who has the God
of Jacob as his helper.*

PSALM 146:5 TLB

Sometimes I almost wish Thomas Jefferson had not inserted those words in the American Declaration of Independence about "the pursuit of happiness."

He was correct, of course: God has given us the right—or at least the freedom—to pursue happiness. The problem is that millions think this must be the primary purpose of life, and they spend their lives frantically pursuing it. In the end, however, their search ends in disillusionment.

Happiness is a byproduct of something greater, not an end in itself. Happiness cannot be pursued and caught anymore than one can pursue a sunny day, put it in a bottle, and then bring it out on a rainy day.

True happiness comes from a different pursuit—the pursuit of God. He has promised, "You will seek Me and find Me, when you search for Me with all your heart" (Jeremiah 29:13). That promise is true—because God also pursues us. He even sent His Son into the world to pursue us and bring us to Heaven.

Only God gives true happiness.

True Belief

You believe that there is one God. Good! Even the
demons believe that—and shudder.

JAMES 2:19 NIV

It's true. The devil and his demons really do believe in God—and why wouldn't they? They understand that they are engaged in a cosmic battle of titanic proportions, and they know they are up against the Creator of the universe—a truth that makes them shudder. There are no atheists in Hell!

But their belief is a far cry from the kind of belief you and I are called to have. They believe God exists; they even believe in the facts of Jesus' birth, life, death, and resurrection. But their belief is not a saving belief: it has not led them to turn to God in repentance and trust Christ alone for their salvation.

True belief—saving belief—involves not only an intellectual acceptance of certain facts about God and about Jesus. It also involves trust and commitment—trust in Christ as our Savior and commitment to Him as Lord. Is your belief a saving belief? Make sure by trusting Christ and committing your life without reserve to Him.

Needed: Godly Leadership

Righteousness exalts a nation,
but sin is a disgrace to any people.

PROVERBS 14:34 NIV

I don't intend to vote this year," his letter to me stated. "I don't have much use for politicians, and anyway, my vote won't make any difference."

I can understand his attitude; it's easy to become cynical about government or feel that our vote is insignificant. But what would happen, I reminded him, if everyone had his attitude? What kind of leadership would we likely get then? We need leaders who are men and women of integrity and wisdom, and we should thank God that we live in a country where we have the privilege of choosing our leaders. We must never take that responsibility lightly.

The Bible tells us to pray for "all those in authority, that we may live peaceful and quiet lives in all godliness and holiness" (1 Timothy 2:2 NIV). Pray as you vote, and pray regularly for all those who are in positions of political leadership. And if God leads you to become involved in politics in some way, take your responsibilities seriously and seek His wisdom in all you do.

Are you calling Jesus "Lord"—but not doing what He wants?

The Uncertainty of Life

Teach us to number our days,
That we may gain a heart of wisdom.

PSALM 90:12

We are not the masters of our fate. We think we control our lives—but we don't. In an instant—a car accident, a heart attack, a pink slip, a child's raging fever—life can radically change. Frustrated researchers conquer one deadly virus, only to discover one even more lethal.

The psalmist pointed out our basic dilemma: "The length of our days is seventy years—or eighty, if we have the strength; yet their span is but trouble and sorrow, for they quickly pass, and we fly away" (90:10 NIV). Even if we live to a ripe old age, he said, we seldom know peace.

No book is more realistic about the human situation than the Bible. It won't let us get by with frothy platitudes or unsupported optimism. But it also gives us hope. It tells us that Christ can change our lives and that He has prepared a perfect place for us in Heaven.

Even your next breath is a gift from God. Don't take life for granted, but "gain a heart of wisdom."

God's Amazing Love

God demonstrates his own love for us in this: While we were still sinners, Christ died for us.

ROMANS 5:8 NIV

Have you ever asked yourself what you would do with the human race if you were in God's shoes? How would you treat them in light of their rebellion, neglect, and mockery of you?

We can't really put ourselves in God's shoes, of course; He is far greater than we are. But if you were God, wouldn't you be tempted to wipe out the human race and blot them from your memory? Why would you even try to do anything good for them, knowing they'd probably reject it?

But this isn't God's way—and the proof is Jesus Christ. You've heard the statement that God hates the sin but loves the sinner. When Adam and Eve rebelled against God, He punished them by sending death to the human race. But He also refused to stamp them out, and even promised an eventual way of salvation. That way is Jesus Christ, who loved us so much that He gave His life for us. Thank God today for His grace to you—grace that is greater than all your sin.

Satisfying the Soul

Direct me in the path of your commands,
for there I find delight.

PSALM 119:35 NIV

The Bible teaches that a person is more than just a body—each of us is actually a living soul! And our souls are created in the image of God. God Himself has implanted His own nature within us!

Just as our bodies have certain characteristics and appetites, so do our souls. The characteristics of the soul include intelligence, emotions, and will. The human soul or spirit longs for peace, contentment, and happiness. Most of all, the soul has an appetite for God—a yearning to be reconciled to its Creator and to have fellowship with Him forever.

In our world, we give most of our attention to satisfying the appetites of the body and practically no attention to the soul. Consequently we are one-sided. We become fat physically and materially, but spiritually we are lean, weak, anemic.

The soul actually demands as much attention as the body. It demands fellowship and communion with God. It demands worship, quietness, and meditation. Nothing but God ever completely satisfies, because the soul was made for God. Don't starve your soul.

The Weapons of Faith

This is the victory that overcomes the world, our faith.
1 JOHN 5:4 RSV

One of Satan's sly devices is to divert our minds from the help God offers us when we struggle against evil, telling us we have to fight the battle alone. But God knows we need His help.

The Bible warns, "Be sober, be vigilant; because your adversary the devil walks about like a roaring lion, seeking whom he may devour" (1 Peter 5:8). What would you do if you met a lion? You'd probably run, and you'd probably grab any weapon you could to fend it off if it attacked.

And that should be our strategy in our struggles against evil. When evil and temptation stalk us, our first response should be to flee. And when they still attack, we should use every weapon we have to drive them away. The good news is this: God has provided the weapons! His Word, His angels, His Spirit, the encouragement and prayers of our brothers and sisters in Christ—these and more are weapons God provides.

We aren't in this battle alone—so why act like it?

Every Moment of the Day

On my bed I remember you;
I think of you through the watches of the night.

PSALM 63:6 NIV

One of the habits I have always urged new Christians to develop is the discipline of spending time alone with God every day—reading the Bible, meditating on its truth, and turning to God in prayer. Even if it's only a few minutes at first, nothing can calm our souls more or better prepare us for life's challenges than time spent alone with God.

But the Bible also urges us to walk with God every waking moment.

"Pray continually," Paul urged the Thessalonian Christians (1 Thessalonians 5:17 NIV). "Night and day I constantly remember you in my prayers," he told Timothy (2 Timothy 1:3 NIV).

The psalmist noted that the righteous person takes delight in God's Word, "and on his law he meditates day and night" (1:2 NIV). Often when I'm speaking to someone or preaching to a crowd, I find myself praying for them in my heart.

Jesus promised, "I am with you always" (Matthew 28:20). Ask God to help you be aware of His constant presence and to turn your heart and mind toward Him.

What Is Joy?

The joy of the LORD is your strength.
NEHEMIAH 8:10

Some people think Christians should always be smiling and happy and that something is wrong if they aren't.

But this isn't necessarily true. Jesus stood outside the tomb of His friend Lazarus, and we read that "Jesus wept" (John 11:35). As He approached Jerusalem, "He saw the city and wept" (Luke 19:41) because of its spiritual blindness and guilt. He knelt in the Garden of Gethsemane and was "in agony . . . [and] His sweat became like great drops of blood" (Luke 22:44).

Don't confuse happiness with joy. Happiness comes with happy circumstances; joy wells up deep inside our souls as we learn to trust Christ. Joy does not mean that we are never sad or that we never cry. Joy is a quiet confidence, a state of inner peace that comes from God.

Life's troubles may rob us of our happiness, but they can never rob us of the joy God gives us as we turn in faith to Him and seek His face.

Respecting and Encouraging

Respect those who work hard among you,
who are over you in the Lord.

1 THESSALONIANS 5:12 NIV

Have you ever noticed that often when a new pastor takes up his responsibilities, almost without fail people first begin looking for his faults? How sad!

No pastor is perfect, of course; even the apostle Paul admitted to the Christians in Corinth, "When I came to you, brothers, I did not come with eloquence or superior wisdom" (1 Corinthians 2:1 NIV). His young pastor friend Timothy was apparently somewhat shy (1 Timothy 4:12).

If you are a pastor or church worker or you teach a class in your church, be honest about your weaknesses and ask God to help you overcome them so you can serve Christ more effectively.

Instead of criticizing your pastor and others who have leadership in your church, show respect for them. God gave them their gifts and their responsibilities. Pray for them regularly and sincerely. Encourage them as well, thanking them for what they're doing and expressing appreciation for their service. And encourage and pray for their families; they, too, are part of your church's ministry.

Boundless Blessings

He gathers the lambs in his arms
and carries them close to his heart.

ISAIAH 40:11 NIV

T he Old Testament gives a wonderful picture of God
as our Shepherd. One psalm begins, "Hear us, O
Shepherd of Israel, you who lead Joseph like a flock"
(80:1 NIV). The almighty Creator of the universe stoops
to be the Shepherd of His people!

A shepherd protects his sheep, feeds them, and pursues them when they stray. At evening he brings them
into the fold, secure against every enemy. Without the
shepherd, the sheep would scatter and wander into
danger.

In the best-known of all the psalms, David made the
relationship personal. "The LORD is my shepherd," he
cried exultantly, "I shall lack nothing." He then told of
God's constant care, until that day when "I will dwell in
the house of the LORD forever" (23:6 NIV).

But the New Testament tells of another Shepherd—
the Lord Jesus Christ: "I am the good shepherd. The
good shepherd gives His life for the sheep" (John 10:11).
Jesus guides and protects us and even gave His life for
us so we will be safely in His fold forever.

Dealing with Anger

An angry man stirs up dissension,
and a hot-tempered one commits many sins.

PROVERBS 29:22 NIV

We all know what it is to be angry, and we all know the damage it can cause. Anger makes us do things we ordinarily wouldn't do, and even when we think we have it under control, anger can build up within us until it bursts forth in all kinds of hurtful ways. Anger damages everyone it touches and opens the door to many other sins.

No wonder God wants to help us deal with our anger! How can this happen? First, we must admit our anger, and then we must hand it over to God. We can't deal with it by ourselves—not fully and finally. We need God's help, and the first step is to ask Him for it.

Then ask God to help you see others the way He sees them and love them as He does. Their wrongdoing may have caused your anger—but God still loves them. Ask Him to fill you with His love, because anger and love can't coexist. The Bible says, "Above all, love each other deeply, because love covers over a multitude of sins" (1 Peter 4:8 NIV).

Excusing Our Sin

Woe to those who call evil good,
and good evil;
who put darkness for light,
and light for darkness.

ISAIAH 5:20

Is God behind everything that happens to us?

This question isn't easy to answer. On one hand, God is sovereign, and in ways we can only dimly understand this side of eternity, He is at work behind the scenes. The psalmist wrote, "He guides me in paths of righteousness for his name's sake" (23:3 NIV).

On the other hand, the Bible warns us against assuming that everything that comes our way is from God. Recently a woman wrote me about a man she had fallen in love with, and they were now living together. "God brought us together," she stated—in spite of the fact they both were already married. But she was wrong; God never leads us to do anything that is contrary to what He has told us in His Word. This woman was excusing her sin by claiming it must be God's will.

Don't be deceived; don't ever "call evil good, and good evil." Sin is serious—so serious it sent Jesus Christ to the cross. Flee from sin, and stay close to Christ.

Banishing Worry

*The L*ORD* is near to all who call upon Him,*
to all who call upon Him in truth.

PSALM 145:18

Think of the things you do not worry about. Perhaps you never worry about whether you will be able to get water out of the faucet in your kitchen, or maybe you do not worry about a tree falling on your house. You may be a worrier by nature, but even the worst worrier in the world doesn't worry about some things!

Now ask yourself why you do not worry about those things. Is it because, in the case of running water, it has always been there when you wanted it? Or that a tree has never fallen on your house before? Certainty breeds trust, doesn't it? (You may even live in a place where there are no tall trees.)

We can be just as certain and just as worry free about God's love and protection. What is the evidence? It is the cross, where God fully expressed His love for us. The Bible says, "He who did not spare his own Son, but gave him up for us all—how will he not also, along with him, graciously give us all things?" (Romans 8:32 NIV). God's love is certain. He has never gone back on a single promise, and He never will.

Refusing the Remedy

As Paul discoursed on righteousness, self-control
and the judgment to come, Felix was afraid and said,
"That's enough for now! You may leave. When I find
it convenient, I will send for you."

ACTS 24:25 NIV

Paul was under arrest, and the Roman governor Felix had full authority either to release him or keep him in jail. Rather than flatter Felix or try to win his favor, however, Paul instead spoke openly to him about Christ. Finally, Felix had had enough; he ordered Paul to leave, promising to listen more fully "when I find it convenient."

Hoping for a bribe (which Paul wouldn't give), Felix did send for him repeatedly—but two years later Paul was still in jail, and Felix was still an unbeliever. Like a patient who consults his doctor yet refuses to take his prescription, Felix listened to Paul but refused to repent of his sins and commit his life to Christ. The cost was too high; he wasn't willing to give up his sins and begin following Jesus.

Don't wait until a more convenient time to give your life to Christ; the devil will make sure it never happens. Instead, commit your life to Him—today.

Created in His Image

If anyone is in Christ, he is a new creation.

2 CORINTHIANS 5:17

Is it not logical to believe that the only One who can re-create us is the One who created us in the first place? If your watch were out of order, you wouldn't take it to a blacksmith. If your car needed overhauling, you wouldn't take it to a plumber. If you needed an operation, you wouldn't go to a machine shop.

Our spiritual problems can only be solved by the God who originally created us. He created us in His own image and likeness, and He knows all about us.

Today, by the grace of His Son, God can re-create us in the likeness of Jesus' resurrection. Through faith in Christ, we are re-created and become partakers of His life. Just as we were born again by the Spirit of God, so we grow and become more like Christ as the Spirit works in our lives.

"If anyone is in Christ, he is a new creation; old things have passed away; behold, all things have become new" (2 Corinthians 5:17). Don't be chained to the past. You are a new creation in Christ!

A Home in Heaven

*You yourselves had [in heaven] a better
and lasting possession.*

Hebrews 10:34 AMP

Paul once wrote, "If only for this life we have hope
in Christ, we are to be pitied more than all men" (1
Corinthians 15:19 NIV). If there is no life after death, no
Heaven, no promise of a better world—then life in this
world is empty, hopeless, without meaning or purpose.

But this life is not all! Ahead is Heaven, and someday "we shall always be with the Lord" (1 Thessalonians
4:17). Someday we will go to a home where all is happiness, joy, and peace. How barren our lives would be if
we didn't have this hope.

Knowing Heaven is real will make a difference
in the way we live. For one thing, we won't become
attached to the things of this world. We will say with
Paul, "I have learned in whatever state I am, to be content" (Philippians 4:11).

But Heaven should also give us a burden for those
who do not have this hope. Every day you meet people
who do not know Christ. Will you tell them?

Depending on the Truth

This is the testimony: God has given us eternal life,
and this life is in his Son. He who has the Son has life.

1 JOHN 5:11–12 NIV

Imagine that you had a wealthy relative, and one day her attorney called to tell you she had died and left you a million dollars. The money, he added, was now deposited in a bank in your name, and you could draw on it at any time.

What would you do? Would you say, "Oh well, it can't be true; I'll just forget about his call"? I doubt it. Instead, you'd act, accepting by faith that what the attorney told you was true—that you were now a millionaire. And what a difference it would make!

In a far greater way, God offers us a gift—the gift of salvation in Jesus Christ. Christ has done everything possible to provide it for you; all you must do is receive it. Have you taken that step and, by faith, received Christ into your life?

But God's generosity doesn't end there. God wants you to draw upon His riches every day—the riches of His wisdom, strength, truth, and presence. Don't live like a spiritual pauper any longer!

Honoring Our Parents

Honor your father and your mother, as the
LORD your God has commanded you.

DEUTERONOMY 5:16

One of the signs of the latter days before Christ returns, the Bible says, is that "people will be . . . disobedient to their parents" (2 Timothy 3:2 NIV). Instead of obeying the commandment to "honor your father and your mother," they'll bring dishonor to them.

Does this command become irrelevant as we grow older? Is it only meant for young children? No, not at all. As long as our parents are alive, we are to honor and respect them. They weren't perfect parents—but they were the ones God gave you, and you should honor them because of that.

If your parents are still living, ask God to help you let them know you love them and you honor them for the sacrifices they made for you. I'm saddened whenever I visit a nursing home and the staff begs me to visit some of the residents "because their children have just dumped them here and never come to visit."

If your parents are no longer living, ask God to help you befriend an older person who feels lonely and forgotten.

A United Family

*All your children shall be taught by the L*ORD,
And great shall be the peace of your children.

ISAIAH 54:13

The family is the basic unit of society. But from the very beginning, since man sinned against God, the family has been in trouble. The first crime we read about in the Bible occurred when Cain killed his brother, Abel. Instead of love, family life is all too often marked by conflict and tension.

For best results in marriage and in building a stable home, follow the instructions of the One who performed the first wedding in the garden of Eden. Those instructions are in the Bible. The reason the family is in critical condition today is that we have neglected God's rules for a successful home. We have put self in place of sacrifice. We have valued things more than we have valued people.

You can have the right kind of home. Your home can be united if it is now divided. The place to begin is on your knees, asking Christ for forgiveness and then asking God to give you a new love for each other—and for Him. Don't let your family drift apart. With God's help, resist the pressure and come together around the cross.

Cling and Hope

The LORD will be a shelter for His people.
JOEL 3:16

The late British historian Arnold Toynbee shared his personal slogan with the world when he said, "Cling and hope." With all the ideals we held a few years ago crumbling, he advised the human race to cling and hope.

But cling to what? Millions cling to the wreckage they have made of their lives, thinking they have nowhere else to turn. Others cling to false ideologies or deceptive cults. Still others cling to possessions, or relationships, or pleasures. Yes, cling and hope—but what if you are clinging to something that is sinking?

In contrast, thousands of people find refuge from the storms of life by their living faith in a living God!

The true Christian does more than cling and hope. He knows that, with Christ, he is secure forever. Is your hope in Christ?

The Cost of Discipleship

*"If anyone would come after me, he must deny
himself and take up his cross daily and follow me."*

LUKE 9:23 NIV

These are sobering words. Jesus was warning His disciples that it would be costly for them to follow Him. It would be costly because they would have to give up their own plans and goals; it would be costly also because they must share in Jesus' rejection and death. No wonder "many of his disciples turned back and no longer followed him" (John 6:66 NIV).

The cost of following Jesus has not changed. We want to cling to our plans—but He says they must go. We want to live for ourselves—but He says we must live for Him. We want to enjoy a life of pleasure and ease—but He says we must follow Him to the cross.

But why not be His disciple? Why not follow the King of kings and the Lord of lords? Someday your life will be over, and all the things you accumulated will vanish. Don't waste your life. Instead, give everything you have and everything you are to Christ, for He alone is "the way and the truth and the life" (John 14:6 NIV).

Overcoming Discouragement

> [Elijah] came to a broom tree, sat down under
> it and prayed that he might die. "I have had
> enough, LORD," he said.
>
> 1 KINGS 19:4 NIV

We all experience discouragement, and sometimes it can be almost overwhelming.

Look at Elijah. He had been one of God's most faithful servants, never wavering in the face of disaster or King Ahab's threats. Then God used Elijah to confront the pagan prophets of Baal and demonstrate to all the nation that God alone was worthy of their worship.

But only days later, discouragement and depression almost overwhelmed him. Fearing Queen Jezebel's rage and convinced the people's hearts were unchanged, Elijah fled to the desert and concluded he was a failure: "I have had enough, LORD."

How did God answer? First, He provided rest and food: Elijah had neglected to take care of himself, and it affected his emotions. Second, God showed Elijah His glory, reminding him of the greatness of the God he served. Finally, God assured him that He still had work for him to do. When discouragement comes and you wonder if you can go on, remember Elijah—and be encouraged.

God in Human Form

*[Christ] has gone into heaven and is at
the right hand of God.*

1 PETER 3:22

What proofs did Jesus offer that He was truly God come in human form?

First, there was the proof of His perfect life. He could ask, "Which of you convicts Me of sin?" (John 8:46)—and no one could answer.

Second, there was the evidence of His miraculous power. His power was the power of God Almighty.

Third, there was the evidence of fulfilled prophecy. Hundreds of years before His birth, the prophets of the Old Testament spoke precisely of His death and resurrection.

Fourth, there was the evidence of His resurrection from the dead.

Fifth, there is the proof of changed lives. Christ alone, the divine Son of God, has power to change the human heart. And He does.

Faith in Christ is not a leap in the dark. It is a decision based on the solid facts of Christ's life, death, and resurrection. Thank God we have a solid foundation in Him!

Life's Hard Reality

The length of our days is seventy years . . .
yet their span is but trouble and sorrow.
Psalm 90:10 niv

There it is in black and white: life is hard, and our years on Earth are marked by "trouble and sorrow." As someone has said, there is no false advertising in the Bible!

We wish it weren't so, of course. Maybe that's why we're so quick to believe the advertisements that promise happiness if we'll only use their product. And sometimes life can bring us a measure of happiness. As the Bible says, "The Lord bestows favor and honor; no good thing does he withhold from those whose walk is blameless" (Psalm 84:11 niv). But I've never met a person who didn't have problems of some kind. We live in a world that is broken because of sin, and we share in its brokenness.

What difference should this make? First, it should give us greater compassion for others. All around you are people whose lives are filled with trouble and sorrow, and they need your compassion and encouragement. Second, it should make us yearn for Heaven. There our troubles and sorrows will cease, and we will be safely with Christ forever.

"Even So, Come!"

"Behold, I am coming quickly!"
REVELATION 22:7

What would you say about a person who had made a hundred promises to you and already kept ninety-nine of them? You would probably think that person was honest enough to fulfill the last promise as well, wouldn't you?

Jesus Christ has fulfilled every promise He ever made—except one. He has not yet returned. Will He?

In both the Old and New Testaments, there are references to the return of the Lord. Isaiah, for example, looked forward to the day when the Messiah's Kingdom would be a reality: "Behold, I create new heavens and a new earth; and the former shall not be remembered or come to mind" (65:17).

John quoted Christ as saying, "I go to prepare a place for you. And . . . I will come again and receive you to Myself" (John 14:2–3). The entire book of Revelation tells of the glorious return of Christ. And we can say with the apostle John, who wrote that book, "Amen. Even so, come, Lord Jesus!" (Revelation 22:20).

Are you looking forward to His return? And are you seeking until that day to be His faithful servant?

Dealing with Eternity

I will see Your face in righteousness;
I shall be satisfied when I awake in Your likeness.
PSALM 17:15

When English patriot Sir William Russell went to the scaffold in 1683, he took his watch out of his pocket and handed it to the physician who attended him in his death. "Would you kindly take my timepiece?" he asked. "I have no use for it. I am now dealing with eternity."

This world fades into insignificance in light of eternity. All the things that preoccupy us are no longer important, and only one thing counts: our relationship with the Lord.

But we should live every day in light of eternity! As Peter wrote in his last letter, "Since all these things will be dissolved, what manner of persons ought you to be in holy conduct and godliness? . . . Be diligent to be found by Him in peace, without spot and blameless" (2 Peter 3:11, 14).

How different would today be if you knew it would be your last one on Earth before meeting God face-to-face? We should strive to live every day as if it were our last, for one day it will be!

Life's Toughest Job

Train a child in the way he should go,
and when he is old he will not turn from it.

PROVERBS 22:6 NIV

I'm president of a large corporation," he said to me, "but the hardest job I've ever tried to do is be a good parent." Then he added, "If my home was as successful as my company, I'd be elated." Being a parent is hard; every child is different, and every day brings fresh challenges. It's especially hard if one parent is missing; being a single parent is surely one of the most difficult responsibilities imaginable.

But sometimes we overlook some basic truths about parenting that we need to keep before us (or, if we're older, pass on to others).

First, see your children as a gift from God. He entrusted them to you; receive them as a gift (and responsibility) from His hands. Second, let your children know you love them. Show them affection; teach them right and wrong; spend time with them. Third, be an example of faith. Pray with them, read the Bible to them, and let them see that Christ is important to you. With God's help, you can be the kind of parent they need.

The Glory to Come

Our days on earth are as a shadow.

1 CHRONICLES 29:15

C. S. Lewis once observed that this life is only "shadow lands" compared with the glory to come. Even life at its best is but a shadow of Heaven.

Does that mean we turn our backs on this world and have nothing to do with its delights? Not necessarily. Sometimes (as Lewis was suggesting) the good things God gives us are a foreshadowing, a hint of what is to come. We experience the joy of marriage, knowing it is the foretaste of an even greater joy: the Heavenly marriage feast of the Lamb (Revelation 19:9). We enjoy the beauty of God's creation, knowing it is the foretaste of an even greater beauty: the glory of Heaven (Revelation 21:23).

Take delight in the good things God gives you. Don't be too preoccupied to smell the roses! The Bible reminds us, "Every good gift and every perfect gift is from above, and comes down from the Father of lights" (James 1:17). And every one of His good gifts should remind us of the glory to come!

The Body of Christ

Christ is the head of the church, his body,
of which he is the Savior.
EPHESIANS 5:23 NIV

When we come to Christ, we come as individuals. We alone repent of our sins; we alone believe Christ's death on the cross will save us; we alone decide to become His follower.

But once we come to Christ, we are no longer just individuals. We are now members of His family—what the Bible here calls "the church, his body." We are now part of that vast group of people through the ages who have trusted Christ and are our brothers and sisters in His family. Although we'll never meet most of them on this side of eternity, we're still united spiritually with them. This community transcends any local church or denomination; it includes all who truly belong to Christ.

Christian fellowship is one of God's greatest gifts to us. Are you sharing in it—worshipping with others and growing closer to Christ through fellowship with them? No local church is perfect, of course—but don't use that as an excuse to avoid fellowship with others. The Bible tells us to "encourage one another and build each other up" (1 Thessalonians 5:11 NIV).

Faith and Reason

For since the creation of the world God's invisible qualities—his eternal power and divine nature—have been clearly seen, being understood from what has been made.

ROMANS 1:20 NIV

Is faith illogical?

If you listen to some people, the answer would appear to be yes.

Every year books hit the best-seller lists announcing that faith in God is dead; every year college students write me wondering why their professors reject God; every year talk show hosts promote the latest self-help gurus claiming to solve all our problems.

Is faith illogical, as some would have you believe? No, not at all.

Some of the most brilliant people I have ever known were also men and women of deep faith in Christ, and without exception they said they believed in the gospel because it made sense.

But there was another reason for their faith. They were convinced Jesus Christ was who He claimed to be: God in human flesh, sent to save us from our sins. Don't be misled, but rejoice that in Christ "are hidden all the treasures of wisdom and knowledge" (Colossians 2:3 NIV).

Sweet Slumber

I will both lie down in peace, and sleep;
for You alone, O Lord, make me dwell in safety.

PSALM 4:8

By any measure, drug and alcohol dependence has become one of our greatest social problems. The issue isn't just illegal drugs; many people depend on alcohol or over-the-counter or prescription drugs just to face each day or to get to sleep at night.

I'm not a doctor, of course, and I fully realize that some drugs have a legitimate place under careful medical supervision. But in my experience, far too many people turn first to drugs or alcohol instead of to God. Rather than face their problems and deal with them (with God's help), they use drugs or alcohol to escape.

But such "solutions" never work; in fact, they only make things worse. No wonder the book of Proverbs warns that alcohol "at the last . . . bites like a serpent, and stings like a viper" (23:32).

Don't let anything substitute for God. He loves you, and He wants to give you peace—the peace that comes from knowing Him. Jesus' promise to His followers is true: "I will give you rest" (Matthew 11:28).

Sunshine and Shadow

If you should suffer for righteousness' sake,
you are blessed.
1 PETER 3:14

All the masterpieces of painting contain both light and shadow. Artists use light and shadow to highlight certain features of their subjects; they provide contrast and harmony to reveal beauty or character.

A happy life is not one filled only with sunshine, but one in which both light and shadow produce beauty. Suffering or persecution can become a blessing because they can form a dark backdrop for the radiance of the Christian life. The greatest musicians, as a rule, are those who know how to bring song out of sadness. Fanny Crosby, her spirit aglow with faith in Christ, saw more with her sightless eyes than most of us do with normal vision. She gave us some great gospel songs that cheer our hearts and lives.

Paul and Silas sang a song of praise at midnight in a rat-infested jail in Philippi, their feet in stocks, their backs raw from the jailer's whip. But their patience in suffering and persecution led to the conversion of the heathen prison warden and his family.

Don't despise the shadows God brings into your life. He can use them to produce a masterpiece.

Still Serving

*Now Barzillai was a very old man, eighty
years of age. He had provided for the king
during his stay in Mahanaim.*

2 SAMUEL 19:32 NIV

You've probably never heard of Barzillai. He lived in an obscure, isolated village, and virtually his whole life was behind him when we meet him in the Bible. Even then, his story occupies only a few verses.

But without Barzillai the history of God's people might have been vastly different. In one of the saddest events in the Bible, King David's son Absalom revolted against his father and attempted to take the throne by force. David and his men had to flee for their lives, and by the time they reached the vicinity of Barzillai's home, they were out of supplies and in danger of starvation. But Barzillai came to their aid, and David's army was saved. Absalom's rebellion collapsed, and David—Jesus' ancestor—was restored to the throne.

Barzillai was eighty when this happened, and he easily could have said, "I'm too old to do anything" or "It's too risky. What if Absalom wins?" But he didn't.

Are you older, perhaps retired or nearing retirement? Don't waste those years, but ask God to use you—just as He did Barzillai.

Abiding Peace

"Fear not, for I am with you;
be not dismayed, for I am your God."
Isaiah 41:10

Whenever I think of God's faithfulness in the midst of suffering, I am reminded of my dear late friend Corrie ten Boom, the remarkable Dutch woman who, with her family, hid Jews from the Nazis. After being imprisoned in the infamous concentration camp Ravensbruk, Corrie traveled the world telling her story of suffering, forgiveness, and joy.

For thirty-five years she never had a permanent home, but when she was eighty-five and in declining health, some friends provided her with a lovely house in California. It was a luxury she never dreamed she would have (and one she never would have pursued on her own).

One day her friend, the late movie director James Collier, was visiting. He said, "Corrie, hasn't God been good to give you this beautiful house?"

She replied firmly, "Jimmy, God was good when I was in Ravensbruk too!"

Most of us will never experience the horrors Corrie knew. But no matter what we face, we can depend on God's promise: "Fear not, for I am with you."

A Solid Center

But these [miraculous signs] are written that you may
believe that Jesus is the Christ, the Son of God, and
that by believing you may have life in his name.

JOHN 20:31 NIV

Jesus Christ is the Bible's central message. The Old Testament looks forward to His coming; the New Testament recounts His coming. Without Christ the Bible is only another book of ancient history—but beyond that it has little relevance. But Christ gives the Bible its value, because before time began God planned to send Him into the world for our salvation (Ephesians 1:4).

But Jesus Christ isn't just the center of the Bible; He is the center of our lives. By believing in Him, John said, we "have life in his name." What does this mean? First, it means eternal life. Without Christ we have no hope of Heaven; as the Bible says, "The wages of sin is death" (Romans 6:23). But when we yield our lives to Christ and trust Him alone for our salvation, we know we will be with Him through all eternity.

But Jesus Christ also gives us life right now—not the artificial, unstable life the world offers, but a life of purpose and peace and joy. Is Christ the center of your life?

How Do You Define Success?

*Therefore, holy brothers, who share in the heavenly
calling, fix your thoughts on Jesus. . . . He was
faithful to the one who appointed him.*

HEBREWS 3:1–2 NIV

Recently a friend of mine went on the website of one
of the major booksellers and searched for books
with the word *success* in their title. Literally thousands
were listed. Our world is obsessed with success.

What is success? The world has its measures:
financial success, athletic success, business success,
professional success, social success—the list is almost as
endless as my friend's website search. And most people
spend their lives pursuing at least one of these.

But how does God define success? His measure is
very different from the world's measure, and it can be
summed up in one sentence: in God's eyes, success is
faithfulness to His calling. Paul was a failure in the
world's eyes—but not to God. Even Jesus was a failure
as far as most people were concerned, but "he was faithful to the one who appointed him"—and that is all that
mattered.

What is your definition of success? Is it the same as
God's? And are you pursuing it?

Thankful in Prayer

*Devote yourselves to prayer, being
watchful and thankful.*

COLOSSIANS 4:2 NIV

Prayer isn't just asking God for something we want. Prayer should also include confession of our sin and praise to God for who He is and what He has done for us.

But prayer should have an additional element, and that is thanksgiving. Repeatedly the Bible commands us to give thanks. The psalmist said, "Oh, give thanks to the LORD, for He is good! For His mercy endures forever" (107:1). Jesus only distributed the bread He had miraculously provided for the crowds after "he had given thanks" (Matthew 15:36 NIV). At the Last Supper with His disciples, before facing the horror of the cross, Jesus "gave thanks" (Luke 22:17, 19).

It's easy to be thankful when God blesses us with something good—a swift recovery from an illness, for example, or an advancement at work. But the Bible says we should "give thanks in *all* circumstances, for this is God's will for [us] in Christ Jesus" (1 Thessalonians 5:18 NIV, italics mine).

Thankfulness drives away a sour or prideful spirit. Make it part of your prayers every day.

The Grace of Gratitude

It is good to give thanks to the LORD.
PSALM 92:1

The Pilgrim Fathers who landed at Plymouth in America in 1620 knew nothing of the bountiful prosperity that so many people enjoy today. During that first long winter, seven times as many graves were dug for the dead as homes were built for the living. Seed, imported from England, failed to grow, and a ship that was to bring food and relief brought thirty-five more mouths to feed, but not an ounce of provisions. The Pilgrims caught fish and hunted wild fowl and deer. They had a little English meal and some Indian corn.

Yet their lives were marked by a spirit of constant thankfulness. On one occasion William Brewster, rising from a scanty Plymouth dinner of clams and water, gave thanks to God "for the abundance of the sea and the treasures hid in the sand."

According to today's standards, the Pilgrims had little, but they possessed a sense of great gratitude. Gratitude is one of the greatest Christian graces; ingratitude, one of the most vicious sins. Ask God to open your eyes to all the blessings He has bestowed on you and to give you a fresh spirit of gratitude—not just at this season of the year, but always.

The Spirit of Gratitude

Give thanks to the Lord, for he is good;
his love endures forever.

PSALM 107:1 NIV

One day when Jesus was on His way to Jerusalem, ten lepers approached Him and pleaded for Him to heal them. In an instant they were restored to perfect health, but only one, "when he saw he was healed, came back, praising God in a loud voice. He threw himself at Jesus' feet and thanked him" (Luke 17:15–16 NIV). All the others left without a single word of thanks. They were preoccupied with themselves and gripped by a spirit of ingratitude.

Such ingratitude and thanklessness are far too common in our world. Children forget to thank their parents for all they do. Common courtesy is scorned. People take for granted the way others help them. And, above all, we fail to thank God for His blessings. Such an ungrateful heart is cold toward God and indifferent to His mercy and love. It is a heart that has forgotten how dependent we are on God for everything.

Be like that one leper: take time to give thanks—and mean it. It brings glory to God, warmth to relationships, and a special awareness of God's love and grace toward you.

Make It a Habit!

I have learned the secret of being content in any and every situation, whether well fed or hungry, whether living in plenty or in want.

PHILIPPIANS 4:12 NIV

The next footsteps, he knew, might be those of the guards taking him away to his execution. His bed was the cold, stone floor of the dank, cramped prison cell. There was never any relief from the constant irritation of the chains and the pain of the iron manacles cutting into his wrists and ankles.

Separated from friends, unjustly accused, brutally treated—if any man had a right to complain, it was this man, languishing almost forgotten in a harsh Roman prison. But instead of complaints, his lips rang with words of praise and thanksgiving!

This was the apostle Paul, a man who had learned to give thanks even in the midst of great adversity. Look carefully at what he wrote during his prison experience: "Sing and make music in your heart to the Lord, always giving thanks to God the Father for everything, in the name of our Lord Jesus Christ" (Ephesians 5:19–20 NIV).

For Paul, giving thanks was a regular habit that made him joyful in every situation. It can do the same for you. Start developing that habit today!

God's Holiness

*Holy, holy, holy is the L*ORD *of hosts;*
The whole earth is full of His glory!

ISAIAH 6:3

The Bible teaches that God is absolutely holy and pure. From Genesis to Revelation, God reveals that He is so holy He cannot even look on sin.

Christ cried from the cross, "My God, My God, why have You forsaken Me?" (Mark 15:34). What a horrible moment, as the blackness of human sin—now laid upon Christ—caused the Father to turn away in disgust. In that moment Jesus endured the ultimate punishment for our sins—the punishment of being banished from the presence of His Father on our behalf.

If you were asked to list the things you are thankful for, what would you include? Perhaps your family, health, friends, church—and those wouldn't be wrong. We should be grateful for every gift God gives us.

But the greatest gift of all is God's gift of His Son, who endured the penalty we deserved for our sin, so we could be reconciled to a holy God. Never take that gift for granted! "Thanks be to God for His indescribable gift!" (2 Corinthians 9:15).

The Right Attitude

Now, our God, we give you thanks,
and praise your glorious name.

1 CHRONICLES 29:13 NIV

The Pilgrim Fathers who landed at Plymouth to settle in what became the United States of America can teach us an important lesson about giving thanks.

During that first long winter, seven times as many graves were made for the dead as homes were made for the living. Seed, imported from England, failed to grow, and a ship that was to bring food and relief, brought instead thirty-five more mouths to feed, but no provisions. Some Pilgrims caught fish, and others hunted wild fowl and deer. They had a little English flour and some Indian corn.

Yet William Brewster, rising from a scanty dinner of clams and water, gave thanks to God "for the abundance of the sea and the treasure hid in the sand."

According to today's standards, the Pilgrims had almost nothing, but they possessed a profound and heartfelt gratitude to God for His love and mercy. Gratitude is one of the greatest Christian virtues; ingratitude, one of the most vicious sins.

Our English words *thank* and *think* come from the same word. If we'll stop to think, we'll be more thankful.

True Thanksgiving

Oh, give thanks to the Lord, for He is good!

Psalm 107:1

Separated from friends, unjustly accused, brutally treated—if any man had a right to complain it was this man, languishing almost forgotten in a harsh Roman prison. But instead of complaints, his lips rang with words of praise and thanksgiving!

This was the apostle Paul—a man who had learned the meaning of true thanksgiving, even in the midst of great adversity. Look carefully at what he wrote during that prison experience: "Sing and make music in your heart to the Lord, always giving thanks to God the Father for everything, in the name of our Lord Jesus Christ" (Ephesians 5:19–20 NIV).

Think of it! "Always giving thanks . . . for everything" no matter the circumstances. Paul's guards and fellow prisoners must have thought him crazy—but that didn't stop him. Thanksgiving for Paul was not a once-a-year celebration, but a daily reality that made him a joyful person in every situation. May that be true of us as well.

Give Thanks!

Enter [God's] gates with thanksgiving
and his courts with praise;
give thanks to him and praise his name.
PSALM 100:4 NIV

Throughout the Bible, we are commanded to be thankful. A spirit of thanksgiving is one of the most distinctive marks of a Christian whose heart is attuned to the Lord.

First, we are to be thankful for the material blessings God gives us. Some people are never satisfied with what they have, but what a difference it makes when we realize that everything we have has been given to us by God!

Second, thank God for the people in your life. It is so easy to take them for granted or to complain or become angry because they don't meet our every wish. But we need to give thanks for our spouse, our children, our relatives, and our friends. Most of all, thank God for Christ and His love for you.

Third, thank God in the midst of trials and even persecution. We draw back from difficulties, but not one of us is exempt from trouble. Yet in the midst of trials we can thank God because we know He has promised to be with us and help us.

For the Christian, every day is Thanksgiving Day!

Gratitude for His Gifts

Thanks be to God for His indescribable gift!
2 CORINTHIANS 9:15

The apostle Paul warned that the time would come when "people will be lovers of themselves . . . ungrateful" (2 Timothy 3:2 NIV). What a description of our own time! Rather than being grateful, we get wrapped up in ourselves and take for granted what others do for us. Of course, it shouldn't be this way, but it often is.

I know of a couple without children of their own who—at great sacrifice—helped put their two nieces through college without ever hearing a single "thank you." If something like that happens to you, I hope you will find satisfaction in knowing that you made a difference in someone's life—and that someday that person will appreciate what you did and perhaps even see the Lord's hand in it.

While we're thinking about gratitude, though, I find myself thinking about how ungrateful we often are to God. He has given us everything we have, but are we truly thankful? Most of all, God sent Jesus into the world to die for us. Have we responded by thanking Him for His love and giving our life to Him?

Gratitude in Word and Deed

*If anyone has material possessions and sees his
brother in need but has no pity on him, how can the
love of God be in him?*

1 JOHN 3:17 NIV

Whenever we sit down for a meal, let us not forget
that at least half the world goes to bed hungry.
When we enjoy the comfort of our home, let us not forget that millions have no home to go to. As we ride in
our car, let us not forget that many people in the world
cannot afford even a bicycle.

Whenever we go to church to thank God for our
material and spiritual blessings, let us remember that
millions have never heard the gospel, the good news of
salvation in Christ. Let us remember as well those who
follow Jesus but risk their lives by owning a Bible or
attending a worship service. Let us also remember that
missionaries in many parts of the world are suffering in
order to take the gospel to those who have yet to hear
about Jesus.

And let us always be grateful not only in word but in
deed. May our gratitude find expression in our prayers,
our service, and our commitment to live wholly for
Christ.

God's Love

In this the love of God was made manifest . . . that
God sent his only Son into the world.

1 JOHN 4:9 RSV

From Genesis to Revelation, from Earth's greatest tragedy to Earth's greatest triumph, the dramatic story of humanity's lowest depths and God's highest heights can be couched in twenty-five beautiful words: "For God so loved the world that He gave His only begotten Son, that whoever believes in Him should not perish but have everlasting life" (John 3:16).

Many people misunderstand God's attribute of love. "God is love" does not mean that everything is sweet, beautiful, and happy or that God's love could not possibly allow punishment for sin.

God's holiness demands that all sin be punished, but God's love provided a plan of redemption and salvation for a lost and sinful world. According to that plan, Jesus Christ came from Heaven to give His life as the final and perfect sacrifice for sin.

But we must respond. We must believe. We must commit our lives to Jesus Christ and trust Him as our Savior and Lord. Have you put your faith in Him? If so, everlasting life is yours!

Thanking God in Everything

He has shown kindness by giving you rain from heaven and crops in their seasons; he provides you with plenty of food and fills your hearts with joy.

ACTS 14:17 NIV

God delights in giving—even to His enemies. God gives people food—but they give Him rebellion. God gives people wisdom—but they serve the devil with it. He gives people strength—but they waste it in evil pursuits.

All of God's giving, however, should drive us to thanksgiving. Whatever material things we enjoy came from God, and He gives them to us to remind us of His goodness. Some people ask, "Why should those who have plenty pray, 'Give us our daily bread'? We can understand why a poor person would pray such a prayer, but why should a rich person pray it?" The reason is clear: to remind us all of our constant dependence on God. The bread is in our hand, yet both the bread and the blessing are from God's hand.

No matter what we receive from God, it should drive us to give humble thanks to Him, from whom all blessings flow.

Wisdom from Above

The wisdom that is from above is first
pure, then peaceable.

JAMES 3:17

Today there is more knowledge in the world than ever before. Computers and fiber optic cables can transmit information in a matter of nanoseconds. More facts have been discovered in the past century than in all of the other centuries of human history combined. Yet that same century also recorded the most devastating wars and the fiercest genocides in human history. We have never been further from solving our basic problems.

The Bible says there are two kinds of wisdom in the world. First, there is wisdom that is given by God, a wisdom that views life in terms of eternity. Of this wisdom, the Scripture says, "The wisdom that is from above is first pure, then peaceable, gentle, willing to yield, full of mercy and good fruits, without partiality and without hypocrisy" (James 3:17).

The second is the wisdom of the world. This wisdom excludes God and His moral standards from human decisions, and seeks to solve society's problems apart from Him. But where has it gotten us? Which kind of wisdom will you choose?

The Ticket to Heaven

The Lord will . . . preserve me for
His heavenly kingdom.
2 TIMOTHY 4:18

Preparing for Heaven is much like going on a journey. First, you must decide you want to go there. Next, you must purchase your ticket.

But wait! How will you purchase it? Can you buy it by being a good person? By going to church or acting religious? By giving money or volunteering your time to help others? The Bible says none of these will suffice, because the ticket to Heaven is expensive—far too expensive for any human being to afford.

Does that mean we can never go there? No—and the reason is because Someone else has already purchased the ticket for us. That person was Jesus Christ, and the price He paid was His own blood, shed on the cross for us.

Now He offers us the ticket to Heaven free and fully paid! Why refuse it? Why try some other way? Jesus' invitation is still open: "'Come!' Whoever is thirsty, let him come; and whoever wishes, let him take the free gift of the water of life" (Revelation 22:17 NIV).

Giving to God

Honor the LORD with your possessions,
And with the firstfruits of all your increase.

PROVERBS 3:9

God doesn't need our money to get His work done. He is sovereign and can do it without our help. Yet He has arranged it so that His work often depends on our generosity.

At least two things happen when we give. First, when we give with the right attitude, God reminds us that what we have isn't really ours. He gave us everything we have, and it actually belongs to Him. King David prayed, "All things come from You, and of Your own we have given You" (1 Chronicles 29:14). We need to learn that truth.

Second, when we give, we help meet the needs of others whom God also loves. By giving to others we testify to God's love for them, and we point them to the greatest gift of all—God's gift of His Son for our salvation.

Someone has said that our lives should resemble channels, not reservoirs. A reservoir stores water; a channel distributes it. God wants us to be channels of blessing to others. Are you?

A Heavenly Address

"I am going there to prepare a place for you."
JOHN 14:2 NIV

I live high on a mountain in a log cabin in North Carolina. I may travel all over the world, but I know that when I come home, I will return to a precise location. It will still be there at the end of my journey, and I always look forward to coming home!

In saying that He was going to prepare a place for us, Jesus was telling us that when we die, we are going to a precise location. We do not evaporate or disappear. In fact, Jesus said, "In My Father's house are many mansions" (John 14:2). We are going to have a place in Heaven if we have trusted Christ as our Savior—and not only a place, but a mansion!

When we Christians die, we go straight into the presence of Christ—straight to that place, straight to that mansion in Heaven to spend eternity with God. We are simply changing our address!

The Hope-Filled Truth

"Surely I am with you always, to the
very end of the age."
MATTHEW 28:20 NIV

On the purely human level, there is little hope in the world. Immorality and lawlessness seem to be increasing. Wrong seems to be winning and right seems to be losing the battle for the minds and hearts of people.

Many of us have put our faith in money, jobs, status, gadgets, pleasures, and thrills. Many of us—and society as a whole—have tried to bypass God, and now we are paying the inevitable price. We are in trouble because we have left out God; we have left out the Ten Commandments; we have left out the Sermon on the Mount. Now we as individuals and as a culture are reaping the tragic results.

But the living Christ can bring glorious hope to us and to our world. After His resurrection, Jesus promised, "I am with you always." In those words is the encouragement for the discouraged, the hope for the hopeless, and the help for the helpless. There is purpose and guidance and peace and power.

Turn to Jesus. He is with you . . . always.

The Faith of a Child

He called a little child and had him stand among
them. And he said . . . "Whoever humbles himself like
this child is the greatest in the kingdom of heaven."
MATTHEW 18:2–4 NIV

I s it of any use to talk to young children about God and
encourage them to give their lives to Jesus? Perhaps
you are a parent, or you've taught a children's class in
your church, and you've asked yourself this question. Or
perhaps you made a decision for Jesus when you were a
child, and you wonder if it really counted for anything.

Jesus welcomed the children who flocked to Him:
"Let the little children come to me, and do not hinder them, for the kingdom of heaven belongs to such
as these" (Matthew 19:14 NIV). Their openness, their
enthusiasm, their trust—all these delighted Jesus.

A young child may not understand everything
about God—but he or she can understand something.
A young child understands love, and also understands
what it means to obey someone. They—like us—can
confess Jesus as their Lord, and believe that Jesus came
back to life for them. Don't ignore the children God
brings across your path, but by your words and by your
example, tell them about Jesus.

God's Truth

You are my hiding place . . .
I hope in Your word.

PSALM 119:114

God's Word never changes. Jesus said, "I tell you the truth, until heaven and earth disappear, not the smallest letter, not the least stroke of a pen, will by any means disappear from the Law" (Matthew 5:18 NIV). Jesus also declared, "Heaven and earth will pass away, but My words will by no means pass away" (24:35).

This is not because God is an inflexible or insensitive tyrant. It is because He knows what is best for us. He knows how we function, and He knows the pitfalls and dangers we face. If He didn't love us, He wouldn't try to guide us in the right path. But He does!

Only God's Word can help us avoid moral and spiritual danger and lead us in the right way. The psalmist testified, "Your word is a lamp to my feet and a light to my path. . . . The entrance of Your words gives light" (119:105, 130).

Let God's Word shape and guide you. God loves you too much to leave you in the dark!

DECEMBER

The Secret of His Strength

*"But when you pray, go into your room, close the door
and pray to your Father, who is unseen. Then your
Father, who sees what is done in secret, will reward you."*
MATTHEW 6:6 NIV

Recently I heard about the owner of a small factory who was greatly respected by his employees—not only for his business skills, but for his integrity and his concern for his employees. They knew that he went out of his way to be fair to them and that more than once during hard times he sacrificed the company's profits to keep his workers employed.

After his death one of his longtime employees was showing the man's grandson around the factory. "Do you want to know the secret of your grandfather's success?" he asked. "Certainly," the younger man replied, wondering what gems of wisdom he might learn. Wordlessly, the employee led him to the rear of the factory. In one corner was the door to what looked like a small storage closet. "This was the secret of his success," the employee said. "Every morning he slipped in here before anyone else arrived and spent at least half an hour in prayer. Prayer was the foundation of his life."

What is the foundation of your life?

Infinite Grace

Grace and truth came through Jesus Christ.

JOHN 1:17

The word *grace* means more than just God's kindness or gentleness toward us, more than just His mercy, even. It means His undeserved favor: God owes us nothing, and we deserve nothing. When the Bible says "by grace you have been saved" (Ephesians 2:5), it means our salvation was totally unmerited. It came solely because of God's grace.

The motive of grace is the infinite, compassionate love of a merciful God, but the work of grace was Christ's death on the cross. When I imagine Christ hanging from the cross—the spikes in His hands, the crown of thorns on His brow, His blood draining from His body, the soldiers mocking Him—then I begin to see the depth of God's grace. Then I know that nothing can equal the infinite love of God for a sinful world.

But God's grace is also exhibited when we humbly bow before Christ in repentance and faith, for then we find forgiveness. Thank God for His grace, for without it we would have no hope!

We Shall Be Changed

> *We know that when he appears, we shall be like him,*
> *for we shall see him as he is.*
>
> 1 JOHN 3:2 NIV

It's natural to wonder what Heaven must be like. Are the streets really paved with gold? Will we know each other? What will we do with our time?

These and a hundred other questions crowd our minds—and to be honest, the Bible doesn't answer all our questions about Heaven. Heaven is so glorious, and our hearts and minds are so limited, that we can only dimly perceive its grandeur. I often think of the apostle Paul's statement: "Now we see but a poor reflection as in a mirror; then we shall see face to face" (1 Corinthians 13:12 NIV).

But one truth about Heaven is absolutely clear: we will be safely in God's presence forever. All the fears and insecurities and sorrows and disappointments that afflict us here on Earth will be banished. So, too, will all the weaknesses and sins and failures that mark our lives right now. We will be changed—for we will be like Christ! When life weighs you down, turn your heart to Christ—for someday you will see Him, and all life's burdens will be lifted from your shoulders forever.

From Time to Eternity

We give thanks to God . . . because of the hope
which is laid up for you in heaven.

COLOSSIANS 1:3, 5

Once I stood in London to watch Queen Elizabeth return from an overseas trip. I saw the parade of dignitaries, the marching bands, the crack troops, the waving flags. I saw all the splendor that accompanies the homecoming of a queen.

However, that was nothing compared to the home-coming of a true believer. At that moment of death, the believer enters Heaven itself, carried upward by the angels to the glorious welcome awaiting the redeemed (Luke 16:22).

From our human viewpoint, death is always tinged with sadness. It is not wrong to mourn the loss of a loved one; Jesus wept at the grave of His friend Lazarus (John 11:32–35).

But the Christian should never consider the death of a fellow believer a tragedy. Paul said we should not "grieve like the rest of men, who have no hope" (1 Thessalonians 4:13 NIV). Yes, we have hope! The way to Heaven may lie through the valley of the shadow of death, but the angels accompany us all the way—and beyond that shadowy valley is Heaven, our glorious home.

An Open Door

"What he opens no one can shut, and what he shuts no one can open. . . . See, I have placed before you an open door that no one can shut."

REVELATION 3:7–8 NIV

When God opens a door, what possible excuse can we have for not going through it?

All over the world God is opening doors of opportunity today, making it possible for us to take the gospel to millions who have never heard of Christ. Some live in lands that have been freed from the grip of atheism in recent years; others are immersed in a rising tide of secularism or religious oppression. But in spite of the barriers—and they are real—God is opening doors today in unexpected ways for the preaching of the gospel. Will we fail to go through them?

God may not call you to be a preacher or missionary (although He may). But what will you do to help the Church of Jesus Christ move through those open doors? Will you pray? Will you give? Will you go on a short-term mission project? Jesus said, "The harvest is plentiful but the workers are few. Ask the Lord of the harvest, therefore, to send out workers into his harvest field" (Matthew 9:37–38 NIV).

Sin's Deadly Heritage

The creation itself will be liberated
from its bondage to decay.

ROMANS 8:21 NIV

Recently some computers in our office were attacked by a major computer virus. Thinking they were opening a legitimate e-mail, the staff suddenly found their computers running amok, unable to function as they were designed to do. Only a major reprogramming of their corrupted hard drives, I was told, would restore them to usefulness.

I couldn't help but compare this to another virus—the virus of sin. God created our first parents perfect and without sin, their every need met and their relationship with God unblemished. But then they rebelled against God, and sin entered the world. Since that day, the human heart has been infected with the deadly virus of sin. Our fellowship with God was destroyed, we became morally weak and corrupt, and even all creation was affected.

But Christ came to conquer the virus of sin! When He enters our lives, He begins to remake us from within. The virus no longer has absolute control. And someday God will remove the virus of sin forever, and all creation will be renewed.

Peace in Pain

So walk in Him, rooted and built up in Him.
COLOSSIANS 2:6–7

Not far from my home in North Carolina is Mount Mitchell, the highest point in the eastern United States. On its ridges are old trees that have been stunted and gnarled by the hostile climate and the rocky soil.

But local craftsmen have told me that when one of these trees finally dies, its wood is highly prized—and the reason is because it is so strong. The tree resisted those fierce alpine winds for decades, and they strengthened it.

What happens when the winds of adversity blow in your life? Do they flatten you, knock you down, stop your growth? Or, like those trees, do you grow stronger?

What makes the difference? The trees that survive, I am told, are those with the deepest roots. The roots are like an anchor helping them survive the storms, and they also draw up the soil's nutrients, helping the trees grow stronger.

Make sure your soul is firmly planted in Christ, so you may be "rooted and built up in Him and established in the faith" (Colossians 2:7).

The Exact Image of God

"Anyone who has seen me has seen the Father."

JOHN 14:9 NIV

Many people respect Jesus' moral teachings; they may even respect Him for His impact on civilization. But one part of His teachings shocked and offended many of His hearers and still does today.

The offending teaching? It was Jesus' teaching about Himself. Repeatedly Jesus made the most startling claim imaginable: He was God in human flesh. He wasn't just a man (although He was that); He was also God. Think of it! The great and powerful God of the universe came down to Earth and took upon Himself human flesh!

But Jesus' teaching about Himself didn't stop there. He went on to say that, because He was divine, He was without sin—and because He was without sin, He could become the sin-bearer for the human race. All our sins would be placed on Him, and He would take upon Himself the death and Hell we deserve. And this is exactly what happened.

Don't ever lose sight of who Jesus was: God in human flesh. And don't ever lose sight of what He did: He died for you, because He loves you.

Twice Born

*"Unless one is born again, he cannot
see the kingdom of God."*

JOHN 3:3

We cannot fully explain the mystery of physical birth, but we accept its wonder, and we accept the fact of new life. What is it, then, that keeps us from accepting the reality and wonder of spiritual rebirth—of being "born again"? To those who have experienced it or seen it happen in others, it is just as real as physical birth.

Just as surely as God implants the life cell in the tiny seed that produces the mighty oak . . . as surely as He instills the heartbeat in the life of the tiny infant yet unborn . . . as surely as He puts motion into the planets, stars, and Heavenly bodies—so He implants His divine life in the hearts of those who earnestly seek Him through Christ.

This is not conjecture; it is fact. But has it happened to you? If not, you are not only unfit for the Kingdom of God, but you also are cheating yourself out of the greatest, most revolutionary experiences known to any human being. By a simple prayer of faith, ask Christ into your life right now. He will come in, and you will be born again!

Danger Zone

In them is fulfilled the prophecy of Isaiah:
"You will be ever hearing but never understanding;
you will be ever seeing but never perceiving."

MATTHEW 13:14 NIV

The people who are in the most danger spiritually are the ones who don't see any need for God. They may enjoy life; they may be successful and looked up to by others. They may be moral, honest, and even be outwardly religious (although only outwardly, because God's truth hasn't touched their hearts).

But these individuals live only for the moment, giving no real thought to eternity or the place God should have in their lives. They may give a fleeting thought to such things when they have to attend a friend's funeral—but for practical purposes, they are like the hard ground in Jesus' parable on which the Word of God falls, but "the devil comes and takes away the word from their hearts" (Luke 8:12 NIV).

Do you know people like this—even in your own family? Only God can break through the barrier of a heart that has no place for Him. That is why the most important thing you can do is to pray for them. Don't give up; God is able to do what we cannot do.

Don't Cheapen God's Grace

What shall we say, then? Shall we go on sinning so that grace may increase? By no means! We died to sin; how can we live in it any longer?

Romans 6:1–2 niv

If God will forgive us when we sin—no matter what we do—then why bother trying to be good? All we need to do is ask for forgiveness, and He'll grant it, won't He? So why try to avoid sin?

But the Bible tells us that this kind of thinking makes a mockery of God's forgiveness and grace. It makes a mockery, too, of Jesus' death on the cross, for Christ died not just to forgive us but to free us from sin. The Bible says, "Sin shall not be your master" (Romans 6:14 niv). When we keep on sinning without ever attempting to turn from it or restrain it, it is because we are still sin's slaves.

Never forget that sin is God's enemy—and Satan's friend. Sin is so serious that it caused Jesus Christ to leave Heaven's glory and come into the world to die as the final and complete sacrifice for sin. Don't take sin lightly. Repent of it when it rears its ugly head and, with God's help, cast it out of your life.

God Sees All

Great is our Lord, and mighty in power;
His understanding is infinite.

PSALM 147:5

Some years ago a friend of mine was standing on top of a mountain in North Carolina. The roads in those days were filled with curves, and it was difficult to see very far ahead. This man saw two cars heading toward each other. He realized they couldn't see each other. A third car pulled up and began to pass one of the cars, although there wasn't enough space to see the other car approaching around the bend. My friend shouted a warning, but the drivers couldn't hear, and there was a fatal crash.

This is how God looks upon us in His omniscience. He sees what has happened, what is happening, and what will happen. He also sees us when we foolishly think we can get away with breaking His moral laws or when we act out of sinful pride or lust or anger. Like the man on that mountain, He shouts His warnings at us—but we are too busy or too stubborn to listen.

God sees the whole picture. He knows what is best for us, and He knows what will destroy us. Don't think your way is better than His, but listen to His Word—and obey.

Serving with a Pure Heart

*Delight yourself in the L*ORD
and he will give you the desires of your heart.

PSALM 37:4 NIV

How do you draw the line between your own desires and God's will for you? It isn't always easy.

Take, for example, people who love to sing. They are good at it, they enjoy it, they love being around people who like to sing also. Would it be wrong for them to join the church choir? Would they be doing it just because they enjoyed it . . . or even because they liked to show off their talent and have others praise them? Or because they were sincerely seeking to serve God?

This may not be your problem; you may be like I am—hardly able to carry a tune! But the question of our motives—why we do what we do—is always with us.

It's not wrong to enjoy something, as long as it's good and honorable. God may even have gifted you in certain ways, and it would be wrong to deny those gifts. But always commit your motives to Christ and seek His will in everything—even in things you enjoy.

Training Our Children

Train up a child in the way he should go,
And when he is old he will not depart from it.

PROVERBS 22:6

Children need to know right and wrong, and the
best place to learn it is at home. If they don't learn
it there, they may end up without any moral and spiritual anchor.

Children also want their parents to care enough
for them to be strict. Parents who refuse to discipline
their children are actually sending a signal, saying they
don't care what happens to them. The Bible says, "He
who loves [his son] disciplines him promptly" (Proverbs
13:24).

The Bible also says to train our children in God's
ways "precept upon precept, line upon line . . . here a
little, there a little" (Isaiah 28:10). In other words, when
a child is about to become a teenager, we can't suddenly
say, "I've ignored it so far, but now I'll cram religion and
morals into my child." It must start the very moment he
or she has any understanding.

But what we do is as important as what we say, for
children usually acquire their parents' characteristics
and habits. What are our children and grandchildren
learning from us?

Life Is but a Breath

*Show me, O Lord, my life's end
and the number of my days;
let me know how fleeting is my life.*
PSALM 39:4 NIV

I was speaking at a university, and afterward the students were invited to ask questions. I'll never forget the question one student asked: "What has been the biggest surprise of your life?" Almost without thinking I replied, "The brevity of life."

It's true: life is short, and the older you get the more you realize it. Events that happened thirty years ago seem like they took place just yesterday—but when your mind turns to the future, you realize just how short life is. None of us knows how much more time we'll have, but even if God gives us a long life by most standards, our time is still brief. In the psalmist's words, "Each man's life is but a breath" (39:5 NIV).

Don't waste your life on things that have no eternal value. Draw closer to Christ, and make each day count for Him. See each day as a gift from His hand, and use it for His glory. The Bible says, "Teach us to number our days aright, that we may gain a heart of wisdom" (Psalm 90:12 NIV).

Our Journey to God

*He is able to keep what I have committed
to Him until that Day.*

2 TIMOTHY 1:12

The Bible speaks of death as a departure. When Paul approached the valley of the shadow of death, he did not shudder with fear; rather, he announced with a note of triumph, "The time of my departure is at hand" (2 Timothy 4:6).

The word *departure* in Paul's time literally meant "to pull up anchor and set sail." Everything that happens prior to death is a preparation for that journey. Just as a ship would be loaded with provisions and the voyage carefully mapped out before its departure, so our time on this Earth should be spent carefully preparing for our journey into eternity.

Many times I have said farewell to my wife and children as I have departed for a distant destination. Separation always brings a tinge of sadness, but there is the high hope that we shall meet again.

Such is the hope of every believing Christian as we stand at the grave of a loved one who has departed to be with the Lord. We say good-bye, but only until that new day dawns and we are together with the Lord.

Follow—Now!

> *Another disciple said to him, "Lord, first let me go
>   and bury my father."*
> *But Jesus told him, "Follow me, and let the dead bury
>   their own dead!"*
> MATTHEW 8:21–22 NIV

A t first Jesus' words here sound harsh. If this man's father has died, wouldn't it be compassionate to let him go and arrange for his burial?

But in all likelihood this man's father was still alive, and what the man was saying was that someday in the future—maybe months or even years later—he would be willing to follow Jesus. (In those days, burial was usually carried out within hours of a person's death, so if the father had already died, his son probably wouldn't be away from home listening to Jesus.) But Jesus told him that nothing—absolutely nothing—must stand in the way of being His disciple.

Many people are willing to have Jesus be part of their lives—as long as it doesn't cost them anything. But Jesus calls us to follow Him every day. What keeps you from being His disciple?

The Christmas Crunch

*When they saw the star, they were overjoyed. On coming
to the house, they saw the child with his mother Mary,
and they bowed down and worshiped him.*

MATTHEW 2:10–11 NIV

It may sound like Scrooge—but do you almost hate to
see Christmas coming? It's such a busy time, and our
spending easily gets out of control. Instead of a season
of peace and goodwill, it becomes a season of exhaustion and resentment.

Of course Christmas shouldn't be this way—nor
does it need to be. One key is good planning: keeping
track of commitments, saying no to things we don't
really need to do, knowing in advance what we have to
spend—and sticking to it. And don't leave everything to
the last minute!

But there is a deeper solution to having a good
Christmas—and that is to rediscover its true meaning.
At Christmas we celebrate the birth of Jesus Christ,
who came down from Heaven to save us from our sins.
May you see His glory this Christmas season!

The Victor

"Is anything too hard for the LORD? I will return to you at the appointed time next year and Sarah will have a son."

GENESIS 18:14 NIV

Can you blame Abraham and Sarah for doubting God's promise? Sarah had been childless all their married life, and now she was approaching the age of ninety. Could anything be more impossible? Ninety-year-old women simply do not bear children.

But God gently reminded them that He is sovereign and nothing is too hard for Him. And the following year the impossible happened: Isaac was born. God's promise to Abraham that he would become the father of a great nation (and the ancestor of Jesus Christ) could now be fulfilled.

Remember Abraham and Sarah the next time you encounter what seems to be an insurmountable problem. Nothing was too hard for God then—and nothing is too hard for Him today. If it were, why would we pray? God is still sovereign over His creation, and He is still at work. That doesn't mean He always answers the way we wish He would—but never doubt His power, and never doubt His love.

The God of All Comfort

*Praise be to the God and Father of our Lord Jesus
Christ, the Father of compassion and the God of all
comfort, who comforts us in all our troubles, so that
we can comfort those in any trouble.*

2 Corinthians 1:3–4 niv

Does God honestly care about what is going on in our lives? When hard times hit or illness strikes, does He really care?

The answer is yes—a thousand times yes! When the apostle Paul wrote the words above, he had just endured one of the hardest times in his life: "We were under great pressure, far beyond our ability to endure, so that we despaired even of life" (2 Corinthians 1:8 niv). But in the midst of it, God assured Paul of His compassion and presence, and in time God brought Paul through the trials he was experiencing and opened the door to new opportunities.

But why did God allow Paul to go through this experience? One reason is so he would be able to "comfort those in any trouble." Are you going through a difficult time? Thank God for His compassion, and then ask Him to teach you how to comfort others in their trials. Remember: God knows what it is to suffer, for His Son suffered on the cross for you.

Living in Harmony

Finally, all of you, live in harmony with one another;
be sympathetic, love as brothers, be compassionate
and humble . . . because to this you were called.
1 PETER 3:8–9 NIV

Have you ever asked yourself why some people aren't interested in becoming Christians? There are many reasons, of course, running the gamut from violent rebellion against God to ignorance of the gospel.

But if you took a poll of people you pass every day on the street, many would say that the main reason they aren't attracted to the Christian faith is the Christians they know. Some believers repel people with their self-righteousness; others show no love or compassion; still others show little concern for the world and its problems. Most of all, these observers will point out, Christians can't seem to get along with each other. Why should we believe in Christ, they say, when He doesn't seem to make any difference in the lives of His followers?

Some of what they say isn't valid—but some of it is, and it should be a rebuke to those of us who claim to follow Christ. Our primary calling is to demonstrate to an unbelieving world the transforming love and power of Jesus Christ. Do others see Him in you?

The Peril of Preoccupation

Behold, God is great, and we do not know Him.

JOB 36:26

One evening in Jerusalem, I looked out my hotel window and saw the lights of Bethlehem in the distance. I thought about the response of the innkeeper when Mary and Joseph wanted to find a room where the Child could be born. The innkeeper was not hostile or opposed to having them, but his inn was crowded, his hands were full, and his mind was preoccupied.

Perhaps he told them, "I wish I could help you, but I must keep my priorities. After all, this is a business, and this coming Child is no real concern of mine. But I'm not a hard-hearted man. Over there is the stable. You are welcome to use it if you care to. That is the best I can do. Now I must get back to my work. My guests need me."

And this is the answer that millions give today. It is the answer of preoccupation—not fierce opposition, not furious hatred, but a lack of concern about spiritual things. Some of us are simply too preoccupied with other things to welcome Christ into our lives. Don't let that happen to you!

Joy, Hope, Patience, and Prayer

Be joyful in hope, patient in affliction, faithful in prayer.
ROMANS 12:12 NIV

Discouragement and depression can come for many reasons—losing someone to death, facing a problem that overwhelms us, or even chemical imbalance.

When we feel discouraged or depressed, we need to turn to God in prayer and commit the situation into His hands. This isn't a substitute for medical treatment if we need it; God can use the insights of medical science to bring relief and healing. But ultimately our lives are in His hands, and when we face problems of any kind, we need to turn to Him.

God wants us to be aware of His presence and His love when we walk those lonely roads. Knowing He is with us gives us hope—and from that hope, joy. We also find patience when we rest in His sovereign power. Besides, where else can we turn but to Him?

Whatever you're dealing with right now, may you discover in a new way the truth of God's promise: "The eternal God is your refuge, and underneath are the everlasting arms" (Deuteronomy 33:27).

The Promise of Rest

The LORD is my shepherd; I shall not want.
He makes me to lie down in green pastures;
He leads me beside the still waters.
He restores my soul.

PSALM 23:1–3

No psalm is better known or better loved than Psalm 23, which probably owes its origin to David's boyhood years as a shepherd. But has it become so familiar to us that we have forgotten its riches?

Look at the verses above. They tell us that God is like a shepherd to us—guiding us, keeping us safe, protecting us from our enemies, giving us everything we need to sustain our lives. But they also hint at our tendency to wander and get in trouble, like the lost sheep in one of Jesus' parables (Luke 15:1–7). So our Good Shepherd "makes" us lie down in green pastures, and He "leads" us to still waters—things we might not do on our own.

What kind of sheep are you? Rebellious, prone to wander, resisting the gentle prodding of the Shepherd? Or gratefully submitting to His wisdom and His ways? Remember Jesus' words: "I am the good shepherd; I know my sheep and my sheep know me" (John 10:14 NIV).

Where Is His Peace?

"Glory to God in the highest,
and on earth peace to men on whom his favor rests."
LUKE 2:14 NIV

On that memorable night in the Judean hills of Bethlehem two thousand years ago, this was the song of the angels. Though the centuries have rolled by, still the world longs for and looks for the peace that the angels announced. Where is this peace?

Clearly, it is not evident in the world, with its constant fighting and conflicts. This peace abides instead in the hearts of all those who have trusted in God's grace. In the same proportion that the world has trusted Christ, it has peace. There can be no lasting peace until Christ has come to the hearts of all people and brought them His peace.

There is no discord in Heaven, there is no strife in Heaven, for Christ reigns supreme there. Similarly, in the heart where Christ abides and reigns, His words become a reality: "Peace I leave with you" (John 14:27). The truth of these words has been proven in human experience over and over again. Thank your Heavenly Father today for the times they have proven true for you.

God Sent His Son

In Him dwells all the fullness of the Godhead bodily.

COLOSSIANS 2:9

On that first Christmas night in Bethlehem, "God was manifested in the flesh" (1 Timothy 3:16). This manifestation was the person of Jesus Christ.

What an incredible truth! Think of it: the God of the universe came down from Heaven in human form! As the words of the familiar Christmas carol declare, "Veiled in flesh the Godhead see; hail th' incarnate Deity."

If you want to know what God is like, then take a long look at Jesus Christ—because He was God in human flesh. In Jesus are displayed wisdom, power, and majesty, justice, mercy, grace, and love. "The Word was God. . . . And the Word became flesh and dwelt among us" (John 1:1, 14).

To His disciples Jesus said, "You believe in God, believe also in Me" (John 14:1). This sequence of faith is inevitable. If we believe in what God made and what God said, we will believe in the One whom God sent.

The Anthem of His Name

God also has . . . given Him the name
which is above every name.

<small>PHILIPPIANS 2:9</small>

Over two thousand years ago, on a night the world has come to call Christmas, a young Jewish maiden went through the experience countless mothers had before her: she brought forth a child.

But this birth was like no other in the history of the human race. For one thing, this Child had no human father. As the angel had promised, "The Holy Spirit will come upon you, and the power of the Highest will overshadow you" (Luke 1:35). In humble obedience the Virgin Mary had responded, "Let it be to me according to your word" (Luke 1:38).

But this birth also was like no other because of the One who was born. This was no ordinary child. This was the unique Son of God, sent from Heaven to save us from our sins.

Amid the glitter and busyness of the season, don't lose sight of the miracle of that first Christmas. With the wise men, let us fall down and worship Him (Matthew 2:11).

He Will Be Called Wonderful

> *He will be called*
> *Wonderful Counselor, Mighty God,*
> *Everlasting Father, Prince of Peace.*
>
> Isaiah 9:6 NIV

My dictionary defines *wonderful* as "so unusual or magnificent that it causes wonder and amazement." What a description of Jesus!

First, Jesus was wonderful in His pre-existence. As the perfect man who was also God, He existed from all eternity. Only He is equally at home in Heaven and on Earth.

Jesus was wonderful in His birth. To right the wrongs of the world and redeem a fallen race, God sent not angelic armies but a tiny baby, His Son, to accomplish this majestic purpose—born not of man but of the Holy Spirit.

Jesus was wonderful in His life. His enemies could not find a single flaw in His character. His miracles and His teaching both testified to His divine authority.

Christ was also wonderful in His death. He died for others just as He had lived for others: to make our salvation possible. And this death led to the wonderful, glorious resurrection, opening for us the door to Heaven and eternal life. Jesus is wonderful indeed!

God in the Flesh

The Lord himself will give you a sign:
The virgin will be with child and will give birth to a son,
and will call him Immanuel [which means "God with us"].

ISAIAH 7:14 NIV

Jesus Christ lived on Earth only thirty-three years, yet He transformed civilization. And after two thousand years, countless millions worship Him.

Where did Jesus come from? His birth in a stable in Bethlehem was not His origin; that was His incarnation—His coming in the flesh. The Bible teaches that Jesus is God in human flesh, God Incarnate. Jesus—the eternal Son of God—never had a beginning; He will never have an end. He always was, and He always will be.

When Jesus walked this Earth, He made the blind to see, the deaf to hear, and the dumb to speak. He was the greatest teacher of all time, and He was also a man of compassion, love, and selflessness.

Yet consider the emphasis on His death. Three chapters in the book of Matthew, three in Mark, three in Luke, and six in John are devoted to the last twenty-four hours of Jesus' life. Why? Because Jesus was born to die as the final and perfect sacrifice for your sins and mine.

Praise Him this holy season!

The Night of Light

"I am the light of the world. He who follows Me
shall not walk in darkness."

JOHN 8:12

This month the birthday of Jesus Christ will be celebrated all over the world. It will be celebrated in various ways, in many languages, by people of all races. For a few hours many in the world will stop talking of satellites, rockets, and war. For a few hours they will talk of peace on Earth and goodwill toward men. People will exchange gifts and talk about the Prince of Peace.

Imagine the scene in Bethlehem two thousand years ago. It was the night of nights, yet it had begun as every other night before it.

But it was to become the greatest, most significant night of history. This was the night when light would conquer darkness and bring in the day when there would be no more night. This was the night when those who lived in darkness would see a great light. This was the night God brought into the world the One who is "the light of the world."

May Jesus' light shine in your life this Christmas season!

The Christ of Christmas

*"Today in the town of David a Savior has been
born to you; he is Christ the Lord."*

LUKE 2:11 NIV

Famed movie director Cecil B. DeMille once told me
that his film *The King of Kings,* made during the
silent-movie era, was seen by an estimated 800 million
people. I asked him why he didn't remake *The King of
Kings* with sound and color. He replied, "I will never be
able to do it, because if I gave Jesus a southern accent,
the northerners would not think of Him as their Christ.
If I gave Him a foreign accent, the Americans and the
British would not think of Him as their Christ. As it is,
people of all nations, from every race, creed, clan, can
accept Him as their Christ."

Jesus came for us all—and today He can be your
Christ. Today you and I can know the Christ of
Christmas—who alone can wipe away our tears, lift our
burdens, solve our problems, forgive our sins, and make
us new. Your Christmas will be joyful indeed as you discover these truths!

One more thing: To whom will you introduce the
Christ of Christmas?

Our Loving, Compassionate God

"I am the bread of life."

JOHN 6:35

Jesus came to the world so we could know, once and for all, that God is concerned about the way we live, the way we believe, and the way we die.

God could have told us in other ways, of course—and He had, throughout the pages of the Old Testament and in the lives of His people. By His written Word He declared His love for us.

But Jesus was the Living Word. By His life, death, and resurrection, Jesus demonstrated God's love in a way we could never ignore or deny. Paul wrote, "God demonstrates His own love toward us, in that while we were still sinners, Christ died for us" (Romans 5:8).

Every time Jesus fed the hungry, He was saying, "I am the bread of life." Every time He healed a suffering person, He was saying, "It hurts Me to see you in pain." Every move He made, every miracle He performed, every word He spoke was for the purpose of reconciling a lost world to the loving, compassionate God.

Mary's Example

> *The angel said to her, "Rejoice, highly favored one, the*
> *Lord is with you; blessed are you among women! . . .*
> *And behold, you will conceive in your womb and*
> *bring forth a Son, and shall call His name JESUS."*
> LUKE 1:28, 31

Mary was no more than a teenager when the angel Gabriel appeared before her with this astounding announcement. And her response is one of the most remarkable demonstrations of faith found in the Bible.

Mary was a virgin, engaged to a godly man by the name of Joseph, yet she was to be made pregnant supernaturally by the Holy Spirit. People would talk, shame would be attached to the pregnancy, and Joseph would probably leave her. But by faith Mary said to Gabriel, "I am the Lord's servant. May it be to me as you have said" (Luke 1:38 NIV).

Mary accepted God's will for her life, no matter what it might cost her. I pray that God would give me grace and courage to follow Mary's example and be faithful to Him no matter what price I may be called on to pay. May that be your prayer as well.

The Remedy for Sin

Bless the LORD . . .
who forgives all your iniquities,
who heals all your diseases.

PSALM 103:2–3

J esus came into the world to save all kinds of people: rich and poor, black and white, educated and illiterate, sophisticated and ordinary—and anyone in between.

Yet only two groups of people gathered at God's invitation to pay Him homage when He was born. One was the shepherds—lowly, at the bottom of the social ladder, uneducated, unsophisticated. The other group was the wise men—intellectuals, from another race and country, wealthy, respected. The two groups could hardly have been more different!

God brought both groups to Bethlehem—one by an angelic announcement, one by the appearance of a miraculous star. And by bringing both, God was telling us that Jesus is the Savior for everyone. Every person stands in need of His forgiveness and new life—and every person can know it, if he or she only repents and makes that journey to the Christ of Christmas.

No matter who you are, you need Christ. And no matter what you have done, He loves you and stands ready to welcome you.

The Joy of Christmas

When they saw the star, they rejoiced with
exceedingly great joy.

MATTHEW 2:10

E very year people write me saying how much they dread Christmas. Often their complaint stems from how busy they will be or how much money they will spend.

Did those wise men who journeyed hundreds of miles across the desert to seek out the infant Jesus ever feel that way? After all, it took months to make the arduous trip, and they had gone to great expense to provide gifts of gold, frankincense, and myrrh for the new child.

I doubt it. In fact, as their journey neared its end we read they had "exceedingly great joy." What made the difference? Their focus was totally on Jesus, the One who would be called "Immanuel . . . 'God with us'" (Matthew 1:23).

Don't let this Christmas season overwhelm you. Don't feel you have to do everything or go into debt just to impress other people. Focus instead on Jesus. Take time every day to read the prophecies of His coming and the wonderful story of His birth. Make this Christmas one of "exceedingly great joy"!

The Prince of Peace

"Your faith has saved you. Go in peace."

LUKE 7:50

During the First World War, on Christmas Eve, the battlefield was strangely quiet. As the soft snow fell, the young men were thinking of home and their families.

Softly one lad began to hum "Silent Night." Others took up the chorus until the trenches resounded with that Christmas song. When they finished, they were astonished to hear the song echoing from the trenches across no-man's-land: In their own tongue, the other soldiers also sang "Silent Night." That night they were thinking of the Prince of Peace, the Christ of Christmas.

How different this world would be if we could unite together around that "Holy Infant so tender and mild." Earth can be as Heaven with Christ. Discord can be as peace when Christ is near. Midnight gloom can be transformed into noonday brightness when He abides with us.

Full peace will come only when Christ returns. But until that day we can know His peace in our hearts and be messengers of His peace in the world.

A Rainbow of Hope

The LORD is near to all who call upon Him,
To all who call upon Him in truth.

PSALM 145:18

Have you ever thought about what has happened because Christ came into the world? That baby in the manger of Bethlehem grew up to become our crucified and risen Savior—and the world has never been the same.

Jesus' compassion has made the world more compassionate. His healing touch has made the world more humanitarian. His selflessness has made the world more self-effacing. Christ drew a rainbow of hope around the shoulders of men and women and gave them something to live for.

If Christ had not come, our world would indeed be a hopeless world. If Christ had not come, ours would be a lost world. There would be no access to God, there would be no atonement for sin, there would be no forgiveness, and there would be no Savior.

Yes, Christ came into the world and made it a better place. And He will do the same for you if you will open your life to Him.

The Incarnation

The Word was God. . . . [And] the Word became
flesh and made his dwelling among us.

JOHN 1:1, 14 NIV

The word *incarnation* comes from the Latin word *incarnatus*, meaning "to be made flesh." This great mystery of God's incarnation—of God coming to Earth in the person of Jesus—is the message over which rationalists stumble, humanists are offended, and the world is bewildered. The unbelieving mind is confused by this truth, which runs counter to human wisdom.

The apostle Paul, reasoning with intellectual Greeks and Romans, said, "Beyond all question, the mystery of godliness is great: He appeared in a body, was vindicated by the Spirit, was seen by angels, was preached among the nations, was believed on in the world, was taken up in glory" (1 Timothy 3:16 NIV).

Sinful people are incapable of coming to God by their own efforts, so God in love and mercy descended to Earth to save us. The creature could not go up to the Creator, so the Creator came down to redeem His creation. May the Holy Spirit of God confirm in your heart the wondrous mystery of the incarnation.

The King of Kings

A scepter of righteousness is the scepter
of Your kingdom.

PSALM 45:6

From His very birth, Christ was recognized as King. Something about Him inspired allegiance, loyalty, and homage. Wise men brought Him gifts. Shepherds fell down and worshipped Him. Herod, realizing that there is never room for two thrones in one kingdom, sought His life.

During His ministry, Jesus' claims upon people's lives were total and absolute. He allowed no divided loyalty. He demanded and received complete adoration and devotion. Mature men and women left their businesses and gave themselves in total obedience to Him. Many of them gave their lives, pouring out the last full measure of devotion.

Jesus' words caused even His most avowed enemies to say, "No man ever spoke like this Man!" (John 7:46). And yet He was more than a poet, more than a statesman, more than a physician. We cannot understand Christ until we understand that He is the King of kings and the Lord of lords. Like Thomas, our response must be to bow down and confess, "My Lord and my God!" (John 20:28).

God's Perfect Timing

When the time had fully come, God sent his
Son, born of a woman.

GALATIANS 4:4 NIV

Someone once asked me why Jesus wasn't born many centuries earlier, in a less populated world, and at a time when He might have had a much greater impact. That's an interesting thought, but Jesus was born when He was—neither sooner nor later—because God knew it was the best moment for Him to come.

Take, for instance, the fact that Jesus was born during the height of the Roman Empire. Unlike previous empires, the Romans had built roads from one end of their vast territory to the other. These highways enabled early Christians to spread the news about Jesus throughout the civilized world in only a few decades— something believers never could have done if Jesus had come earlier.

Also, by then the human race had tried all kinds of religions and philosophies, yet none had satisfied the deepest longings of the human heart or taken away the burden of guilt. Many people were now open to Jesus' message of hope and new life.

Know that God's timing is always perfect. It was then—and it is today.

God with Us

Behold, the virgin shall conceive and bear a Son,
and shall call His name Immanuel.

ISAIAH 7:14

I never celebrate Christmas without thinking of the thousands of people who are lonely and troubled. I have had psychiatrists tell me their schedules are over-loaded with people who find the Christmas season almost more than they can bear because of their loneliness and isolation.

But Christmas is God's reminder that we are not alone. God revealed in the life, death, and resurrection of Jesus a reconciling love that rescues us from separation and loneliness. We are not alone! God has come down from Heaven to tell us He loves us!

During this Christmas season, you can be assured that Jesus Christ is here. He is here to give us hope, to forgive our sins, to give us a new song, to impart faith, and to heal our wounds if only we will let Him.

The Christmas message has not changed in two thousand years. Christmas still reminds us that God is with us. If you are lonely this Christmas, welcome Christ into your life. Then ask Him to help you reach out to someone else who is lonely and show that person His love.

Heavenly Herald

*"I have come that they may have life, and that
they may have it more abundantly."*

JOHN 10:10

Christmas is not just a date on the calendar. It is not just an annual holiday. It is not a day to glorify selfishness and materialism. Christmas is the celebration of the event that set Heaven to singing, an event that gave the stars of the night sky a new brilliance.

Christmas tells us that at a specific time and at a specific place, a specific person was born. That person was (in the words of an ancient Christian creed) "God of God, Light of Light, very God of very God." That person was the Lord, Jesus Christ.

And from the lips of Him who came fell these words: "The Son of Man has come to seek and to save that which was lost" (Luke 19:10). Like piercing trumpets, these words heralded the divine. They declared that Heaven had come to our rescue and that God had not left us to stumble alone on Earth's pathway. What a wonderful and glorious hope we have because of that first Christmas!

A Healing Word

"I have called you friends."
JOHN 15:15

Christ came into a world that had problems much like the ones we grapple with today. Life was short, disease was rampant, nations chafed under the heel of Roman rule, slavery was universal. Widows, orphans, the disabled, and the chronically ill had no social safety net to see them through the rough times.

To those people without the joy of living, Jesus said, "I have come that they may have life, and that they may have it more abundantly" (John 10:10).

To those who bore sin's burden of guilt, He said, "Be of good cheer; your sins are forgiven you" (Matthew 9:2).

To the friendless He said, "No longer do I call you servants . . . but I have called you friends" (John 15:15). Jesus had a healing word for everyone.

On the surface the world has changed radically since that first Christmas. But deep inside, our problems are the same—for they are problems of the heart. And Christ still comes to us to cleanse our guilt, give us hope for the future, and heal our hurts with His love.

Finding Peace

"Glory to God in the highest,
and on earth peace."

LUKE 2:14

The centuries have rolled by, and still the world longs for and looks for the peace the angels sang about on that first Christmas morning. Even the land of Jesus' birth often seems torn by violence and conflict. "Where is His peace?" people ask.

I'll tell you where it is. It abides in the hearts of all who have trusted in God's grace. And in the same proportion that the world has trusted in Christ, it also has peace. Yet our world continues to be torn by wars and unrest. I know of no country that is completely safe or completely at peace.

The greatest war of all, however, is the war between God and us, as we stubbornly rebel against His authority and defiantly seize control of our lives apart from Him. But now the war can be over, as we yield ourselves to Christ as our Lord. Now we can have peace—peace with God, peace in our hearts, and peace with one another. Is the war over in your life?

The Summit of Love

How great is the love the Father has lavished on us,
that we should be called children of God!
1 JOHN 3:1 NIV

Mary and Joseph deeply loved the Child God gave them, even becoming refugees to spare His life when King Herod tried to kill Him (Matthew 2:13–15).

But their love was almost nothing compared to God's infinite love for His Son. The Bible declares, "The Father loves the Son, and has given all things into His hand" (John 3:35). Can you even begin to imagine the Father's emotions that first Christmas as His dearly loved Son left Heaven for Earth, knowing Jesus would one day go to the cross, "despised and rejected by men, a Man of sorrows and acquainted with grief" (Isaiah 53:3)?

We rightly focus on God's love for us. But don't lose sight of what it cost the Father to send His beloved Son into the world. Why did He do it? Because "God so loved the world that He gave His only begotten Son, that whoever believes in Him should not perish but have everlasting life" (John 3:16).

God loves the Son—and He loves you as well.

No Vacancy?

There was no room for them in the inn.

Before we denounce the unaccommodating citizens of Bethlehem, we should admit that many people still refuse to make room for Him. Millions remember Jesus' birthday and speak His name in holiday greetings, yet they consistently close their hearts to Him, saying in effect, "There is no room in my soul for Christ."

We hear great cries for tolerance—but consider the bigotry toward followers of Jesus. There is no room for His Word in our culture: our children are without reverence for God or faith in the Bible. There is no room for our Lord's creed of purity and self-denial: the media sends forth a constant barrage of profanity, indecency, and materialism. There is no room for the promise of His cross and His blood: the angel's statement that "He will save His people from their sins" (Matthew 1:21) is rejected by those who deny that the Child in the manger is our Emmanuel, "God with us."

What will you do to make more room in your heart—and in your life—for Jesus?

A Message in the Night

*And there were shepherds living out in the fields
nearby, keeping watch over their flocks at night.*
LUKE 2:8 NIV

The first Christmas worship service was conducted not in a temple, cathedral, or synagogue, but in the great outdoors. The tidings of Christ's birth echoed in the skies as the angel of the Lord proclaimed the good news to lowly shepherds.

Do you think it strange that this glad word was not first given to the priests, the scholars, or the Pharisees? The reason is clear: God speaks to those who are prepared in their hearts to listen. Apparently these humble shepherds were prepared and therefore able to discern the voice from Heaven above the noisy din of Earth's confusion.

It is also significant that this angelic message was delivered at night. It was night not only because the sun had gone down, but because the world was shrouded in spiritual and moral gloom—just as it is today. Often when things are darkest, God makes Himself known.

Is it night for you this Christmas season? If so, may Jesus reveal Himself to you in a powerful and real way.

Room for Jesus

She brought forth her firstborn Son . . . and
laid Him in a manger, because there was no
room for them in the inn.

LUKE 2:7

No room for Jesus? No room for the King of kings? No, but room for others and for other things. There was no room for Jesus in the world that He had made—imagine!

And things have not really changed since that Bethlehem night over two thousand years ago. God is still on the fringes of most people's lives. We fit Him in when it is convenient for us, but we become irritated when He makes demands on us. If God would only stay in His little box and come out when we pull the string!

Our lives are so full. There is so much to be done. But in all our busy activities, are we in danger of excluding from our hearts and lives the One who made us?

May this be our prayer: "Oh, come to my heart, Lord Jesus; there is room in my heart for You."

That First Christmas

*So [the shepherds] hurried off and found Mary and
Joseph, and the baby, who was lying in the manger.*
Luke 2:16 niv

It would have been logical to expect God to tear open
the Heavens and descend to Earth in majesty and
power on that first Christmas night—but He didn't.

Instead, on that quiet night in Bethlehem, a virgin
mother lay her newborn baby in a manger designed to
feed cattle. The lowing cows, the sweet-smelling hay, and
the dark sky illumined by a magnificent star provided
the setting. Humble shepherds joined the carpenter-
husband to witness the miracle and praise God. The
most significant drama of the centuries was unfolding—
the drama of salvation that would ultimately take this
child to the cross.

Truly, God works in mysterious ways. The wheels of
His mercy and justice move quietly, but they do move.
The birth of Jesus Christ—the Son of God, our Savior—
went unnoticed by the vast majority of the world that
first Christmas night, but no event in human history
was more significant. May His birth—and all it means—
not go unnoticed in our lives!

Welcoming the Christ

Then, being divinely warned in a dream that they should not return to Herod, they departed for their own country another way. . . . Then Herod, when he saw that he was deceived by the wise men, was exceedingly angry.

MATTHEW 2:12, 16

In his fear and raging jealousy, King Herod responded to the newborn Jesus with bloodthirsty hostility: "Destroy Him! Let Him die while He is still in His cradle!" This response grew and swelled until one day many years later it became a mad mob's terrifying roar: "Take him away! Take him away! Crucify him!" (John 19:15 NIV).

In many hearts, this cry is still being shouted. The world rejects its Messiah. If He would remain a gentle and mild Jesus, that would be all right. Or if He remained a mystical dreamer, that would be all right. But a reigning Christ, an invading Christ, a revolutionary Christ, a life-changing Christ—that is unacceptable to millions of people. That is a menace to their way of life. It damages their self-determination and strikes at the roots of their stubborn independence.

During this Christmas season, however, may you welcome this reigning Christ, invading Christ, revolutionary Christ, life-changing Christ into your life anew.

Why Did He Come?

God was reconciling the world to himself in Christ,
not counting men's sins against them.

2 CORINTHIANS 5:19 NIV

Christianity has its roots in the deep, firm soil of history. Jesus' incarnation—God invading human history in the form of a man—is on the record. Every time you write the date, you attest to the fact that God entered human history.

Jesus came into the world so we might know that God cares how we live, what we believe, and how we will die. Jesus came to demonstrate to us that we were made to have a personal relationship with God. He came to bridge the gap that separated us from our Creator.

Every time Jesus fed the hungry, He was saying, "I am the bread of life" (John 6:35). Every time He healed someone, He was saying, "It hurts Me to see you in pain." Every time He lifted the burden of sin, He was saying, "Your Heavenly Father is grieved when you remove yourself from His grace."

Every miracle Jesus performed and every word He spoke reminds us that He came to reconcile a lost world to our loving, compassionate God. Has this happened to you?

The Suffering Servant

He was wounded for our transgressions.

ISAIAH 53:5

Jesus' life began in the midst of persecution and peril. He came on a mission of love and mercy, sent by the Father. An angel announced His conception and gave Him His name. The Heavenly host sang a glorious anthem at His birth. By the extraordinary star, the very Heavens indicated His coming. He was the most illustrious child ever born—the holy child of Mary, the divine Son of God.

Yet no sooner did He enter our world than Herod decreed His death and labored to accomplish it. Warned by God in a dream, Joseph fled Bethlehem at night, taking Mary and the baby Jesus to Egypt until Herod's death finally made it safe to return.

The only Son of the eternal Father, Jesus entered time and was made in the likeness of man. He assumed our human nature with all its infirmities, and weakness, and capacity for suffering. He came as a child of the poorest parents. His entire life was one long pathway of humiliation.

But now Jesus reigns in Heaven, no longer limited by time and space. And someday He will come again—this time in glory—to take us to Himself.

The True Light

"You are the Christ, the Son of the living God."
MATTHEW 16:16

Christ came into this world as God's ambassador, sent from Heaven to tell us of God's love and to bring the war between us and God to an end.

Now we, as "ambassadors for Christ" (2 Corinthians 5:20), boldly echo the apostle Peter when he confessed, "You are the Christ, the Son of the living God." The title *Christ* means "anointed one." It is the Greek term for the ancient Hebrew word *Messiah*—the anointed one whom God would send to save His people.

Peter and his fellow Jews, the first believers of the early Christian Church, recognized Jesus Christ as the Messiah promised in the Old Testament. Their world was one of discouragement and despair, but the promised Messiah shone as a beacon in the darkness, and His light has never dimmed. "In Him was life, and the life was the light of men" (John 1:4).

No matter how dark the world gets and no matter how dark our paths may seem, Jesus is still our life and light.

God's Infinite Knowledge

*How unsearchable are His judgments and
His ways past finding out!*

ROMANS 11:33

T he end of another year is approaching, and people are already predicting what the new year holds. A year from now most of them probably will have missed the target!

The fact is, no one knows the future—except God. We human beings know so little about the world in which we live. No doubt scientists will continue to uncover astonishing facts about the universe. But even then, they will know only a miniscule amount compared with the total sum of potential knowledge.

But God is infinite! He knows it all—because He created it in the first place. We will always be bewildered and confused by what we don't know, if we are honest. We don't even know our immediate futures; as James said, "You do not know what will happen tomorrow" (James 4:14).

What should this mean? It should give us humility before God, and it should give us trust—trust in the God who does know our futures and who works all things for His glory. You can trust all your tomorrows to Him!

Good News!

> *If every one of [the things Jesus did] were written down, I suppose that even the whole world would not have room for the books that would be written.*
> JOHN 21:25 NIV

In light of these words of John, we should not be surprised that we have four accounts of Jesus' life in the Bible, for each of the four gospels gives us details about our Lord that are not found in the others.

As they wrote under the inspiration of the Holy Spirit, Matthew, Mark, Luke, and John each gave us a distinctive portrait of Jesus. Matthew, for example, shows us Jesus as the Messianic King, sent by God to fulfill the Old Testament's prophecies about a Savior. That is why Matthew quotes from the Old Testament so much, for "this has all taken place that the writings of the prophets might be fulfilled" (Matthew 26:56 NIV).

Never forget that these four accounts of Jesus' life aren't merely interesting stories. Instead, they are accurate, historical accounts of the most important event in human history: the coming of God's Son into the world. Because He came, we can know what God is like. And because He came, we can be saved from our sins. This is good news—which is exactly what the word *gospel* means.

Pass Along Comfort

Blessed be the God . . . of all comfort.
2 CORINTHIANS 1:3

A dear friend and trusted counselor once told me that sometimes the greatest test comes to us when we ask God the question, "Why?"

As Charles Hembree has pointed out, "In the full face of afflictions it is hard to see any sense to things that befall us, and we want to question the fairness of a faithful God. However, these moments can be the most meaningful of our lives."

Alexander Nowell once said, "God does not comfort us that we may be comforted but that we may be comforters." We are to pass along the comfort with which God has comforted us.

Look around you. There are countless opportunities to comfort others, not only in the loss of a loved one, but also in the daily distress that so often creeps into our lives. One of Paul's companions on some of his missionary journeys was named Joseph, but "the apostles called [him] Barnabas (which means Son of Encouragement)" (Acts 4:36 NIV). Will you be a Barnabas to someone in your life?

Fix Your Eyes on Jesus

"The Spirit of the LORD is upon Me,
because He has anointed Me
to preach the gospel to the poor."

LUKE 4:18

The Man who read aloud these words from Isaiah 61 and made this claim is Jesus of Nazareth, the Compassionate Christ. As Isaiah had prophesied, Jesus made the blind to see, the crippled to walk, and the deaf to hear. We live in a world filled not only with physical suffering, but also with problems like guilt, loneliness, emptiness, and fear. Jesus is interested in suffering people. If we are believers, we should be too.

Jesus is also the Crucified Christ. Good works won't get us to Heaven. Only what Jesus did when He died in our place and shed His blood can open Heaven's door for us.

In addition, Jesus is the Conquering Christ. He rose from the dead as the conqueror of sin and death and Hell. Because the risen Jesus holds the keys of Hell and death, we don't ever have to experience them for ourselves.

And finally, Jesus is the Coming Christ. Someday He will return to establish His Kingdom of peace and blessing.

May your faith and hope be in Christ—today and always!

Bring Glory to God

Present . . . your members as instruments
of righteousness to God.

ROMANS 6:13

When you serve sin, your body is dedicated to the service of sin. Your appetites, whetted by Satan, rage unthrottled. Your God-given creative impulses are sacrificed to Satan on the altar of lust. A sinner, in a sense, is a dedicated person, yielded to his appetites and selfish desires.

But when Christ comes into the human heart, we are to yield our bodies to Him. Our human frame is often a rebellious and unruly servant. Only through rigid discipline and the help of the Holy Spirit are we able to master it and bring it into complete subjection to Christ. We must guard against appetites that blight the conscience, wither the soul, and weaken our witness for Christ.

Perhaps many things are lawful, but are they moral? Are they a harmful example to others?

As long as we are in this world, our old nature will try to defeat us and turn us away from Christ. But learn to recognize the warning signs, and commit your mind and body to Christ "as instruments of righteousness."

God's Gifts to Us

We have different gifts, according to the grace given us.
ROMANS 12:6 NIV

If you are a parent, you've undoubtedly had the experience of having your children complain after Christmas is over, disappointed they didn't get the gift they wanted or bored with the ones they did receive. This is not an easy problem to solve!

God our Father has given gifts to each of us, and I pray we may never become discontent or bored with them. The greatest gift of all, of course, is the gift of His Son. But the Bible also teaches God has given us other gifts—gifts that come from the Holy Spirit's ministry in our lives. These are the gifts of the Spirit, and they include everything from the gift of preaching to the gift of hospitality. None of us has every gift, but every Christian has at least one, to be used for one purpose: to build up Christ's body, the Church (Ephesians 4:11–12).

What spiritual gift has God given you? Don't worry about those gifts you don't have. Be content with those God has given you, and use them for His glory.

Our Unchanging God

"I the Lord do not change."

Malachi 3:6 NIV

God is the same yesterday, today, and tomorrow. And because He is unchanging, He is also utterly trustworthy and faithful.

God is unchanging in His holiness: "Holy, holy, holy is the Lord Almighty!" (Isaiah 6:3 NIV).

God is unchanging in His demand for holiness and integrity in our lives: "Consecrate yourselves and be holy, because I am holy" (Leviticus 11:44; 1 Peter 1:15–16).

God is unchanging in His judgment: He will judge all the Earth, welcoming some into His eternal presence and sending others to eternal death (Matthew 7:22–23).

God is unchanging in His love: "God demonstrates his own love for us in this: While we were still sinners, Christ died for us" (Romans 5:8 NIV).

God's way of salvation has not changed. The message of Jesus' sinless life, His sacrificial death, and His victorious resurrection still transforms lives today.

May our commitment to our unchanging God never waver but only grow stronger as we walk with Him!

The City of God

There shall be no night there. . . . And they shall reign forever and ever.

REVELATION 22:5

Many years ago I was visiting the dining room of the United States Senate. As I was speaking to various people, one of the senators said, "Billy, we're having a discussion about pessimism and optimism. Are you a pessimist or an optimist?" I smiled and said, "I'm an optimist." He asked, "Why?" I replied, "I've read the last page of the Bible."

The Bible speaks about a Heavenly city whose builder and maker is God, where those who have been redeemed will be superior to angels. It speaks of "a pure river of water of life, clear as crystal, proceeding from the throne of God and of the Lamb" (Revelation 22:1). It says, "There shall be no night there: They need no lamp nor light of the sun, for the Lord God gives them light. And they shall reign forever and ever."

As another year ends, no doubt you have had your share of joys and disappointments. Don't live in the past, but "be patient and stand firm, because the Lord's coming is near" (James 5:8 NIV).

Looking Back

*But one thing I do: Forgetting what is behind and
straining toward what is ahead, I press on toward
the goal to win the prize for which God has called me
heavenward in Christ Jesus.*

PHILIPPIANS 3:13–14 NIV

What are your thoughts as you look back over the past year? Was it a year of heartache and loss, tragedy and sorrow? Or happiness and joy, success and achievement? Or something in between? Do you close the book on this year with regret or with relief?

No matter what your answer is, I hope you will pause and prayerfully ask yourself two important questions. First, how do you think God looks on this past year in your life? Did it bring you any closer to Him? Did it expose any weaknesses or find you wandering from His way? Was He disappointed in your responses to its challenges?

Second, what lessons will you take from this year into the next? What did God teach you? What did He try to teach you? What needs to change—and how will it happen?

Don't be bound by the past and its failures, but don't forget its lessons either. Like Paul, forget the past and press on in obedience to Christ.

Notes

Notes

Notes

Notes

Notes

Notes

Notes